LATINING AMERICA

SERIES EDITORS

Jon Smith, Simon Fraser University
Riché Richardson, Cornell University

ADVISORY BOARD

Houston A. Baker Jr., Vanderbilt University
Leigh Anne Duck, The University of Mississippi
Jennifer Greeson, The University of Virginia
Trudier Harris, The University of North Carolina, Chapel Hill
John T. Matthews, Boston University
Tara McPherson, The University of Southern California

LATINING AMERICA

Black-Brown Passages and the
Coloring of Latino/a Studies

CLAUDIA MILIAN

THE UNIVERSITY OF GEORGIA PRESS
Athens & London

© 2013 by the University of Georgia Press
Athens, Georgia 30602
www.ugapress.org
All rights reserved
Designed by Walton Harris
Set in 10/14 Chaparral Pro
Printed digitally

Library of Congress Cataloging-in-Publication Data

Milian, Claudia.
Latining America : black-brown passages and the coloring
of Latino/a studies / Claudia Milian. — 1st edition.
  pages   cm. — (The new Southern studies)
Includes bibliographical references and index.
ISBN-13: 978-0-8203-4435-5 (hardcover : alkaline paper)
ISBN-10: 0-8203-4435-4 (hardcover : alkaline paper)
ISBN-13: 978-0-8203-4436-2 (paperback : alkaline paper)
ISBN-10: 0-8203-4436-2 (paperback : alkaline paper)
1. Hispanic Americans—Ethnic identity. 2. Hispanic Americans—Race identity.
3. Hispanic Americans—Study and teaching (Higher)
4. Hispanic Americans—Intellectual life. 5. Ethnicity in literature.
6. American literature—Hispanic American authors—History and criticism.
7. Race—Social aspects—United States. 8. Cultural pluralism—United States.
9. United States—Ethnic relations. 10. United States—Race relations. I. Title.
E184.S75M545 2013
305.868′073—dc23   2012028061

British Library Cataloging-in-Publication Data available

CONTENTS

ACKNOWLEDGMENTS
vii

INTRODUCTION
The Copiousness of Latin
1

CHAPTER ONE
Southern Latinities
25

CHAPTER TWO
Passing Latinities
59

CHAPTER THREE
Indigent Latinities
93

CHAPTER FOUR
Disorienting Latinities
123

EPILOGUE
@
151

NOTES
159

WORKS CITED
259

INDEX
289

ACKNOWLEDGMENTS

Latining America: Black-Brown Passages and the Coloring of Latino/a Studies came to fruition because my guiding forces, Jon Smith, Riché Richardson, and Nancy Grayson, willed it into being. I recognize, first and foremost, my deepest gratitude and appreciation to Jon, Riché, and Nancy for their bold vision, wholehearted commitment, promptness, and tremendous support.

To add to the pleasures of getting this text off the ground, the University of Georgia Press fortuitously rewarded me with two splendid interlocutors. I would like to duly credit and submit my overdue thanks to the anonymous reviewers solicited by the Press, who dedicated hours reading and laboriously thinking about this study, proffering substantive, cogent, and lightning-fast critiques that refined this work.

Particular thanks are due to Beth Snead at the University of Georgia Press for her ever-present resourcefulness, attentiveness, and editorial talents. Continued thanks to Erin Kirk New for her dedication to the production of handsome books. Super thanks, Susan Silver, for your expert eagle eye, meticulousness, and professionalism.

This project was also made possible by a Donald C. Gallup Fellowship in American Literature from the Beinecke Rare Book and Manuscript Library at Yale University. Many and most sincere thanks to the Beinecke staff for their unsparing assistance, especially to Leah Jehan for her archival know-how and more-than-generous willingness to help me with my endless requests.

For financial support that made this volume's visual economy possible, I thank the Center for Latin American and Caribbean Studies at Duke University.

I have drawn on and revised parts of two previous publications for this writing. Parts of chapter 3 are gathered from "Playing with the Dark: Africana and Latino Literary Imaginations," in *A Companion to African American Studies*, edited by Lewis R. Gordon and Jane Anna Gordon (Oxford: Blackwell, 2006),

543–67, used by permission of Wiley-Blackwell. Portions from chapter 4 and the epilogue build on "Central American–Americanness, Latino/a Studies, and the Global South," *Global South* 5, no. 1 (Spring 2011): 137–52, and appear here courtesy of Indiana University Press.

I am incalculably indebted to José David Saldívar for being an enthusiastic advocate of this monograph from the beginning. José David is herewith proclaimed as this book's *padrino*. The influence and presence of his phenomenal scholarship also permeates throughout these pages.

I have been indefatigably aided and abetted along the way by the superb and gracious Arturo Arias, whose inestimable efforts and contributions to Central American studies have opened the door wide in clear encouragement to future generations.

I gratefully acknowledge the camaraderie of my confreres in the Department of Romance Studies at Duke University for taking a chance on an unknown scholar, for institutionally "homing" me, and for nourishing me with a truly dynamic space. Infinite thank yous, respect, and admiration to Roberto Dainotto, Esther Gabara, Margaret Greer, Walter Mignolo, and Richard Rosa for enriching my workdays and for caring about this book nearly as much as I have.

A great and special homage to the wise and fabulous Antonio Viego for the spirited exchange of ideas, engaged support, music recommendations, and terrific inspiration.

I have been quite fortunate to count on the generous Karen Inouye, Sean Metzger, and Maritza Stanchich as early listeners and as an invaluable community of preliminary readers. I am obliged to them for shepherding me to the present stage of this endeavor and for being so detailed and rigorous.

It has been a privilege to work with Marc Schachter and to rely on him as a treasured friend. My gratitude to him is boundless for his kindness and benevolence, unflagging interest, and illuminating comments. He organically harvests, without exception, meaningful fruits of collaboration.

The supportive and wonderful friendship of Francisco-J. Hernández Adrián has meant the world to me: it underscores that writing is hardly accomplished in isolation. A standing ovation to him for being an unbroken source of intellectual stimulation, for furnishing me with his genius and inimitable wit, and for helping me through all my rough patches.

Platinum-level gratefulness to Anna Krylova, my critical titan, for her receptiveness and intellectual moxie, which contributed to the story of this book.

My profound word of thanks to the marvelous and peerless Izel Vargas for his exquisite oeuvre. His imaginative and intuitive eye helped me achieve what I visually wanted for this volume.

Enormous and heartfelt thanks to Holly Ackerman, Eduardo Bonilla-Silva, Michaeline A. Crichlow, Leslie Damasceno, Sarah Deutsch, Natalie Hartman, Pedro Lasch, Randall Love, J. Lorand Matory, Mark Anthony Neal, Diane Nelson, Charles Piot, Richard J. Powell, Charles Thompson, Priscilla Wald, Catherine Walsh, and Jenny Snead Williams. I send an equally lasting mention, too, to Bunmi Fatoye-Matory, Edna Goldstaub, and C. T. Woods.

I cherish the intellectual solidarity and motivation along the way from María DeGuzmán, Emilio del Valle Escalante, Jacinta Escudos, Licia Fiol-Matta, Jane Anna Gordon, Paget Henry, Norman Holland, Ifeoma Kiddoe Nwankwo, Marvette Pérez, Alberto Sandoval-Sánchez, Kirsten Silva Gruesz, Faith Smith, and Susan Smulyan.

Lewis R. Gordon deserves countless praise for teaching and mentoring me well and for being an inexhaustible voice and pillar of support.

An extra special note of colossal thanks to the vibrant and extraordinary students, current and past, from whom I have also acquired knowledge and whose career trajectories dazzle and inspire me. I salute your immense intellect, your ethic of care, and your friendship. I owe much to Carina Barnett-Loro, Christopher Clayton, Michelle Crow, Rebecca Feinglos, Andrew George, Anna Gravier, Bronwyn Lewis, Joanna Lichter, Catherine Nelson, Andrea Piskora, Jacob Spinner, Camila Vignaud, and Dominique Villegas for revealing that teaching is relational, for giving life to this project, and for joining me in this journey.

A resounding shout-out to Phoebe Lawless and Scratch Baking in Durham for hooking me up with a clean "desk" each morning and setting the right harmonious tone for my working hours. Big thanks to Karen Caffrey, Curtis Cushman, and Hilary Ragin for their warmth, humor, impeccable artistry, and skillful expertise, which consistently accomplishes glorious microfoam high notes.

I extend a tip of the hat to the usual suspects, Austin Bouton, Kyle Cox, Alex Junho Kim, Sumer Mishue, Amanda Lee Morris, Serena Qiu, Courtney Satterfield, and Katie Weeks, for their talented awesomeness.

Thanks, a thousand times over, to friends across multiple geographies who provide joy and comfort: Jane Cruz, Ronaldo Cruz, Bruce Fuller, Wendy Fuller, Holly Kunkel, Nadine Nelson, and Debbie Zambetti.

A fond acknowledgment to the late Humberto Cruz for his gentle presence and selflessness during our formative years at Hampshire College.

For reminding me of the revolutionary power of words and the text beyond the academy, I honor the memory of the late Saúl Solórzano, U.S. Central American community activist and leader. My unceasing gratitude to him for recognizing my potential and for mentoring me. I wish that I could have personally presented a copy of this book, the fruits of my labor, to Saúl, made possible by his magnanimous spirit and foresight.

For the gifts of lifelong friendship, moral support, and all-purpose wisdom, my interminable gratitude and affection go to the exceptional duo Frank Augustine and Aliza Augustine.

I thank my earliest intellectual comrade, Gloria Chacón, for her steadfast sisterhood and for sustaining me emotionally, professionally, and spiritually since our days at Hampshire. Her joie de vivre, kindness, and perspicacity continue to nurture me.

The making of this investigation benefited immeasurably from the dexterity, tolerance, and beauty of Miguel Segovia, my super-smart and never-tiring sounding board. No thanks are enough, Miguel, for living and enlivening every phase of this enterprise with me, for giving up your time to forward the crafting of this book, for sharing your insightful interpretations, and for shaping my thinking in new ways.

I reserve a simple and loving thank you for the magnificent Eduardo Contreras, my secret and critical weapon. Thank you for your humbling goodness, patience, brilliance, creativity, curiosity, and faith in my work. None of these pages could have been conceptualized or written without you.

For years of companionship, I offer this perfect-bound tribute to Theodor W. Adorno, the feline love of my life, for pouncing on my keyboard and reminding me that there is time for writing and time for play.

Dedicated to my mother, Betsy Arias, my source of strength and aspiration. *Dedicado a mi madre, Betsy Arias, fuente de fortaleza y razón de mi empeño.*

LATINING AMERICA

INTRODUCTION

THE COPIOUSNESS OF LATIN

The word "Latin" has migrated North.
What happens when that happens?
—PEDRO LASCH (2008)

Not only has the word "Latin" migrated northward but, historically speaking, so have multiethnic racialized subjects. *Latining America: Black-Brown Passages and the Coloring of Latino/a Studies* examines how multidirectional processes of Latinness travel, break, and alter at the level of meaning, geographies, and peoples. Through a Latin, Latin-American, Latino, and Latina triangulation, I seek to chart a different but coeval path and lexicon for how cultural signifiers for the U.S. Latino or Latina have been accessed by an unexpected circle of Latin participants: U.S. African Americans and "problematic" subgroups like Central Americans.[1] No theoretical language or sustained academic endeavor in Latino/a studies has yet critically traced and accounted for the multiple and simultaneous frames of reference at work for the Latin body, particularly within a national language of race invested in "color" as well as "coloring."

Attempting to revise the reigning black-white and white-brown model of social analysis, I pursue how a panoply of U.S. African Americans, Latinos, and Latinas walk in and out of their traditional designations. Sociologist Saskia Sassen has argued that "the modern twenty-first century citizen . . . is . . . being remade in bits and pieces," and I take this prescient statement as a point of departure for constructs of Latin and Latinness as weaved into U.S. Latino and Latina subject and cultural formation (2009: 230). These subjects do not operate under a single referent of an ontological grammar of race and sociocultural existence. Latinoness, Latinaness, Latinidad, blackness, and Africananess are literally more than they are or have turned out to be.² The detours Latinoness and Latinaness take—through blackness, dark brownness, indigence, Indianness, "second-tier" Latino status, and unmappable southern geographies—demand to be rigorously gauged. Problematizing and rearticulating the discursive order of Latino/a studies and perspectives as we presently know them is my principal purpose here.

The kinds of crossovers this project disentangles are evidenced in two incidents in the lives of brownness and blackness and their permeable borders. One brief anecdote entails Maya Soetoro-Ng, the half-white, half-Indonesian sister of President Barack Obama. Trying to live up to the category that stringently situates her, time and again, as Latina but that also exposes this term's laxity, Soetoro-Ng told the *New York Times Magazine*: "[P]eople usually think I'm Latina when they meet me. That's what made me learn Spanish" (Solomon, 2008). The second relates to Harvard University–educated actor Natalie Portman. The Academy Award winner made headlines not for her latest multimillion-dollar Hollywood release or for the type of exclusives aired on celebrity and entertainment news. According to one outlet, the hearsay boiled down to an apology Portman issued "after she was branded 'insensitive' for apparently saying she knows what it feels like to be black" (Femalefirst.co.uk, 2004). The "it" referred to Du Boisian double consciousness. In Portman's appropriation of the actor as metaphor, her conceptualization surfaced when confronted by the demands of a fame-chasing, consumerist world and the strains of trying to pass with the rest of the populace.³ Unlike Soetoro-Ng, a public redress was urged from Portman for summoning a theory that deliberates, to slightly swerve from Priscilla Wald's course in *Constituting Americans*, on "the stranger as self, the self as stranger" and that can only originate from U.S.-situated African American blackness (1995: 7).⁴

These seemingly arbitrary examples of a black consciousness and the enactment of a brown language make way for a highly deliberative moment where many people locate, practice, and live a "Latinity" that meddles into the customary affairs of Latinidad. That Soetoro-Ng speaks Spanish does not institute a definitive form of Latinaness any more than Portman's double consciousness would readily materialize U.S. African Americanness.⁵ Yet Soetoro-Ng and Portman encapsulate the crux of my efforts. Their locations directly intercalate an indirect knowledge that displaces intrinsic ethnoracial narratives of being. There is no precise categorical beginning, or end, for these identities-in-the-making. They speak to the power of social situations and relations as an excess of the imaginary and attest to the need for further inquiry about visual and sensory perceptions with regard to what has been constructed as ethnoracial. Soetoro-Ng and Portman induce evolving processes of identities that will be discharged again and give rise to the following questions: What makes mixed subjects singularly brown or black? Which kinds of bodies gain entrance into manifestations of Latinidad? Do these black-brown bodily migrations, which can be arranged under philosopher Alejandro de Acosta's (2007) incitation of "mobile meditations," provide a new exegesis for projects that account for other peoples and power relations vis-à-vis intertwined journeys in black, brown, and dark brown?

To be sure, we are witnessing the appearance of something vying for our attention. A multiphasic something that is letting us know that whatever might be ascribable to blackness, Latinoness, and Latinaness is being dissolved. It is becoming more expansive and tinged with a host of ethnoracial and cultural dichotomies openly encouraging a way out of a brown Latino and Latina impasse.[6] This additional something might be going, as Gustavo Pérez Firmat has it in connection to Cuba as proxy for a Latin atmosphere, to a "pan-Latin 'somewhere,' a locale without location" (2010: 18–19). This Latin venue sans location is enigmatically concretized by the emanation of a Latin subject. Ed Morales succinctly—but no less abstractly—sums up the coming of this Latinity: "[T]here may be more styles and variations of being Latino than there are different Latin American countries" (2003: xi). Morales's overview of Latin surplus cannot be wiped off the Latinidad map. It rightfully lacks the social scripting of one Latino, Latina, or Latin-American subject as well as a single unit of cultural and geopolitical articulation.

The notion of recognizable U.S. Latinos and Latinas is subject to revision from a Latinities standpoint that takes another look at the ethnoracial logic shaping this population. Literary critic Marcus Boon has asked, "[S]uppose copying is what makes us human—what then? More than that, what if copying, rather than being an aberration or a mistake or a crime, is a fundamental condition or requirement for anything, human or not, to exist at all? If such is the case [. . .] then the activities known as 'copying,' the objects known as 'copies,' and those who find themselves making these copies would all need to be revalued" (2010: 3–4). Boon's questions on copies and their equivalencies lead us to this introduction's title as well as to my analytic maneuver: to constellate the manifold complexities of Latin signification and make use of the practice and acquisition of Latinness in ways that exceed generic brown Latinoness and Latinaness.[7] The copiousness of the Latin does not merely imply large and abundant quantities. It is also connotative of how Latinities are led astray and spurt out of the structuring content of U.S. Latinoness and Latinaness. The meticulous or inaccurate transference of Latin copies — the styles and variations that Morales touches on — is beside the point. These Latinities, as copies that cling to different actors and give rise to new representations, do not slip away from their "rightful" U.S. Latino and Latina brown proprietors. This copiousness can be understood as a set of new possibilities in the referents and sources for Latinness, as a new understanding from which different types of Latinoness and Latinaness are redirected and picked up. The copies are not final. They are a recurrent activity of Latined living — a participatory contact that is edited, revised, and reoriented. The copiousness of Latin thusly calls forth a new and much bolder conversation, for lest we forget, Latinoness and Latinaness slip out of brown bodies and the Spanish language.

What merits ongoing deliberation is not *who* are *the* Latinos and Latinas but *how* do "they" become as such? At what moments do these Latinities, with indiscriminate sites of attachment, emerge? I am interested in how other liminalities activate the inflection Latinity and how this word's paradigm affixes itself to — and migrates in the direction of — U.S. Latino, Latina, black, dark brown, and discursively parenthetical bodies. Notice that I intentionally refrain from employing in this instance the term "Latinidad," as it is unquestionably tied to a collective ethos located no further than its surrounding U.S. Latino and Latina criterion. This does not mean that Latinidad, as a category and incubator of Latino/a thought, will be completely ignored or dispensed with. Its currency in the academy, especially in Latino/a studies' guardianship and organization of Latino/a knowledge, impels my desire to investigate how it crosses paths with blackness, dark brownness, and marginal U.S. Latino and Latina subgroups. To cite Latinidad and its limits, as currently theorized, I need to identify and critique it as such.

The Latinities herein are highly mindful of the different reflections of living as a form of U.S. Latino or Latina but not as Latino and Latina. These Latinities provide illuminating traces and insight into what unstable Latined lives look like and might mean in this century. But these Latinities by no means suggest an endless line of peripatetic individuals walking in and out of a U.S. Latino and Latina turnstile. Rather, this book gestures toward new formulations of Latinoness and Latinaness that do not solely depend on a definite, firm color and national origin or that, in some cases, are even specific to the United States. The core of my study refigures how Latino/a studies' construction of Latinoness and Latinaness looks outside this field and its relation to ideological white Americanness to think of new possibilities beyond national identities and brown symbology.[8]

In asking about national identities, I also inquire about which types of incipient denationalizations of (Latin) citizenships are taking place, to return to Sassen's proposition (2009: 229). U.S. public and political perceptions cast Latinos and Latinas as foreigners from a "separate nation, 'as a country that is separate and apart from the United States'" (Dávila, 2001: 83).[9] For Sassen, denationalization captures "something that remains connected to the 'national' as constructed historically, and is indeed profoundly imbricated with it but is so on historically new terms of engagement" (2009: 229). These new terms of engagement deliberate on the incompleteness of "minoritized citizens" or migrant status, which "brings to the fore the work of making, whether it is making in response to changed conditions, new subjectivities, or new instrumentalities" (228).[10] I solicit Latinities as one mechanism that culls on the kinds of incompleteness essential to the "normalization" of a particular mode of Latino/a studies. Brownness as designative of U.S. Latino and Latina identities, as presently manifested, cannot adhere, and neither can blackness as appropriate only to a U.S. African American context. Blacks, browns, and dark browns enter, move into, and interfere with one another's color lines, and not unidirectionally either, or horizontally, but vertically as well.[11] These black-brown–dark brown color lines pass for and cross through one another.[12] They reshape and are not sedimented, even though I recognize that this book's methodology still brings to light an ever-present, dissolving line. A line, as established by the *Oxford English Dictionary* (*OED*), is "a long, narrow mark or band" in mathematics. But it is also "a straight or curved continuous extent of length without breadth." Its curvature—effectively, a *bending* line—can connect "all points having a common property on a map or graph." The *OED* also qualifies a line as "a sphere of activity; a direction, course, or channel."[13] The crossing lines summoned here, as domains of activity, often strip the weighty signifiers that ostensibly jell the Latino and Latina place in U.S. social imaginaries and political memberships.

My premise, mapped in four chapters, is that Latinities offer a conceptual framework that plots other subjectivities and localities that have yet to be charted within and beyond the configurations of Latinidad. This task proves demandingly difficult to chart, insofar as such an approach has not been delineated or critically diagrammed within Latino/a studies.[14] Since Latinidad has yet to graph these other ways of activating and wrestling with the ambiguities undercurrent in the construct of Latinness, Latinities are introduced as a potent and voracious symbol that circulates and changes among porous populations and geohistories.[15] Brownness, variations of the Spanish language, and Latinness enact a working ambiguity—a Latinity—that does not conceal, reject, or erase its uncertainty and equivocation. Instead, the vagueness of these Latin possibilities makes and remakes itself precisely because Latino and Latina are a product of ambiguity.

Latinities, with its variable currents and transfers of meaning, parse the vocabulary subscribed to U.S. blackness, brownness, and dark brownness. Latinities operate as questioning incitations that give careful consideration to new, even "unknown" and unsituated Latino and Latina modalities. Doing so entails theoretical efforts that aim to capture my contributions to Latino/a studies. My critical feat results in an analytic search that tracks the shifting contours of Latinoness and Latinaness in a language heretofore unacknowledged. Other than Latinidad, there are no additional key terms in Latino/a cultural studies that encapsulate the nuanced ways that Latinoness and Latinaness have been entered, recalibrated, exited, entered yet again, and en*liv*ened by different groups. This approach requires new avenues for understanding why concepts like Latinities have been solicited to provide a scholarly recontextualization of how "perturbative" forms of Latinoness and Latinaness are lived and come alive in creative and undetermined patterns. The same applies for the proposed verb advancing this book's title, "Latining." These designations methodologically perform the ways that the signifier Latin hosts a free flow of people and stirs with or without the easily assumed Latino and Latina subject in Latinidad.[16]

Such open-ended possibilities demand a distance from U.S. Latino and Latina authenticity and the ontological grammar of Latinidad. Thus, Latinities emerge and their meanings alter depending on the context and in the process of subjectivation. There is not one decisive way of presenting and defining a particular Latinity at hand. But this approach should not be misread as a colloquial cop-out. To demand transparent and sharp certitude around the ever-evolving terms and terrains of Latinities is to restrain black-brown–dark brown passages and limit their unpredictable prospects. The unrestricted flexibility of Latinities cannot be linearly smoothened in the same manner as the more reliable and complete Latino and Latina equation and narration proffered in Latinidad. A necessary requisite, Latinities give this analysis elucidative insight, as the point of continuous excavation is the idea of Latinoness and Latinaness as provisional.[17] Latinities are held together by their acknowledgment of just how much these subjectivities are consistently moving and remapping the U.S. terrain and its imaginary.

As such, *Latining America: Black-Brown Passages and the Coloring of Latino/a Studies* raises two central concerns: What is a Latino or Latina? And how do these social actors arrive at such a discourse? Versions of Latinities are manifested as a reprise, in plural form, appearing by necessity in each of the chapters. Latinities are an outwardly verb that signals the adjective "Latin," which is enumerated by the *OED* as pertaining "to those countries of Central, North, and South America in which Spanish or Portuguese is the dominant language, spec. as Latin America."[18] Needless to add, this is not an account of the Latin language (cf. Clackson and Horrocks, 2007). The "Latin" in Latinities is not meant to sinew, within the realm of Latinoness and Latinaness, a canonical language akin to how Latin has played out in the West's cultural history and development. As a common but evaluative thread among various populations, Latinities are an overlay of meaning that parses the grammar subscribed to blackness, brownness, and dark brownness. I pun on Latin as much as the Latins, who are thought to cohesively populate a community of "Spanish people" through the latter's affiliation with a body politic in which traces of a black and brown (ethnoracialized) vernacular evolve into new conceptions. These Latinities can constitute what Nicholas Ostler approximates through the phrase *ad infinitum*, meaning "on and on, without boundary" (2007: 317). Repetitive though they may be, these Latinities take form through continuity and rupture, differing in each context and eroding into another formation. They are not U.S. Latino and Latina specific, although they draw on the brown formulations of U.S. Latinidad to tease out the troubling limits of such an articulation.

By contrast, Latinidad bears an ideology impaired by its own referents or illusory connection as an inherited, unitary lineage that devolves into an intelligible U.S. Latino and Latina membership. And yet Latinoness and Latinaness often pose a dilemma, as these tend to be contested sites because of the trappings found in the nationalistic appendages that come with the category.[19] Latin body politics are repeatedly disputed spaces that empty out the identificatory categories of Latino and Latina—taking them to the meanings and classifications that have been presumably expunged from Latinidad: blackness and dark brownness.[20] The problem for second-tier groups who have "no" intellectual history or clear genealogical evidence of U.S.-grounded Latino and Latina life and experience is that their Latino and Latina experiential situations must be retold so as to wrestle with the lacks and insufficiencies found in the present Latino/a studies project. The color palette this study considers may appear to preclude other groups such as Asians.[21] My goal, however, is hardly exclusionary. I seek to build on the idea and practice of Latinoness and Latinaness through dark brownness and blackness. These signifiers stand associatively close to—and paradoxically distant from—each other in the production of a Latinidad that, as Richard Rodriguez sees it, is reconciled through brownness as the primary habitus for Latino or Latina personhoods (2002: xii).[22]

A further clarification is in order. My intent is not to focus on U.S. Afro-Latinos or Afro–Latin Americans from the Hispanophone Caribbean. Rather than exclusively turning to the Spanish-speaking Caribbean for clear-cut and solidifying experiences and representations of blackness, I set my course toward the study of the more subtle but still resonant preoccupations with the semiotics of blackness and dark brownness in the Mesoamerican geographies of Mexico and Central America and U.S. Latinos and Latinas tracing their heritages to those regions. I do not refute or deny that there is a black presence in these areas or within U.S. Latino and Latina populations.[23] For my purposes, I am concerned with the rhetoric and invocation of blackness, brownness, and dark brownness in Mesoamerican contexts.[24] I am also interested in how a supposed parenthetical blackness, often presumed as being antithetical to brown Latinoness and Latinaness, passes through different bodies beyond the categorical delineations of "standard" blackness. My objective is to initiate a dialogue with writers, narratives, and experiences that have been previously ignored or written out of Latino/a studies: the southern, the black, the dark brown, the indigenous, and the Central American. The idea of problematic blackness for U.S. African Americans and problematic dark brownness for U.S. Latinos and Latinas within Mesoamerican contexts has not been fully investigated in this field. The academic tendency in Latino/a studies has been to orbit around the Hispanophone Caribbean, seeking to neatly point and comprehensively index blackness in the American hemisphere through this geography. Here, blackness and indigenous darkness are shepherded to the forefront as they inhabit the presumably browned Latinized body.

My monograph's quest does not set to endeavor with the institutional or intellectual history of U.S. Latino/a studies.[25] It is not an account for how the field of Latino/a studies becomes "Latino/a studies." The book interrogates *what* enters as Latino and Latina in the field and how Latino/a studies rearranges or unplugs *Latin* significations from the premises of Latinidad.

With this explanation of my motives and timely contributions, I now turn to critically review the theories and components of Latinidad. Getting back to these basics marking the premises of Latino/a studies affords a genealogical entry into my intellectual initiatives. It also situates the framework for Latinities as a conceptual language.

Grammar Matters: Latinidad and Latinities

Promoted by France, Latinidad and its variants, Latinity and Latinitée, were launched during the second half of the nineteenth century, initiating imperial and colonial differences in the region that Walter Mignolo skillfully modifies as "'Latin' America." Mignolo puts across that "'Latinidad' was the ideology under which the identity of the ex-Spanish and ex-Portuguese colonies was located (by natives as well as by Europeans) in the new global, modern/colonial world order" (2005: 58). This credo has been an example "of the kind of modern/colonial translation that captures and transforms people, cultures, and meanings into what is legible and controllable for those in power" (144). The organizational hierarchies of this world order suggest that U.S. Latinos and Latinas, much like Latin Americans, have operated, as Mignolo assesses it, as copies of the Latin in the European sense. "*In the imperial imaginary*," he remarks, "'Latin' Americans are second-class Europeans while Latinos/as in the U.S. are second-class Americans." But while Latinidad operated as a previously colonizing tool for European imaginaries that pushed a "colonization of being," it has now emerged, for U.S. Latinos and Latinas, as a "decolonizing project" (64).

This decolonizing project is made up of, as historian Virginia Sánchez Korrol claims, established U.S. Latino and Latina populations such as Mexican American, Puerto Rican, and Cuban American, that are also matched with "relatively recent arrivals, predominantly from the Dominican Republic and Central and South America, with long-time U.S. residents; English speaking with Spanish speaking; aliens with citizens; and documented individuals with undocumented immigrants" (1996: 5). At the center of this ever-evolving panethnic category stands the cultural and political necessity for what sociologist Felix Padilla conjectured, during the mid-1980s, as "Latinismo." This model grants "an ethnic-conscious identity and behavior distinct and separate from the individual ethnic identity of Mexican-Americans, Puerto Ricans, Cubans, and other Spanish-speaking groups" (1985: 1). Although Padilla's tenet is comparativist in scope, his Latinismo's parameters are clearly drawn by Hispanophone ties. Yet Latinismo "represents a collective-generated behavior that transcends the individual group's national and cultural identities" (162).

Grounding Latinismo a decade after Padilla's case study, Suzanne Oboler's *Ethnic Labels, Latino Lives* takes up this outlook as "the forging of unity among Latinos in the struggle for citizenship rights and social justice in the United States." Of equal importance is "the need to provide second and later generations of Latin American descent with a broader framework for examining the meaning and implications of their respective national, racial, linguistic, class, and gendered diversity in the process of constructing that unity" (1995: xix). This deployment of Latino, Latina, and Latin American unity of thought incites discussions on the aggregate nationalities, ethnoracial locations, and institutionalizations of the U.S. Latino and Latina public face, as it were. Sociologist Agustín Laó-Montes posits that Latinidad, "as a form of identification lies in its historical production as a U.S.-based constellation of identities of peoples of Latin American and Caribbean descent" (2001: 15). He explicates that "it is crucial to conceive Latinidad not as a static and unified formation but as a flexible category that relates to a plurality of ideologies of identification, cultural expressions, and political and social agendas" (8).[26] While Laó-Montes's Latinidad appears more permissive — what Sánchez

Korrol also introduces as "a heightened sense of awareness and receptivity"—a U.S. Latino and Latina subject can be largely informed by some nationalities that may have more visibility and historical presencing than others (1996: 5). Such subjectivity can also draw from the more aurally "visible" and acceptable modalities of the Spanish language.[27]

In this sense, Latino and Latina lives—already homogenized by the aforementioned umbrella demarcation—can become more uniform in the production of a Latinidad that subsumes its subjects through the sole emphasis of coalitional alliances. This leads one to wonder whether there can be a Latino or Latina self separate from a—or even *the*—Latino cause. Such approaches could lock a subject in a Latino- or Latina-specific inflexible Latinidad and in a direction that is unable to meet other ways through which widespread Latin spheres are being accessed, interrupted, and reconfigured. Conceptually speaking, this is what Latinities aim to elicit: to move beyond the limiting locations of Latinidad and result in a larger "ethic of care," as Joan C. Tronto envisions it.[28] Tronto's precept infers "everything that we do to maintain, continue, and repair our 'world' so that we can live in it as well as possible. That world includes our bodies, our selves, and our environment, all of which we seek to interweave in a complex, life-sustaining web." An ethic of care necessitates "daily and thoughtful judgments about caring." It is a process of being active. Tronto elaborates that it also entails "care as an action, as a practice, not as a set of principles or rules [. . . . It] can occur in a variety of institutions and settings. Care is found in the household, in services and goods sold in the market, in the workings of bureaucratic organizations, in contemporary life" (1998: 16). The potential to care about collective, everyday *life* surfaces within and outside the reliable and predictable criterion that falls under Latinidad.[29] These emergent commonalities and practices of care, informed by the myriad spaces of Latinities, would raise questions not only on how one *knows* Latinidad but also on how one is capable (or perhaps even incapable) of getting it "right" and, indeed, of achieving it—living it—"rightly."[30]

As presently mapped, studies of Latinidad—concisely phrased by Deborah Paredez as "the process of Latina/o identity making"—generally focus on the organized pursuit for consensus building (2009: xiii). Through social movements and community affiliations, Latinidad (or, in the Spanish plural, Latinidades) stress these loci of political activity: (1) uncriminalized, fully functional U.S. citizenship rights; (2) governmental representation at the local, state, and federal levels; (3) socioeconomic equality; and (4) dissenting, analytic voices regarding the mainstream media's disparaging representations and commodification of U.S. Latino and Latina body politics. But as anthropologists Nicholas De Genova and Ana Y. Ramos-Zayas have demonstrated, there are multifaceted—not to mention contradictory—tensions within the variegated and highly selective sociopolitical imaginaries storing the contemporary uses of what grows into an enclosed Latinidad. De Genova and Ramos-Zayas focus on the contours that Latinidad takes within Chicago's Mexican and Puerto Rican populations. They identify these groups' dissimilar approaches to a panethnic partnership through any of these platforms: (1) a Latinidad as the "American" abjection of the U.S.-born; (2) a Latinidad composed through migrant illegality as well as a Latinidad without Puerto Ricans; (3) a Latinidad in opposition to African Americans; (4) a Latinidad as an articulation of working-class solidarity; (5) a Latinidad as a strategy of middle-class formation; and (6) a fractured Latinidad through institutional contexts, whiteness, and power (2003: 178–210).[31]

These Latinidades allude to, as María Lugones has stated in the context of the forging of alliances, a Latino and Latina panethnic logic of narrow identities assuming an "epistemically shallow sense of coalition based on coincidence of interests" (2006: 76). As outlined, the aforementioned pan-Latino identifications set forth what José Esteban Muñoz has called "the affective overload that is Latinidad" (2000: 73). Muñoz doubtlessly punctuates a noticeable schism that leads one to interrogate why such political activism and social expectations can be theorized as "Latinidad" in light of their expeditious deletions. Furthermore, there are no analytic terms available for the theorizing of collective Latino and Latina dissonances, variances, and disagreements. Lugones incisively explains that people of color in the United States learn maxims "to deal with white supremacy in rather narrow enclaves" (2006: 78–79). Such an outlook clarifies, to some degree, why this coincidence of interests—posited, at first glance, through an extensive arrangement of Latinidades with divergent boundaries in terms of Latino and Latina national as well as political affiliations, different generations, and sexuality—remain specific to Latino brown and white American objectives.

A similar binary is also entrenched in a Latinidad that connects to U.S. Latino and Latina cultural practices. Myra Mendible explains that a cultural

Latinidad is "implicated in a history of U.S. marketing and entertainment distortions of Latino/a cultures." These representations have "met resistance from many Chicano and Latino critics [who] have questioned the usefulness and effect of such labeling, for example, its tendency to homogenize peoples whose histories, language usage, and circumstances may differ significantly or to alienate U.S.-born Latinos, who may not speak Spanish or share other identifying criteria. There are also legitimate reasons to suspect bureaucratic attempts to regulate, profile, and monitor a growing constituency of over 40 million people" (2007: 4). These findings are informative, but central to my efforts is the attempt to call attention to and investigate more precisely brown-white Latinidad distortions from within brown, dark brown, and black Latino and Latina states.

Latinidad, as presently articulated and generally adopted, is hardly useful for my analytic purposes. Its dual-directional model of identity and working signifiers are ensnared in the logic of white and brown. This book dialogues with recent approaches to Afro-Latinidad—for example, Agustín Laó-Montes (2001, 2007), Miriam Jiménez Román and Juan Flores (2010), and the Afro-Latin@ Project—to the extent that it is concerned with the Africana diaspora in the new world.[32] But it also constructively departs: Afro-Latinidad scholarship has the tendency to give primacy to Caribbean geographies in the Americas. Discourses on Afro-Latinidad, moreover, are often dependent on tangible, phenotypic black bodies to study Latinoness and Latinaness from one location: blackness. While some work on Afro-Latinoness has approximated, in part, what I am trying to articulate, such studies have not investigated in an extended way the kinds of cross-identifications that propel me. I scrutinize how the U.S. color line crosses paths with a Global South and unravel how habitually perceived brown subjects cross into, circulate, and revamp the operational semiotics of both blackness and brownness. In this way, discourses on Afro-Latinidad and Latinidad are expanded, as they shift to new articulations of Latinities north and south.

One could consider, as a brief illustration, the expressive sketches of Latining that Junot Díaz demonstrates in his Pulitzer Prize–winning *The Brief Wondrous Life of Oscar Wao*. The novel centers on Oscar de León, a nerdy, sci-fi-loving, pop culture aficionado, and his family's migration from the Dominican Republic to northern New Jersey. The shadow of Rafael Leónidas Trujillo's dictatorship follows Díaz's subjects. In their deeply meshed past and present, Oscar's family struggles with the effects of the inescapable new world curse, *fukú americanus*, "or more colloquially, fukú" (2007: 1). But the origins of fukú americanus, which as speculatively written in the book's inaugural sentence, imply myth or hearsay—"they say it came first from Africa"—is not a mere punch line propitiously executed in Latin. It provokes thoughtful inquisitiveness on its sources and lineages, on what accounts for its presence, and what it means for the Latined diaspora of lowercase americanus to be conjoined by an interminable fukú. Díaz globalizes this emergent but fairly obfuscated subject adjusting its "who-ness," "what-ness," and "how-ness," but not necessarily guaranteeing a clear (read: Latino) outcome.

The types of americanus encountering, in some measure, the evenly spaced and distributed fukú—"because no matter what you believe, fukú believes in you"—eclipse Afro-Latinoness, Latinidad, and a formal nationality (Díaz, 2007: 5). In one telling instance, Oscar de León, whose name appears to have an ironic alliteration with the Venezuelan salsa performer Oscar D'León, is acknowledged as a new species through the visionary greeting, "Hail, Dominicanis."[33] This acknowledgement gives prominence to the open conditions of Oscar's traveling Latinities. Under Díaz's pen, this Latin subject is a revision of both Dominican and American subjectivity. It is a "God. Domini. Dog. Canis" and takes a new, "illegible" speciation depending on the geographic, physiological, and linguistic barriers at hand (171).

Like Oscar's Latinities, there is no fixed form or stable geography to Díaz's text, which like Gabriel García Márquez's *One Hundred Years of Solitude* (1998), was first conceived in Mexico City.[34] Its multiple story lines, cultural vacillations, and interlacing linguistic styles admit a Spanglish marked by an urban vernacular or a bigger language that bears the influences of literary and nonliterary texts and practices from the United States, the Caribbean, Latin America, and Europe. Not to be discounted is Díaz's use of footnotes as well, which gives a scholarly quality to the story line. Yet the quick-witted annotations amuse through their historical and political irreverence in the plotting of the similarities and differences of Dominican, Dominican American, and U.S. Latino and Latina life.[35] The novel's open-ended resources exceed local and national circumstances. They are a new source of explanation for the "Latino" and "Latina" plenum and how it has been read. Communicative Latinities emerge through a Latined mode of rewriting, from the Dominicanis archive, the variable form and content of Latinidad and its memberships. Like Díaz's hero, the literary lineage of *The Brief Wondrous Life of Oscar Wao* moves across the boundaries of cultures, creating a Latined literary history that draws out, borrows from, and is steeped in a vast range of relationships and discourses that may, as a popular phrase goes, pop in — or pop out — anywhere.[36]

The Latinities evoked chronicle the various ranges of the Latin that currently fissure Latinidad. By passing through different bodies, geographies, and cultures within and beyond the United States, we see how black, brown, and dark brown "passing lines," to recall Brad Epps's term, point to the limitations of the white-black, the brown-white, and the brown-black dyads (2001). They defy confining classifications and living states of interregnum that also amount to what Veronica Gonzalez has called "twin time" (2007). Such Latinities demand a shift in the brown vocabulary we presuppose and understand as Latino or Latina today, since Latinity calls for *re-cognition* in ever-widening global migrations. "Re-cognition" is inserted here, rather than misrecognition, because a given, recognized Latinity is not "wrong" per se. Through re-cognition, the ambiguous Latin subject has been acknowledged for what it can also be, which is interpreted as an admissible Latinity.[37] It is another formulation of Latino and Latina, not so much because the classification cannot index a subject's definitive identity, but because its incoherence is also hauling another meaning (cf. Muñoz, 2000). Latinities steer toward a dynamic mode of analysis that is attentive to emergent subjectivities as well as the categories needed to affirm them. What I have said thus far can and does sound provocative, particularly when Latino/a studies seems to be at stake. In view of this concern, I ask what we in this field are to do with this type of questioning and analysis. As a reassessment of the tools of Latinoness and Latinaness, my approach calls for different ways of thinking about and orienting the changes engulfing Latinidad to open a space for moving Latinities.

Latinities offer a conceptual shift in multiple interwoven discourses and how these shape the subject. They are a "re-articulatable" panethnic space where the subject is constituted in relation to blackness, brownness, and dark brownness but also in terms of language, ethnicity, nation, class, gender, sexuality, and race, depending on the context. Latinity is the action of the "thing" that "becomes" re-cognized in locations outside its own ethnoracial and cultural particularities. Latinities are re-articulatable because they become a different discursive element and provide a necessary distance from how normative U.S. African American and U.S. Latino and Latina projects have been bounded and represented. Routine life practices and occasions must be revisited and rewritten, reminding us that "blackness transcends North America—and even Africa," just as much as Latinness surpasses Latin America (L. Gordon, 1995a: 2). Seen in this manner, the irreducibility of African and Latin signifiers transverse, slip, and disperse. They generate Latinities that swirl around us without parochial boundaries—taking us to the immense yet contradictory sites and passages of being and dwelling in the Americas.

In Short/Breve Faciam

Latining America: Black-Brown Passages and the Coloring of Latino/a Studies delves into the cultural connections and global crossing color lines of blackness, brownness, and dark brownness. Latining speaks to the Latinities that have yet to play out in—and pass through—the U.S. social structuring of Latinos, Latinas, and African Americans.[38] To be Latined, according to the *OED*, is to be versed in Latin. To "Latin it" stands for speaking or writing in Latin and therefore corresponds with a Latining. A Latining of the Americas, as signified in *Latining America*, circulates the need for becoming better acquainted with and versed in the marginal black-brown–dark brown literary passages that are seldom read in comparative form and in English and Spanish within U.S. academic contexts.[39] Angie Chabram-Dernersesian gives observant care to this matter, most notably as it corresponds to Spanish and Latin American departmental politics and their relationship to U.S. Latinos and Latinas. She writes that "the time-honored practices of traditional [Spanish] departments that appeal to *la hispanidad*" often allure to "an overarching unity of Spanish-speaking peoples while delivering curriculums that selectively foreground elite Spanish, Latin American, and Latino traditions." While these elements of "elite traditions" are not sharply defined, Chabram-Dernersesian taps into how Latina/o studies is articulated and positioned in the U.S. academy. She notes, "Other legacies considered to be too popular, indigenous, domestic, working class, or too American for Spanish (American) Eurocentric tastes are ignored, underrepresented, or directed to ethnic studies departments" (2003: 107).

I give precedence to these U.S. Latino and Latina concerns in relation to Africana blackness. This Latining tackles a Latin vagueness paradoxically grounded in what has come to be extracted as "that other negativity, U.S.-based Latin American working class" or as a U.S. Latinoness and Latinaness that simultaneously "suggests a broad and aged otherness to Anglo American modernized norms—but an otherness constituted as almost an absence within the Western episteme" (Zimmerman, 1992: 14). A passage also means to not be impeded by or restrained from activity and movement. The black-brown passages inferred are biographical journeys into each presumed prohibitive U.S. Latino, Latina, or African American space, admitting us into the various passings that have been activated in the unsteady, daily stages of blackness, brownness, and dark brownness.[40] Finally, a word on the last part of this book's title: *The Coloring of Latino/a Studies* is a nod to the "colored folk" euphemism for black. It also indicates a diversification in the multiple forms of Latinities "re-coloring" the particles that have been airbrushed from the production of Latino and Latina brownness. This coloring takes two striking forms: the ethnoracial and cultural paradigm of black versus brown and the normative terms that write off other Latino and Latina subpopulations from the Latinidad map.

The subsequent chapters explore how Latinness is being triggered through an illustrative, but hardly definitive, quadrant of these renderings: Southern Latinities, Passing Latinities, Indigent Latinities, and Disorienting Latinities. These Latinities build on Mignolo's (2005) idea of "Latin" America as they take on the ways that the region has been conjectured. They also depend on Lugones's (2006) incisive rearrangement of hyphenated Latin-American beings and worlds. As a referent, Latin-American is a stimulus for the constitution of Latin subjects—within and outside the United States—that may be regionally, culturally, or racially intangible.[41] An amalgamated invisibility gives form to U.S. Latinos and Latinas as well as Latin Americans in the United States and Latin America. "Latin" America (in the U.S. Latino and Latina sense) and Latin-America (in the América Latina or Latinoamérica denotation) are extant interpretations of Latinness that have been Americanized in the United States. I hyphenate Latin-American to point to the conflation of U.S. Latinos and Latinas as well as Latin Americans, while building on Latinized representations for the worlds that ("southernly") Latins dwell in and migrate from.

Latining America is organized around four chapters, where each directs attention to different themes and composites that describe divergent and neglected forms of Latinidad. There is dynamism in play along each unrestricted and flexible Latinity. This approach enacts the nonlinearity, continuing contexts, and relevance of corresponding Latinities from chapter to chapter. The book's structure conceptually spans the twentieth century. It investigates, as a whole, how certain lives and traveling bodies have taken shape as "black" or "brown" or been relegated to the U.S. Latino and Latina margins. The study defies U.S. Latino and Latina stasis, if not the unilateral genealogy of Latinidad. The volume progresses from the black-white color line and brown-black passing lines, as accessed by black Latinos, U.S. African Americans, and dark Latinos, to the empire line, as confronted by U.S. Central Americans.

The first chapter, "Southern Latinities," builds on the Du Boisian color line. I extend this color line to broader crossings where the movement of racially marked bodies, geographies, and critical awareness install an emergent Latinity within a "local" south (i.e., the U.S. South) and engage with it through the conceptual category of the Global South. My use of the latter builds on theories and geographies to account for alterations to — and by — the black, Latino, and Latina subject. I recognize, as Jonathan Rigg has observed, that the Global South "is also known, variously, as the Third World, the poor world, the less developed world, the non-Western world, and the developing world." Through these constructions it is also difficult, as Rigg details, "to begin the process of thinking about the Global South without also irrevocably linking it with the challenge of development and the stain of poverty" (2007: 9–10). Not dissimilar to Rigg, my intellectual attempts are neither about poverty nor development. As an analytic concept, the Global South, paired with the adoption of what Raewyn Connell (2007) identifies as "Southern theory," allows for epistemological overlaps where the parameters and geographic extensions advancing the idea of the U.S. South — for example, a plantation economy, processes of racialization, U.S. South–U.S. North migrations, and the creation of empire — highlight changes in U.S. national dynamics and in regional characteristics. Global peripheries are thus reconfigured, often analogously to the U.S. South in an open-ended charting of the geographic and geohistorical. The Global South's contours allow me to rigorously question how regional spaces are mapped and how certain geographies are imagined as the main purveyors of absolute blackness and brownness.

Chapter 1 also draws on Evelio Grillo's (1919–2008) *Black Cuban, Black American* (2000). It relocates the Southeast's black-white color line through Grillo's continuous crossings of black-Latin-white divides, spanning the 1920s onward. The value of this autobiographical cartography is not simply attributed to Grillo's black Cubanness. The memoir's cultural weight is also due to this differentiation: the "recovery" of Grillo's Hispanic/Latino life, as reclaimed through Arte Público Press's Recovering the U.S. Hispanic Literary Heritage series. This editorial effort by "the premier center for research of Latino documentary history in the United States" functions, in the press's words, as "a national project to locate, preserve and disseminate Hispanic culture of the United States in its written form since colonial times until 1960" (Latinoteca.com, 2010). I bring into focus the value of the heterogeneity of blackness as it brushes alongside the heterogeneity of Latinoness and Latinaness. In examining Grillo's "Latinization" or "Hispanization" within literary studies, my interpretive lens does not attempt to signal that there are no black Latinos in the United States. Grillo's entry into the double locations of Latin-blackness and Americanness needs to be emphasized as one paralleling the multidirectional Latinities that surface in his rather exiguous publication. Grillo's double perspectives situate an interdependent Latin blackness derivable from a shifting historicized black-and-white South and a seemingly dehistoricized brown, alien South.

The ("*Nuevo*") alien South that I rethink approximates Africana and Latino/a disciplinary distance and can more affirmatively articulate what I call open double consciousness. That Du Bois's double consciousness is already "coterminous with his career-long effort to think outside the space and time of the nation" is hardly questionable (Cooppan, 2005: 300). Yet my figuration of "open" to a racialized double consciousness "extends it beyond its origins" (Gooding-Williams, 2005a: 205). My synergistic call to investigate Du Boisian double consciousness in relation to Latino/a and African American studies (and by association American studies as well as Latin American studies) need not be superficially dismissed as an old new thing, meaning a recycled undertaking of an "old notion."[42] More than a century after Du Bois propounded what Vilashini Cooppan has recognized as "the necessity of learning to think doubly about the scene of political identification," double consciousness is a resource for emergent subjects who, characterized as aliens and American intruders, are situated outside the U.S. national symbolic of white and black

(2005: 299). Du Bois's work, Robert Gooding-Williams also concedes, "invites appraisal from many disciplinary perspectives [. . .] because its impact and significance cannot be reduced to the terms available to just one such point of view." His pertinence continues "to shape valuable discussions of black literature and racial politics in postsegregation America" (2005a: 204).

But Latino and Latina oppositions in postsegregation America differ from Du Bois's. The doubling of the Americas, north and south, is one instance that cues us on the exigency to open a double consciousness for populations who have not been historicized within the U.S. black-white dyad. Latino and Latina polarities—or twenty-first-century peculiarities—range from U.S. American/foreigner, Anglophone Americas/Hispanophone Americas, and U.S. Latinos/"Other Latinos" to black English speaker/brown Spanish speaker, African American Southeast/Chicano Southwest, and black-white America/incompatible Latinities in, and colorings from, the Americas.[43] I assign "open" to double consciousness to allow the entry of other subjects from varied geographic directions and ethnoracial configurations who must also labor with the meaning of how they may or may not fit in the foundational American coupling of white and black. Allow me to say that open double consciousness does not—nor does it pretend to—substitute Du Boisian double consciousness. It is meant as a rhetorical move that opens up room for the discursive maneuver of Latino and Latina collective "alienness." It strives to flesh out the everyday relationship of double consciousness (i.e., of being black and American) to new embodied doublings that are dislodged from the "American" landscape and that should go away from the United States. The openness of open double consciousness vies for the open constitution of mobile subjectivities as well as for the possibilities of transnational citizenships in the "active making of diverse kinds of rights-bearing subjects" (Sassen, 2009: 230).

Chapter 2, "Passing Latinities," broadens the meanings of Chicano and Chicana border theory to two central figures of the Harlem Renaissance: James Weldon Johnson (1871–1938) and Langston Hughes (1902–67). The Harlem Renaissance, also variantly known as the New Negro Movement and the Negro Renaissance, is widely considered, as Winston Napier presents it, as "the most dynamic cultural event in the history of black America." It propagated "a literary and cultural explosion that would establish the black writer as a seminal social force" (2000: 2).[44] Through a South-South discussion, my primary task is to inspect how a passing, transitory South informs Johnson's and Hughes's African Americanness. This reading, dating from the 1910s to the 1930s, allows for an intraethnic comparative examination of how the shifting shades of color of these eminent authors gesture toward an evolving Latinity in Nicaragua, Mexico, and Cuba. I link these cultural workers' contributions to larger U.S. Latino/a and Latin-American literary oeuvres like the *crónica* and border art, considering the former's prominence as a genre in Latin America and the latter's emblematic marker on Chicano and Chicana identity and imagination. This interpretive means does not elide the literary genealogy of U.S. African American cultural producers. Somewhat echoing the crónica form at the beginning of the twentieth century, African American literary thinkers wrote "mainly in magazines established to report on their society" (Napier, 2000: 1).[45] The crónica, as Paul Allatson qualifies it, is "an accepted and popular literary genre in Latin America, but less common in the Anglophone world." This writing form includes "short meditative pieces, autobiographical in scope, and characterized by a combination of personal confession, everyday observation, and a memorializing drive" (2004: ix). My underscoring of such Latino/a and Latin-American interdisciplinary modes of expression points to larger forms of cultural exchanges that exceed their specific "brown" or "black" fields of study. In channeling U.S. African American cultural production into Latino/a studies and its literary traditions, I am trying to also expand the Latino/a canon's signifying practices.

The penultimate chapter, "Indigent Latinities," proceeds with an inquiry of how the meanings and resonances of undesirable blackness, dark brownness, indigence, and Indianness are signified in post–World War II Chicano and Chicana subjectivities. I am preoccupied with what become South-South crossing lines of contention vis-à-vis the ideological construction of a Chicano and Chicana brownness that extends to U.S. Latinoness and Latinaness. The Latino and Latina category has been generally regarded as an "overly vague idea" (Jiménez Román and Flores, 2010: 2). Along these lines, brownness can be clearly added to this indeterminate ethnoracial Latino and Latina qualifier. This third chapter thus makes a case for the obligatory dark brown and black counterparts of a more populous brownness. My undertaking seeks to understand what has produced the spread of Latino- and Latina-specific brownness. Developing my analysis through autobiographical works by Gloria Anzaldúa, Cherríe Moraga, and Richard Rodriguez, I take to task the cultural representation of dark brownness and its leap to brownness. A parenthetical disclosure: Piri Thomas's canonical memoir, *Down These Mean Streets*, does not have a foundational presence in this section. His autobiography has undeniably served as the quintessential text in Latino/a studies to categorically demonstrate an "Afro-Latino" identity.[46] Although the scope of *Latining America* is not the Hispanophone Caribbean or Nuyorican subjectivities, I recognize, nonetheless, that Thomas is doubtlessly an authoritative resource in Latino/a studies. And I rely on Thomas, in an abbreviated but far-reaching way, to show how the disparate ethnoracial categories in his Puerto Rican and Cuban household—that is, black ("*negrito*"), dark brown, almost black ("*moreno*"), Negro ("*moyeto*"), and dark-skinned ("*tregeño*," "*tregeña*")—speak to Chicano and Chicana subjectivity and Mesoamerican representations of pejorative Indianness, "*lo indio*," and disparaging blackness, "*lo negro*" (1997: 340).[47] Such comparative conversations addressing the various Latino and Latina color lines have yet to be sufficiently reflected on and augmented in Latino/a studies.

The concluding chapter, "Disorienting Latinities," explores late twentieth-century migrations and the formation, post–Cold War, of U.S. Central Americans as "new" Latino and Latina invisible subjects. It looks at how Latino and Latina subgroups like Central Americans arrive at Latinidad. By doing so, a cultural and intellectual unmappable South is wrestled with in terms of the regional significations of Central America and the discursive deportability of the isthmus's bodies. If U.S. Central American migrations, among others, are almost exclusively understood, in Juan Gonzalez's (2000) terms, as a "harvest of empire," this part of the book is concerned with how to turn the assumed protracted appearance of such groups into a U.S. Latino and Latina "harvest of knowledge," as Sánchez Korrol posits (1996: 8).[48] The perceived lateness of Central Americans is theorized through Arturo Arias's arrangement of the new Central American–American paradigm, a diasporic consciousness that can be likened to wide-ranging Latino and Latina cultural politics and displacements (2003: 185). Arias's concept embarks on a possibility of re-cognition for groups marked by a hierarchical separateness—denoted in this chapter as a "Guatepeorian Latinidad"—that stands in categorical opposition to (normative) Latino and Latina otherness.

These Latinities, by no means coherent and complete, canvass the remains of overlooked blackness and dark brownness in a Latino and Latina context and the vestiges of other groups, like Central Americans, who, up to now, have not discursively passed into—or are problematically situated within the makings of—Latinidad.[49] The horizon of identity is always in the process of becoming, as it crosses paths with an otherness "of color" as much as with the "white otherness" Du Bois spoke of in *The Souls of Black Folk* (1996b). I attend to the struggles of the body as it walks in and out of the dormant voids written out of Latinidad's grammar. Each resituated repetition of Latinity in this work becomes, in a manner of speaking, an archeology of Latinities attendant to life stories that propound, in Gerard Aching's words, "an aesthetic elaboration of 'facts'" (1997: 116). Memoirs, autobiographies, and life-changing happenstance lay the groundwork for my revisiting of black-brown stories that have remained unchronicled despite their seeming collaboration and efforts to widen our understanding of Latin intersections.

Jane Gallop's theorizing of the anecdote upholds its fruitfulness. Emphasizing pivotal moments that tell stories about theory, Gallop acquaints us with a threefold language milieu that accounts for the critical insights such lived incidents offer, recognizes them as both "literary and real," and renders them "'interesting' precisely for their ability to intervene in contemporary theoretical debates" (2002: 2–3). Her elucidation forcefully moves along with this Global South discussion through the disentanglement of the quotidian, what Rigg, in his pursuance of "a grammar that makes living decipherable," also calls, as his book title puts forward, *An Everyday Geography of the Global South* (2007: xv). With it, Rigg "explores the details and minutiae of local lives and livelihoods and the local structures and processes that create such everyday lives and which are, in turn, created by them" (7). His scholarly immersion in the commonplace is fueled through "everyday living," as "the everyday begins and ends with the personal." Rigg depends on anecdotal daily occurrences for the fashioning and retelling of "'ordinary' people" (17).

To this end, *Latining America* draws on chronicled lives, narrative production, travel dispatches, urban tags, and television programs from a cultural studies perspective. This variety gives insight into how Latined, dark brown, and black lives sculpt and voice Latinities in the Global South. My overarching intention is to treat the accounts referenced here as cultural bodies of thought departing from certain constructions of literature that bind it to such strict methods as close examination. This book's interpretive angle centers on specific cultural and historical moments, concentrating on textual approaches like discourse analysis and conceptual exploration to evaluate how individuals engage in and theorize everyday processes of subject formation.

While *Latining America* is in conversation with U.S. African American studies, it remains crucial to remember that it is an intervention in and a contribution to Latino/a studies. I position my work as a critic and theorist within the rubric of a flourishing Latino/a studies that also turns to the signifying economies of absence: blackness, dark brownness, the U.S. South, and Latin America's other Souths, like the Central American isthmus. Ifeoma Nwankwo (1999–2001) has noted that the two contemporary domains encircling U.S. African American scholarship are African American studies as a field and a hemispherist approach to American studies.[50] Latinos and Latinas, in like manner, seem to fall between the space of Latino/a studies and a continentally driven American studies. But to which routes will African American and Latino/a studies be pushed, especially within Latin America studies, too? How will these disciplines dual-directionally cross over? And what will allow for their continuity, as Latinities proceed with their flood of departures and points of arrival? My engagement with Latino/a studies proffers an investigative space by which to think through the role of African Americanness and blackness in the production of the Latino and Latina citizen-subject as well as the field of Latino/a studies. As Nwankwo has also reminded us, U.S. African Americans are not provincial, and neither are Latinos and Latinas (2006).[51] They do not exist in a single place. By bringing African American studies discourse to Latino/a studies arenas, we are able to shift from the "pure" aims or seemingly inert black or brown predicaments from these disciplines, deliberate through new concepts and enunciations, and enable new histories in the making.

CHAPTER ONE

SOUTHERN LATINITIES

> People live — I mean, really live —
> in spaces that aren't on a map.
> —CRISTINA HENRÍQUEZ (2009: 129)

This chapter delves into the challenges and contradictions that emanate from U.S. African American, Latino, and Latina boundaries in discourses of the U.S. South and its place across an untrammeled Global South. I trace the articulation of these identifications and differences in a twofold manner: (1) seemingly intact ethnoracial bodies tied to specific landscapes and (2) the distinct means and extensive array through which southernness and Latinness run out of their "naturalized," confined spaces. The exigencies that arise as these proliferating bodies open up to Latinities and encounter the limits of the fields that examine the southern, the black, the American, and the Latino and Latina are a cornerstone for remapping how certain disciplines have been anchored.

Such regional analysis and its convergence with overlapping blackness-and-brownness focus on the increasing approaches to the Global South as an area of academic investigation pushing for broader geographies, flows, circulations, and epistemologies that reconsider U.S. southern studies, American studies, African American studies, Latino/a studies, and Latin American studies. In disentangling the fixity of peoples and geographies, a pair of questions animates this work. First, if U.S. southern/southeastern identity has been rooted in black-and-white dynamics — and the U.S. Southwest has been understood as brown and white — can we afford to reproduce these spaces as the main purveyors of blackness and Latinness? Second, how does the social reality of living in shifting geographies and color lines, as subjects pass through and relive the weight of difference, radically reshape how U.S. African American, Latino, and Latina political identities in the "Nuevo South" come to be understood?[1] These lines of interrogation disrupt "legible" Latinoness, Latinaness, and blackness and retrace the passages and routes accounting for the different types of southern Latinities that are being brought into due relation and conversation.[2]

I assess, from there, the racial and regional nomenclature in the South's production of a black-and-white conjunction. I argue that these deeply ingrained characteristics need to be reconstituted through projects that refocus on Latino and Latina peripheries and their relation to other minoritized spaces. This contention does not propose that these lives are eternally doomed to the ideological fringes of this "binary region," to use Helen B. Marrow's language (2009: 1038). Rather, my objective questions the logic governing Latino/a and black boundaries in U.S. intellectual practices, disciplines, and methods.[3] I struggle to burgeon forth new theories and knowledges that think through blackness-cum-brownness not as polarizing antagonists, but as cohabiting forces. I also literarily inquire how Latinos and Latinas have navigated ethnoracial, cultural, and class conflicts along the U.S. North/U.S. South divide and the white-black-Latin color line. I gesture toward open double consciousness as a theoretical content that embraces the unpredictable movements of southernness and Latinness, ineluctably stepping outside the requirements of blackness and brownness.

More concretely, I take up Evelio Grillo's memoir, *Black Cuban, Black American* as an emblematic example of divergences in the categories, moments, and ambits that sustain the rationalization of the separateness adhered to Latinness, blackness, and the U.S. southeastern landscape. Editing the tenor of oppositional blackness and Latinness, this octogenarian's retrospective study ushers us into instances that can be regarded as a Latined course of events along the U.S. color line, slightly more than a decade after W. E. B. Du Bois's introduction of the term. Despite Grillo's lived black and Latin instability, Arte Público Press attenuates a Hispanic past and veers him to the U.S. Hispanic ("non–African American") archive.[4] At stake are not just the development and systematizing of a U.S. Hispanic literary canon but also the tarrying of possibilities for reading, thinking, and framing new questions on Latined black-brown–dark brown discourses. I conclude by canvassing the discursive continuity of black-white problems through the vectors of Latino and Latina being, mulling over what may make a Latined open double consciousness feasible. This move is allowed after my rendering of Grillo's publication to give prominence to other formulations of the U.S. African American experience opening up in multiple and different directions. Building on the great inheritance of double consciousness, open double consciousness is devised not to rival Du Bois's framework but to work with it, particularly through the notion of bringing about a moving knowledge in the twenty-first century.

The measure of my argument thus established, I would like to briefly set up my analytic direction by recounting a passing but edifying anecdote about the perceived recentness of Latinos and Latinas in the U.S. South.[5] Their late occurrence coincides with the regional denomination of the Nuevo South, a phrase that I frequently hear since my arrival to Durham, North Carolina, in 2006. The episode touches on the founding yet rupturing assumptions of the U.S. South as a coherent "tight place," to extend Houston A. Baker Jr.'s insight, that parochially preserves its black-and-white composition and non-fluid racial categories (2001: 15).[6] I intentionally retell this experience in an investigation that is knotted to the dismantling of self-contained ideas about geographies, bodies, and cultures and that may as well function as an ethical call for the reception of the openness of being. This bid applies multidirectionally to U.S. African Americans as much as to U.S. Latinos and Latinas and mainly to spaces that have entered and participate in a "new borderland urbanism" caught between the forces of economic globalization and traditional black-white mainstays of the plantation South (Herzog, 2003: 120).[7]

Aboard a return flight to North Carolina fairly recently, I sat next to a Durham-born African American woman. I learned from our conversation that she had relocated to Texas, where she is a nurse. She told me that she seldom returns to the "City of Medicine" since her mother's death. "Each time I come back," she said, "I find a different city. It's all Hispanic now, and I ask myself, 'Where are the African Americans?'"[8] My flight partner expressed urgency about the deracination of U.S. African Americans in her urban space's new ecology, which she quipped, used to be prominently black.[9] She revealed apprehension for how unrecognizable Durham had become. Through her Southwest-Southeast migrations, I wondered if, for her, "Hispanics" were more acclimated and physically bounded to Texas than North Carolina.[10] Yet this dislocation of southeastern culture could be attributed to a hyper-Latin visibility juxtaposing the South's nuevo status with a new physiognomic regional alienness, or a new Latinness set in an unfamiliar ("southernly") time. This alien South racializes Latinos and Latinas, even though what is being described, for the most part and yet again, is the South's socioeconomic transformation vis-à-vis an unfamiliar mixing of local and regional actors.[11] Weighed against this historicopolitical national frame, Latinos and Latinas are stamped as rarefied bodies in a host city.[12] But this encounter also marks the limits of the South's operative logic. It pushes us toward a new turning point for this geography as well as for the supplementary fields and modes of thought touching on James L. Peacock's deliberations. He asserts that if "the old question for the South and for southerners was, 'How do I relate to the nation,' [t]he new question is, 'How do I relate to the world?'" (2007: x). Likewise, in which spaces do southerners from the U.S. South and numerous dispositions of southern life establish an association with seemingly just formed Latino and Latina beginnings?[13]

Some historians and anthropologists trace this South to the late 1980s and early 1990s. It has been documented that between 1977 and 1992, the South's economy surpassed other regions in the nation, steering a strong economic boom, or in Raymond A. Mohl's description, "Dixie's dramatic demographic, economic, and cultural transformation" (2005: 67). Meanwhile, the United States, as a whole, faced an exigency to admit refugees from Southeast Asia, the former Soviet Union, Eastern Europe, and Africa. The State Department selected the South "as a target area in which to settle refugees who were not being sponsored by family members in other parts of the country." Mexican and Central American migration is also attributed to a thriving economy "dependent on abundant, inexpensive labor and a population willing to fill such positions" (Duchon and Murphy, 2001: 1). These developments lead to "a growing conviction that there is more value in studying the South as a part of the world than as a world apart" (Cobb and Stueck, 2005: xi).

The type of twenty-first-century urban South–transforming cities such as Durham refers to a Latino and Latina resident alienness thought by the popular media to be displacing U.S. African Americans.[14] The rather recent history of this new South obscures the present economic moment that also impacts Latinos and Latinas. This Latino and Latina now, adhered to a nuevo genealogy, is perceived to be without a history. Leon Fink underlines this temporariness in his work about Guatemalan and Mexican migrants' employment in the poultry plants of Morganton, North Carolina. "A lot of people" in that industrial town, he writes, first looked at the "Hispanics as a 'temporary thing'" (2003: 21).[15] Despite these volatile markers, the circulating bodies of Latinos and Latinas direct our attention to how different ethnoracial and U.S. identities are emerging at different points in time. Our task, then, is to adjust our lenses and see the ethnoracial and cultural history of the South beyond the U.S. black-and-white binary from an approximational point of view that inquires: How have Africana, Latino, and Latina groups arrived at, found, and formed their "North" not so much in this Nuevo South, but in what Marshall C. Eakin appreciatively calls this "Newest South" (2003: 21)?[16] What types of relationships and knowledges do those that remain "unnativized" in the U.S. South and America activate in this Newest South?

As I sketch out and ask about Latin bodies through customary understandings of U.S. Latinoness and Latinaness, just as I probe into generic characterizations of the U.S. South and African Americans, I want to pause momentarily and elucidate on my claims. My examination of this terrain and its "new" peoples and journeys—referred to by journalist Paul Cuadros as a "silent migration"—corresponds with how "the" Latin and Latinness are being opened up to Latinities (2006: 10).[17] Certainly Latinities include Latinos and Latinas, a U.S. panethnic group and category that tends to fall into specific nationalities. But Latinities also appear and are put into use beyond this assemblage of individuals and the Latino or Latina classification. Let me be clear. I do not deny the sociocultural histories and manifestations of blackness, Latinoness, and Latinaness. I am, more readily, talking about Latinities, which include these groups and categories but are not reducible to them. In simple terms, Latinities move. And as this study moves to explore the fluid Latinities of the U.S. South and African Americanness, I am interested in Latinities as remnants that play out through what Brent Hayes Edwards has termed as *décalage* for Africana diasporas. Décalage is "the kernel of precisely that which cannot be transferred or exchanged, the received biases that refuse to pass over when one crosses the water" (2003: 14).[18] The lingering remnants of Latinities, however, are not always lived by, located through, and ladened with an intrinsic Latin American diasporic population.

The migratory meanings of Latinness spread out to Latinities through bodies as well as geohistorical and disciplinary crossings. Beyond the scope of one panethnic and cultural identity and one particular diaspora, Latinities' porousness is exposed. It denaturalizes the restrictions ascribed to blackness, Latinoness, and Latinaness. Latinities may be mapped through "passing lines," to echo but distinctly build from Brad Epps's notion. Passing lines cross the boundaries of national and cultural differences. They are

> the stories, moves, and gestures that may be deployed in border crossings, borders that include what Gloria Anzaldúa calls a "1,950 mile-long open wound" between Mexico and the United States, but that also include the waters of the Caribbean, the naval base at Guantánamo, Coast Guard boats, "international" airports, INS offices; borders that are even, maybe even specially, streets and parks and schools and stores, banks and clinics, courtrooms and emergency rooms, borders that are our minds and bodies, our words and our deeds, our thoughts and our thinking. Borders that are "our" own and that provoke these lines, here and now. (2001: 117)

I summon passing lines as more than a means to subvert national ideologies and daily normative/unnormative transactions. The act of crossing over is not necessarily unidirectional, and passing lines do not travel punctiliously one way. They have the potential to rearticulate moving Latinities and the delayed signifiers that upset the fictive nature and operating truisms ascribed to ethnoracialized groups. Continuously in flux, these passing lines reconfigure what has been unveiled from the dispersals of archetypical and time-honored borders. They form a knowledge through what is otherwise unmanageable in conventional black or brown identity registers.

Passing has generally signified crossings from subaltern blackness to normative whiteness within black-and-white identity discourses. As parallel routes, passing lines can become a strategy that passes through frameworks (e.g., border theory and the Global South) and bodies with different markers and ranges of Latinities.[19] The distance between these theoretical accounts and subjects is thus minimized and bears in mind Linda Schlossberg's point that "passing is not simply about erasure or denial, as it is often castigated, but rather, about the creation and establishment of an alternative set of narratives" (2001: 4).[20] The promise of these narratives outline Thomas Bender's heed to revise the nature of nation formation through "alternative solidarities and social connections," since they could also move in the direction of political kinships (2002: 1).

The U.S. South's social identity can be assessed along these passing lines of thought, as an extended south — a Global South — tracing and recording "adopted political relatives" from a global stage. These figurative in-law family relations are known, in Spanish, as "familias políticas" (Sommer, 1999: 84).[21] Through political kindred, U.S. ambiguities come to the fore as they coevally establish a recognizable American nation and a paradoxical disconnect between domestic subjects and alien intruders. This set of hypothetical in-laws could unsettle the dividing lines between domesticity and alienated foreignness, dissolving the determinant factors that reproduce national distinctions about those who are (alienated) "at home" because of the (alien) presence from "abroad" (Kaplan, 2002: 1). But this study is not due because Latinos and Latinas are now part of a sociocultural totality localized in the black-and-white historical circumstances of the U.S. South. Questions of legality, citizenship, and racial categories and distinctions commonly noted in southern "colonial statutes referring to 'negroes, indians, mulattoes, and mestizoes'" have touched upon reference points outside the rigidity of U.S. blackness and whiteness, alongside linguistic and classificatory equivalencies for what become U.S. Latino and Latina identities (D. Gibson, 1993: x).[22]

Southern Latinities are linked to this Latin permeability and accumulation of signifiers, to bring in Henríquez's quote from the epigraph. While these types of Latinities surface and can be charted, they do not forever function and dwell in "spaces that aren't on a map." They foreground being off and on the map, and they are "really live[d]" and relived differently. Read this way, my analysis of the U.S. South and Latin ways of living are a generative source for acknowledging and veering toward a Global South where migratory movement — up, down, across, and vice versa — does not occlude new subjectivities and new narratives of migration.[23] Southern Latinities invite a reconceptualization of the U.S. South's normative construction that hallmarks "the centrality of the antebellum South in the narrative of Southern history" and issues a temporariness to Latinos and Latinas (Eakin, 2003: 10). The continuous, systematic narrative of the past and "the politics of the late nineteenth and early twentieth centuries" have "long distorted our notions" about the U.S. South's exceptionalism and its innate detachment from Latinos, Latinas, and Latin America (18). Such blind spots have impaired "our ability to see [the] multi-centered, multi-ethnic, multi-cultural emergence of the U.S. South" and its resonances with Latin America, not to mention the manifold and divergent Latinings that propel this monograph (10). Southern Latinities propose the rethinking of the U.S. South, the United States, and Latin America to highlight the changing relationships among the diverse subjects and cultures moving to and passing through these locales. These Latinities inflect us with conceptions of Latin genealogies, as they try to cobble through the idea of when particular groups become southernly as well as to theorize how a pool of ever-growing southern resources might be studied, a point to which I now turn.

Transamerica: Southern Theories and American Studies

Marshall C. Eakin provides a fitting historical detail for these southern concerns, laying a path for what can be conjectured as malleable Latined regions and subjects. Eakin imbricates thematic turns that form a nexus with the U.S. South and Latin America. His exegesis on hemispherist isolation — what has been included and excluded in U.S. southern and Latin American historiography — serves as a starting point for a discursive contiguity with the parameters demarcating southernness. Eakin's appraisal and undoing of each of this field's narrative choices in the production of what becomes a bounded geohistory reads,

> Narrowly defined, the Old South is eleven states, if one sticks to membership in the Confederacy as the ultimate measuring stick. Missouri, Kentucky, and Maryland get left out (as does the anti-secessionist West Virginia). Those who emphasize the heritage of slavery as the essential feature bring those three states (and Delaware and West Virginia) back into the region (because all were still slave states in 1860). If one places greater emphasis on certain cultural and social patterns such as language, religion, and sense of identification, some sections outside these states qualify as Southern. Some places that are clearly within even the most traditional political boundaries do not (such as southern Florida or northern Virginia, or even sections of Appalachia). As in the case of Latin America, political boundaries often trump cultural patterns when one defines the region.
>
> Latin American specialists face the same problems, sometimes the mirror image of the dilemma in Southern Studies. Texas and Florida, for example, are on everyone's list of Southern states, yet they were parts of the Spanish

Empire in the Americas for three centuries. Despite their long histories under Spanish colonial rule, scholars of American Studies count them as part of the U.S. South. In spite of their long histories under Spanish colonial rule, many scholars of Latin America do not include them in standard treatments of Latin America. These regions do not suddenly become Southern and leave Latin America in the 1820s and 1830s. (2003: 17–18)

This comparative take alludes to a resurgence of these areas of interest and their respective disciplines, southern studies and Latin American studies. From a literary and historical standpoint, Deborah N. Cohn has gauged the two regions she patches together as the South and Spanish America as "neighboring spaces" due to their "similar 'personalities' deriving from shared histories" (1999: 2). In broadening the mental map of the U.S. South not only to Latin America but also to the Global South, a remappable terrain is drafted. This approach partakes in the furthering of transnational research projects and the excavation of multidisciplinary and multilingual topics and histories. In U.S. domains, the Global South theorizes how Latino and Latina figurative alienness functions and is transported in African American studies programs and, conversely, how blackness figures in Latino/a studies.

Global is inserted into both fields' equations not because U.S. Latinos, Latinas, or African Americans lack either a globalness or globalization, which can be conceived as "the tendency toward a world-wide market economy (facilitated by the institutional frameworks of the World Trade Organization) and dominated by transnational corporations and transnational criminal organizations" (Dear and Leclerc, 2003: 6–7). The history and memory of the two Souths, to trope on Cohn's book title, is premised on the parallels between the South and Latin America. Cohn delineates these regions' differences. But her study gives more pronounced attention to their shared history "of dispossession, of socioeconomic hardship, of political and cultural conflict, and of the export of resources to support the development of a 'North'" (1999: 5). The outcome has shown "a semi-colonial dependency on the North" as well as "subordination to foreign governments and, increasingly, to transnational corporations" (6). U.S. Latinoness, Latinaness, and African Americanness are placed in a Latined Global South framework to denaturalize and dislocate the visual grounds and backgrounds that instantiate where they "authentically" belong. In this way, a renarrativization of southern platforms is promoted through the comparability of black-and-brown Latin analogies. Building on a more generous mapping of the U.S. South, a Global South can speak to the negotiation of political identities—and the passages of political families—across borders.

The scope of these concerns, suffice to say, has a genealogy. Some of the working premises of the Global South can be traced not only to the 1950s "but to the early modern period of the 1890s through the 1920s, when 'American Studies' was being first constituted as a field in the academy in the midst of a surge in immigration, new forms of racial segregation and industrial labor, a more varied mix of students attending universities, and the closing of the western 'frontier' coupled with newly global ambitions for U.S. power" (Singh and Schmidt, 2000: 4). The 1992 quincentenary also marked a propitious turn, fueling a spate of "interest in a hemispheric approach to the literatures of the Americas," the growth of New World studies as a field, and the establishing of programs like Florida International University's African–New World studies.[24] But as Rachel Adams and Sarah Phillips Casteel have propositioned, "the hemisphere's northernmost member, Canada" has been omitted, in many cases, from comparative orientations that have "more typically focused on relationships between the U.S.A. and Latin America" (2005: 6).[25]

The Global South's insights lie in equivalent approaches that, as Jon Smith and Deborah N. Cohn claim, "look away from the North in constructing narratives of southern identity" and exercise the function of America in a continental perspective. They outline "the experience of defeat, occupation, and reconstruction" as qualities that "the South shares with *every* other part of America" (2004: 2). While the Global South is evoked in this present undertaking, the reference is not meant as a totalizing international identity. It goes without saying that the term could not operate as all-embracing, given the situatedness of a U.S. Americanist discourse within the circumstances and historical factors that advance U.S. Latino, Latina, or African American subjectivities. But it is incongruously at this fragmentary juncture—in light of family and cultural remittances, massive deportations, return migrations, and technological shifts—where we can scrutinize what forms of overlapping and distinctive Americanizations and un-Americanizations may mean beyond the U.S. map. The Global South's unboundedness acts as an instructive point of orientation.[26] And, as José David Saldívar incisively puts forth in *Trans-Americanity*, there is "something speculative and risky in reading through the critical and theoretical approaches of scholars, activists, and social theorists" from the Global South. An exigent Global South, as Saldívar brings to mind, "is the intellectual property of no specific national field-imaginary yet" (2012: xvi).

The Global South, as a framework of great analytic import, acquiesces to an integrated locus of citizenships, memberships, and neighboring spaces examining the multiple Souths within the United States and outside of it too. This type of South within the U.S. North deviates from New England as largely designative of "the North," as Nilo Cruz suggests (2003: 35). It may look like the Dominican New York/New Jersey borderlands Junot Díaz chronicles in *Drown* (1996) and *The Brief Wondrous Life of Oscar Wao* (2007).[27] It bolsters Ana Castillo's consideration of "what the history of the United States would read like, in fact, what shape the country would have taken if it had developed in the Southwest with the Spanish" (2005a).[28] This South elevates silences as well. Recall the South articulated through the perspective of female absence, an epistemic void that Patricia Hill Collins gives rise to with the question, "Why are African-American women and our ideas not known and not believed in?" (1990: 5).[29] The Global South also addresses, as David Palumbo-Liu sets forth, a racial frontier hinged on the modernizing project of America and its expansion of the East and Southeast Asian regions, otherwise configured as the Pacific Frontier, Pacific Rim, and Asia Pacific (1999: 6).[30]

As Latino and Latina identities become invariably tied to U.S. Souths, they are paradoxically "southernized" — or resouthernized — but in the Latin American sense of regularly characterizing an alienated Latin "abroadness." And yet this overlay of Souths helps in facilitating new conceptual spaces. That is why superimposed southern imaginaries are summoned here: the U.S. Southwest, the U.S. South/Southeast, the Global South in a Global North, and Latin America's Souths. These Souths are placed in dialogue with one another to survey methodological moments of "pedagogical encounter" and to reroute the epistemic orbits of these "marginal" worlds (Gallop, 2002: 4). I am aware, as Matthew Pratt Guterl has written, that the "'South' is an imagined location, an inherently unstable unit of space." Despite this fleeting geography, "most people in the United States feel they know exactly where it is: just below the Mason-Dixon line and just above the Gulf of Mexico. But the phrase 'South' defies such directional certainty; it has multiple meanings, competing positions, and personalities" (2007: 230).

Wherever and whenever these multiple Souths are invoked, they point to institutional ideas, political statements, and terms that may proceed "as frustratingly mobile, sometimes overlapping spots on a map" (Guterl, 2007: 230). Such Souths communicate a North/South demarcation, a meaningful dualism for U.S. Latinos and Latinas, a group that should be positioned within a new category of the "split state" since "more than half of the Latin American nations now have in the United States permanent diasporas." This North/South fissure "seems particularly important to situate U.S. Latinos within the historical blueprints of American imaginaries, given that their unsuspected gaze upon America often cuts through the North/South divide" (de la Campa, 2001: 376). But this North/South motif is applicable within the United States, and markedly so for African Americans. Amy Kaplan grounds this North/South American fulcrum as one that denotes the mapping of U.S. imperialism "not through a West/East axis of frontier symbols and politics, but instead through a North/South axis around issues of slavery, Reconstruction, and Jim Crow segregation" (2002: 18).[31] To disrupt the structure of white-and-black lines, the Global South is visited with a keen eye to theorize the complex ways that individuals respond to the said crises that heighten the sociopolitical identities and hierarchies that organize their being.

North and South continue to spread out and coexist within these geographic demarcations. But North and South can project South-South locations also. A South-South dialogue advances the Global South and its permeability.[32] Chicano/a border studies and African American studies are two approaches that constitute approximate genealogies passing one another in their interrogation of notions of rootedness and unrootedness as well as the historical legacies of conquest, expansion, slave trade, and plantation and postplantation economies.[33] From their respective geographic points of entry—the U.S. West and Southwest for Chicano/a studies and the U.S. Southeast for black American cultural productions and intellectual thought—these discourses move to theorize regional identity formations through the tense encounters and uneven divisions between North and South.[34] The mapping and conceptual constructs of the South and the North have operated within the realm of Latino, Latina, and African American subjectivities. In these configurations, the North is, perhaps, discernible in its

North American connotation of the United States, while the South has generally symbolized the U.S. Southeast, the U.S. Southwest, and as Chicano and Chicana thought has theorized, Mexico.

Our levels of engagement, then, shift to generating knowledges that account for social bodies in practice: bodies that do not seamlessly assimilate into normative Americanness, widespread ideas of U.S. southernness, or academic discourses wedded to strict blackness and brownness. How, I ask, do Latinos and Latinas fit the scholarly bill of U.S. African American studies, and what are the modes of belonging for African Americans in U.S. Latino/a studies? Culling through the correlational spheres of contention for blacks and browns, I weigh in on these concerns through a number of questions driven by what María Lugones has adverted as a "double perception and double praxis" that necessitate "one eye [that] sees the oppressed reality, [while] the other sees the resistant one" (2006: 78). Is it not possible for African Americans, in their navigation — and passages into a horizon — of color lines and Latinities, to have a consciousness of borders, passing lines that have historically pointed to differences (and promises of economic prosperity), much like the United States and Latin America, akin to the U.S. North and South?[35] Why should there be a "purist" theoretical model, geography, and approach to how itinerant groups have rethought deracination and marginality?[36]

The variegated carvings of a continental, southernized American studies go beyond the limits of a standard America and open intersecting windows of genealogical interrogation. Yet these approaches do not adequately reference fluid associations among moving bodies in mercurial American worlds. "Transamerica," the descriptor used for this section, is a play on the 2005 film bearing the same title.[37] It is also a nod to the field-imaginary of trans-American studies, where "diasporic and border writers and thinkers" provide a new narration of the world (J. D. Saldívar, 2012: xx). The "trans-American imaginary" challenges the normative literary pedigree of a U.S.-centered America through hemispherist scrutiny — vide, as illustrations, J. D. Saldívar (1997, 2012); Brickhouse (2004); Moya and Saldívar (2003); and Gruesz (2002). Far more than a play on words, this part of the discussion was framed as such to emphasize not only that a "trans" theoretical language has come to the fore. An unrestrained thematic subject has also surfaced, one premised on the regrounding of continuous cultural transactions and self-relocations in the Global South.

In the film *Transamerica*, for example, Felicity Huffman portrays the life of Bree, a preoperative male-to-female transsexual. The movie centers on Bree's gender-reassignment surgery and her inconvenient discovery that she had fathered a son several years earlier. The offspring turns out to be a New York City teenager and hustler named Toby, whose mother has committed suicide and consequently needs Bree's help. Plot twists soon demand that Bree pass for a female and a Christian missionary, not disclose her identity as Toby's father, and take the proverbial all-American road trip. Her cross-country foray evokes other geographies and citizens from the American landscape, provocatively bringing about Bree's immersion in a Latin life. *New York Times* movie critic A. O. Scott has inadvertently keyed into this Latin optic, first noting that the voice of Huffman's character "is soft and breathy." Bree's female representation, as he sees it, "avoids cursing and peppers her conversation with Latinate words and foreign phrases" (Scott, 2005). The *Oxford English Dictionary* illuminates that Latinate consists "of, pertaining to, or derived from Latin; having a Latin character. Also, occas., resembling an inhabitant of a Latin country." Bree's Latinities are evinced through her living environment. She resides in a Los Angeles Latino neighborhood, earning her dollars and cents as a server in a Mexican restaurant.

Cinematically speaking, however, Bree's Latinities are seemingly peripheral, nearly "soft and breathy" secondary exchanges. Yet these parenthetical moments cannot be readily dismissed. U.S. Latinoness, Latinaness, and Latin-Americanness are blurred and coeval signifiers. *Transamerica*'s Latinate character walks, passes into, and ruptures the normative constituents of Latinness. In two telling moments, Bree arouses desire not from the admiring gaze of white American masculinity, but from the marginal yet appreciative stares of Latino and Native American males. In this navigation of a moving America, the film's Latined beginnings reframe the native, the migrant, the transgender, and the transnational into a linked territory of complex relations and accumulated knowledge whose geopolitical subject matter is not immutably structured through heterosexual mobility alone. *Transamerica*'s "trans-ness" goes across and through the United States. It curves around a vexed America and drifts against laws, regulations, and customs, as this transamerican imaginary is staged by prohibitive beings from the shifting Americas. The film transmits a counter-reading through the different ways in which this new space is desired, inhabited, and narrated—reassembling the ensuing stage of America's Latined body politics.

The Southern Latinities undertaken herein may appear to have no epistemological material to work with. But if seen as a process and a practice that results from institutional schisms, new states of knowing emerge, which Walter Mignolo champions as "geo- and body-politics of knowledge." These forms of awareness are brought through "geo-historical and bio-graphical configurations in processes of knowing and understanding [that allow] for a radical re-framing (e.g., decolonization) of the original formal apparatus of enunciation" (2009: 4).[38] Kathryn McKee and Annette Trefzer advocate, to that end, a southern studies and American studies that resituate "the histories and literary interpretations of a regional culture such as the U.S. South" through "a two-way process [where] the dimensions of the global refer simultaneously to the importation of the world into the South and the exportation of the South" (2006: 679–80). This interruption of southern studies and American studies echoes the divergence between American studies and Latin American studies. Such disciplinary separations lend themselves to "new metaphors and unexpected narratives" that in de la Campa's view "can still claim these territories," mostly from the sphere of American studies. But the question remains "on whether new constructs and unexpected subjects will aid in the blurring of these lines" at the level of the Americas (2001: 374). McKee and Trefzer claim that "a new Southern studies [is] based on the notion of an intellectual and practical Global South, a term that embeds the U.S. South in a larger transnational context" (2006: 678). The Global South is suitable because it aims to be more expansive—and dissonantly spacious—to the extent that it reconfigures "the legendary South of two isolated and homogeneous races" (Peacock, Watson, and Matthews, 2005: 1).

In this sense, the Global South's content operates as a complementary point of encounter supplementing the Chicano and Chicana borderlands, U.S.-situated models of American studies, and approaches to inter-American studies.[39] One of the most compelling facets of Chicano/a border thought, as Héctor Calderón and José David Saldívar (1998) have demonstrated, is its ability to centrally ground Chicano and Chicana cultural productions in frameworks that figure the U.S. West and Southwest—or as José Limón (1998) has further shown, "Greater Mexico"—in relation to U.S. and Latin American literary traditions. This landscape is fundamental to Chicano and

Chicana writing and cultural imaginings. Its articulations must be understood in a broader mapping that charts "the borderlands of theories and theorists," since the perspectives that Chicanos and Chicanas have designed need to be admitted and legitimized in literary canons and the U.S. academy (Calderón and Saldívar, 1998: 7).

But such efforts fall noticeably short in corresponding and interacting with other Latino and Latina groups who lack a specific U.S. sociopolitical and cultural identity term like Chicano and Chicana. Such a comparison would also prioritize the interactional dynamics among Chicanos, Chicanas, Latinos, Latinas, and African Americans in a globalized United States. Calderón and Saldívar's attempts are vital, nonetheless, in their detailing of a "global borderlands" that generates "allegiances outside the sphere of Chicano studies [. . .] because ideology itself involves networks of meaning and borders through which society is knitted together" (1998: 6). The globalness of the borderlands, they attest, "must be reinterpreted against the influx of Third World immigrants and the rapid re-Hispanicization of important regional sectors of our Mexican America and the wider United States" (7).

My motive is to dissect how blackness, brownness, and dark brownness operate in multiple Souths. By doing so, I am not looking at the "globalness" of the borderlands but at the global dimensions of Latino, Latina, and African American and how we come to know them as such. "Speak of the South as you will," forewarns Carol Stack, "but you will have to speak of it" (1996: 18). Motioning to not just speak of it but with it, we accordingly progress to what social scientist Raewyn Connell judiciously names "Southern theory." This premise takes up unmappable global peripheries, "where the majority of the world does produce *theory*" (2007: ix). The "south" in "southern" is tied to the political dilemmas of "relations—authority, exclusion and inclusion, hegemony, partnership, sponsorship, appropriation—between intellectuals and institutions in the metropole and those in the world periphery" (viii–ix).

Adopting Connell's insights to the Global South's general theories demands that the concept-metaphor found "everywhere," as Matthew Sparke puts it, be graphed "somewhere, located at the intersection of entangled political geographies of dispossession and repossession." This is why I move in the direction of southern ways of thinking, where open double consciousness, to cite one source, refocuses on the ways in which one keeps finding geographies and reconfiguring the modalities and theories from which social actors operate. As Sparke observes, the Global South "has to be mapped with persistent geographic responsibility," which occasions "a call to track critically and persistently the open-ended graphing of the geo" (2007: 117). Sparke's distinctive inclination requires that this "critical capsizal of colonial cartographic conventions" apply a Du Boisian double consciousness in "the over-mapping of the Global South: acknowledging the power of the over-mapping by dominant imaginative geographies while also disclosing the critical possibilities of the other geographies that are covered up" (119–20).[40]

Installed in the Global South, Sparke's summoning of double consciousness is attentive to dominant and nondominant geohistorical and political territorial relations. Du Bois himself was heedful to such models of double consciousness, since his "colored" geography had global implications.[41] Du Boisian double consciousness and its manifold associations, however, are not always a given. Its relationality to an ilk of double consciousness, as it were, needs to be localized and intensively engaged in each state. I underscore, for this reason, the urgency to forge an open double consciousness that maneuvers Sparke's "open-ended graphing of the geo." Open double consciousness resonates with double consciousness, but it is a double consciousness with othered differences and entries. It might be argued that as an avowed Pan-Africanist Du Bois was a global citizen whose double consciousness was antecedently enhanced with a plurality of critical visions. I do not dissent from such contentions.[42]

It is useful to clarify that my aim is not to unearth, tally, and fully register the number of consciousnesses already imparted in Du Boisian double consciousness. My call for open double consciousness concentrates on how such awareness can be teased out and opened in light of the absences of certain populations who have had no place within prevailing U.S. black-white articulations of double consciousness.[43] This erasure has not been of Du Bois's own making, of course, but a projection of how such a binary has been structured and the ways in which it operates. As such, how do groups like Latinos and Latinas, who are black, white, and with varying shades between these designations, pass through the very black-white dyad that has determinedly omitted them from double consciousness? The abstract Americanness of U.S. Latinos and Latinas demands hermeneutical openings—however small, modest, or great in scale—in the black-white, U.S.-situated North/South order that has orbited around double consciousness. Open double consciousness, as an ever-rising tide of information and critical self-formation, creates orifices in the domains that trap how Latin subjects walk into and move, sometimes incompletely, between the traversing black-brown–dark brown color lines. As an ongoing process, open double consciousness is an unfinished intellectual incorporation of the contemporary flow of subjects whose personal journeys also draft a map of changing consciousnesses, contingent on their U.S. circumstances, world events, and political developments and crises. In this light, we might also investigate the circuitous paths double consciousness has taken and the pressing necessity of its return for "new" populations.

Spanning spatially and at the subjective level, open double consciousness captures extended sites of *sabidurías populares*, as Ramón Saldívar designates them (2007: 406). Saldívar's "popular knowledges," in connection to other selves and places, form a part of "vernacular wisdoms" (or "dialogized collective wisdoms"). They are central in the countering of what Connell dubs as "the idea of global difference." Global dissimilarity conveys the "difference between the civilization of the metropole and other cultures whose main feature [has been] their primitiveness" (2007: 7). What does it mean to live in the Global South—or, in Connell's words, through a general theory that tries to theorize and formulate "a broad vision of the social, and offers concepts that apply beyond a particular society, place, or time" (28)—as a U.S. African American, Latino, or Latina individual?[44] What kinds of southern epistemologies can account for relational black, Latino, and Latina identities? While sifting through this number of questions, I am not saying that the U.S. South becomes global by virtue of the perceived contemporary Latino and Latina browning of the region and the rest of the United States. I take my cue from a highly applicable—and productive—question posed in *The American South in a Global World*. In it, the editors inquire, "what does this world mean for arts and culture?" (Peacock, Watson, and Matthews, 2005: 3). Indeed, what would this world mean for the location, relocation, and cognitive mapping of global Latined imaginations?[45]

Latin Is, Latin Isn't: The Autobiography of an Extra-Colored Man

Despite these scholarly moves toward the open sea of a conceptual Global South, the indexing and cognitive mapping of Latino and Latina life is saliently marked and memorialized through U.S. Americanness. The tracking of a U.S. Hispanic literary heritage, as Arte Público Press has it, ironically exposes how the conflicting impulses toward Latinoness and Latinaness demand a re-cognition of the terms and experiences that are sanctioned to revise, archive, and secure preeminent bits of the Hispanic American narrative space and body politic.[46] But Evelio Grillo's *Black Cuban, Black American* stands outside the purview of U.S. Americanness, blackness, and Cubanness. There is no guarantee that his most intimate and public rendition of black Americanness infinitely stays or ends in that titular space and place. Grillo's passages merit a review of the irregularities of the brown-white and black-white ensemble, for he heralds the vertiginous detours of Latinness. His passing lines are not unbroken admittances into black Americanness. They demonstrate another timbre that does not follow the traditionally anticipated forms and norms of adhering to one ethnoracial identity. Grillo (1919–2008) accentuates Latinities that are not inseparable from other forms of Latinoness, Latinaness, or blackness. Nor are they isolated, above all, when they move toward U.S. Americanness.

Just as we are trying to understand the makings of a U.S. South devoid of the Latinities that inform it, we also endeavor to evaluate how Latinoness and Latinaness garner national meaning. At first glance Grillo's memoir about an Ybor City, Florida-born man striving to "join black American society" to gain "American roots" at a time when his black and white options were limited, reads rather straightforwardly (2000: 12). But Grillo's ostensibly unassuming plot admits an opportunity to go over and open the possibilities that are imported within the linear narrative of black assimilation attached to this story. Grillo's fragmentations emphatically allow for the undoing of fixed ideas about the Latino subject's place and placement in the U.S. ethnoracial and literary landscape as entirely inanimate. By pushing a disentanglement of the fractured categories that inform the book's title, *Black Cuban, Black American* brings about a forceful question. Can we unerringly map U.S. African American, Latino, and Latina subjects when these errant bodies, like Latinities, are incessantly and at any time mobile? Grillo furnishes illuminating glimpses of a black Latin/black American record that is represented, in the introduction, as "the story of one Afro-Cuban's adventures in identity reconstruction." This self-alteration is ultimately situated as a "triumph over racial and ethnic ambiguity," even as the narrator comments on the chasm that existed for black Cubans and black Americans (Dworkin y Méndez, 2000: viii).[47]

Grillo speaks of a region that is not generally hypothesized as part of the U.S. South. Much of Ybor City's economic expansion was, as Kenya Dworkin y Méndez has observed, "directly attributable to 'Latin' immigrants, who in 1886, brought with them the cigar-making industry. This revolutionized the local economy and turned Tampa into the 'clear Havana' cigar capital of the world, a dynamic new city in the New South" (2000: viii).[48] The history of Cuban working-class migrations prior to the 1959 Cuban Revolution localizes Cuban Americanness within U.S. racial economies and politics. Overlapping with U.S. blackness, Cuban Americanness, mainly one grounded in Florida, cannot be reductively thought of and dismissed through anti-Castro viewpoints that have been attributed as "too passionate, over the top, [and] even a little crazy" (Fontova, 2007: xi). Grillo's version of Cubanness advances an exploration of how Latinness comes to be known. The twenty-first-century Nuevo South of recent origins becomes a Global South that has had a previous Latin knowledge but whose regional Southeastern existence is now being recovered. Grillo's account can be read as an activation of Latined cultural signs performed by a black subject that is conjectured, many times, through "un-Latinized" blackness.

Narratively speaking, Grillo's life motions toward the memorialization of U.S. African Americanness, while the text contradictorily moves toward Hispanization. Institutionally restored by Arte Público Press, *Black Cuban, Black American* is not merely about diasporic blackness in its Cuban American and U.S. African American affirmations. Archival practices on Hispanization emerge through the press's publication and distribution of stories that are, under its editorial rubric, Recovering the U.S. Hispanic Literary Heritage (RUSHLH) and contributing to its Hispanic Civil Rights Series. This literary emendation unquestionably has great value. Nicolás Kanellos, RUSHLH's director, submits that this program's goal is to "make accessible an archive of cultural productions by Hispanic or Latino peoples who have existed since the sixteenth century in the areas that eventually became the United States." He suitably reminds us that RUSHLH has "found, accessioned, and made accessible tens of thousands of books and documents that were heretofore unknown." Kanellos also calls attention to an important characteristic of the program: that it is "not creating an 'ethnic' archive, per se, in order to build an ethnic, minority, or subcultural identity" (2012: 371). RUSHLH's reconstituted archive "aspires to recover all written culture, not just literature, and it intends to restore to local and national institutions what was lost or suppressed during the ethnocentric and racial construction of the nation through such ideologies and practices as manifest destiny, slavery, segregation, and capitalist construction of the government and economy" (372). These are persuasive and cogent reasons, and I share Kanellos's ideas on and commitment to this subject.[49] Yet the archival resources also point us to a literary struggle: to that of the constitution of a cumbersome Hispanization in which a person speaks from a particular ethnoracial location that seems historically inert.[50] How, one must urgently ask, would Grillo be restored in the African American archive as well?

We know that this is true: Grillo is a black Cuban whose roots end at black Americanness, because he tells us so in a book published by "the nation's largest and most established publisher of contemporary and recovery literature by U.S. Hispanic authors" (Latinoteca.com). But Grillo's Hispanization does not end there or at black Americanness. Priscilla Wald's study on processes that constitute both America and Americans—the manners and viewpoints that fashion a recognizable American nation and subject—assists us in reformulating narrations of the self that suggest ethnoracial linearity (1995: 3–5). Wald focuses on the official stories that create "We the People" and that impel the telling and retelling of untold stories by those who have been deemed socially unacceptable and have faced political censorship, personal prohibitions, and cultural conventions (1). For Wald, the authority exercised in official stories gives form to Americans.[51] Might the ethnoracial authority exerted in *Black Cuban, Black American* come from the Hispanic publishing house that is also constituting a collectivity of U.S. Hispanics? Is the authorial "I" and its official, archival direction shared—or split—between Grillo, the contemporaneous black American, and the (Hispanic) American publishing house?

I raise these considerations not to minimize either the significance of Grillo's account or of the press. My reflections stem from the dissonances posited in Grillo's "deep archives of memory," as Michael Dear and Gustavo Leclerc (2003: 4) might say and in Arte Público Press's Hispanic Americanization. If Grillo and the publishing house constitute a dissimilar "I," what relational models are at work, and for which relational ethnoracial and literary constituencies? Henry Louis Gates Jr. and Nellie Y. McKay's question on African American literature equally fits here. "What relation," they ask, "does the canon of African American literature bear to that of the American tradition" (1997: xxxvi)? The textual politics and the expansive ethos of Grillo's "Hispanic" book with the U.S. Hispanic literary corpus and the African American literary tradition need to be unfolded. Nancy K. Miller notes that autobiographies present a "model of relation that organize[s] the experience of reading." Miller's schema attends to "the kinds of bonds and desires that connect readers to the contemporary memoir" and occasions "identifications (which include disidentifications and cross-identifications), conscious or unconscious, across a broad spectrum of so-called personal experience" (2000: 423). The experience of reading *Black Cuban, Black American* is broader than Arte Público Press's categories and Grillo's own absorption into blackness. The double investment of these two "I's"—the published "me" of both the press and the author—are constricted by their "important form of collective memorialization, providing building blocks to a more fully shared national narrative" (424). But Grillo's story unwittingly departs toward the commemoration of the struggles of the constitution of a *Latined* American "We the People," going against the interpretive grain envisioned in his title.

Readers enter Grillo's domestic world through the eyes of a boy who, once upon a time, was affectionately nicknamed "Chuchi." Irresoluteness is at work: the elder Grillo, as author, appears to remind Chuchi, the authenticating child witness, of a sensorial life that establishes accuracy and validity around his Cubanness. "It had to be a Saturday afternoon," the memoir initiates, "because of the way the house smelled, the way that it felt, and the way that it sounded" (2000: 3). Yet the content, smells, and sound of the Grillo household lend themselves to familial lacunae. As the narrator speculates on his family's menu for that day, "*biftec a la palomilla*," Grillo's beginning is set through a gastronomic atmosphere: "thin slices of sirloin seared rapidly in olive oil and smothered with onions, rice, cold boiled string beans, and a simply magnificent salad of lettuce, vine-ripened tomatoes [. . .] and large avocado slices." The appetizing Cuban meal is never consumed, and the visual representation of inanimate edibles lingers like an epicurean still life. Just as quickly, the smells of dead human flesh in Cuba bring Grillo's domestic vignette to a sensorial end. He describes the refrigerated casket carrying his tuberculosis-stricken dead father, with water dripping "into a bucket placed under it, to catch the melting ice" (4). Being recollected is Grillo's awkward steps to remake a familiar domestic sphere in the United States that has been unmade. He gives life to the Spanish-speaking household that indulges him with comfort food and draws a bodily still life of his father.

This beginning does not lead one to believe that Grillo has annulled his Cubanness and that he has wholly and incontestably assimilated into U.S. African Americanness. What comes out of Grillo's Cuban, black, and American triangulation is a Latined décalage that operates in all of these ethnoracial liaisons. At stake is the vocabulary that informs not so much Hispanicness and Latinoness, but Latinities' intermittent and elastic Latinness. This Latined grammar is noted as "the past" in the text. Its cultural and ethnoracial dispersals, however, account for the "un-passed" lingering moment that affixes to, opens up, and forms through Latinities. Grillo's Latin equivalencies are crucial for the theorizing of mutually dependent Latinities sliding through blackness as much as through brownness. His passing line from Afro-Cubanness to U.S. African Americanness is not a closure. It is an open-ended temporality that provides glimpses of, as Jane Gallop has it, the "uncanny detail[s] of lived experience" (2002: 2). Grillo's narrative reformulates his Hispanization and gives prominence to a black Latined Americanness.[52] By black (or brown/ dark brown) Latined Americanness, I do not mean that the alterable black subject moves toward U.S. Latinoness, Latinaness, or whiteness only or does so in a tidy manner. Nor do I mean to say that the black body is eliminated through dispersed Latinings. I refer, instead, to how each Latinity falls from one spectrum to another. Moving back and forth, there is no determinacy in this association of blackness-cum-brownness and its multiple dwellings.

Grillo's southern Latinities show that his altering black Cubanness, and/or black Americanness, clings to each Cuban or U.S. African American Latinity that pauses through the comma evoked in his title. The joint states of being black do not end at black Americanness. The comma that connects, pauses on, or splinters black Cubanness from black Americanness is a measuring point that quantifies the limits of each black Cuban or black American side and adjusts the emergence and enactment of Latinities. On the one hand, the comma's arrangement, under Grillo's representation, has stretched and morphed into a U.S.-situated blackness. But then again this comma is a clause with a stipulation beyond the narrative's set function of identity.[53] It marks the ever-shifting ambits of Latinities that exceed Grillo's black Cuban and black American specificity.[54]

Take note of how black Americans "Latinize" Grillo, thereby suggesting that U.S. African Americans are un-Latinized. Grillo draws on the ambivalence of un-Latinized blackness to allow for different forms of U.S. Americanness to emerge precisely through his Latined blackness. Grillo's model of Latinized/un-Latinized African Americanness was exposed to him when his black American classmates would refer to black Cuban students as "tally wops." This phrase, Grillo explains, is "a combination of two slang terms applied to Italians."[55] The term

> rang out in the schoolyard whenever black Cuban children were being addressed derisively. Our [black] schoolmates found it difficult to distinguish between the Spanish and the Italian languages, so since we sounded Italian to their ears, they attached a misnomer to us. [. . .] [T]he mean and combative black American students called us *tally wop* in loud and jeering voices and with great delight. They never physically abused us, but they did substantial hurt to our feelings. (2000: 39)

The focal point of this Latinness convoking a Latin "sign community" is linguistic (Carby, 1987: 17). It is more connected to Italy than to the Spanish-speaking Americas and takes us, to borrow from Mignolo, "beyond the question of bi- or pluri-lingualism or multiculturalism." Mignolo insists, "It is more, much more. Language, epistemic, and subjective borders are the foundations of new ways of thinking, of an-other thinking, an-other logic, an-other language" (2005: 107).

Since Grillo sounds Italian, he moves from a "paradigm of newness to the decolonial model of co-existence" (Mignolo, 2005: 107). Such decolonial paradigm alludes to a shared Latin signifier by a set of presumably discontinuous, socially Latinized communities. This Latin language with different Latin actors, to summon Hazel V. Carby's comments about Afro-American women novelists, is not "divorced from the shared context in which different groups that share a language express their differing group interests." To be sure, each Latin actor and Latinity at work is "accented differently." The sign becomes "an arena of struggle and a construct between socially organized persons in the process of their interaction; the forms that the sign takes are conditioned by the social organization of the participants involved and also by the immediate conditions of their interactions" (1987: 16–17). How these Latin sign communities expand into Latinities is central to this discussion. This analytic bent, however, does not aim to consolidate people. It vies to speak of a renewed circulation of meaning and an ensemble of individuals who, as different narrators of dynamic sign communities, dehabitualize and destabilize the "true" selfhoods housed under U.S. African Americanness, Latinoness, Latinaness, and Americanness.

Grillo's pejorative (black) Latinness, signaled in a public school climate, demands local and national allegiances that un-Latinize him. But his questionable Latin allegiances publicly shift later on, when he enrolls at a Catholic school for blacks and at Xavier University in Louisiana, one of the Historically Black Colleges and Universities (HBCU). Grillo accesses a distinct black Americanness. And perhaps to verify his political membership, the words to James Weldon Johnson's "Lift Every Voice and Sing," commonly identified as the Negro national anthem, are duplicated in his volume. The "melodious, passionate song," Grillo notes, "stirs deep feelings among black Americans." It guided students "to develop comfort with our identity as black Americans" (2000: 45–46). Through his education and familiarization, readers can concur with Grillo's own appraisal: that he was "fully integrated with our black American schoolmates. We were blacks, subsumed for all purposes within a monolithic group" (40).[56] Grillo offhandedly presents his black Cuban incorporation as one allowed into the narrow confines of monolithic black Americanness. An argument could be made that Grillo's story remains truthful to that period's black-and-white racial identity and legal and social segregation. Yet the prevalence of the one-drop rule also encompassed a blackness that "included people whose physical appearance was other than black" (Lewis and Ardizzone, 2001: 27).[57] Surely, then, such a group cannot remain so homogeneous and unbroken within its own parameters if it is also permissive of other digressions. And what of Grillo's own undergirding Latin knowledge and Latined vacillations between black Cubanness and black Americanness?

He writes that his generation's choices "became clear," to either "swim in black American society or drown in the Latin ghettoes of New York City, never to be an integral part of American life" (2000: 12).[58] Grillo draws on black cultural and literary producers to account for his black socialization and U.S. intellectual formation. He concedes, "Our identity as black Americans developed strongly," adding an encyclopedic list of cultural figures that are key to his identity construction. To prove an unequivocal loyalty to black Americanness, he also acknowledges, "I remember but one black Cuban hero, Antonio Maceo, the general who had led the fight for Cuba's independence from Spain. There were no photographs in my home of historically significant Cuban blacks. My heart and mind belonged to Nat Turner, Frederick Douglass, Harriet Tubman, Sojourner Truth, Paul Laurence Dunbar, John Brown, Paul Robeson, Langston Hughes, W. E. B. Du Bois, Allison Davis, Alain Locke, and the two brothers, James Weldon Johnson and James Rosamond Johnson, who wrote the song very dear to my heart, 'Lift Every Voice and Sing'" (16–17). Grillo's references demonstrate a knowledge that has comprehensively incorporated into U.S. blackness—publicly and institutionally, that is, for the absence of "historically significant Cuban blacks" in the privacy of his domestic world invites other admittances. The range of vision "very dear" to Grillo's heart encourages one to think about the significance of notable black Cuban erasures, as these have not been completely effaced. Like Grillo's transient Latined Americanness, historically notable people have yet to be named, and not fully as black Cuban or Cuban American either but through broader key figures and moments that are Latining America.

Grillo's transitions modify the passing lines of black and brown. Passing into blackness does not lead into a renunciation of Cubanness, black Cubanness, or Hispanicness. It is a deviation of Du Bois's color line that goes through Latinities' various crossings. Passing into blackness means accessing and enacting "that" black Latined being that is unimaginable and unmappable within some U.S. Latino and Latina relations as well as within the markers of U.S. African Americanness. Such a process is also about what returning entails. This does not express a return to the same former space or group. It is a different type of comeback that draws on this rejected subject matter so as to reinterpret and shape new constellations of Latinoness and Latinaness. They are resignified through the subject's open articulation and consciousness of what Latinities effectuate outside Latino- or Latina-specific domains. Passing is not an end point, but a slightly pausing, nonalphabetical symbol—the comma between black Cuban(,) and black American—that carries great promise for further inquiry into the self and all encountered there. Such passing lines within the "divided borders" (to use Juan Flores's [1993] phraseology) between blackness and Latinness expose the proximity these boundaries have with one another and the ways in which these voids speak in U.S. Latino/a and African American literary productions. The multiple apertures also push for the "living borders" (to return to Flores) that interrogate and reshape identifications outside arranged binaries (see Flores and Yúdice, 1990).

Formwise, Grillo's text, at 134 pages, is a rather slim and staccato depiction. It traces a nascent self that can be "privileged as the definitive achievement of a mode of life narrative." Grillo's autobiography "celebrates the autonomous individual and the universalizing life story" through efforts that serve as entryways for acceptable forms of U.S. Americanness (Smith and Watson, 2001: 3). His is a recollection of an accomplished life whose achievements bounce from binary to binary, ranging from the assumed nonblack forms of Cuban whiteness to American blackness; from U.S. citizen to migrant "other"; from U.S. South to U.S. North (and their global and South-South locations); from a Latin South (Cuba) to a Latined black South (Florida); and from a lingering Latinity of supposed unassimilability into U.S. African American assimilation. As a life that strives to be fashioned after black American success, Grillo's career path ought to be conceived as one of a race man whose uplift depends on the distinguished mobility of both Latined blackness and brownness. His educational and institutional movements attest to epistemic migrations into black-white-Latin spaces of socialization, knowledge, activism, and policy.

These successes, though, are construed as a body of facts at Grillo's point of conclusion. His noteworthy passages are commemorated in an epilogue that reads like narrative curriculum vita. Grillo separately recounts black American and Hispanic success. His college education at Xavier came about because of "what 'a colored southern boy [could] do'" (2000: 90).[59] Migrating to the North, Grillo earned a graduate degree in Latin American history from Columbia University, arguably Latining his education by expanding on his areas of expertise. He served his country by joining the military in World War II, where he fought "the opening battle in the primary war for black U.S. troops [. . .]: the war against segregation within the United States Army!" (93). His American civic service also extended to his work as an executive assistant for the U.S. Department of Health, Education and Welfare (HEW) during the Carter administration. His brushes with the executive branch of the U.S. government are illustrated too. The book's last image includes a 1978 official White House photograph of Grillo shaking hands with former president Jimmy Carter (1977–81). Grillo mindfully returns to Arte Público Press's readerly constituency when writing, "with respect to Hispanic-Americans, I had a major role developing the Community Service Organization," a California-based Latino civil rights group. Boosting his Latino career contributions, Grillo adds that his professional experience also includes "the Spanish-speaking Unity Council, which became the most outstanding development flowing from my work with Mexican Americans" (133).[60]

The memoir's insights lie in Grillo's interdependent black-brown Latinities. These Latinities cannot be easily omitted, nor do they pass unnoticed. Even Grillo's portrayal of his mother and his subsequent motherless state offer some clues bearing the inadequacies of his constructed adaptation/transformation and delayed Latin unassimilation at the literary level. His Cuban/Latin mother, Amparo (the name translates as "I protect" in English), becomes less and less detailed. But she does not fully leave Grillo's stage. Amparo operates as the transitional presence into black Americanness. She is described as "beautiful, very agile, and very smart." Yet Amparo is "seldom graced by a smile, her face reflected resignation to a difficult, somewhat onerous obligation" (2000: 18). Her toilsome appearance is masculinized: she is "tall, thin, erect" (19) and "strong-willed," and because of this "humor had no place among her techniques for handling her brood" (23).[61] Grillo casts light on Amparo's proclivity for strict rules of conduct by addressing her in a formal fashion. She is "mother," not mom, or *mami*. He recalls that she rarely treats her son "with tenderness." Ultimately, the stern Cuban matriarch, who as a tobacco worker, habitually reeked of her means of employment, is substituted for the nurturing black American mother figure, Mrs. Byna, "a stout woman of about sixty." She gave Grillo "kind and caring love," allowing him to feel "very safe and secure" (19). Amparo's son is kindly, caringly, and lovingly looked after—protected—elsewhere. As Grillo's Cuban family life becomes more and more blurry, what takes precedent is his just formed political family. His mother's textual exit takes the orphaned Cuban character into another biographical way of being that does not manifestly and unaffectedly lead to black Americanness.

This biographical mode is a break in one's geographic and biographic temporalities. It is aligned with what sociologist Lynn Davidman has proposed, in the context of the loss of a maternal figure, as "biographical disruption." Davidman's approach allows for "continuous movement back and forth between [one's] own memories, feelings, and responses," as one's life is rebuilt "after experiencing a major, unanticipated" bereavement (2000: 6–7). This fracturing creates a need to flesh out and "refashion [one's] biography, thereby aligning [one's] sense of self with [one's] social world" (26). The biographical disruption I build on concerns the interruption of what is constitutive of peoples' lives and selfhoods in terms of geography, nation, family, memory, and cultural conventions. For my stringent focus is the discontinuity in touchstone narratives by biographical ethnoracial groups whose accounts produce further inquiry about their excess, deletions, and transitions. Grillo's irreconcilable selfhoods transport him to other literary and national processes of becoming—to other ways of being constituted as a Latined subject from the Global South. How the shifting terrains of black-brown personhoods are conceived at the theoretical level, not so much to arrive at formal identities but to articulate a Latined milieu of representation and emergence, is the focus of this chapter's last section.

Like a Problem: Passing Lines of Knowledge and Open Double Consciousness

Allow me to now compositionally embark on this chapter's concluding subheading with a luminous yet unvarnished question posed to me by a student: Are Latinos and Latinas a problem?[62] Faced with this heuristic task, I harked back to whether Latinos and Latinas can rely on an account of this group through the same Du Boisian contours of being problems and the fashioning of the critical visions and political world consigned to double consciousness. My use of Du Bois's double consciousness and concern for problematic populations does not eclipse his theoretical use of twoness.[63] I turn to the meaning of the problem because it also guides subjects on how to have a consciousness of their otherness and their efforts to make the American way of life more manageable. Lewis Gordon has stressed that "consciousness is, always, consciousness *of* something" (2000: 73). By working through the construction of "political problems" in Latin-American contexts, I am also forging an "epistemological openness" for new problems that have the capacity to engender consciousness in different American locations (72, 90). Latino and Latina sociopolitical emergence and American formation share genealogies of being. They are a type of derivative but overblown problem germinating from the black-and-white color line. This color line crafts new political families that are now moving into a family of problems. The revised ruminations thus call into question: How do Latino and Latina problems come about? What types of problematic practitioners do they become? And how to treat an evolving double consciousness when markers outside black and white pass through that dichotomy, cutting across and disturbing the facticity of those two main categories?

Unmistakably, we have a problem. But this is a serviceable problem. It works to problematize the existent black-white economy we endeavor to interrupt in everyday life to produce epistemic lines for this entangled composite of blackness, brownness, and dark brownness.[64] As broached with Grillo earlier, blackness and brownness are irreducible. They are not at a distance. Joint black-brown problematic routes engulfed Grillo's two opened states, which were continually structured as disjointed. Yet the narrative's black-brown rift intervenes and arranges an opening for double consciousness.[65] This openness for mobile subjectivities is quintessential to an open double consciousness in the context of Latinities. I affix "open" to double consciousness so as not to cut and isolate one set of U.S. African American, Latino, and Latina relations from another. Du Bois serves as my interlocutor. But I also branch off his thought, as the germane moments of—and thresholds for—double consciousness must be articulated through the multiple genealogies that admit Du Boisian critical awareness as historical knowledge.

Open double consciousness can be framed as a passing line of knowledge—or, a knowledge that has been passed on—through black-brown mutability. The link between blackness and brownness becomes a shifting relationality insomuch as the peculiar meanings of blackness have been passed on to its substantive others, brownness and dark brownness. The openness of double consciousness is dispersed in motley directions. Its place as a knowledge has to be uncovered, as does the probing of what allows for the introduction and continuity of certain problems. Open double consciousness turns to different memberships of belonging that, as Susan Bibler Coutin puts it for "variegated national populations," are multidimensional, since the contemporary United States encompasses inhabitants "whose legal statuses and national affiliations are diverse" (2003: 58). Even the American intentions and allegiances of Latined subjects with transnational connections and practices are not solely embedded in the United States.[66] Open double consciousness is therefore needed as a driving force for a more detailed analysis of black-brown-dark brown incoherence. We must take into account that blackness has run out of African Americanness, that brownness has migrated from Latinoness and Latinaness, that the South has become more southernly, and that America is deliquescent outside the United States.[67]

Open double consciousness transpires in a wide array of "translocations," where self-awareness and self-alteration move not so much to reinscribe one's life to patterns of opposition. I make use of Agustín Laó-Montes's proposal of the "politics of translocation" to render visible links to—as well as the transactions within—the "geographies of power," established "at various scales (local, regional, national, global) with the subject positions (gender/sexual, ethno-racial, class, etc.) that constitute the self" (2007: 317). Open double consciousness, as I submitted elsewhere, embraces itself in its unstable, autobiographical "I": what it is, what it is not, and what it can be. It is a fused first-person pronoun that also suggests ensuing interactions of what is to come and what is to become (Milian, 2006). It is a pathway that charts places where Latinos and Latinas are a nonnarrative, an incoherence, a disruption. But open double consciousness is not exclusively pertinent to Latinos and Latinas, as its Latined portal continues to be renewed. While irreconcilable strivings may remain, the function of open double consciousness is its resourcefulness in taking to task the recontextualization of new twenty-first-century problems responding to the Global South's volatile compositions and movements.

When Du Bois affirmed that between him and "the other world there is ever an unasked question [. . .] unasked by some through feelings of delicacy," aspects of the "other [white] world" may be brought to bear on Latino and Latina worlds of color, whose shades of blackness move to other racial variations that "flutter around" problematic blackness, or deviations thereof. For José Esteban Muñoz, Du Bois's articulation of his difficult location in "the other world"—repeatedly emphasized through what Du Bois finds as that world's *unasked* question of "How does it feel to be a problem?" (1996b: 3)—emits the idea of "feeling like a problem."[68] This feeling becomes what Muñoz calls "a mode of belonging through recognition," namely "a mode of minoritarian recognition" (2007: 441). Muñoz puts across that "there may be considerable value in thinking about the problem of feeling like a problem as not simply an impasse, but instead, an opening" that could "index a communal investment in Brownness" (441, 445). Placing the promise of the "opening" that the problem could grant aside for a minute, I respectfully digress. Du Bois did not so much *feel* like a problem. He articulated blackness as part of a hermeneutical turn that, as Gordon points out, does not pertain to "*being* black but about its *meaning*" (2000: 63). One could contend that the lingering feeling of the meaning of a problem is simultaneously felt by the "other world" that first identifies and provides a diagnosis of, as Richard Wright put it, the "white problem" (Rowley, 2001: 332).[69]

Du Bois's blackness was what gave bodily form to the problematic predicament. But since he does not provide a response to the question of *being* a problem ("I answer seldom a word"), the "feeling" is the way in which Du Bois controls his emotions from the "outrages" stemming from "the other world." He admits, "At these I smile, or am interested, or reduce the boiling to a simmer, as the occasion may require." For this feeling to be analytic and reasonable, the bothersome subject must also "unfeel" the weight of that blackness. The sensation of feeling like a problem must subside so that a theory on blackness (like double consciousness) emanates, which is what Du Bois also vied for in *The Autobiography of W. E. B. Du Bois: A Soliloquy on Viewing My Life from the Last Decade of Its First Century* (1968). In this self-illustration written during his ninetieth year, Du Bois introduces his lived experience as one that must be grasped as a *theory* of his life (1997: 12).[70] "Feeling brown," as Muñoz suggests, thus needs more than a feeling or "a way of being in the world" (2007: 444).[71]

Latino and Latina troublesome status, under Muñoz's critical eye, emerges from "the idea of feeling Brown," of "feeling like a problem," that is, "feeling together in difference." This form of "Brownness registers as a mode of affective particularity that a subject feels in herself and recognizes in others" (2007: 443–44). In effect, "a 'group investment' in Brown feeling requires a certain transmission as affect and this happens through various sensory circuits" (447). These circuits open up the space for brownness as "a mode of consciousness that responds to the historical pressure of the historical" (449–50). But what is the historical weight of problematic brownness if Latinoness and Latinaness seem to gradually pull away from African American problems?

Du Bois's twenty-first-century millennial problem runs through a menagerie of a villainous, Latin (Americanized) freakery. These multisymptomatic problems have widened—squeezed into the rubric of a Latinness that is "freaking out" America. They provoke un-American distress and stand outside the national sphere of acceptable heteronormativity. They informally become a "freaking problem" for the nation that John Leguizamo calls "America[,] home of the freak, land of the depraved" (2006: 195). A brief but blatant pattern of examples, ranging from Gloria Anzaldúa and Miguel Piñero to Leguizamo and Junot Díaz, substantiates that Latinos and Latinas concur with feeling *like* a problem. But they also differ in "feeling like a freak," something outside the grasp of America (Leguizamo, 2006: 188). They are, plainly said, freaks of an un-Americanized nature.

Anzaldúa's transgressive abnormalities gave way to a collective subjectivation put forward by a "weird" universal deformity that socially arranges her being. A disproportionately built populace materializes, comprising "the squint-eyed, the perverse, the queer, the troublesome, the mongrel, the mulatto, the half-breed, the half dead" (1999: 25). Piñero, a Nuyorican poet and playwright, amassed a "freakery" situated in Manhattan's Lower East Side, where "the hustlers & suckers meet / the faggots & freaks will all get / high" (1980: 7). His lyrical ode to "ghettocide"—urban alienation—actively makes him a problematic individual of "ethnic proportion" (10). Despite being an extension of what makes him, under a Du Boisian diagnosis, a U.S. "ethnic" problem, Piñero, the self-proclaimed "Philosopher of the Criminal Mind," critically reasons through and humanizes his "criminality" (8). He embodies "the Cause" that makes him "a problem of this land" (23–25, 8). From the purview of a Dominican South in the U.S. North, Junot Díaz's cluster of social aberrations are charted as "the fat, the ugly, the smart, the poor, the dark, the black, the unpopular, the African, the Indian, the Arab, the immigrant, the strange, the femenino, the gay" (2007: 264). These different sets of disabling anomalies from different geopolitical locations (or demographics that compose a Global South), propound an open double consciousness that allows for the enabling entry of subjects who exceed the unbending oppositions of black-and-white and brown-and-white. Raising this preoccupation animates the need to more carefully probe into and rejuvenate moving epistemologies that deflect from and align with what Paul Miller has called "the famished souls of a geography of now-here" (2008: 5).

I have attempted in this inaugural chapter to afford Latinos and Latinas another avenue into Du Bois's sculpting of double consciousness and the parallel lines "of color" that accompany the color line in the U.S. American order. These southern Latinities revise porous Norths and Souths and bear in mind Peter Davidson's contention that if "North is always a shifting idea," so are the South, the Nuevo South, the Newest South, the Global South, and the open Latinities that are passing through them (2005: 8). The transformative migrations that have been researched are but one example of these living southern Latinities. The very movement from myriad vantage points indicates how the geography of white-black-Latin relations triggers an open double consciousness among these passing groups and their passing lines.

These evanescent passages point to the need for a more nuanced focus on biographical patterns opening up larger southern conversations. Narratives like Grillo's highlight how both blacks and browns pass into and are admitted in worlds with fairly limited possibilities of being. How they walk in and out of these worlds and the types of knowledges they carry have doubtlessly been the key points of exploration. As Danzy Senna cued us—following James Baldwin's signal at the end of *Notes of a Native Son* that "[t]his world is white no longer, and it will never be white again" (1984: 175)—U.S. African Americanness "is black no longer too" (2009: 195). The Latino and Latina ethnoracial world, as diagrammed, has ceased to be a binding brown also. The next chapter explores this premise. It surveys the Latinities of blackness and how these shift from blackness to brownness—pursuing these geographic and racial movements from Central America and Mexico.

CHAPTER TWO

PASSING LATINITIES

> My, my. A body does get around.
> —WILLIAM FAULKNER (1990: 30)

If the reader has accompanied me through chapter 1, it should by now become apparent that this project is observant of cross-cultural, passing acquaintances. My topic of study pursues altering scripts of working ambiguities that involve coming to, getting to, or turning to a new appreciation for quotidian attributes of arriving at Latinities from conflicting geographies and alternative entryways. I inquire into "Passing Latinities" through what William Anthony Nericcio has devised as "'miscegenated' semantic oddities" that codify not just brown folk but black folk too (2007: 16). This black-brown point of intersection reorients black-white passages beyond this dual-directional schema and focuses on how Latinities permeate these blurred encounters. Mary Bucholtz's take on passing identifies it as "*the active construction of how the self is perceived when one's ethnicity is ambiguous to others.*" She adds, "an individual may in certain contexts pass as a member of her 'own' biographical ethnic group by insisting on an identity that others may deny her. Furthermore, passing of this kind is not passive. Individuals of ambiguous ethnicity patrol their own borders, using the tools of language and self-representation to determine how the boundaries of ethnic categories are drawn upon their own bodies" (1995: 352–53).[1] Passing Latinities, however, do not depend on ambiguity alone to tinge an individual with an other's ethnoracial signifiers. Such Latinities tackle ideas of an authenticating essential core used as a baseline assumption to visually produce and hermetically seal a particular group's semiotics. The tools of language and self-representation in these passing but cohabiting Latinities speak to the incoherence underlying other Latin constructs that interrupt the eyes and inaugurate new biographical knowledge formation as well as conceptual cultural terms.

As I seek to broaden the premises of border cultures and cultural communication, my principal aim is to intervene in this horizon to make room for two crucial figures of the Harlem Renaissance: James Weldon Johnson (1871–1938) and Langston Hughes (1902–67). I steer toward this interpretive nexus, because as foundational approaches to the black diaspora have demonstrated, U.S. black literary and theoretical accounts seemingly impart a transcontinental cultural turn mainly encompassing Europe, the United States, Africa, and the Anglo- and Francophone Caribbean (see, e.g., Edwards, 2003; and Gilroy, 2003). The Hispanophone Americas and U.S. Latino/a studies are rarely configured in these mappings of diasporic blackness.[2]

Taking the roles of Johnson and Hughes as points of orientation, I begin by centering on how these eminent literary figures have traversed Latin-American borders, consciously mindful of the ways that "other" Souths informed their multifaceted literary and political work. Knowledgeable of Spanish, both Johnson and Hughes were preoccupied with the formation of black aesthetics exceeding U.S. boundaries. Analytically attentive to questions of blackness in global dimensions, they assumed a stance that is of paramount significance for my investigation of the Global South. Such sharp interests allowed these cultural producers to understand that the hemispheric imaginings of blackness constituted a variable spectrum "of color" that worked alongside and often in stark contrast to U.S. African Americanness. Turning to other understandings of race outside the United States, one enduring concern is how both Johnson and Hughes were mindful of these southern Latinities in U.S. and Latin-American terrains. My primary intention also considers the manner in which their U.S. ethnoracial markers stand in relation to national landscapes as well as the traveling and exchanging meanings of Latin-Americanness: how their subjectivities and bodies move, act, become known, evade, or "get around," as Faulkner's epigraph to this chapter suggests. My work examines the semiotic burden and the interdependency of blackness and brownness within conceptions and deployments of Latinidad and U.S. African Americanness.

Given this scope, I study how Johnson's and Hughes's bodies "spoke" their blackness-cum-brownness in the Latin topographies of Mexico and Cuba, in

Hughes's case, and Nicaragua in Johnson's. Their blackness-cum-brownness is not reducible to brownness-*not*-blackness. Blackness and brownness are mutually encoded and in close company with each other. Johnson and Hughes dared to enter these nations in the Americas and point to processes of becoming that are not strictly black or brown. They actualized, in this manner, a passing Latinity. But these black-brown passages do not equate a process of deracialization. Through their overlaps, we see how the firm grip of blackness and brownness is loosened and muddled. Blackness enables a continuum of Latin interventions and acquires a Latinity that ceases to be durably brown in the U.S. Latinidad sense that entraps the fixity of the Latino and Latina body. Johnson's and Hughes's moving bodies jettison the essence of Latino and Latina brownness, altering Latin spaces. Latinness is perpetuated differently, and newly emergent Latinities—that is, passing Latinities—are revised through polymorphic passages, turns, and interactions. The disorder and interplay of blackness-cum-brownness widen the Latin imaginary and put this touchstone into useful practice: why can't black and blackness also be bearers of Latin?

The previous chapter inspected other axes of blackness that are not anchored in unidirectional Latinoness, Latinaness, and African Americanness. The present one interrogates how U.S. black bodies have crossed and commingled with Latin-America's color lines. Such an investigation raises a critical but as of yet unasked question: what are the national implications of U.S. Latinoness and Latinaness when that ethnoracial group's markers have been passed through by U.S. African Americans? I bring this question to other aspects of the South not simply as an analogous correlation between first and third world peripheries but as a maneuver that undoes what has passed as static and monolithic for far too long: the meanings of Latino, Latina, and Latin as devoid of blackness. If, as Arlene Dávila has contended, U.S. "ethnic group after ethnic group has been pressed to distance itself from African Americans, or else has been distanced from 'blackness' by others," the goal is not just to disentangle the distanciation and disassociation between Africana blackness and Latin blackness–dark brownness (2008: 7). My parameters of inquiry set in motion their potential through the reexamination of the disparate locations of Latinness and its unleashing vis-à-vis broader cultural sites and social actors installing Latinities as a different formation.

My research interests derived from perceived moments of literary discretion by both Johnson and Hughes that suggested far more about the marginal renditions of Latin life than what I was reading in perfect bound form. In the introduction to Hughes's *The Big Sea* (1940), for example, biographer and literary critic Arnold Rampersad writes that the poet was a "reluctant autobiographer," who resisted such a project, granting that he hated "to think backwards" (1993: xiii). Hughes's Mexican intervals are marked with inertia—notwithstanding the fact that Rampersad paradoxically interprets Hughes's pages on that nation as animated purveyors of "Mexican Technicolor" (xvii).[3] His appraisal is based on an instance that amounts to textual lethargy, wherein Hughes confessed, "I didn't do much that summer but read books, ride my horse Tito, eat [. . .] apple cake, feel lonesome, and write poems when I felt most lonesome" (1993: 58). Hughes's public self-summarization retains a matter-of-fact tone, an oscitancy that turns Mexico into a happenstance of a cursory forty pages (39–79). But Hughes's trove of private papers at the Beinecke Rare Book and Manuscript Library, as I soon explore, indicate far more precious insight.

Johnson's writerly voice in *Along This Way* (1933) also inspires. It has the proclivity to be a formal narrative of social triumph modeled for the black race as much as for the consumption and normative acceptance of black success.[4] Divided into four parts, *Along This Way* appears as a linear yet passing explanation of achievement. The book centers on Johnson's interwoven geographies (Haiti, Bahamas, Africa, and the United States), growing up in Jacksonville, Florida, and attending Atlanta University. Johnson's life also motions toward a series of distinguished posts such as educator and administrator, U.S. consul in South and Central America, literary figure, as well as NAACP field secretary in 1916 and, latterly, executive secretary in 1920. Johnson's and Hughes's documents provided extraordinary perspicacity into other facets of their lives, to less guarded but still poignantly observant moments where these writers were sharply aware of Latin geographies. My examination of once-private pages demonstrated a series of interior monologues and critical reflections that expand our frames of reference: how we situate, study, and bring together the Africana diaspora and a Latinidad that because it has yet to be theorized from the flowing encounters and responses beyond brown and white, must be "deLatinized" from the normative entanglements that underlie U.S. Latinoness and Latinaness.

Though Johnson primordially served in this same capacity in Puerto Cabello, Venezuela, in 1906, I emphasize his diplomatic career as U.S. consul to Corinto, Nicaragua (1909–14), since my key preoccupation is his appointment as that city's inaugural consul during the Theodore Roosevelt administration. Johnson's years in Central America raise, for me, a host of issues about U.S. processes of Americanization and ethnoracialization from the Latin American experience of lived brownness, or mestizaje.[5] Taking the upper-class affiliation that his post afforded him because of his U.S. consul status, my analytic lens is focused on the kinds of foresight that Johnson's account on ethnoracial interactions, economic stratification, and American ideology at home and abroad furnish for the Hispanophone Americas in the diaspora. I pay attention to how his diplomatic skills contribute to his navigation of Nicaraguan-American color divides and shifting borders. Johnson's profession in the realm of international relations further prompts self-reflection on his black Americanness as well as his brown Americanness. His prominent role stands out as much today, perhaps, as it did then. Try catching sight of this unfathomable scene in U.S. foreign relations, during Jim Crow segregation, recalled by Johnson himself: "a white man (the Vice-Consul) [is] seated at a long table just to the right of the entrance. And, up center of the room, a Negro (myself) seated at a desk, just back of which an American flag draped the wall" (2000: 259).[6]

At the time, President Roosevelt believed that "America's greatness was being threatened not only by rampant poverty but also its cozy affluence." Whereupon Roosevelt submitted the idea that "some day we will realize that the prime duty, the inescapable duty, of the *good* citizen of the right type is to leave his or her blood behind him in the world; and that we have no business to permit the perpetuation of citizens of the wrong type" (quoted in Bruinius, 2007: 6). Johnson's consular tasks set aside doubts on his being "of the wrong type" in a historical moment of segregation, eugenics, and American empire.[7] He had a decisive role in protecting U.S. interests during the 1912 Nicaraguan revolution—engaging in what was also known as "Dollar Diplomacy"—where a force of 2,700 U.S. Marines landed in Corinto and the Bluefields.[8] The United States maintained an occurring presence in Nicaragua until 1933, when the anti-imperialist campaign led by Augusto César Sandino (1895–1934) served to remove forces from that nation.[9]

Johnson proves important in these pages, for he was fostering a literary trajectory alongside his consular job. While in Nicaragua, Johnson learned that his novel, *The Autobiography of an Ex-Coloured Man*, was going to be published by the Boston-based Sherman, French and Company in 1912.[10] The prevailing view among literary critics of passing literature during the Harlem Renaissance has been to situate the mixed, black and white American subject as one who uninterruptedly moves into whiteness (see, e.g., Kawash, 1996). Yet Johnson demonstrated that passers are not only tapping into whiteness but to other Latinings too. Johnson implicitly introduced the notion in *The Autobiography of an Ex-Coloured Man* that shades of U.S. African American blackness can be read as forms of U.S. Latino and Latina brownness. Johnson's literary intent, as conveyed to his publishers, could fall under this explanatory aegis spreading and "re-Latinizing" the boundaries of Latinidad. His advance notice to the Sherman, French and Company read, "Not yet has a composite and proportionate presentation of the entire race, embracing all of its various groups, showing their relations with each other and to the whites have been made; this I have endeavored to do" (1912b: 17 Feb.). The proposed anonymity of Johnson's hero, as it appears, develops into a flowering of anonymities, since the unnamed protagonist surpassed reductive misreadings by the dominant gaze.[11] Because he had a fluent command of the Spanish language, he educated Cuban cigar workers in the "one trade in which the colour line is not drawn" (1989: 67). This interpretive disposition becomes a Latinity, a spoken act and linguistic performance of brownness that is enacted by a black, Latined subject.[12]

As in Johnson, my comparative exercise also takes me to Hughes's 1920 chronicling, as an eighteen-year-old, of his first trip southward, spanning Jim Crow Texas, Nuevo Laredo, Saltillo, Vanegas, San Luis Potosí, and Mexico City. This border crossing is highly significant and bears considering. What these types of passings mean in the theorization of race and culture within the fields of Chicano/a, Latino/a, and African American studies inform my analysis of "new" Souths. They pose larger emphasis on the necessity to rethink what it means to become a Latino from the specter of U.S. African American blackness. My points of discussion and findings, then, are provoked by questions such as these: What is involved for these bodies as they look for and study, as Du Bois put it, the "North American Negro" and the Latin American *negro* in Latined spaces (1998: 205)? Where do their own personal archives — their probing archaeology of blackness and Latinness in

North, Central, and South America—focusing on interdependent Negro/*negro* elements take us? What becomes of brownness as an unalloyed Latinidad ceases to continue as we know it and shifts toward an ongoing, open Latinity marked and passed by different agents?

Hughes's Mexican journey primarily stands out because the reader is able to assess the arduous labor he undertook in learning Spanish and conversing, depending on the national context, like a native. Moving between and across blackness and brownness, Hughes proceeded to ask himself, during his 1930 trip to Havana, "What constitutes Negro blood?" (1930). These southern migrations furnish us with rare glimpses—comparable to a stream of consciousness—that, journalistically speaking, are involved with the world as events immediately unfold. The then and thereness of these encounters thrusts us into the intersectional value of the here and now as an antidote to homogenizing U.S. African American or Latino/a thought. They instruct us to update the semiotics of the peoples we come to believe and know as Latino, Latina, and black, no less significantly because the people we also come to believe and know as Americans continue to evolve.

Although politically engaged, Johnson and Hughes press us to think about their ruminations from a literary standpoint.[13] The authors transport us to a Latin American narrative style known as the crónica, or chronicle. The crónica is an interdisciplinary, investigative medium combining literature, anthropology, cultural reporting, and criticism. It is a writing form that disrupts aesthetic boundaries, generally combining memories, travel notes, interviews, testimonials, documentary narrative, fiction, and essays. Mónica Bernabé (2006) has postulated that the crónica can be considered as a space where literature emblematizes an encounter broadening the realm of other discourses. The value of the crónica was intensified from the end of the nineteenth to the beginning of the twentieth century, when Latin American writers like José Martí (1853–95), Rubén Darío (1867–1916), and César Vallejo (1892–1938) set out to decipher the meanings of modern city life, or as more properly worded by Julio Ramos, "the different ways of representing the fin de siècle city" (2001: 126). The teasing out of the city as a concept becomes, under Ramos's elucidative structure, "an archive of the 'dangers' implicit in the new urban experience; an ordering of daily life as yet unclassified by instituted forms of knowledge" (113). These urban segments translate to what Ramos also deemed as *la retórica del paseo*, the rhetoric of taking a stroll. Such strollings merge with the crónica through the act of taking a literary or poetic stroll — or, simply, any stroll of investigation and exchange — which, for our purposes, becomes, as Frank Andre Guridy has it, a "cross-border, transnational" Latin-American zone (2010: 7).[14]

As critical thoughts that pass through subjects in geographies from which they are weeded out, the crónicas that Johnson and Hughes offer — in their efforts to transform Latin metropoles into a personal, or as Johnson shows, an unusual space — interlock U.S. Latino/a and African American writing. The crónica fits Johnson's and Hughes's arrangement of Nicaraguan and Mexican political and sociocultural matters, while also lending an open-endedness that defies simple subject, writer, and genre recognition. Hayden White has pointed out in a different context bearing relevance here that chronicles "have no *inaugurations*; they simply 'begin' when the chronicler starts recording events. And they have no culminations or resolutions; they can go on indefinitely" (1975: 6). The indeterminateness of Johnson's and Hughes's crónicas depends and takes shape next to their passing Latinities, which are reentered and discharged differently on each occasion. Their autobiographical moments challenge, break, and modify the story of blackness and brownness. At the same time, it needs to be duly noted that this study is not intended as a biographical attempt on Johnson's or Hughes's life.[15] My analytic sketch endeavors to unravel how Latin imaginations are summoned in these literary workers' genealogies to produce U.S. black cultural and intellectual thought. In this sense, I concur with Gregson Davis, who qualifies and employs the term "biographical" as constitutive of "the life of the mind — the intellectual and aesthetic evolution" of the writer, an instructive point from which I base this critical platform (1997: ix).

This chapter moves to discuss Johnson's Nicaraguan crónicas at a time of political crisis. His firsthand exposition of Central America operates as a barometer of irreconcilable contradictions mediated by U.S. diplomacy. Under this art of managing negotiations between nations, Johnson directly accounts for his Americanness but tacitly articulates his Negro Americanness. While his musings appear reconcilable by virtue of his distinctive title of U.S. consul, they also stand for the limits of his un-Americanness. In his letters, Johnson confers primacy to the "realness" of his consular Americanness and how it may transfer to the United States after the successful completion of his assignment. Johnson brings out an important line of inquiry and its relation to the Latined constitution of his "ex-coloured man": the alienating absurdity of Nicaraguan/Latinness coupled with ideological forms of American modernity. Johnson, literarily speaking, transnationally keeps his American selfhood, while Nicaragua retains its inherent Nicaraguanness. This Latinness, far from coherent, is managed for creative purposes in American letters and black-white tensions and representations. Johnson shows that the schismatic passing figure from *The Autobiography of an Ex-Coloured Man*, who acquired narrative form in Central America, consists of unrestricted passages and corresponds to more places in the world than the United States.

Hughes's Mexican and Cuban travel notes follow. His first southern passage leads to cultural processes of "Becoming Mexican," as Hughes calls them, from a Negro, black, and Latined perspective. George J. Sánchez has written that Mexican Americanness has been historically treated as "a tenuous site of cultural exchange, always a prelude to the attractions of a 'purely' Mexican or a 'purely' American stance" (1993: 8). But Mexican Americanness has actively worked against the assumed stasis of Mexican, American, or Chicano. It has highlighted continuous "movement between Mexican and American cultures," creating "a place of opportunity and innovation" for what has been scholarly framed as a Mexican and American border culture (9). The depth of Hughes's reflections evidences irregularities in the production of such a fixed Mexican and American characterization. His interpretations of and evolving access into Mexicanness cannot be bypassed, as we indisputably become intimate guests to his Latined milieu.

I now put into cultural and formative relation Johnson's and Hughes's varying worlds of creative writing and affinities with creative Latined living.

A Voice from Another South:
James Weldon Johnson's Nicaraguan Literary "I"

> I was eager and curious over the new
> experience I was about to enter.
> —JOHNSON (1989: 70)

In a rather depreciatory note, dated 2 August 1929, Langston Hughes opined that "No one needs to know me—everything I have to offer worth the offering is in my work; the rest is slag and waste." There is dissimilarity with

Johnson in that numerous individuals knew the polymathic Floridian in different and prominent competencies outside literary arenas. Johnson's laudable trajectory appears as a prudent voice of precisionist professionalism. No spontaneous and lasting journalistic notes or magnificently revelatory observations and reports exist by the author during his formative and professional years. The Beinecke Library explains that Johnson's written communication "was not systematically preserved throughout his career and the amount of extant material varies for different periods of his life. There is no correspondence for the period before 1904, and between 1906 and 1920 Johnson saved only those letters that he felt were important" (Cunningham, 1973).

I thus elected to research a constant and dependable source of interlocution in Johnson's life during his tenure in Nicaragua. I perused his epistolary interaction with his wife, Grace Nail Johnson, or la niña Graciela, as Corinto residents knew her during the nearly two years she lived there with her husband.[16] Third parties were not intended as beholders of their exchanges. Skimming through Johnson's private dispatches, it is likely that the couple's terms of endearment and longing might make some researchers blush, as archivists strive to examine pressing matters in the Western Hemisphere. In addition to general archival material, I consulted intermittent periods in Johnson's correspondence. They conveyed supplementary information about significant anecdotal moments relating to Latinities, both in the United States and abroad, that fashioned Johnson's view of, to reference the diction of the time, the colored race.

Literary critic Harilaos Stecopoulos has contended that for Johnson "the black-white divide could never completely encapsulate the U.S. South" (2007: 39). This claim is important for understanding Johnson's body of work, which is in line with the types of Latin knowledge he possessed, assisting him as a U.S. government official in Latin America. *The Autobiography of an Ex-Coloured Man* and *Along This Way* are two literary models from different genres that are demonstrative of Johnson's crossings into continental adaptations of informative Latinities. There is, to be sure, the influence of bilingualism from a young age through his father, James Johnson, an autodidact who was born a freeman in Richmond, Virginia. The Johnson patriarch had gained "a working knowledge of the Spanish language [. . .] to increase his value as a hotel employee" (Johnson, 2000: 17). Thereafter, Mr. Johnson taught Spanish to his two sons, James and Rosamond. The learning process entailed, as Johnson recalled, sitting "for an hour at a time while he drilled us." The utility of these Spanish lessons was confirmed when the Johnson family hosted a Cuban boy with a "light bronze complexion" named Ricardo Rodriguez Ponce. The family helped familiarize the visitor with the United States as well as gain English-language proficiency. With the three boys soon "carrying a bi-lingual conversation," Johnson noted, "meals were little less than exciting" (59). This Latin environment conferred on Johnson a certain cachet, and he intuited, as a college student, its social value. "I possessed a prestige entirely out of proportion to my age and class," he inferred at Atlanta University. "Among the factors to which this could be attributed were: my prowess as a baseball pitcher, my ability to speak a foreign language, and the presumable superiority in worldly wisdom that having lived in New York gave me" (75).[17]

Rodriguez Ponce's brownness, as subsequently evinced, provided an entry for Johnson into the sinuous gradation of the colors of Latinity. This access and excitement, as the epigraph for this section suggests, was couched in *The Autobiography of an Ex-Coloured Man* through the nameless protagonist's immersion in the Latin world, which meant, in those pages, the "artistic skill of cigar-making by Cubans" (Johnson, 1989: 70). The character went on to "not only make cigars, but also to smoke, to swear, and to speak Spanish." He elaborated, "The rapidity and ease with which I acquired Spanish astonished my associates. [. . .] In fact, it was my pride that I spoke better Spanish than the many of the Cuban workmen at the factory" (72–73).[18] This passing Latinity attests to a fascinating dynamic: that those who have crossed are better with the identity they possess at the moment than the "original." But it is not just Johnson's hero alone who crossed the U.S.-Cuban divide. Cuban exiles spoke "English excellently" and frequently surprised Johnson's storyteller "by using words one would hardly expect from a foreigner" (71).[19]

This characterization differed from the unassimilability attributed to the puerile Rodriguez Ponce in *Along This Way*. "He was something of a puzzle," Johnson declared in referencing the young Cuban with the unmistakably un-American pitch (2000: 66). At that time, students who enrolled at Atlanta University signed a pledge akin to the politics of respectability, where they had "to abstain from alcoholic drinks, tobacco, and profanity" (71). Rodriguez Ponce could not desist from smoking. He told the school's disciplinary authority, as Johnson phonetically mimicked it years prior to the 1953 debut of "the fastest mouse in all Mexico," Speedy Gonzalez: "that education or no education, he couldn't get along without smoking. [Ricardo] clinched his statement by saying, 'Meester Francis, I wass born weet de cigarette in de mout'" (73).[20] Decidedly divergent in this portrayal is Cuban uncrossability into the institutional and cultural Americanness of which Johnson forms a part. It is as though Rodriguez Ponce has been shut in or denied his "passability." Johnson, by contrast, had the ability to audibly tap into degrees of Latinities through his proficiency in Spanish, which administered a cryptic blackness. Boarding a first-class train car, Johnson once headed to Atlanta University with Rodriguez Ponce. The conductor notified the men of color that they had to change cars. But upon hearing Johnson translate for Rodriguez Ponce in Spanish, "his attitude changed." Johnson noted that the railroad official "punched our tickets and gave them back, and treated us just as he did the other passengers in the car" (2000: 65).[21]

This linguistic and ethnoracial mix up led Johnson to the conclusion that "in such situations any kind of a Negro will do; provided he is not one who is an American citizen" (2000: 65). This viewpoint may communicate, as Stecopoulos interprets, that Johnson "makes clear that 'Negroes' who seem Latin American 'will do' far better than any others in the Jim Crow South" (2007: 41).[22] But it is not that other kinds of *negros* (note the slight modification here to U.S. orthography and pronunciation of the term Negro by shifting, in italicized form, to its Latin counterpart, *negro*) will fare better in the segregated South. Instead, this episode — or to recycle a common expression, this train of thought — urges the possibility that for a *negro* to become an acceptable kind of Negro, he or she must have an interpreter, as was the case with Rodriguez Ponce. He counted on Johnson as more than an English speaker but as someone who, in this act of translation, exalts his Latin@ness: Latin-*at*-ness.[23] Something is "lost," not gained, for a Latino or Latina, since his or her Latinness has no place within the long continuance of black-and-white matters. The Latin matter, as a problem that belongs somewhere else, is postponed for another time and, undeniably, another place. It is not that these passing Latinities "will do" or that they promptly move into whiteness. Johnson's Latinity is more like a trespassing, as he brings in and redraws different equations to the rigid color line. Not merely a notional "fine line," as in a clearly arranged and limiting straight line, this demarcation is not simply black-and-white. It is a coloring line where one thinks along similar lines.[24]

Johnson's autobiography attests that this cultural agent was increasingly absorbed by efforts that decode the colors and meanings of blackness. A meticulous inspection leaves the impression that he lived—given the recurrence of the qualifier "brown"—in a brown world of difference. His father's aspect was described as "light bronze, a number of shades darker than that of my mother" (2000: 18). His grandfather's disposition was recorded as "dark brown" (20). The coloring of his maternal grandmother's side of the family was pictured as "lighter in complexion" and "light brown" (46–47). Certain neighbors were also perceived as "brown." Others "looked white but were not" (32–33). Upon arriving at Atlanta University, Johnson spotted the tertiary color now appended to U.S. Latinas and Latinos. "The bulk" of his classmates, his synopsis affirmed, "ran the full gamut of all the shades and nuances of brown" (75).

Johnson was consequently admitted as señor consul with a keen knowledge of the various ways in which blackness and Latinities are crossing lines that disquiet the insidious inactivity of the color line. Stecopoulos's adroit analysis constructs Johnson as a figure who is "eager to link the federal administration of the domestic South with U.S. intervention abroad" (2007: 35). He adds that "while critics have read the novel in light of myriad issues—publication history, the unreliable narrator, African American music, the representation of male sexuality, and, of course, the vexed question of racial passing—they have never considered how the *Autobiography* might speak to the contemporary question of empire" (38). Fair enough. One point I posit is that Johnson is more than an agent of empire. How his experience looks from the context of diplomacy is equally salient. I wish to decipher, for instance, how Latinness is looked at from a diplomatic space and from a racial vocabulary that insists, as Johnson notified his publisher, on the capitalization of the term "Negro." "My dear Sirs," Johnson advised the Sherman, French and Company, "I also wish to request that the word 'Negro' be capitalized throughout the book" (1912b: 23 Jan.). Not simply a stylistic convention, the formalized name emphasizes the "arrival" of the Negro at a U.S. workforce that develops intellectual labor. Quite the opposite, lo negro, the Negro's lowercase counterpart in the Americas, remains locked in undistinguishable typescript. Johnson's consular location in Nicaragua may be regarded as a literary agent that advances the Negro race as it coevally forges and cements the creation of a literary canon. Johnson acknowledged this striving in *Along This Way*. "When I had no official duties to perform," he said,

"I made it my business to use that period in getting ahead with my writing, to do which had been one of my chief reasons for entering the Consular Service" (2000: 237).[25]

Through his literary vocation, Johnson could make a lasting imprint, thereby exceeding his work as a foreign service officer. While in Nicaragua, "a great idea" occurred to him about selling his recently published *The Autobiography of an Ex-Coloured Man* to American military figures there. But the thought came "too late." He lamented that "I should have had 2 or 3 dozen copies of the book sent here to me while the big fleet was here. I could have sold a number of copies, but better still, it would have been a splendid 'ad' to have given autographed (initials) copies to the Admiral and other high officers" (1912a: 16 Nov.). Johnson wanted as much recognition for himself, as an American consul, as for his American novel. Lacking determinative responses to Johnson's hunger for military readership, I remain, nonetheless, overpowered by these queries: What might this type of audience intimate about the intellectual ascendance of the "race narrative" within U.S. military personnel? Just as individuals were speculating whether or not *The Autobiography of an Ex-Coloured Man* was "real," what would such a novel imply not only in reference to how (and when) one passes, but whether such infiltrations — that is, the ethnoracial equivalent of "don't ask, don't tell" — are also happening within the U.S. armed forces? Would the fallacy of the production of race turn the U.S. Army's gaze inward and help the Negro at home?

Johnson was satisfied with his technical skills in writing a fictional story that was to be read as nonfiction. He was emphatic in retaining the author's anonymity for *The Autobiography of an Ex-Coloured Man* and instructed his wife that she, with his father and brother, could do "a great deal" to help the book. He persuaded, "Ask friends and acquaintances — in a casual way, 'Have you read The A of an Ex-Col Man? If not be sure to read it.' You can write to friends in the same way. If Rosie [J. Rosamond Johnson, his brother, 1873–1954] goes out on the road he can do an enormous amount of advertising. But in it all, the absolute secrecy of the authorship must be maintained" (1912a: 26 May). Almost two decades after this book's initial publication, Johnson continued to garner a larger audience for his novel. He had become, by 1930, the Adam K. Spence Professor of Creative Literature and Writing at Fisk University. Exchanging a few words with the Head Office of the Fox

Film Corporation in New York on 27 April 1931, he followed-up on the "possibilities of making *The Autobiography of an Ex-Coloured Man* into a picture" (1931a).²⁶

Two years down the line, and while promoting another narrative, his own autobiography, Johnson drafted a letter to Eleanor Roosevelt, petitioning the First Lady to deliver on his behalf a copy of *Along This Way* to President Franklin D. Roosevelt. His missive began rather modestly, introductorily declaring, "It is hardly probable that you would recall me." But, he interjected and pushed on, "I remember with distinct pleasure that at a dinner given by Edward Bok some years ago in New York [. . .] I had the privilege of sitting at your right." The immediate connection to Bok (1863–1930), the Dutch-born editor of the *Ladies Home Journal* and Pulitzer Prize winner, situates Johnson among an influential group of individuals with parallel literary affinities and American achievements. This reference's importance also puts forward the merits of Johnson's own life story. Bok was awarded the Pulitzer in 1921 for *The Americanization of Edward Bok: The Autobiography of a Dutch Boy Fifty Years After*, published by Charles Scribner's Sons.²⁷ In it, Bok mentions one case in point that cues us in on Johnson's perceived value of U.S. presidential readership. Bok acknowledges seeking "a noteworthy list" of contributors for "each number" of his publication, the *Brooklyn Magazine*, which he conceived as "an organ of the society." Among the notable voices included in the magazine's premiere issue was that of the nineteenth U.S. president, Rutherford B. Hayes. His offering "astonished" Bok's patrons, "since up to that time the unwritten rule that a President's writings were confined to official pronouncements had scarcely been broken" (1927: 65–66). Not dissimilar to Bok, Johnson formally pursued his wish to include the thirty-second U.S. president as a reader of his oeuvre. He wrote "with the hope" that the First Lady would "be good enough to bring it to his attention, and with the hope also that you with him may be able to find the time to read the book" (Johnson, 1933b). Nine days later, on 15 November 1933, Mrs. Roosevelt responded to Johnson's request, assuring him that "I shall be very glad to give it to the President and hope to find the time to read it myself" (1933a).

Johnson's quest for an audience affiliated with the executive branch of the U.S. government intimates a search for a kind of American citizenship validation that unites the literary with the nation. There may be an ulterior political motive at work, as Johnson coveted FDR's literary eye. By and large, though,

Johnson seemed partial to presidential blurbs. In 1917, a few years after the *New York Times* publication of "Fifty Years," the Cornhill Company published this titular verse collection.[28] A publicity announcement from this publisher included a succinct, yet peculiar paean by President Theodore Roosevelt, who conspicuously turned Johnson's enterprise into an inanimate object with the phrase: "It is a striking thing" (Johnson, 1915).[29] The reader is forced to speculate on Johnson's private reaction to such tepid acclaim for his first book of poems. Johnson, after all, had confidently divulged this expectation to his wife: "If I get my poems properly launched, I believe they will make a reputation for me, the kind of reputation that I really want, the reputation of a writer and a thinker. Don't doubt — I'll win it — It's hard, slow work, but I know I'll succeed" (1912a: 26 June).

Johnson's Central American years substantiate an urgency to write, despite living in a torrid zone. Worthy of comparison to Johnson's guarding of U.S. national interests is the type of optic he applied to Nicaragua. "My first view of Corinto," he divulged in *Along This Way*, "sent my heart down like a plummet. What I saw was not a city or a town, but a straggling, tropical village" (2000: 255). He appeared to live in a world with a recursive assembly line of assistants named Pancho, telling his wife, "I have a new office boy, another Pancho by name. I expect to get Julia to clean up after me."[30] Safety proved a concern. "I am alone in the house at nights," he said, "but I don't mind much. I have a good revolver" (1912a: 4 Apr.). His attendance at Nicaraguan social gatherings signaled a North American–Central American line of difference, which was quite an arresting disengagement, since Johnson spoke Spanish and had, during his service as principal of the Stanton School in Florida, introduced Spanish as a modern language in courses (2000: 129). He recalled this occasion, using the first-person plural, thus: "We English speakers kept to one side of the corridor pretty much of the time and danced away ourselves almost entirely — It's so much less trouble — I danced with one native girl" (1912a: 8 May).[31]

One wonders what "native" constituted in this instant of rhythmic diplomacy highlighting U.S.-Nicaraguan linguistic — and no doubt political — tensions. Women appear, in Johnson's world, as intermediaries of culture, arguably evoking La Malinche, who translated for Hernán Cortés during the Spanish conquest of Mexico. This representation was also present in Johnson's account of how his wife learned Spanish, which attributed a passing-like quality for the Anglophone subject. Johnson wrote, "Her absorption in acquiring the language went far toward making many of the discomforts of life in Corinto less apparent. She enjoyed the trips we made to León and Managua, and meeting people there; to be able to talk with them better on each succeeding visit became an interesting game" (2000: 268–69). Under Johnson's watchful eye, Nicaraguan women are clearly differentiated. They stand in opposition to the continuous "sameness" reproduced in Nicaraguan men through the name Pancho.

Johnson declared that "in the tropics, 'Do not do today what *can* be put off till tomorrow,'" circulating, for his audience, the "maxim that contains many grains of wisdom" (2000: 237). Notes to his wife, who also spoke Spanish, bemoaned the tropical sultriness and humidity.[32] "My but this is going to be a scorcher," he protested, while ascertaining that the visibility of his body, as a race man, was deemed presentable and dignified.[33] Johnson seemed pleased with himself when he remembered, "It's a good thing I got the full dozen of those undershirts, for I take two shower baths and change from head to foot every day; it's the only way to keep feeling half decent. Helps in looks too" (1912a: 26 May). Discontentment with the pesky weather persisted four months down the road. He told Mrs. Johnson, "My it's hot today. I remember how you used to suffer from this heat" (11 Sept.). Likewise, Johnson reminded *Along This Way* readers that Nicaragua was no place for la niña Graciela, who "was dazed with disappointment" upon seeing Corinto for the first time. Johnson added that he "knew that no woman from a northern climate ought to stay longer than two years at a time in the tropics" (2000: 273).

The Nicaraguan post, in sum, was an assignment of utmost displeasure. At one point Johnson flatly declared, "Well, Corinto is the same, and I've told almost everything tolerable" (1912a: 8 May). Central America and its monotony did not fare with the rest of the world, especially Europe. Aboard a Pacific mail steamer one day, he sailed through Costa Rica and decided that "the change from Nicaragua to Costa Rica was comparable to a change from Costa Rica to France" (2000: 265). But what stood out the most in La Pequeña Suiza—or the Little Switzerland, as Costa Rica is dubbed—was finding "a jet-black Negro," who proved to be "the most curious sight [. . .] in Catholic San José" (275). Ever observant of black bodies—each time he found Negroes in the region he referred to them as a "sight"—Johnson was impressed that *negros* in Panama were not just "working as janitors or laborers, but doing clerical work" (254). He concluded that Nicaragua's wealth, "as in each of the Central American republics," was located "on the Pacific rather than the Atlantic side," which has a predominant Caribbean presence (260). Johnson's pages on Central America refrain from descriptive varieties on brownness, and what produced inquisitiveness, for the señor consul, was when he detected perceptible jet-black *negros*.

Nonetheless, it was in Nicaragua where Johnson could pace and display his spectacular Americanness. He devoted the third section of *Along This Way* to his consular duties abroad. He disclosed a fair amount of official details about the 1912 revolution in which the United States intervened to support the conservative president Adolfo Díaz. Johnson's correspondence with his spouse, however, revealed his other qualities and impulses during that tumultuous affair, given that he also had to protect "American lives and property" (1912a: 4 Aug.).[34] The first letter to Grace Nail Johnson on the topic of revolution was dated on 1 August 1912. Updating her from the five-hundred-ton armed warship Annapolis, Johnson began with the already expected. "Well, here it is again," he confided. "But this time it looks like something serious, not play. I've been on the wire three times today with the capital. Things look rather bad. Never saw the same amount of intense excitement as there is here tonight. The Com. was hiding at my place for a whole day. Don't worry though, I'm all right." Things continued to be, in his words from 4 August, "shaky." Johnson was advised that "in case of extreme danger," he should "take the custom house under [his] wing." Almost two weeks into the conflict, Johnson recapitulated Nicaragua's military attack in this way: "Well, there's no 'comic opera' about it. The bombardment of Nicaragua was terrible, people left the city by the thousands. All of the American refugees are here in Corinto" (17 Aug.). His account captured the event's severity:

> The Consulate was open day and night and was full of American refugees from Managua and those seeking safety in Corinto. The women and children were placed aboard the ships each night. We slept by turns for an hour or so each, and then we slept on our arms. But, in spite of it all, the strain, irregular meals, and lack of sleep, I feel splendid, my nerves are a bit on edge, but I'm all right, now with our troops here and the great weight of responsibility which I carried being lightened I'll be back to my old standard in a day or two. The Consulate

is still an armed camp, a detachment of Marines with a machine gun is here day and night.

But Johnson was also reserved about the political intricacies involved during the delicate situation, even with his wife. "I'll not attempt to write you about it," he remarked. "I can only tell you when we meet." Just before ending this letter, however, Johnson was decorous in his estimation of Adm. W. H. H. Southerland, the commander-in-chief of the Pacific fleet who did not treat him merely "as a very nice *colored* man." He had recognized Johnson "in the fullest degree as a man and officer." Johnson stated that he had been "called into every consultation" with the general, who had taken "no important step or action without asking [his] opinion and advice." Johnson's highest point was when Southerland had "issued a general order to all the American forces occupying Corinto, and in that order he commanded that the Consul was to receive the same naval honors as those accorded to the officers of the fleet; so whenever I pass the men on duty come to 'present arms' and I salute. A little thing, but it means a great deal." Johnson, the American authority on Nicaragua, uses the possessive pronoun when referring to "our government." He boasted to his companion, "I *know* this revolution from A to Z, and I've studied it out to my fullest ability—from the point of conditions, of international law and the policy of our government" (31 Aug.).

Nicaragua's historical "encounters with the 'northern' colossus" suggest that U.S.-Nicaragua experiences, like the black-white color line, bear parallels with a tense locus of Americanization processes in tandem with the un-Americanization of ideologically differentiated bodies and geographies (Gobat, 2005: 5). Just as Johnson symbolically stood as an American abroad, his un-Americanness "at home" coincided with Nicaragua's military, economic, political, and cultural negotiation of U.S. imperial rule. These complex appropriations of Americanness, Michel Gobat has pointed out, demonstrate Nicaragua's "competing forms of pro- and anti-Americanism" (2005: 5). Nicaragua's "variegated experiences with U.S. intervention" date as early as 1788, when Thomas Jefferson "proclaimed his country's interest in using the San Juan River and Lake Nicaragua to build a canal that would link the Atlantic and Pacific oceans" (1). The 1849 California gold rush exacerbated Central America's importance, as the isthmus became "a major transit for westbound fortune hunters." U.S. expansionism was strengthened through the 1846–48 U.S.-Mexican War, with Latin America becoming "the new 'frontier.'" Filibusters initiated private military expeditions during that period. This era's most notorious apostle of Manifest Destiny, the Tennessee-born William Walker, attempted, between 1855 and 1857, to Americanize Nicaragua "by replacing the native populace with U.S. colonists and implanting U.S. institutions such as slavery" (2).

By the start of the twentieth century, the interoceanic American route projected for Nicaragua was ultimately built, in 1914, by the United States in Panama. Political and strategic interests in Nicaragua led to that country's U.S. occupation from 1912 to 1933. The takeover staged "the greatest U.S. effort to turn Nicaragua into 'a little United States'" (Gobat, 2005: 3). This intervention brought, as Gobat has surveyed, "a U.S.-orchestrated regime change that blocked Nicaragua's incipient democratic opening; a U.S. invasion and subsequent military occupation; the takeover of Nicaraguan public finances by U.S. dollar diplomats; the spread of U.S. missionary activities and culture industries, especially Hollywood; a second full-scale U.S. invasion; the U.S. military's campaign to promote democracy; and a six-year guerrilla war" (10). Responses to U.S. influence and intervention differed and shifted. There was, for instance, the "elite Nicaraguans' infatuation with the U.S. road to modernity" (5). But this "Americanization from within" Nicaragua "did not simply adapt U.S. consumption and leisure patterns—the typical contemporary definition of Americanization" (7). Nicaraguans, rather, modified economic and cultural anti-Americanisms by being partial to U.S. "liberal institutions and practices that, in their view, had allowed the United States to become so prosperous and modern" (7–8). In this sense, we come across Nicaragua, the largest Central American nation, and Johnson, the plenipotentiary U.S. consul, as they both struggle for an incomplete American ideal outside U.S. boundaries.

Focusing on Nicaragua from Johnson's conflicting perspectives warrants a look at the ways that certain occupations facilitate processes of mainstreaming—*passing*—into ceremonial whiteness. But does Johnson truly pass when he has to account for an "exotic" locale as the space in which he accessed a particular kind of Americanness? Previous scholarly contributions such as Ileana Rodríguez's sustained work, *Transatlantic Topographies: Islands, Highlands, Jungles* (2004) and Stephen Benz's anthologized essay in *Tropicalizations: Transcultural Representations of Latinidad* (1997) have examined how the idea of Central America has been disseminated by imperial projects launched by the United States and Europe. Johnson may be perceived as having advanced such an agenda, but his time in Nicaragua is an unwitting link to his writing. Despite its tropics, underdevelopment, and second-rate Latinness, Nicaragua is an annex to Johnson's "American" literary geography. That republic impelled Johnson's carving out of new writerly lines. And while Nicaragua continued, for Johnson, as an unchanging backwater, a geography of ugly duckling proportions, that Latin space allowed him to slightly adjust his paradoxical standing of un-Americanized Americanness. Nicaragua functioned as an unpassable Latinity, as a witness to Johnson's awkward Americanness and to having lived a rendition of Americanness elsewhere. Johnson did not properly shed the other signifiers blocking his entrance into the type of Americanness practiced in the United States. But then again his passing Latinity was novelistically mediated through *The Autobiography of an Ex-Coloured Man*.

Given the austerity to which he had been subjected in the isthmus, Johnson had rigorous American standards and claimed from "our government" his due share of the American Dream. "I feel that something good is coming of it all. We just simply can't lose out; we've worked too hard, and played the game too straight to lose," he emphasized meritocratically (1912a: 11 Sept.). Johnson confirmed that he "set out to do a certain thing" and that he felt "satisfied with the way I've done it." Referencing his duty as a "game," he noted that "it's finished now, and I either win or lose — but I believe I've won" (16 Nov.). A winning factor was Johnson's victorious representation of his nation. This "win" allowed him to pass as a full U.S. citizen abroad. Yet Johnson's cultural representations pass into the realm of U.S. Latinities, as he illustrated in *The Autobiography of an Ex-Coloured Man*.

But if "ours is the era of the passing of *passing* as a politically viable response to oppression," as Carole-Anne Tyler asserts, Johnson proves otherwise in *Along This Way* (1994: 212). Nicaragua's Latinities remained what was professionally unpassable for Johnson. That country was a reminder that within consular hierarchies, Johnson had reached his zenith, notably after President William Howard Taft was not reelected in 1912. Facing the politically inevitable, he acknowledged after realizing that he had not received his coveted posts — Bordeaux, Reims, Nantes, and Calais, in that order (1912a: 4 Apr.) — that "I have seen the list of promotions, and to say that I was bitterly disappointed would be putting it very mildly." Although such was the case, Johnson's consolation was Americanness itself, as it continued to be stamped by Admiral Southerland. Johnson told his spouse that the naval officer had "increased my authority and official dignity 100 per cent. You ought to see these soldiers and blue jackets come to a 'present arms' when your old son goes by. The whole of Nicaragua knows that *I* am the American Consul" (10 Sept.).

The Americanness Johnson attempts to describe and fulfill is reduced to personal narrative, epistolary writings controlled by Johnson. Americanness becomes a part of his storytelling, whereas Nicaraguanness functions as an allegorical stage for how Johnson's Americanness is induced and then dwarfed in domestic U.S. venues. What of his passing Latinities? The Latinities he knows and accesses have no place in his consular appointment and tasks, which include "promoting American trade, helping American shipping, protecting and often disciplining seamen, and assisting American citizens who fell into trouble in their consular districts" (Kennedy, 1990: vii). Johnson's Americanness assumes the writerly form of a passable, autobiographical experience *in* Nicaragua, while Nicaragua's inadmissible Latinness enters Johnson's complex, fictive world of alteration and intercommunication. And yet Latinness, novelistically speaking, has been fictionally penned in opposition to Americanness and blackness — but not before readers have seen that Latinness is not on its own. Johnson, in other words, has been privy to — and has set up — Latined openings as they shift right across the black-brown boundary.

Really Becoming Mexican/Becoming Mexican, Really: Langston Hughes's Latin Passages

> You see, unfortunately, I am not black.
> —HUGHES (1993: 11)

Embarking on what would no doubt turn out to be an uncertain or unusual experience, Hughes began a 20 July 1920 journal entry with the hopeful title, "A diary of Mexican adventures (if there be any)." We now know, to briefly recall his autobiography, *The Big Sea*, that the main subject of this discussion was en route, via Cleveland-Mexico, to visit his father, James N. Hughes, from whom he had heard only after an eleven-year absence. Years earlier, the Hughes progenitor had relocated to Mexico, where, in his son's words, "a colored man could get ahead and make money quicker" (1993: 15).[35] This move led the Hughes patriarch, "who had legal training in the [U.S.] South," to gain admission in the Mexican bar and practice law, acquiring, in this process of socioeconomic ascension, "property in Mexico City and a big ranch in the hills" (39). For the elder Hughes, his Mexican success—a transnational version, in the opposite direction, of the American Dream—pointed to a form of achievement and self-recreation that, in his estimation, other U.S. blacks should aspire to and emulate.[36] Hughes remarked that his father's "favorite expression," not unlike the obiter dictum time is money, "in Spanish or in English, [was] hurry up"—or, in Mexican vernacular, *ándale*—so that tasks could be executed quickly and efficiently (45–46).

Fast-tracking now to Hughes's 1920 train trip, which overlapped with the political instability of the Mexican Revolution (1910–20), the young writer began this journey with a comment on the local scenery: "All day long I've been riding through Texas, heat and cotton fields, little forlorn villages with a large public well in the center of the main street" (1920).[37] Hughes's traveling thoughts soon turned to the ethnoracialized dynamics on the railroad, highlighting, "I am a Negro in the car. Of course being in Texas I am not allowed to forget my color." His blackness surely not forgotten, the supposed unyielding duality of the black-and-white color line promptly took another direction. A fellow passenger took note of a passing resemblance. He informed our chronicler that "he had known at once that I was a Mexican."[38] Hughes did not refute the designation, bringing to mind an incident of re-cognition and admitting, "I did not tell him otherwise."[39]

Years later, in the wake of *The Big Sea*'s publication, Hughes noted in this book's opening pages that when he first visited Africa, "the great Africa of my dreams," in 1923, "the Africans looked at me and would not believe I was a Negro" (1993: 11). The multiple entries into Hughes's ethnoracial significations are striking. Not only do they suggest an elasticity of Latinness through a blackness that can pass for many things except a U.S.-situated whiteness, but also a "Negroness" that, prior to being questioned in Africa, was manifestly expressed as Mexican three years earlier. And so whether or not that train passenger—or, we, as readers—stand corrected is not the point. What concerns us here is the manner in which one becomes an "ethnic" as well as the type of ethnic one can become. As Hughes's black body demonstrated, there are mutual implications to blackness and brownness and how they are understood in the shifting installments of everyday life. Indeed, as Hughes looked for a dwelling space further in Texas, he avowed, "We are nearing San Antonio. There I shall cover up my hair and really be Mexican or else they will not sell me a berth to Laredo and the trip is a long one. I know enough Spanish to ask for a 'cama en el tren.'" The process of "really becoming" Mexican in Texas and beyond is deeply provocative. On the one hand, Hughes seemed to speak to the contemporary types of South-South border passings on the way to the United States, where "distant" Latin American nationalities try to pass, along the two-thousand-mile U.S.-Mexico border, as Mexicans, or as is common now in the six-hundred-mile Mexico-Guatemala boundary, as Guatemalans.[40] Hughes's efforts at "really becoming" direct us to think about how he conceives Mexicanness and the kinds of markers that are appropriated and "indigenized" through his fluid blackness.

Unlike Hughes's short story "Passing" in *The Ways of White Folks* (1940), these black-Mexican crossings are far from tragic. In this account, Jack, a light-skinned narrator (in effect, Hughes's own version of "an ex-coloured man"), writes a letter to his dark-skinned mother. Mother and son pass each other in a downtown Chicago street but remain silent. A German American girl accompanies Jack, and under this circumstance his talking to a Negro may raise suspicions about the "purity" of Jack's new racial configuration (1990: 51). The reader learns that such crossings are never racially settled. Though appearing as strangers in the social world, Jack and his mother continue their communication at the epistolary level. They divulge their secrets, passing through the public sphere in ways that make the rigidity of such a world *passable*. What takes primacy is the realm of (written) communication, as it becomes part of an ongoing familial archive that retains the informal word for mother, *Ma*. Jack writes in one missive, "I will take a box at the Post Office for your mail. Anyhow, I'm glad there's nothing to stop letters from crossing the color-line. Even if we can't meet often, we can write, can't we, Ma?" (55). Jack's physical abandonment of his mother must occur in the interest of an emerging biographical self. The offspring recreates a ruptured "orphaned" state. Jack's protective affiliation ceases to be maternal: it is the social relations and political affiliations that now must reconstruct and vouch for the new subject's altering narrative of whiteness.

By 21 July 1920, Hughes found himself in Nuevo Laredo, at a hotel "that is not half bad according to Mexican standards. Of course it's far from being the Ritz-Carlton, but then I couldn't stop there anyhow for I am colored. But here nothing is [barred] from me. I am among my own people, for Nuevo Laredo is a dark skinned city and Mexico is a brown man's country." As Hughes "Mexicanized" himself, he morphed into a border subject, poetically conferring us with a variant of, to borrow from Walter Mignolo (2000), "border thinking." Hughes's contemplative note spoke of the militarization of the U.S.-Mexico border, exposing, to play on the misspelling, its "shams." Hughes and the border are somehow spurious. Each blueprint for Mexican, black, and American is not squarely what is purported to be. Hughes juxtaposed the round-the-clock patrolling of the border with a heavenly constellation pointing to an experience beyond Uncle Sam's guarded horizon. The Missouri-born poet and playwright elaborated:

> A giant government hydroplane has been circling about all day, guarding Uncle Sam's border. One can see the towers of the very powerful wireless that the army has erected at Laredo. It towers high above the flatness of the Texas city, even as the Eiffel towers above Paris. And Paris has nothing on the two Laredos when it comes to stars, for tonight the sky with those lovely jewels which Evening wears upon her velvet gown. High above the Rio Grande, above the two cities, above the two countries they sparkle and glow, and one big star is winking and twinkling as if he were laughing at my littleness — at the little of all men with their *schams* [chasms] of hatred and war, and their eternal bickerings [emphasis added].

Politicians conceived of the Eiffel Tower as a "symbol of industrial civilization," whose Frenchification was also illustrated through its explicit dependence on "French labor, materials, and technology" (Jonnes, 2009: 25–26). Gustave Eiffel's project was initially dismissed in the City of Light as an antiartistic endeavor in opposition to French genius. The tower, it was said, resembled "a lighthouse, a nail, [and] a chandelier." It was seen as more "in character with America (where taste is not yet very developed) than Europe" (23). In time, Roland Barthes pointed to it as a Parisian statement: *"the Tower is there."* That generic, everyday "there" can be linked to the Mexican image of the "other" side, the U.S. border. Like the Eiffel Tower, "Uncle Sam's border" is a towering American statement of modernity, of communication and miscommunication, and of "phallus [. . .] confronting the great itineraries of our dreams." It is "incorporated into daily life" as an "incontestable" existence. Barthes claimed that the Eiffel Tower remains "friendly" through its presence for the entire world (1997: 3–4). The iron behemoth imparts "the huge and amazing" and what everyone desires, "the incredible" (Jonnes, 2009: 23).

On the other side of the Atlantic, the incredible becomes the extraordinary American Dream. But the fixed image of the U.S. border differs. In the U.S.-Mexico split contact and movement between nations and subjects are monitored, restricted, and criminalized, no less during the years following the Mexican Revolution. This tumultuous political struggle impacted the United States through immigration from north-central Mexico. Julie M. Weise writes, "North-central Mexico, most affected by the revolution, sent the majority of the era's migrants to the United States. These poor, rural emigrants journeyed to all parts of the United States during the 1920s, from Arizona to Alaska, Michigan to California, and the U.S. South was no exception" (2009: 252). The "inevitable sign" of America, then, is not "to join" but to reinscribe the inadmissible (Barthes, 1997: 4).[41] By 1925 the U.S. Congress had approved the creation of the border patrol in an effort to halt undocumented migrations and "to 'secure the nation's borders,' especially those to the south" (LeMay, 2006: 23). Hughes's triangulation of the United States, Mexico, and Paris proves ironic. The guarding of border crossings is ineffective as Hughes's recalcitrant Latinities cross and recross U.S.-Mexico boundaries. His "diary of Mexican adventures" underscores the permeability of guarded borders and how "the spatiality of citizenship," as Mary Pat Brady invitingly presents it, is lived out (2002: 86).[42]

Hughes ultimately reached his destination on 23 July to "a pale white glow against the sky"—meaning, Mexico City's lights. His entry may have ended at that incandescent point, but these crónicas provide stories that demand a familiarization within the identificatory standpoints of Mexican, Latino, and black. These "adventures" did not operate as mirthful, southern escapades, as Hughes's crimson-colored, pocket-sized journal, dating from 1934 to 1937, made known afterward. There, Hughes methodologically wrote lines and lines of words in Spanish. The notebook is artlessly and pragmatically titled, "Spanish." Each word and phrase was written in a single line in one-sided pages, often in alphabetical order. Amid lists of verb conjugations and the names and information of his social contacts, the reader finds ample evidence that Hughes was not simply a linguistic abecedarian. He was clearly serious about his Spanish fluency. Hughes wanted to remember proverbs, *refranes* like "'el que canta sus males espanta' ('He who sings dispels his fears')" and "'es como pedir peras al olmo'—the same as asking for pears from an elm tree. Pedir que un niño tenga experiencia [Demanding experience from a child] es como pedir peras al olmo." He wrote fairly straightforward notes to himself, such as "the truth of the matter is: estamos en pleno invierno, we are in the dead of winter."

In like manner, Hughes included folkloric snapshots of Mexican life. These passages resonate, from our vantage point, with the kinds of Mexican and Chicano and Chicana popular cultures that such writers as Sandra Cisneros engage in their work.[43] Hughes, who was christened in 1931 as "El poeta Afro-Estadounidense" by the Mexican review *Cristol*, could just as well be denominated "El poeta fronterizo" (Rampersad, 2002: 302). Some of the Mexico City vignettes he recounted included these musings:

> When the Latins mourn, they really mourn. Black dresses, black veils. Black suits, black hearts of crepe on the arm, black ties, black hats.
>
> The Meat Market Jerusalem, next to the Palestine Grocery.
>
> The lottery tickets everywhere—National, Queretaro, Toluca.
>
> The pat, pat, pat of hands making tortillas.
>
> The child vendors.
>
> The lovers in the parks.
>
> The Song Vendors with their guitars.
>
> Chickens on the roofs.

Hughes progressed with two pages of what he called "Mexico Names of Shops." Among the memorable store designations and pedestrian happenstance are

> The Two Magicians United Furniture Shop.
>
> The Christ Died to Save Us Candy Store.
>
> The Strong Man of Chapultepec Saloon.

Messenger of the Gods Charcoal Stand.

Pictures of the dead and wounded on front pages of newspapers.

Knock on the door and a head pop out of an upper window.

And yet inserted between these quotidian scenarios were observations on the North's ever-present ethnoracial landscape. Thinking about white normativity while abroad, Hughes remarked in one *apunte*, or note, "Me And The White Race / No hate — not bitter / Many friends / White step-mother / Father lent money to whites / Prostitutes — Cleveland to Vicksburg / Race and bad manners / Race and economics / Race and ego / Race and religion — Y's."

The excavation of the race question by the black body eliciting Latinness exposes the miscellaneousness of racial assignments and the porous borders of brownness. Hughes itemized his 1930 "Expenses of [the] Havana Trip," which tabulated the amount of money spent on taxis, wires, postcards, stamps, meals, and tips. He also tallied an untitled list of racialized distinctions in Cuba. This type of delineation was absent from Hughes's notes on other international trips, although *The Big Sea* exhibits an acute ability to characterize bodies in ways that diverge from the type of colorings regularly attributed to blacks and Latins. The reader is introduced in that literary project to someone who might as well function as an individualized piece of candy, or as Hughes calls him, a "chocolate-covered Puerto Rican" (1993: 4). Hughes's expressive palette flexibly stretches to Mexico, underscored through the nuances he addressed in such a qualifier as brown (79).

The persons Hughes encountered were typified through a wide array of shades that resonate with Cisneros's conception of the presumably deracialized term *caramelo*, as her novel bearing the same title shows. For Cisneros, the Mesoamerican color of caramel relates to embodied tones as "bright as a copper *veinte centavos* coin. [. . .] Smooth as peanut butter, deep as burnt-milk candy" (2002: 34). Under Hughes's verbal imagery of Mexico, his father's housekeeper was portrayed as having "a kind tan-brown face." The *mozo*, the attendant named Maximiliano, was depicted as a brown Indian, "a silent boy who spoke but little Spanish" (1993: 43–44). The amorphous colorings of caramel are indexed across socioeconomic class stratas. One of Hughes's language students was particularized as "ivory-tan," and Mexican children cumulatively became "cream-colored" (67–68). Hughes's directory of racial specters diagnosed, much like Cisneros's caramelo, a Latin color line that associates with everything but blackness. But this does not mean that blackness is eliminated within those significations. On the contrary, these "caramel marks" are correlational to the extent that they explore the multicolored possibilities—or the multilayered and multidirectional "passabilities"—of blackness, brownness, and its substratum dark brownness.

While in Cuba, Hughes indexed a provocative racial stratum of how black bodies were registered and arranged in the sugar-producing island. Here, too, a caramel juncture surfaces in relation to the Caribbean. One may recall that the Cuban band La Sonora Matancera, founded in the 1920s, monumentalized a song, titled in plural form, "Caramelos." This hit song's verses, performed in 1960 by the late Celia Cruz, the "Queen of Salsa," take the listener to the varieties of flavored candies for sale: "coconut, pineapple (for little girls), lemon, and honey (for the old ladies)" (1997). These sugary, Latin chunks are moments to be savored—"sabrosos pa' tu boquita" (delicious for your little mouth)—in their pretty and bright coloration. They bring about questions on how one becomes a consumer of this wide world of sweets. The caramels render a gathering of bodies randomly exchanging pleasantries and calling out unlimited varieties that also come in "strawberry, vanilla, and chocolate." They force the listener to decide on what will finally pass through one's palate.

But Hughes's Cuban caramel marks are seemingly more pronounced than the ones presented under Cisneros's Mexican and Mexican American lens. They add another type of gazing into Frantz Fanon's "Look! A Negro!" exclamatory encounter, for these caramelos "lighten up" the conversation without the "heavy" burden of race (2008: 89–119).[44] This homage to one's love for sweetness is sprinkled with additional variations on the theme and location of blackness.[45] Hughes's oeuvre includes a contradictory set of explicitly racialized and deracialized abbreviated idiomatic terms like "m. de pasa," which may indicate "moreno de pasa" (or "mulato de pasa"). M. de pasa proves illegible, although the richness of pasa—which means, in Spanish, to come, to go, and to cross from one side to another—also denotes raisin in English. The latter simultaneously implies another caramelo ingredient within the economy of sweets that verbalizes Latin blackness. Ultimately, m. de pasa stands for having "bad hair." "Negro" and "negro prieto" connote "black," as does the disparaging classification "negro bembón" for "nigger."

A handwritten journal index by Langston Hughes on racial classifications from his 1930 trip to Havana, Cuba. James Weldon Johnson Memorial Collection of African American Arts and Letters, Beinecke Rare Book and Manuscript Library, Yale University, New Haven, Conn. Used by permission of Harold Ober Associates.

Interestingly, the term "mulato" is in want of an explanation, a distinction perhaps waiting to be filled later on by the writer. But its vacuity could also imply that an image of the mulato already existed in Hughes's racial imagination and consequently needed no interpretation.[46]

The only other time when an empty space is — to pun on a well-worn expression, in Spanish, *dejado en blanco* — left blank in this cluster of racial patterns occurs in the line allotted for the term "blanco." To cite artist Kara Walker, these unmarked portions assume the form of blank spaces into which individuals project "their fantasies into something concrete." Yet, as she also alludes, their blankness permits the possibility for the mulato and the blanco to "reflect those fantasies back into the projector's unsuspecting eyes" (Sharpe, 2010: 153). Mulato and blanco hint at a complex malleability, where each state may slide back and forth. They are a "more nuanced spectrum of subtle differentiations, in a new global regime where First World and Third World are mutually imbricated. Notions of ontologically referential identity metamorphose into a conjectural play of identifications. Purity gives way to 'contamination.' Rigid paradigms collapse into sliding metonymies" (Stam, 1999: 60).

Just as migrating to Mexico appeared to be a trying ground in 1920, Hughes's 1930 voyage to Havana amounted to a rigmarole of bureaucracy. Prior to heading to Cuba on 22 February 1930, he was informed that "American citizens and tourists of any nationality are admissible with the exception of Chinese, Negroes, and Russians." Henceforth, he underwent an arbitrary—but apparently routine and convoluted process—of governmental formalities to get to Cuba. Hughes was told that there were no tickets available for him. He proceeded to document the reasons that were given to him: "We cannot sell you passageway. There is space available Saturday, but our instructions are that colored people are not admitted."

Undated sheets from Hughes's journal, dating perhaps from mid-February 1930, outlined these setbacks. It should be stressed that Hughes was going to Cuba as a published writer, having released in 1926 his first book of poems, *The Weary Blues*. Just days before finally leaving to Havana, on 17 February 1930, Hughes had also just "turned in his [first] novel [*Not Without Laughter*] to Mrs. Knopf." As he prepared to leave, he wrote, "Now I am free for something new and better." He was not altogether free of the race question, and he poignantly detailed the fallacies that belied how race is understood in the United States. Most revealing from Hughes's meditations on the matter is the way in which he sought to grasp who exactly comprised a Negro in the Global South and who exactly was "there," at the other end, reading and categorizing the Negro/*negro* body. His set of questions solicited proof for the idea of Negro as much as for whiteness. He asked, "What constitutes Negro blood? Can a steamship company under N.Y. State law refuse passage on account of color? Is the American idea of [the] word 'Negro,' meaning anyone darker than white? What about a dark South American? What about Portuguese? Is the interpretation of the law up to the steamship co.? Make them prove that I am a Negro. If a Negro, what is their right of exclusion?"

Throughout this trip to the Caribbean, Hughes had access to the island's literati, meeting figures like Conrado Massaguer "the leading Cuban editor, caricaturist, director of *Social*, *Havana*, and *Carteles*," who presented him with his caricature of "a grand Josephine Baker," poet Nicolás Guillén, and the "Negro-Chinese poet Regino Pedroso."[47] He kept a busy schedule. Some entries specifically named the cultural acquaintances he was meeting and the type of soiree he attended. Consider the evening of Thursday, 6 March, where Hughes was off "to the Plaza bar for Daiquiris. To La something, a famous Havana restaurant noted for seafood. [. . .] To the Valls exhibition on Negro drawings. To dinner [. . .] with [Gustavo] Urrutia and Guillén" (1930).[48] His small, daily register seemed to have what we would now think of as a Post-it note function. Hughes temporarily wrote checklists that form a part of our historical record. In one instance, he penciled a memo to himself about reading, or planning to read, Fernando Ortiz (1881–1969).[49] Hughes designated him as an "Author on Negroes" a decade before his remarkably influential *Cuban Counterpoint: Tobacco and Sugar* (1940) was published.

Loose journal notes from 1929 signal that Hughes was committed to the creation of a black American culture that indigenized blackness to the United States. Hughes's caramelo-like encounters abroad with brownness, dark brownness, and lo negro molded his literary outlook. As historian Frank Andre Guridy has clarified in relation to U.S. black and Cuban exchanges, this cultural and literary reciprocity "made for seminal influences in the ways Cubans and North Americans of African descent came to view themselves both as citizens of their respective countries and as members of the colored race" (2003: 21). His craft, Hughes stated, sought "to create a Negro culture in America—a real, solid, sane, racial something growing out of the folk life, not copied from another, even though surrounding, race" (1929). Part of the creation of this Negro culture included American Negro and Latin-American *negro* exchanges, "linked organically to the historic shift by Mexican, Cuban, and other Latin American poets away from Europe in the depiction of their cultures" (Rampersad, 2002: 47). Hughes collaborated with Guillén on various literary projects, having translated, together with Ben Frederic Carruthers, Guillén's poetic work.[50] Guillén, in turn, translated Hughes's "I, Too, Sing America" into Spanish. Hughes also inspired Guillén, as Michael A. Chaney has pointed out, to "incorporate Afro-Cuban rhythms of the *son* into his first collection, *Motivos de Son* (1930), as Hughes had done with the blues in his own poetry" (2007: 45–46). Hughes "devoted himself to translating short stories by various young Mexican writers" when he returned to that country during his father's death in 1934 (Rampersad, 1997: xviii).[51] But there were various obstacles in this literary quest. Hughes's attempts to place works, including productions by Cuban, Chilean, Haitian, and Spanish writers in

U.S. journals (2002: 48), "came to nothing: to his dismay, he discovered that a market for Latin American fiction did not exist in the United States" (1997: xviii).⁵²

Hughes gave much thought during his time in Cuba to how the construct of race surrounds the Negro abroad. He was interested in learning about the vocations that Negroes had, compiling another type of catalogue. "Occupations of Negroes," he registered in Cuba, "Garbage wagons / On docks / Street cleaners / News boys / Boot-blacks." Meanwhile, he noticed that as these jobs were being performed, "the Americans seem to clot in a dozen or so favorite places" (1930). When reading of Hughes's leaving the island, the reader cannot help but draw parallels with his train ride a decade prior, where the color line was suspended through his "black" body. Boarding a ship back to the United States on 7 March 1930 and taking us to the colors of the Hispanophone Atlantic, Hughes wrote, "Once aboard (3rd class) I find myself in a sort of 'glory hole' with some 20 bunks in the same room, and about 15 fellows from Chile, Panama, etc. Several of them seamen returning at consular or company expense; a Jamaican and his two kids born in Panama, etc. We both eat and sleep in the same room." Hughes's traveling "glory hole" is an inglorious vessel storing an assembly of "etceteras." These assortments are a cavitied constellation of third-rate citizenships that discharge unfolding Latinities. They are recognized through assorted and ungrounded nationalities, not the ethnoracialized hues under which they will fall after arriving in the United States.

Hughes's travels to intermixed Texas, Mexico, and Cuba point to my broader claim to account for the Hispanophone Americas, whose diasporic mappings highlight how other Souths are informed by Hughes's magisterial work. Hughes, like Johnson, took up questions of blackness in a global and aesthetic geography with monumental implications. His vital "nuggets" of history continue to illuminate a conceptually rich literature that has tracked earlier plots of a Global South in the U.S. literary landscape.

In Plain Sight

The magnitude of Johnson's and Hughes's Latined crossings has been hidden in plain sight. And yet their passing lines are recurrent, as these Latinities have been invariably nearby, with access to and a knowledge of each side.

They extract from Juan Flores and George Yúdice's call for Latinoness and Latinaness as a social *movement*. "In order to vocalize the border," they contend, "traversing it is not enough; we must be positioned there, with ready and simultaneous access to both sides" (1990: 70). These black-brown, U.S.-Latin-American crossings are compatible with how current Latinoness and Latinaness can be framed: as an already constituted state of double living. Certainly these dual-directional forms of blackness and brownness echo the traveling bodies of the borderlands, where they "continually walk out of one culture / and into another" (Anzaldúa, 1999: 99). Indeed, what is at stake in these strolls that deliquesce brownness and blackness and exert re-cognition? What do we keep and claim, as Latino, Latina, and black are undone in these mobilities that encapsulate their oscillating togetherness?

Johnson's and Hughes's literary lives did not obey geopolitical demarcations of nations, cultures, languages, and identities. Their intermingling discourses gave way to a torrent of cultural exploration that did not stop at highly guarded borders. Nor did their passages hold back the tide of this living history: the force of a blackness and brownness traveling across moving lines or in the murky waters "of color" in the U.S. imaginary. Their passing lines and free relationships cut through the restrictive inadequacies of black and brown discourses oozing with the interstitial spaces of passing Latinities.

CHAPTER THREE

INDIGENT LATINITIES

Bring back the most repugnant *Inditos* you can find.
— FRANCISCO GOLDMAN (2004: 30)

The previous two chapters touched on the copious Latined elements in the casting and negotiation of blackness and brownness. A black-brown reprisal follows, extending the ways that bodies exist beyond the boundaries and discourses that subject them. This chapter attends to Latino and Latina articulations of and adjustments to configurations of dark brownness and blackness, which get subsumed under a U.S. semiotic of amalgamated brownness. But U.S. Latino and Latina brownness, as a system of ethnoracial and cultural referentiality, is not in gridlock. It houses the corresponding colorings of dark brownness (lo prieto) and blackness (lo negro) — a portfolio that capitulates and confesses to "brownish blackness" and "blackish brownness."[1] The standard U.S. Latino and Latina index, however, eschews problematic blackness, as dark brownness, framed here as a variant of blackness, retains its crucial "afterword," brownness.[2] Yet this register also attempts to pass down this de rigueur concept brimming with referents of indigence to protruding Indianness and a blackness that sprawls to brownness as well as dark brownness.

Because black-brown–dark brown moments of equivalencies have had a long-term relationship, if you will, these characterizations of impecuniousness serve as the cornerstone for a panoptic body of indigent Latinities. These Latinities are by no means inert and inanimate. Indigent Latinities are expressly manifest and assume, to borrow from Danzy Senna, appearances that propagate "a confusion of races" and garner the inexorable spread of "a new world order" on its subjects' faces (2011: 79). Scenes from the iconographic life of brownness rotate around an enmeshed web of association for Latin participants currently obnubilated from the Latinidad map: blacks and dark browns.

Indigent Latinities are neither black nor brown, nor are they meant to connote literal squalor.[3] They are intended as active signifiers within cultural imaginations that dramatize and rupture the meanings of a triumvirate of brownness, dark brownness, and blackness. Richard Rodriguez, Gabriel García Márquez, and Horacio Castellanos Moya annotate from different vantage points the dailiness of this racialized hue's subjugation in informal as well as domestic economies. On the basis of these interlocutors' illustrations, let us briefly turn to the practice and process of dark brownness. They lead us to the semiotic conceptions that inform my treatment of U.S. Latinoness and Latinaness. The then-and-thereness of their take on Latin American dark brownness cues us in on the economy and implications of these representations in our American here and now.

For Rodriguez, an indigent Latinity in Mexico clings to lo indio, an Indianness marked by street vendors. He makes known that "[i]n private, in Mexican Spanish, *indio* is a seller of Chiclets, a sidewalk squatter. *Indio* means backward or lazy or lower-class" (1992: 14).[4] The place of the indigenous comes across through the purchase by García Márquez's family of three Indian servants — Alirio, Apolinar, and Meme — for one hundred *pesos* each. Working in Aracataca, Colombia, the Guajira Indians were, as García Márquez's biographer Gerald Martin has it, "effectively slaves" (2009: 37).[5] Indigenousness is staged through service and domestic duties, and Castellanos Moya's arrangement of this world is no exception. His overlay makes Indianness a dark category peopled, in Central America, by domestic servants. Indianness is also a state affixed to undesirable women "with slanted eyes and toasted brown skin" (2008: 68).[6] But brown is not decidedly brown in every occasion. It has complex and fickle constellations.

These snapshots of the trinity of race, class, and gender resonate with a news event from the summer of 2007. Peace Nobel Laureate Rigoberta Menchú was confused for a street vendor, bag lady, or beggar, in Cancún, Mexico, because of the Maya attire she was wearing. Menchú was subsequently removed from the five-star Coral Beach Hotel. The *Guardian* reported that "the human rights activist was in the Mexican coastal resort at the request of President

Felipe Calderón to participate in a conference on drinking water and sanitation and was due to give interviews at the hotel." The establishment's staff "relented when told who she was. It was said not to be the first time a hotel has tried to throw her out. [. . .] Commentators noted the irony of upmarket resorts discriminating against real Maya while trying to attract tourists with fake Mayan architecture and spectacles" (Carroll, 2007). Indigenous life is reduced to the Mexican landscape, or in Cancún's case, a "'pristine' tropical paradise located in the land of the ancient Maya" (Castellanos, 2010: xxvii). There is no room for an indigenous body that looks and dresses "like an Indian" to leisurely vacation in Cancún as a tourist. Menchú's appearance is ultimately indigenized as a beggar, vagrant, or peddler of indigenous crafts, relegated to "the proletarianization experienced in [Cancún's] service industry" (78).[7]

Indigent Latinities are relevant to imputed blackness in the Americas. Citing Venezuelan use of the proverbial and problematic *mi negra*, Cristóbal Valencia Ramírez analyzed the 2006 presidential campaign in the South American nation. At that point in time, Hugo Chávez's opponent, Manuel Rosales, pitched a welfare debit card that was to be known as Mi Negra (My Black). The Mi Negra plan, as the *Vivir Latino* blog dubbed it, was "complete with a black card and an Afro-Venezuelan *viejita* [little old woman]" (Woodard Maderazo, 2006). The presidential aspirant's stipend called for a deposit between $250 and $450 per month into individual debit accounts for an estimated three million Venezuelans living below the minimum wage. "Rosales claimed that the proposal intended to give marginalized Venezuelans a direct share of the national oil profits," Valencia Ramírez spelled out. "Rosales explained the proposal's name as a reference to oil. However, the advertisements associated with the proposal featured almost exclusively black Venezuelans. Some of the ads showed toothless, grinning Venezuelans hoisting up the black card and singing the praises of Mi Negra and Rosales. The message behind the proposal — that Afro-Venezuelans were indigents — came through in the images and in discourses surrounding the proposal" (2009: 117). Circling the nub of the social production of the gendered *negra* is blackness as a guiding theme for a penurious condition of life. Rodriguez deals with this codified U.S. thematic of economic abjection and structural racism too. He notices that "the garbage men who appeared every Friday morning" in his Sacramento, California, neighborhood were "unmistakably black" (1982: 118).

While the connotations of these indigent overtones may change in meaning and are negotiated and responded to differently, my task is to look at how these ethnoracial and class specific significations continue to dwell within the distinctive cultural and ideological imaginaries for generic U.S. Latino and Latina brownness. Francisco Goldman's epigraph illuminates this context insofar as I am taking and bringing back the idea of "Indito" or "Indita" not just as a marker that adheres to the indigenous, U.S. Latino, or Latina subject. It also indicates other layers of "repugnant" Latinities, blackness. In providing a diagram for black–dark brown bodies, I would like to expound, as I have done in another venue, that I am cognizant of the hierarchies that surface between lighter and darker shades "of color" (Milian, 2004). Black-brown–dark brown populations are knowledgeable of how these racialized states are inhabited. My broad evocation of black and brown — cited in lowercase to trace but to also depart from the visible impressions of these racialized descriptions — does not suppose that these colors and colorings are immutable foundations for fully accountable U.S. African American, Latino, and Latina phenotypes. Black and brown detail the limitations of how these terms operate. But such utilization prompts a larger process encouraging new pedagogical approaches that assess the moving typological lines that challenge the imaging and organizing of the brown-black symbolic.

My deployment of black, brown, U.S. Latino, and Latina denotes the discursive separation of these racially marked peoples and their representation in the academic fields overlooking their associative realities within the corporeal and geographic mappings of Latin-America. The intentional use of such categories as black and U.S. Latino and Latina conterminously works against the presumed ossification of monolithic U.S. African American blackness and Latino and Latina brown fixity. I apply these terms to punctuate moments of close relations that become the seeds of black and brown, shedding light on how these groups are accomplices in knowing each other's color lines. These strands echo the observations of *The Autobiography of an Ex-Coloured Man*'s main character, who comments, "It is remarkable, after all, what an adaptable creature the Negro is" (Johnson, 1989: 153). For our purposes, we should recall that such alterations — Negro, lo negro, lo prieto, and lo indio — also put across the idea that an indigent Latinity is malleable. Among this chapter's preoccupations are the tensions in the adaptability of Latino and Latina brownness within U.S. African Americanness, alongside the inadaptability of blackness and dark brownness in brown Latinidad, which becomes an active exegesis of Latinities, as argued in the introduction.

I engage with how Latinos and Latinas come across, excogitate, and practice their blackness-cum-dark brownness. Blackness and a dark brownness recast as brownness are conceived not as a shared essence but as an open semiotic configuration that molds into porous Latinities in numerous arenas.[8] I build on a blackness-in-transit and how it passes through Chicano and Chicana discourses about dark brownness and brownness.[9] If, as Rodriguez suggests in *Brown: The Last Discovery of America*, U.S. African Americans have been unwilling "to admit brown," this monograph is an exploration not only of the asymmetrical ways browns admit dark brown and black but also of how blacks admit brown (2002: 142). Fundamentally, U.S. Latino and Latina brownness cannot afford an entrance to dark brownness, because it would be an admittance of blackness. Dark brownness exposes an aesthetic and political challenge. Yet curiously, the distinct qualifier "dark" is hardly appended to the U.S. African American acknowledgments of brownness referenced in this chapter, perhaps because darkness and brownness, as embodied by U.S. African Americanness, are unalterably constituted as black.

W. E. B. Du Bois's unraveling of the meaning of blackness as a problem within the white world's problems holds relevance in U.S. Latino and Latina microcosms of brownness. Problematic blackness and darkness also resonate in U.S. Latino and Latina literature with brown leitmotifs. But U.S. Latino and Latina theming of brownness is pervaded not by blackness but by darkness. This dark brownness passes through Latinoness and Latinaness and remains as a repugnant Indian signifier. This relative whiteness—derivative whiteness—does not pass for white. Rather, it passes among whiteness and brownness (R. Rodriguez, 2002: 4). Such manipulation of skin tones is a Latino and Latina concealment that avoids Du Bois's articulation of the "real question" required of blackness: "how does it feel to be a problem?" (1996b: 3–4). The comparable Latino, Latina, and Latin-American query for this deeply embedded U.S. interrogation sonorously shifts to "how does it feel to be dark brown?" The problem that thus warrants further disentangling is the logic of dark brownness and its knots to blackness. I discuss their operational semiotics for the representation of an economy of brownness that gives conceptual form to U.S. Latinoness and Latinaness. How does dark brownness, often unambiguously personified at home, translate into public, ambiguous brownness, a pigmentation lighter than dark brownness?

I push a counternarrative to authoritative U.S. Latino and Latina brownness by thrusting U.S. blackness to that meshed North-South, Global South fusion of Latin referents, Latin-America.[10] I account for signifiers that paradoxically perpetuate the racially crude signification of all things black, lo negro. Please do not misunderstand me here: I do not fathom lo negro as — or confine it to — a commanding phenotypic signifier of blackness in the African diasporic sense. When appropriating lo negro or lo prieto as overarching U.S. Latino and Latina exemplars — especially from groups that have ties to Mesoamerica — I am addressing how these problematic signifiers are denotative of "something" from which brownness moves away. Literature captures the idea of blackness as a derisive, living entity. I lay no claim to speak for the entire U.S. Latino and Latina population on black-brown matters, in the stern and popular understanding of these colorings, wherein blackness is assigned to U.S. African Americanness and brownness to Latinos and Latinas. Nor is my point to dissect, in an amplified fashion, how blacks and browns maintain stereotypes about each other (cf. Mindiola, Niemann, and Rodriguez, 2003). Instead, I search for the *negro* symbolic, endeavoring with how the texts mustered in this chapter voice resistance to the pool of signs ensnared in dark brownness and blackness.

Lo negro and lo prieto suggest a mingling of both blackness and darkness. This merger does not fall into obscurity. It precedes the category and rank of the dark Indian and its rich symbology. Lo negro harbors a loaded location that one does not want to inhabit. Sandra Cisneros inserts this discursive wedge in *Caramelo*, a novel that begins with Mexican-origin subjects alternating North-South geopolitical demarcations, in reverse, from the United States to Mexico. These transnational crossings are plotted as passing color lines between blackness and a caramel tincture that can also conform to the maxims of dark brownness.[11] But these U.S.-Mexican geographic passages cease as caramel-colored bodies are materially grounded through the corporal trappings of a labor based on ethnoracialized colorings. Cisneros intimates that "caramelo" folk recognize blackness through work.[12] Lo negro bears the traces of slavery. A Mexican American character — in another geography of the Global South, Little Rock, Arkansas — is quick to relate a popular saying that connects his arduous physical labor to his U.S. standing. "Today," he announces, "I worked *como un negro*, which is what they say in Mexico when they work very hard" (2002: 211).[13]

The Mexican idiom migrates and crosses genres, going from an oral, commonplace dictum in Spanish to part of an English/Spanglish sentence in American literature. Its familiar meaning is conveyed and preserved in Spanish, which translates, in English to "working like a *negro*." Cisneros's writerly fidelity is aligned with the American ethic of hard work, which has become a dark brown (American) precept of individual effort and asceticism. What takes primacy is not a literal translation of Mexican colloquialisms. It is, instead, the interpretive altering script of how the original text (the Mexican workforce's blackness) migrates to a southern American setting through Mexican caramelo dark brownness. This swerving brownness spaces out these unsubdued bodies and opens them to a semiotic flux that puts brownness *at* work, while putting dark brownness *to* work.

Although the perception is that blackness may not be an inherent element in Mexicanness, its proximity echoes a veridical existence through manual work. Lo negro is an irremediable presence in tandem with a labor that most whites do not — and browns ought not — perform. Through a labor that resonates with blackness, Cisneros's illustration begs a rethinking of subjects whose bedrock foundation may be regarded as strictly brown. Her caramelo subject iterates an Indianness that bespeaks blackness. Indianness accentuates a racializing process that can be manipulated and that may eventually catch up with the rest of the browned Latino and Latina population.[14] Brown is dual-directional and lives among U.S. African Americans too. Its changeable dispositions and resonances bear witness to deliquescent black-brown categories.

The considerations I offer cobble through the discursive uses of blackness and brownness. This third chapter is a scrutiny of brownness as a method of U.S. Latina and Latino identification. So doing, I motion toward the unmappable and unthinkable in Latino/a thought: how Latino and Latina brownness and dark brownness not only commingle with U.S. African American blackness but also semiotically impart blackness. These ethnoracial categories augment one another and demand a new pattern of relational understanding. In summoning these identity formations, I exercise Lewis Gordon's concept of the relational theory of race, where "black people and white people needn't have been the historical black and white people. As long as a group defines itself as white in such a way that it becomes the standpoint from which other races are judged on the basis of the degree to which they are less white, a slippery slope downward begins until the unreal figure of blackness looms at the point beyond which there is only nothing" (1995b: 95). The "unreal figure of blackness" in U.S. Latino and Latina life and its unrelationality to brownness encourages a new emergent relation: a blackness lived through Latino and Latina dark brownness. My examination delves into what kind of a dark American present do U.S. African Americans, Latinos, and Latinas live in and belong to? What is being left behind and withdrawn from the production of a comprehensive (black) U.S. African American and (brown) Latino and Latina future?

Starting from this, my line of inquiry first takes stock of contemporary approaches that produce a way of thinking about brownness as a disobedient and transgressive U.S. site or as a comparative experience formed by an accretion of displacements and political alignments. Some of the theories that are being put forth hinge on ethnoracial U.S. Latino and Latina brownness. Other critical frameworks take up brownness as a cultural sensibility, dissident practice, and shifting solidarity that are not necessarily constituted by Latino- and Latina-specific outlooks. On the whole, however, this chapter reexamines a U.S. Latino and Latina brown vocabulary. I am tackling U.S. Latino and Latina terms of engagement through this group's crafting of — and encasement in — its main narrative component, brownness. How the Latino and Latina brown story is being told protects a "community" that does not open up to dark brown and black beings, rhetorics, and signs.

U.S. Latino and Latina brownness evinces a process of brown becoming, as it incongruously admits dark brown derivatives that pass into brownness. If questions of Latino and Latina origins have been pursuing us since the first chapter through a nuevo U.S. genealogy, the variety and strangeness — alienness — of Latinos and Latinas are being situated in and broadened through a domestic American brownness ushering in a multitude of brown exponents.[15] Yet the trajectory of American brownness through blackness has not been hazarded as an overlapping story that moves outside U.S. African Americanness. This chapter's second objective is to cross-consider, albeit briefly but as a point of incitation, how U.S. blackness is a source of brownness. U.S. African American brownness introduces another look at this Latino and Latina referent, which involves ongoing critical interrogations about new forms of fluctuating brownness and who can narrate it. Third, I intersect U.S. African American brown textual articulations with Latino and Latina literary productions. My focus zooms in on a vexing dark brownness, as lived through the common denominator of the Mexican American domestic spheres chronicled by Gloria Anzaldúa (1942–2004), Cherríe L. Moraga (1952), and Richard Rodriguez (1944). This part of the analysis canvasses how Chicano and Chicana darkness is transformed into brownness as a line of ethnoracial and familial communication.[16]

A Brown Gathering: From the Browning of the Self to the Browning of America

The vast archive of brown, brownness, and brown pride holds such a prominent place in Chicano and Chicana public imaginations and identity configurations that these designations make up one informative entry in Paul Allatson's *Key Terms in Latino/a Cultural and Literary Studies*.[17] Under his grid, "The term brown was adopted by Chicano/as in the 1960s and 1970s in line with the Chicano Movement redefinition of Chicano/as as a mestizo/a people. This racialization also signaled an attempt to insert a third racial category into U.S. racial discourses and debates alongside black and white. The civil rights' celebratory slogan Brown Pride typified this redefinition" (2007: 49–50).[18] This Chicano generation—united as "la raza," or "the people"—laid out an alternative to the social and ethnoracial order, calling those "of Mexican descent to express pride in their ethnic origins rather than try to blend into a homogeneous white mainstream" (Jiménez, 2010: 43).[19]

Ian F. Haney López proposes that "Chicano activists remade [a] Mexican racial identity" set forth by judicial struggles that impelled a nonwhite racial identification (2003: 109).[20] "Had Mexicans not been treated as an inferior race," he brings to mind, "they would not have turned to a politics based on non-white identity" (157). This nonwhite identification gave Chicanos a "space in which to define a positive Mexican identity" (208). Haney López argues that the police shaped the unfolding meaning of Chicanoness, "but the Chicano movement also worked constantly, creatively, and self-consciously to fashion a new racial identity" (205). He adds, "According to Chicanos, and many Mexicans today, Mexicans were racially brown by nature, and contrary beliefs, politics, or attitudes could render one inauthentic but not actually white" (208). Connections with indigenous ancestry were recaptured and the view of a brown people emerged.[21] This nexus was of great significance, as we weigh in Moraga's words that "the majority of Mexicans in the United States and México have historically denied (and been denied) their Native identities" (2011: 7).

And yet the movement's emphasis on indigenousness led "Chicano activists to distinguish themselves from blackness" and "the black experience in the United States" (Haney López, 2003: 211–12).[22] Blackness did not fit at this moment of brown pride and brown power. Neither was blackness accommodated in the nascent stages of Mexican American advocacy during the twentieth century's early decades. At the time, "the idea of being American resonated among middle-class Mexican Americans" who envisioned "themselves as patriotic 'white' Americans" (Ruiz, 2004: 350). The League of United Latin American Citizens, founded in 1929, "maintained the color line between its members and African Americans" (351). Linkages with U.S. African Americans are delayed in what becomes a dyad of (Chicano and Chicana) empowering brownness and (Mexican American) assimilationist "whiteness." The Chicano movement's credo was that "Mexicans should be free from the inferiority imputed to blacks. Though Chicanos did not *want* to be white, neither did they *want* to be black" (Haney López, 2003: 212; emphasis added). I punctuate the verb *want* here. Its meanings—to wish, need, crave, demand, desire, or feel inclined toward—elide the slippages and detours of brownness. The wanting of a homogeneous brown recognition counts on the imposition of how a unified Chicano life should be socially framed and reproduced.

Once a Chicano and Chicana foundational narrative, brownness currently circumscribes a larger U.S. Latino and Latina body politic. Its inventory encapsulates an expansive symbolic. Brownness can refer to an irreversible marker of—and solution to—American uncertainty or to subversive practices that trouble ideological Americanness. By and large, however, brownness has become a metaphoric mapping that profiles Latino and Latina migrants—and the invading waters of immigration—in American public discourse and everyday life. Otto Santa Ana has studied, in-depth, how U.S. Latinos and Latinas have been metaphorically constituted in major mainstream newspapers, such as the *Los Angeles Times*, and the American political stage.[23] He contends that ubiquitous political metaphors like "a sea of brown faces" (2002: xv), "awash under a brown tide" (7), and "invasion of brown hordes" (286), among many others, speak to how "Americans frame their domestic worldview and their [. . .] underlying political and social values" (8). John-Michael Rivera follows this subject of the invasive brown tide and the "excessive growth" of present-day Latino and Latina populations. This new demographic foments a "reality on the landscape of the United States": that "Latinos, and specifically Mexicans [. . .] [will] soon perhaps take over the map—a 'brown tide is rising'" (2006: 6). This public aversion to and dislike of (brown) Latino and Latina bodies implies the spoiling of America.

That unfamiliar and stigmatizing brownness can create a U.S. outbreak that displaces and infects the pure national body has been redirected and transformed as a matter of critical self-inquiry. Richard Rodriguez upholds in his third memoir a suffused brownness that fleshes out a load of his productive "impurity." Formative brown stains as a mode of belonging give credence to various actors and ways: ethnoracially, queerly, nationally, and literarily, to cite but a few of the liberating potentials behind what Rodriguez identifies, post-9/11, as the "combustible dangers of brown" (2002: xiii). Despite this elasticity in signification, Rodriguez inescapably concedes, "Brown is the color most people in the United States associate with Latin America. Apart from stool sample, there is no browner smear in the American imagination than the Rio Grande" (xii). Broadly speaking, the worth of Latin America as a region has been speculated about in terms of excrement. Former president Richard Milhous Nixon once impolitely discharged that "'people don't give a shit' about the place" (Grandin, 2006: 2). This political umbra branches out to Latin-American bodies. In Junot Díaz's indelible words, this fecal condition dates back to "the arrival of Europeans on Hispaniola, [. . . and] we've all been in the shit ever since" (2007: 1). Overall, brown becomes, as Curtis Márez relays, "part of a scatological vocabulary that marks Chicanos as matter out of place" (1996: 109).

Although I note that Rodriguez differs from Nixon's viewpoint, it needs to be reemphasized that he "salute[s] Richard Nixon, the dark father of Hispanicity" (2002: xii). Rodriguez's reverence for Nixon, "the working-class white kid," lies in his administration's coinage of the Hispanic category (95). He acknowledges, "It was not until Richard Nixon's administration that I became brown" (94). Unlike Nixon's ideological posture, Rodriguez's appropriation of and investment in brownness for the twenty-first century gives a shit about the fate of this human and regional "waste" and how it fails to take the allotted place for excrement.[24] Rodriguez takes the color of feces as a consequential constitution and flowing mode of interaction from within (the self) and from without (the American citizen-observer). He welcomes the solid matter and liquefies it, adding more ethnicities, cultures, and modalities into the brown equation. And even though Moraga posits in her canonical essay "La Güera" that "I don't really understand first-hand what it feels like being shitted on for being brown," she shares a likeness with Rodriguez in forging a greater brown terrain of representation (1983b: 30). Brownness, in her view, is "a poverty" akin to "being a woman [and] being just plain poor" (29). Slightly more than two decades after Moraga's vastly influential piece from *This Bridge Called My Back*, Rodriguez domesticates the brown mixture. He charts a new map that fertilizes the American landscape through all that "brownly" confuses, his brown thoughts bleeding "through the straight line" (2002: xi).

Yet Rodriguez does not yield to an "easy optimism" that could be produced by brown as a marker of "a reunion of peoples" (2002: xiii). Its "combustible dangers" signal national infidelities and less than honorable citizenships. The browning of America may direct us toward the future, as Rodriguez insists. But for our intentions here, a multisited brownness is probed as a manifestation that has been nearby all the while and notably from — to paraphrase Mary Douglas — the dangerous contagions of a U.S. African Americanness lived through blackness as much as through brownness. U.S. African American blackness, however, has been read as overdetermined, trapped in the perennial stasis of its "own" blackness. But blackness, like brownness, is also unsettled. As "ambiguous thing[s]," blackness and brownness, sewn together, lead to a "cognitive discomfort" that can be "very threatening" (2002: xi). Since blackness, brownness, and dark brownness move out of their allotted spaces, the habitual order of black and brown is emptied. This revision demands that the perceptions of a brown threat be dismantled and not be generated in an exclusively Latinized mode.

But brownness appears to have "stuck," and not just as a site of U.S. Latino and Latina dread. It is also a signifier of other burdens and beings, incomprehensibilities, distinctions, and divisions. In an instance that could be read as transnational brownness, Cuban American memoirist and history professor Carlos Eire transposes a comparable function of Rodriguez's excremental color to Regla, a poor Havana neighborhood. Regla's viscous streaks, pre-

Cuban Revolution, are textually visualized as brown. Eire tells us, "The only color I remember seeing in that neighborhood was brown. The buildings were brown, the streets were brown, the people were brown. Even the statue of the Virgin Mary enshrined in the chapel of Our Lady of Regla was brown" (2003: 20). Brownness writes in — covers — the town and its dwellers. It blankets its representational contours with a destitute brownness that is remapped in the United States and that could host motley brown contributors.

The practice of a dissident brown aesthetics has also come to the fore. Márez propounds the term "brown style" to entail "a critical discourse that simultaneously counters Anglo repressions, opposes the white supremacist assumptions of highbrow taste, and affirms the qualities of Chicano difference" (1996: 109). It brings forward flamboyance as "a theory of style among contemporary working-class Chicanos" that can be "too ornate, too gaudy, too florid, too loud, too busy, too much — an embarrassment of riches" (110, 122). Additionally, a brown style is a "lowbrow(n)" avowal of popular taste, epitomized through "black velvet bull fighters, tattooed tear drops, bombshell hairdos, lowriders, zoot suits, Christ crucified in 3-D, plastic roses, ceramic black panthers, calendars with Aztec warriors and maidens" (120).[25] It impugns a highbrow style and "names the process of constructing and valorizing racial identities in the context of economic and political oppression" (121).

A brown style builds from a "working-class brown nostalgia" that looks backward into the Chicano heroic and recent past through *ranchera* music, the idealization of rural life, and Mesoamerican iconography (Márez, 1996: 124, 123). Brown nostalgia is not dormant, however. It orients us toward "remobilizations of brown memory" (128–29). Given Chicano and Chicana impurity and mestizaje, "working-class people become mixmasters" of this multifariously expressed brown cultural pattern, a gesture Márez calls a "collage." "Because Chicanos are themselves collages — an amalgam of Indian, Spanish, Mexican, and Anglo elements," he lets it be known, "their cultural products are also mixtures and fragments from diverse traditions. Collage is thus the stylistic corollary of mestizaje, the 'impure' status of racial and national mixture" (122).

Chicano and Chicana mestizaje is marked with substantive brown impurity. Its cultural affirmation occurs through continuous articulations of borrowings that culminate in a brown Chicano and Chicana collage. The greater "we" of the brown world is unclear, as the brown style tangibly sways toward Chicano and Chicana subjectivities. This stylistic shift brings out questions on the genealogy of a brown collage. A collage requires technique, specialized procedures and methods, and execution in the composition and assembling of materials and referents not usually related with one another. What types of non-Chicano, non-Chicana, and non-Mexican provisions and entities get to crossover in this congeries? Where is blackness in this amalgam? Can hip-hop artist David L. K. Thomas, "Kemo the Blaxican," be collaged—mixed and remixed—into this brown style?[26] Márez's brown modality, nonetheless, imports a "decolonial aesthetics," which involves ongoing artistic endeavors that can move in "radically different directions" and respond "to the darker side of imperial globalization." Decolonial aesthetics practitioners engage "in transnational identities-in-politics, revamping identities that have been discredited in modern systems of classification [. . .]. They are dwelling in the borders, sensing in the borders, doing in the borders" (Díaz Neiro et al., 2011).

Outside the unyielding brown premise manifested in Latinoness and Latinaness, the production of brownness can operate in promising ways that subverts, as Hiram Perez has articulated, the "primitive, exotic, or 'brown' body commodified by dominant gay male culture" (2005: 171). Perez's intervention in queer studies—vis-à-vis ungovernable brown impulses that are not based exclusively in Latino/a studies' articulations of Latinidad—presents brownness as a cross-identification marked by "shame and racial embodiment." To engage with Perez's idea more fully, I am interested in this instructive excerpt:

> What color is brown? In regard to race classification, brown is no more a natural color than black or white or yellow or red; brown is a verb. "Brown" designates a kind of constitutive ambiguity within U.S. racial formations—an identity that both complicates and preserves the binary opposition white/other. I use the category here to mark a position of essential itinerancy relative to naturalized, positivist classes such as white, black, Asian. Itself provisional as an identity category (a waiting station of sorts between white and black, or white and Asian, for example), I make use of "brown" provisionally myself—and tactically—to demystify how bodies are situated outside white/black or white/Asian binaries to consolidate cosmopolitan, first world identities. As a reposi-

tory for the disowned, projected desires of a cosmopolitan subject, it is alternately (or simultaneously) primitive, exotic, savage, pansexual, and abject. It is black and not black, Asian and not Asian, white and not white. In an age of weak multiculturalism, it is what it needs to be to maintain existing hierarchies, a race discourse morally divested from politics and social redistribution. That ambiguity designated here as "brown" is opportunistically and systemically deployed at times of crisis — as instanced by the intensified race profiling authorized by 9/11. (175–76)

As a verb, brown is that which is not only situated outside contrasting, racialized oppositions like white-and-black or white-and-other. Brown is a rotation system that surfaces at times of social and political crises. Perez's brownness speaks of U.S. racial formations that rest on seemingly disowned, strikingly unusual, and inadaptable bodies that are scrutinized to promote, depending on the context, desire and governmental power. Brownness, while deeply provocative, unwittingly dialogues with cultural studies premises of Latinidad. Instead of a white-brown dyad, Perez introduces a white-other binary. This otherness applies to a larger range of subjects — a continuous becoming of brown people or a multiethnic progeny — that operate as "primitive, exotic, savage, pansexual, and abject." To be sure, brown is a critical response in this formulation. But this brownness somehow remains static, since it does not apply to interethnic or intraethnic relations or variables, which is the intent behind flowing Latinities that are Latining the continuous motion from, for instance, black to brown to black and other dispositions.

If dread for the browning of the United States ideologically unites white America, the fear of hegemonic America sets off, to quote José Esteban Muñoz, choreographies of the self — narratives of being and becoming — through "brown feeling." This brown sentiment "chronicles a certain ethics of the self that is utilized and deployed by people of color and other minoritarian subjects who don't feel quite right within the protocols of normative affect and comportment" (2006: 676). Muñoz elaborates that brown feelings, as antinormative persuasions, "are not individualized affective particularity; they more nearly express [. . .] a larger collective mapping of self and other" (679). It is under this type of brownness where "different circuits of belonging connect, [as] recognition flickers between minoritarian subjects." Muñoz writes, "Brownness is not white, and it is not black either, yet it does not simply sit midway between them. Brownness, like all forms of racialized attentiveness in North America, is enabled by practices of self-knowing formatted by the nation's imaginary through the powerful spikes in the North American consciousness identified with the public life of blackness" (680). The public life of brownness is being made and remade differently and in various ambits. But what draws my attention is the archival life of brownness. Can brownness be truly trusted to — and entrusted with — the task of, as Judith Butler (2005) might say, "giving an account of oneself," a representation, in this instance, of a newly formed brown folk? How will brown exchanges be inscribed in dark brown and black? Will they uniformly prevail as brown?

At present, the rhetoric of the browning of America is being promulgated at the national level through divergent interpretive propositions. Ronald R. Sundstrom has philosophically broached the public idea of U.S. demographic changes and social justice through Latino, Latina, Asian American, and mixed-race populations, and the ensuing national and ethnoracial transformations vis-à-vis this browning. Such "coloring" consists of conflicting sociopolitical positions around the central demands of race and social justice (2008: 2). For Sundstrom, the browning of America operates, at one level, as a "grand vision," a "social revolution," and a "remedy for all of our racial ills." It entices "those who are tired of racial divisions and who desire a 'color-blind' society." Moreover, this U.S. browning "connects to the popular interest to end so-called reverse discrimination in race-based public policy" (1).

In an equal manner, U.S. "nationalists and xenophobes" are preoccupied with this browning, seeing that it is "a threat to long-established racial and ethnic demographic patterns and associated patterns of the distribution of resources and powers. The browning of America, from their perspective, is the result of generations of chain immigration, illegal immigration, and the lax enforcement of present immigration laws" (Sundstrom, 2008: 1–2). Despite this perceived American fragmentation or restoration, Americans nonetheless take part in this national browning process through "the challenges, threats, and transformations to race, ethnicity, and social justice" (4). Sundstrom argues, "the browning of America offers important challenges to traditional conceptions of racial justice and ethnoracial patterns that expose assumptions based on nativism, xenophobia, and American nationalism predicated on the black-white binary" (6). This "newly *brown* America" allows

Latinos, Latinas, Asian Americans, and mixed-race groups to enter U.S. historical demands for social justice, as previously posed by Native Americans and U.S. African Americans (10). Such considerations exhibit resonances with a "pan-brown"-like coalitional function among the aforementioned minoritized groups whose broad vision is contingent on the ethical responsibility attributed to brownness and the ongoing browning of post–civil rights America.

Earlier, Perez asked "What color is brown?" Duly notable in these brown schools of thought are these accompanying concerns: How does one become ethically (and "ethnically") brown, and with whom? What cultivates and upholds indefatigable brown becomings? What is a brown ethos? Even more, can a brown ethos be dark brown, or even unbrown? The logic of brownness that has taken shape in the renderings discussed previously has occurred through the disavowal of national norms. Brown "origins" detonate outside the self. Although brownness is not always the same, all differences are made coherent and captured under an interim brown pedigree with brown sensibilities. Latinoness and Latinaness are moving toward brown recognition, even as dark brown and black possibilities from within enact different bodily and social forms—fortuitously interrupting and rerouting the Latino or Latina signifier that presumably sediments it.

To familiarize us with the two great problems in brown—blackness and dark brownness—I will now survey the hues and voids of brownness first through U.S. African American cultural productions and then through Chicano and Chicana nonfictional reminiscences. I canvas how a Latino and Latina meditative "I" is modeled and speaks through this darker tertiary tint. I seek to grasp how these bodies stand the familial trials of their dark brown-and-black lives, leading the reader to assume the discovery of a newly created map—of brown fiction, let us say.

A Pile of Problems: The Brownness of Blackness, the Blackness of Brownness

The literary snapshots utilized in this part of my analytic treatment track the story of traditional Chicano and Chicana brownness to U.S. African American blackness. A pivotal question underlying this scrutiny is, in what ways is brownness, literarily speaking, transported and embodied in black? Latino and Latina struggles with the dark body—which can also be read as a discursive black body that in Anzaldúa's stance, opens "the door to old images that haunt me, the old ghosts and all the old wounds"—submit that they have obeyed the familial structuring of constitutive brownness (1983: 198). But Latino and Latina dark brownness is not fully covered up. And we cannot abandon it either, for what remains is the task of unraveling the implications of "that" black infiltration. The wide reach of brownness demonstrates that the contrast and organization of brownness is not whiteness, but dark brownness and blackness.

There cannot be a deferral in how we critically read the centrality of coeval blackness and dark brownness within this group and its relationship to Latinoness and Latinaness. The blackness of brownness has been documented in U.S. African American literature through the rubric of "colored." There, brownness keeps showing up, and the coloring of blackness suggests an intrinsic admixture that invariably points to its different specters. Du Bois, Zora Neale Hurston, Audre Lorde, Richard Wright, and Malcolm X, to cite a few figures, allude to the shifting boundaries of blackness through brownness.[27] What to make of this steady tinge of brownness vis-à-vis blackness? What might this mean for the encrustations of Latino and Latina brownness? The anecdotal life of brownness through blackness furnishes us with a different logic for the brown imagination. The prequel to (Latino and Latina) brownness may as well be (African American) blackness, but we must not be captive to their presumed rigid modes of being. Of particular importance are how blackness and brownness are transmitted in the rehearsal of autobiographical memory and how these hues make the leap into other ontologies that uproot the usually expected Latino, Latina, and African American orientations.

As far back as 1845 Frederick Douglass called the reader's attention to a "plain" fact, whereby "a very different-looking class of people are springing up at the south" (1997: 14). Noting that the plantation is a "little nation of its own," Douglass described the shades of blackness as "black, brown, copper colored, and nearly white" (50, 39). Despite the notable differences that surfaced in the South, the plantation's racial economy demanded that this difference be concealed.[28] Senna offers an eye-catching moment about the story of familial brownness upon discerning in her memoir that brown is the "literal" shade that confounds the black-white divide. Perusing her parents' marriage certificate from 1968—the decade of "Black is Beautiful"—Senna speculates on racial colorings and official documentation. "In both the groom and the bride sections," she narrates, "the third piece of information requested after name and age is 'Color.' While my mother is listed as 'white,' my father is listed as 'brown' rather than 'black' or 'negro.' Apparently my father insisted on this term."[29] She concludes that her father "was trying to make a point about race as a social construct rather than an essential biological category. If they wanted to know his color, he would give them the literal color of his skin. He wanted to call attention to the absurdity of racial categorization, even on this most personal of documents" (2009: 27). Taking a second look more than four decades later, this certificate's edges—its brown marginalia—have migrated to the main text. They are a harbinger of another political message: that brown, intricately appended to blackness, has been politically beautiful all along also. Some points for further deliberation accordingly pass through and reinvigorate old questions in black and white: Where does literal brownness reside? What is the direction of a brown Latinidad when we take into account a brown U.S. African American blackness? Senna similarly underscores a tension at the core of this study: What is the direction of brownness in black?

Side by side, brownness and blackness are continuative. They reopen and cannot be abandoned, especially as projects of epistemological inquiry. Langston Hughes distinguishes himself and his family in *The Big Sea* by saying, "I am brown. My father was a darker brown. My mother an olive-yellow" (1993: 11). Hughes details his color as one of a "copper-brown complexion" (50) and calls himself an *"americano de color,* brown as a Mexican" (78). This kindling of a Mexican-based brownness allows Hughes to pass, as we saw in chapter 2, as a Mexican in Texas. Henry Louis Gates Jr.'s memoir, *Colored People,* connotes a dialogue with brownness through the filters of blackness. The modification of these two colorings proffers a browned blackness that has yet to dialogue with Latino and Latina brownness. Upon first meeting his paternal relations during a family gathering, Gates informs us, "It came as a shock to realize that these mythic characters in Daddy's tales were actual brown and tan and beige people" (1994: 69). These black dissimilarities demonstrate a mixture echoing brown mestizaje. As Du Bois proposes in *The Negro*: "In general the Negro population in the United States is brown in color, darkening to almost black and shading off in the other direction to yellow and white, and it is indistinguishable in some cases from the white population" (1988: 185).

On Latino and Latina cultural fronts, such personal histories as Piri Thomas's *Down These Mean Streets* depict the doubleness in the construction of blackness and dark brownness within the makings of his Puerto Rican and Cuban family. Thomas, a self-proclaimed "skinny, dark-face, curly-haired, intense Porty-Ree-can," provides a glossary at the end of his memoir for "all Spanish and slang terms" (1997: x; ix). He defines six different categories to register such imbricated gradations as white, black, dark brown (both in proper and diminutive form), almost black, and dark-skinned textures (339–40).[30] Esmeralda Santiago's *When I Was Puerto Rican* (what is she now?) retells her first coming-of-age narrative through her nickname, "Negi," an abridged version of *"Negrita"* (1993: 13).[31] While these portraits provide some grounds for how blackness and its other manifestations are thought through at home, John Rechy's memoir, *About My Life and the Kept Woman*, speaks from a Mexican American perspective to a more formal verbalization of whiteness. Recalling the overtones provoked by the (white) name of one of his (nonwhite) sisters, Blanca, Rechy emits the following anecdote:

> Because her name meant "white" and her complexion was darker than my mother's—and certainly my father's—my determinedly "Spanish" grandmother on my father's side ridiculed her. She called Blanca *la India*, inflicting pain that would bruise my sister all her life. [...] Many years later, my beautiful sister Blanca would legally alter her name to Blanche, attempting to banish the pain the grandmother had caused her by mocking her about her darker color. (2008: 64)

The anticipated whitening from the linguistic blanching of Blanca's name does not lead to the discoloration of her dark body. On the contrary, the dolorous meaning of not possessing the phenotypic currency of whiteness continues to gyrate. Through Blanca and its "Latinesque" derivative Blanche, the reader "sees" a genotypic darkness that translates into Indianness. Latino and Latina dark Indianness has been indigenized over and above blackness. If dark brownness portends Latino and Latina Indianness, what does a dark brownness herald in black?

Román de la Campa's life story, *Cuba on My Mind*, raises a telling observation that elaborates how "white" (Cuban) mestizaje subsumes ("non-Cuban") blackness. Cuban ideology, de la Campa explicates, is infused with a white interpretive lens that initiates and stands for blackness: "White Cubans do not doubt the distinct African profile of their music, religion, dance, mode of speaking, and other features, but they see themselves as translators, interpreters, or perhaps guardians of such a cultural legacy. It is a way of acknowledging that African influences define the national culture while continuing to speak for it from the perspective of Cuban creole whiteness" (2000: 11). Díaz parallels de la Campa's point in his compilation of short stories, *Drown*. Blackness is indexed as an imported trait via the Dominican Republic's "blacker" neighbor, Haiti. Subtly and intricately mapping out how blackness plays out within insular brotherly relations evoking larger national practices, Rafa, a main character in the story "Ysrael," pesters his brother with insults that have more to do "with my complexion, my hair, the size of my lips. It's the Haitian he'd say to his buddies. Hey Señor Haitian, Mami found you on the border and only took you in because she felt sorry for *you*" (1996: 5). Slightly more than a decade later, Díaz progresses with black Haitian marginality in *The Brief Wondrous Life of Oscar Wao*. The novel addresses how blackness from abroad enters Dominican life. This particular escape from blackness in the Dominican diaspora is quite probing with regard to the U.S. racial economy, be it black, white, Latino, and Latina. *The Brief Wondrous Life of Oscar Wao* whirls from a complete lack, or denial, of an enunciatory blackness within the Spanish-speaking island of Hispaniola to a hyperreception of the enunciation — if not willingness to craft the self through the excessive use of the referent — "nigger" in the United States.[32]

If stories of the self come into being with a new nation, as William L. Andrews has observed, the personal crónicas analytically catalogued in this section, paired with Díaz's fictional vignettes, show how dark brownness and blackness are visualized in brown Latinidad and how brownness is launched into being in U.S. American mappings of Latino and Latina unlocatable "nations" (1992: 7). In examining a problematic blackness putatively perceived as unsettled in the Americas and unsettling to a brown domestic domain, I veer toward Chicano and Chicana self-portrayals, because in situating the reader in a commonplace — the home — these life stories foreground race in the construction of the personal. They outline how dark brownness and blackness live ambivalently in relation to each other. At the same time, I would like to make clear that I am not reading their perfect-bound experiences as evidential in their undeniable, genuine lives.³³ I am interested, rather, in what has been conceived as brownness and the evidence of the exposed dark brownness that has been left behind on the page. These memoirists account for what become genealogies of human lives exhausted by darkness as they seek to provide coherence to the ideological incoherence reproduced at home. Their processes of rewriting a particular browning of the mestizo or mestiza self trigger new referentialities about the literature, politics, and ethnoracial group to which they "belong."

Literary Homecomings, Brown Becomings

The revisiting of coming-of-age brownness and dark brownness by figures such as Anzaldúa, Moraga, and Rodriguez points to the reevaluation, during adulthood, of formative yet troubling instances during childhood where darkness was to be concealed. These literary cognoscenti cue into what Vicki L. Ruiz identifies as a "color consciousness," one arranged at home through ethnoracial categories that expose the legacy of Spanish colonization in Latin America. "Color consciousness, with white as the hue of privilege," Ruiz briefs us, "is not just a twentieth-century by-product of Americanization, but represents historical consciousness rooted in colonial Latin America" (2004: 348).³⁴ These differentiations are imbedded in Latino and Latina North America and are wedded to the dominant ideologies of new world whiteness. Estelle Tarica has alluded to this level of whiteness as a "selfhood invested in a new power," the power of ideological whiteness simultaneously highlighting its powerlessness (2008: xx). Martha Menchaca has delineated the racial history of Mexican mestizaje in the U.S. Southwest and Mexico. She notes that black slaves, Indians, and mestizos fell, during the conquest, under a racialized order known as "the *casta* system" (2001: 62).³⁵ When the United States annexed the U.S. Southwest, Menchaca observes that "diverse forms of racial discrimination" were instituted on white Mexicans and Mexicans of color "depending on their racial phenotype" (277). Attending to forms of Chicano and Chicana Mesoamerican darkness opens the possibility of expanding our understanding of a Latino and Latina blackness that is not narrowly situated in the Hispanic Caribbean.³⁶

I undertake the production of the core practices and physical journeys of brown through the autobiographical opuses of Anzaldúa, Moraga, and

Rodriguez. They thoughtfully call our attention to how the discourse of dark brownness has not been ethnoracially exhausted. It merits another look through the semiotics of problematic blackness, its dilemmas, and the emotional states that these variations of brownness—dark brownness and blackness—evoke. I would like to clarify that although these figures speak to Chicananess and indigenousness (Anzaldúa and Moraga) and an Americanness of Mexican descent (Rodriguez), I use the panethnic classification Latino and Latina.[37] I engage in a complementary dialogue that, while Chicano- and Chicana-specific, also points to its intersubjective relation to—and commingling with—a broader brown Latino or Latina subject. This does not mean that I conflate the two populations—and the academic fields, paradigms, and histories—that advance the discursive formation and operation of these groups: Chicano/a studies or Latino/a studies.[38] Chicano and Chicana cultural and intellectual life are summoned as a dynamic roadmap that also marks the construction and articulation of U.S. Latinoness and Latinaness.

Anzaldúa, Moraga, and Rodriguez's writings elucidate how Indianness and blackness inhabit their walks of life. They staunchly denote the contradictions that emanate from processes of racialization that also give rise to Chicano and Chicana mestizaje. Rafael Pérez-Torres deems mestizaje as one that "contend[s] with the varying forces that tug and nudge, haul and rend the shape of Chicano culture and identity." Mestizaje is a "conceptual tool" that gives concrete form to "multiple subjectivities," affords "discussions of identity to greater complexity and nuance," and "locates how people live their lives in and through their bodies as well as in and through ideology" (2006: xiii). Pérez-Torres's approach to a critical mestizaje thus "embodies the struggle for power, place, and personhood arising from power and resistance" and highlights "a historical consciousness" (51).

The household uses of black and brown evince a consciousness of what Latino and Latina are not. Anzaldúa gives an example of how racialized categories have been put into motion. "When not copping out, when we know we are more than nothing," she says, "we call ourselves Mexican, referring to race and ancestry; *mestizo* when affirming both our Indian and Spanish (but we hardly ever own our Black ancestry)" (1999: 85).[39] If, as Rodriguez's mother has remarked, brown is "the most important symbol of a life of oppressive labor and poverty" (1982: 119), the guiding general concept has been, as Moraga has put forward, "No one ever quite told me this (that light was right), but I knew that being light was something in my family (who were all Chicano with the exception of my father)." As Moraga imparts the inherently known convictions of her family unit regarding whiteness, there is, concurrently, an explicit view of what can be identified as an inhabited raced category that is classed. Chicano and Chicana become the signifiers for fieldwork and manual labor, as in "braceros" or "wet-backs."[40] Moraga chronicles that for her mother, "on a basic economic level, being Chicana meant being 'less'" (1983b: 28). Although lower-class darkness maintains its dark tone at the field, these categories, while inflated with racial darkness, can be altered and corrected through economic and racial mobility.

In his first life narrative, Rodriguez devotes a chapter to Mexican preoccupation with dark brownness. Blackness, a synonym of darkness, is a silenced marker. It is easier to lighten darkness than it is to "shed" blackness. Calling the fourth part of his book "Complexion," Rodriguez fluctuates between related parenthetical and nonparenthetical admissions, declaring in his introductory paragraph, "My complexion is dark. (My skin is brown. More exactly, terra-cotta in sunlight, tawny in shade. I do not redden in sunlight. Instead, my skin becomes progressively dark; the sun singes the flesh)" (1982: 113). Not unlike Moraga, the motif of indigent darkness operates in Rodriguez's narrative too:

> My mother would see me come up the front steps. She'd wait for the screen door to slam at my back. "You look like a *negrito*," she'd say, angry, sorry to be angry, frustrated almost to laughing, scorn. "You know how important looks are in this country. With *los gringos* looks are all that they judge on. But you! Look at you! You are so careless!" Then she'd start in all over again. "You won't be satisfied till you end up looking like *los pobres* who work in the fields, *los braceros*. (113)

The apprehensions of being compounded by lo negro unmask a personal and familial dread evolving around the fear of being deprived of white-like benefits that are organized along American racial and economic lines.[41] The reminder that Rodriguez looks like a negrito gives greater scope to the employment of this problematic diminutive of *negro*. It is made deliberately smaller. Through a mother's loving tongue, negrito does not offend. Applying negro instead of negrito would otherwise seem more direct and irrevocable. But in another poignant moment, Rodriguez recalls when (racial) dirtiness is to be washed and contained. "My mother would grab a towel in the kitchen and rub my oily face sore when I came in from playing outside. 'Clean the *graza* off of your face!' *(Greaser!)*" (119). Rodriguez sketches his engagement with the politics of lo negro through professedly secondary revelations. Though encased in parentheses, these disclosures are far from parenthetical. They are part of Rodriguez's dark brownness, affirmed in his third annals of the self through the assertion, "I think I probably do. (Have brown thoughts.)" (2002: 47). These immediate first and second thoughts allow the reader to take note of the author's break and continuation of an inner dialogue with the dark brown self.

Rodriguez proceeds to describe his family's different brown colorings. The diverse spectrum in his family circle of "cosmic" and "uncosmic" brownness is mediated through the sorting out of a language that somehow exonerates culpable darkness.[42] Rodriguez states, "There was affection and a kind of humor about these matters. With daring tenderness, one of my uncles would refer to his wife as *mi negra*. An aunt regularly called her dark child *mi feito* (my little ugly one)" (1982: 116).[43] The ugliness of *mi feito* blackens, under a vigilant diminutive, the dark child's skin. The familial dictate of mi negra (my black one) summons a possessive pronoun, communicating his uncle's right to address "that" negra as his. Rodriguez's uncle guards and contains his wife's (deprecatory) blackness within the familial and spousal domain.

Outside the home, Rodriguez is not exempt from the deployment of racial slurs for dark brownness. He recounts an incident where strangers yelled, "Hey, Greaser! Hey, Pancho!" and "I pee on dirty Mexicans" (1982: 117).[44] An undesired dark brown complexion is also synthesized through what Rodriguez suggests as Indianness. Rodriguez, however, sounds encumbered with his dark brown genealogy, appearing as a xenogenic offspring. The sculpting of his family engenders their brown looks. Rodriguez proclaims that his father's face recalls France and that his complexion is white. His mother, "whose surname is inexplicably Irish—Moran—has an olive complexion" (114).[45] But Rodriguez is "the only one in the family whose face is severely cut to the line of ancient Indian ancestors," and, as such, he "grew divorced from my body" (115, 125).

He recalls one night when he locked himself in the bathroom, studying his dark skin. "I began soaping my arms," he recounts. "I took my father's straight razor out of the medicine cabinet. Slowly, with steady deliberateness, I put the blade against my flesh, pressed it as close as I could without cutting, and moved it up and down across my skin to see if I could get out, somehow lessen the dark. [. . .] The dark would not come out. It remained. Trapped. Deep in the cells of my skin" (1982: 124–25). Rodriguez's excerpt has some insights with Moraga, who despite being born with what she appraises as the features of her Chicana mother and the skin of her Anglo father, she calls forth a type of double consciousness (1983b: 28).[46] "It is frightening to acknowledge," she elicits, "that I have internalized a racism and classism, where the object of oppression is not only someone outside my skin, but the someone inside my skin" (30).[47] Moraga leans toward a formative socialization that, to apply Sandra K. Soto's term, permits her to undergo a "self-racialization" (2005: 250).[48] Rodriguez does not strive for a racialization of the self, but his double-sided skin markers surround him. Darkness cannot be shed or cleansed. It nests as a template for dirty.

Indian, Rigoberta Menchú explains from a Maya context, means being measured between combinations of "very dirty" (1994: 3), as was the case with her father, and "filthy" in her situation (92). The locations of these problematic dark and dirty Indian markers are what force Anzaldúa to shelve the rough draft of her essay "La Prieta" (The Dark One) for a year. For Anzaldúa's "sixth generation American" family of Mexican descent, it means eyeing the body from the moment of birth so as to privately wrestle with the meaning of what is detected before the racially unspecified body is publicly presented to the outside world (1983: 198). Put differently, another private part of the domestic sphere is the visualization of the home. Dark brownness is an integral part of the family, but it is a matter that stays behind closed doors. And while dark brownness may be hidden at home, it is still revealed by the main purveyor of said coloring, our now-browned autobiographer.

Anzaldúa opens her essay with this disclosure: "When I was born, Mamágrande Locha inspected my buttocks looking for the dark blotch, the sign of the indio, or worse, of mulatto blood." Anzaldúa mentions mulatto with a double "t," instead of using the Spanish term *mulato* (or in her case, *mulata*) with one "t."[49] This use infers the crossing and circulation of ethnoracial hodgepodges in a U.S. Latino and Latina context. There is not one location for mixture or mestizaje, as dark brown mestizaje coalesces with black mixture. Anzaldúa's *mancha* — racial stain — from babyhood is cordoned off.

Its direction is to be indexed by familial ranks of darkness. Her tone gets compressed to being "dark like an Indian." As inspected by the elder matriarch with detectival skills, Anzaldúa's smear extends beyond the buttocks, and the family's worst fear is confirmed by fiat. Later, Anzaldúa's mother bemoans her daughter's skin color — "morena, *muy prieta*, so dark and different" — and lessons her daughter on how to navigate a nuanced line colored by blackness, Mexicanness, Indianness, and un-Americanness. "Don't go out in the sun," she urges. "If you get any darker, they'll mistake you for an Indian. And don't get dirt on your clothes. You don't want people to say you're a dirty Mexican" (1983: 198). As a substitute for blackness, darkness is grasped as Indian. It is a secretive blackness of sorts, a problematic and undesirable one that can be known and recognized only through Indianness.

Yet, as Moraga notes in *The Last Generation*, "in this country, 'Indian' and 'dark' don't melt" (1993: 57). The linked chain of darkness and Indianness within the constituents of U.S. Latino and Latina, though, does melt at the semantic level. It becomes brown. Moraga allows us to read how she structures her personhood through her mother's brown bloodline as an acting intermediary. Brownness is a necessity that permits Moraga's self-analysis and her use of "that" brown space that her mother seemingly abandoned: "*I am a white girl gone brown to the blood color of my mother speaking for her*" (1983a: 13).[50] The meaning of the blood-color brown endows Moraga with a clear image that entails a collective task of doing — of brown doing or acting brownly in affirmative representations of Chicana lineages to brown indigenousness.[51] It is not coincidental, one might add, that Moraga textually directs our gaze to her mother's "brown hands" (1993: 91).[52]

The Negro problem, in Du Boisian singular or plural terms, is a new brown–dark brown variable. Resistant dark brownness and blackness are vehicles to understanding how Latinoness and Latinaness are semiotically founded within the realm of the familial and then modified outside the household. Anzaldúa is first measured in the domestic realm. Her critical awareness succeeds as one that is sorted out through the internal values along racial lines and gendered alliances. In the eyes of her mother, she admits, and "in the eyes of others I saw myself reflected as 'strange,' 'abnormal,' 'QUEER.' I saw no other reflection" (1983: 199). We find two functioning gazes. One of them reflects what Emma Pérez would reference as a "colonial mind-set" that "believes in a normative language, race, gender, class, and sexuality" (2003:

123). The other, also identified by Pérez, is a "queer-of-color gaze," Anzaldúa's visual scrutiny "that sees, acts, reinterprets, and mocks all at once in order to survive and reconstitute a world where s/he is not seen by the white colonial heteronormative mind" (124). Anzaldúa's queer counterpart to the stigma of dark difference in her family is momentous. She has taken the insulated life of normative brownness to a type of "queer succession," an admixture of illegitimacies — illegalities — that have been denied admittance into her family. Her queerness, radical consciousness, the "blemishes of individual character," race, nation, and spiritual beliefs are the stigma that can now "be transmitted through lineages and equally contaminate all members of a family" (Goffman, 1963: 4). But this "pan-contamination" is the new Anzaldúan mestizaje that doubtlessly adheres to "her" queerness. It transmits, in Alicia Arrizón's language, "spirited connections with others who, like her, reclaim the word *queer*, using it to designate a type of citizenship." We find a political strategy that concretizes Anzaldúa's mestiza body as a "reflection on a 'planetary' citizenship [that] brings local and global meanings to the signifiers *lesbian* and *brown*" (2006: 156).

Anzaldúa's darkness is constituted not just by dark brownness but by a myriad of unsanctioned manchas also. These manchas are undarkened through the unifying potential of their incremental brownification. As Anzaldúa puts it, "We are the queer groups, the people that don't belong anywhere, not in the dominant world nor completely within our respective cultures. Combined we cover so many oppressions" (1983: 209). Anzaldúa conjures the self outside repressive matriarchal restrictions. Our chronicler browns herself and participates in a broader brownification that has, at one level, acquiesced to the grammar of the home. But she has also created a new lexicon that is heightened by a surrogate brownness where the Latina body surrounds herself with other worlds. Hers is not just a mere valuable brownness in the normative sense that her family desires. Anzaldúa denies that brownness and replenishes it with a brownness that voices valuable information about the praxis of browned worlds of differences. This brownness gains more and more importance through the stream of marginal signs that keep flowing and radiating through it: queerness, unbelonging, and nonnormativity.[53]

Anzaldúa catalogues through her prieta status how brown mothers internalize the betrayal of la raza — the Chicano and Chicana race that, to summon Moraga's phraseology, "dissolves borders," since this identity can also be constitutive of "Quichua, Cubano, or Colombiano" (1993: 62). In failing to adequately improve or better the race, Anzaldúa's mother offers the world another virulent dark descendant. Even so, her offspring ceases to be dark through the course of time, as the function of her brood has discursively moved into brownness as an act of signification. But the dark brown space lingers and has not been emptied of its scornful relation to brownness. How Anzaldúa's darkness has passed over into brownness, which is lighter than a muy prieta state and dark brownness, has not been critically put to the question and amended in Latino/a studies.[54] How has this conversion from muy prieta to brownness occurred? If Anzaldúa was once la prieta, how did she pass into brownness—in effect, become "an ex-colored prieta"? What happened to the dark brown/black matter? These black–dark brown questions become particularly hefty and germane. Rodriguez, as a case in point, records that "an uncle had been told by some man to go back to Africa" (1982: 117). He also says that he knew his older sister with dark skin "suffered for being a 'nigger'" (115). "Nigger" is so close to dark brown that it resiliently fits—"represents"—Rodriguez's sister more so than "dirty Mexican" (or even "spic"). How to track this passing from "spic" to "nigger"? What to do with the mirroring form and function of "nigger" in the brown map?

Brownness is far from settled, especially for Latinos and Latinas encountering a dark brownness. If dark brownness is unreliable as a tool for an American way of life, brownness is untrustworthy as a Latino and Latina narrative. Werner Sollors's optic on black-white "interracial literature" can be applied to U.S. Latinos and Latinas, since "the 'mixed-race' space" has been "cleared in favor of monoracial occupancy" (1997: 6).[55] That monoracial occupancy at this juncture is the sociocultural production of a new brownness that has seized dark brownness.[56] By becoming brown, these semiotics of the self are not susceptible to forms and bodies that take the subject away from the predominant content and function of the browned Latino and Latina economy of difference.

Brownness and Latino/a Studies

I have sifted through a new economy of brownness and how its imbued meanings are communicated in Latino/a studies. This chapter's components have argued that decisive brownness as a basic feature and mode of knowledge production poses imprecisions and tremendous challenges for the field.[57] My premise has been that we must make sense of and critically coordinate the symbolic interactions between a joint dark brownness and blackness. In such a way, there would not be one semantic unit framing the subtleties and contradictions in the brown ecology of Latinos and Latinas.

Can the field still afford to hold the same brown thought in all U.S. times and places? Since there are various kinships of brownness, what type of difference will dark brownness make? I have yet to find an epistemically sound framework to be — and think, characteristically and accordantly, in — brown, although I understand that as a Latina, I may be marked not just as brown but also as dark brown "out there." What, I ask, is the substance, the mainstay, of brownness? I raise another set of suitable questions: Do brownness and its different scenarios pose a new problem for Latino/a studies? Does Latino/a studies need brownness as a guiding syntax that inscribes its being in the American landscape? What is a brown methodology? These pressing queries are open ended. They indubitably necessitate further examination and variegated responses. But I direct attention to them so as to rethink and rework the shaky constitution and unstable processes of becoming a U.S. Latino or Latina.

Having identified the cultural indicators and representational emergence of a permissible Latino and Latina brownness that annexes dark brownness, the next chapter concentrates on dark brownness as a literary iconicity scripted for a "new" Latino and Latina generation, U.S. Central Americans. Central Americans are drawn together as a group whose signifying order of underdevelopment, peonization, and illegality is naturalized. They are almost impossible to know within the properties and relations of established Latino and Latina brownness. At stake is the troubling and new understanding of certain subgroups that are allotted a different space in U.S. Latino and Latina everyday life.

CHAPTER FOUR

DISORIENTING LATINITIES

Where were we?
—PATRICK MCGRATH (2008: 130)

Up to this point this volume has demonstrated a link in the semiotic lines of race, culture, movement, and geography. These markers have been scrutinized in ways that exceed the black-white and brown-white dyad, centering on the interchangeable and unsettled presence of blackness, brownness, and dark brownness. I have explored these concerns through the grids of the U.S. Southwest and Southeast (chapter 1); South-South black-brown reciprocal Latin passages in Central America, Mexico, and Cuba (chapter 2); North-South dynamics of problematic blackness through brownness and dark brownness (chapter 3); and now through Central America as an intellectually unmappable South in Latino/a studies. I conclude with this line of thought to disentangle and labor through emendations that I hope reframe the discourse of Latinidad and diaspora not by simply bringing Central Americans into the analytic conversation.

I wish to think through the "centrality" of the limits, by which I mean the canonical boundaries of Central Americanness as a forthcoming project, as an identity- and region-in-the-making that never quite arrive at Latinidad. Central American imperceptibility—its "disorientingness"—provides a locus for how to reorient Latinoness, Latinaness, Latin-Americanness, and Americanness. In this way, the politics and sites of the color line that were introduced by W. E. B. Du Bois in 1900 and that have resonated throughout this work are interwoven with what we can conjure as the empire line broadening the Du Boisian line in the Global South.[1] By 1904 this line had graphed—

in the language of short story writer O. Henry, who coined the "banana republic" term with the fictional Central American republic of Anchuria — such nations as Belize, Costa Rica, El Salvador, Guatemala, Honduras, Nicaragua, and Panama (1922: 132).[2] This is not to say that the question and direction of U.S. Latino/a studies is effortlessly resolved through the inclusion of blackness, dark brownness, and Central Americanness. Neither does it imply that intellectual engagement with these vacuities will make punitive areas of investigation. On the contrary, these chasms punctuate that the potential behind such schemas as Latinidad remain deferred because of the future promise through which particular ethnoracial margins from within the margins will emerge. A knotty point not yet grappled with is that the sidelines of Latino/a studies undertake movement and transformation, while Latinidad, as a potential site of new beginnings, does not.

U.S. Central American emergence as a Latino and Latina group echoes how the isthmus thematically registers as a placeless southern place in imaginaries from a Global North or from a Global South that may host some locales with more "northern" currency.[3] As a region, Central America is cumulatively mapped in ways that connote such areas as Africa. The epigraph to Joan Didion's *Salvador* (1983), as a case in point, carves out her account of that nation through Joseph Conrad's depiction of Africa in *Heart of Darkness* (1902). Recalling the time she lived in Germany, novelist Jacinta Escudos (2005) has written of how when she mailed letters to El Salvador, a postal worker asked her, after long deliberation, "What part of Africa is El Salvador in?" And so while I am inspecting Central American absence in Latino/a studies, I do so fully aware that blackness — in its demonstrably recognizable forms as well as in surreptitious and more nuanced manifestations — is often dwarfed from the governing discourses bringing forward Central American intellectual and cultural thought.

This chapter's underlying claim is that Central America and U.S. Central Americans denote dark brownness not so much through the chameleonic shades of brownness affixed to Latino and Latina colorings. The heart of this darkness lies in the roles of Central Americans as guileless, rustic beings who supply the U.S. and normative Latin American world with strikingly unusual, underdeveloped, and disadvantaged "things" that disorient U.S. Latino and Latina brown bodies. This corporeality is constituted not only by the touchstone paradigm of Mexican American, Puerto Rican, and Cuban American.

It also comes about through the staging of the isthmus nations—to adapt the words of fiction writer Peter Mountford—as "the cucarachas, those chronically dysfunctional Latin American countries like Guatemala, Panama, et cetera" (2011: 30). We find descriptors for a U.S. Central American population as well as a region through what Gustavo Arellano, the architect of the weekly syndicated column "¡Ask a Mexican!," defines in this chain of command and ordered thinking as "Guatemalan: The Germans had the Irish; the Irish had the Italians; the Italians had the Poles. Mexicans have the Guatemalans—our eternal punch line" (2007: 7). Arellano's definition is meant to be satirical, of course. But why are Guatemalans in this cultural template the indispensable subaltern Latino and Latina group that incurs disparagement? Arellano takes us to Mexico as Guatemala's hegemonic north in this demarcation. Guatemala is a permissive site for predictive archetypes of a U.S. Latino and Latina way of life on both sides of the U.S.-Mexico border.

Allow me to explain that my present inquiry does not stage a belligerent analysis of Mexican and Central American cultural and political rivalries or polarities. Rather, my venture calls on and probes textual representations of U.S. Central Americans so as to trouble the types of Latino and Latina differentiations within the "same" rhetorical configurations that pattern U.S. Latino and Latina discursive spaces. My purpose is to illuminate a recognition of Central American forms of communication by posing new questions that tackle the deeply rooted localization of Central America and Central Americans as scions growing downward into lower modes and dispositions of Latinoness, Latinaness, and Latin-Americanness. Their disconnectedness from the Global South's other Americas as well as wider U.S. Latino and Latina populations allows for an interrogation of how the Americanness of Central Americans, together with their Central American un-Americanness in the United States, is produced in a U.S., Latino and Latina, and Latin-American axis. Yet it is not as though the discursive arrangement of Latin-Americanness, Latinoness and Latinaness, or U.S. Americanness—conjectural points that constitute parts of the Global South and Global North—is not irreversible. To that end, *Latining America: Black-Brown Passages and the Coloring of Latino/a Studies* has unraveled U.S. American "northernness" from the specter of its internal multiple Souths and their crossovers to other contexts, communities, and maps.

Before we proceed with this subject, the reader needs to be alerted to two nomenclatures that subjects from Guatemala and U.S. discourses on Central Americanness will take herewith: Guatepeorian and Central American–Americanness. Guatepeorian is being made to vocalize, disturb, and go through the meanings that codify and rift this nation, population, and region. Central American–American is the theoretical "appearance" in Latino/a studies, the space that works — and collides — with sloppy Guatepeorian representations to make itself known and to critically question and deliberate on what is being talked about. I analytically embark, then, on a southern journey that takes up a continental American underdog status for Central America by focusing on how the isthmus's inhospitable southerness is charted in U.S. Latino and Latina creative imaginations. I argue that there are numerous and unsteady Souths that come into view in Latino and Latina literature: some are more "northernly" and socioculturally acceptable than others. I specifically wrestle with the oppositions that arise between Central Americanness and the southern subaltern discursivity of Latinos and Latinas. Central America's alienating local colors are embedded against standardized U.S. American, Latino, Latina, and Latin American manners. My efforts do not aim to sectionalize, assign blame, or send tremors across Chicano/a, Latino/a, and Latin American studies. At stake is the recasting of these fields through a broader and equitable nexus of more globalized and reciprocal southern relations.

Organizationally, I explore the pathos of representing Central Americanness through an "innate" ontological basis that codifies the pathologies of civil war, violence, enduring and widespread poverty, and rural social structures. As a visual and literary experience, this taxonomy suggests the social unrepresentability of U.S. Central Americans, sharing a rhetorical likeness with Patrick McGrath's angle of vision in his novel, *Trauma*.[4] There, Vietnam War veterans await their social translatability and representability in the American world. But first they must absorb their psychological experiences and injuries until they can produce their own language. This chapter's epigraph, to this extent, suggests the continuity and discontinuity of a muddled Latino/a and American conversation on Central Americans. This Latino/a script in relation to America is disoriented by the deep imprints of a Central American presence that perplexes or creates a certain cognitive disturbance. Their precarious situation in both spheres attributes temporariness, since

U.S. Central Americans are not supposed to reside in America. Nicholas De Genova and Ana Y. Ramos-Zayas touch on these contentions when they cite a familial talk, wherein a baffled Mexican child poses the question, "Uncle, the Guatemalans—are they Hispanics like us?" (2003: 184). As subjects of discussion, U.S. Central Americans also disorient the casual conversation about them vis-à-vis contradictions, exclusions, digressions, shifts, resumptions, and terminations. The vernacular question cited earlier—"Where were we?"—also seeks clarification on "Where are we?" and "How are we here?"[5]

As is widely known by now, the mass Central American migrations into the United States are a result of U.S. foreign intervention during the 1980s (cf., M. García, 2006; Mahler, 1995, 1996; Hamilton and Stoltz Chinchilla, 2001; Menjívar, 2000).[6] U.S. interests in Central America revolved around an effort to safeguard the region against communism, which was generally deemed at the time as an East-West struggle. Doug Stokes points out that "The central justification for this support was the U.S.'s stated need to contain alleged Soviet expansionism within Central America." The Carter, Reagan, and Bush administrations resisted making "another Vietnam" out of El Salvador. The 1979 Sandinista victory over Anastasio Somoza Debayle's dictatorship "added to Washington's fears of the spread of subversion in Central America" (2003: 79). In former U.S. ambassador to the United Nations Jeane Kirkpatrick's view, Sandinista control of Nicaragua represented a "major [U.S.] blow," one "of large and strategic significance" (1987: 14). Resisting communism in Central America signified the protection of U.S.-centered American ideologies.[7]

This chapter's discursively disorienting Latinity picks up the baton of political and sociocultural conversation and extends it to literary constructions of a "normalized" Latino and Latina self in relation to a feckless Central American other. Literary sketchings of the U.S. Central American figure as one that intrudes on the established identity and parameters of Latinoness and Latinaness need to be assigned meaning.[8] As follows, this chapter's first section begins with a literary overview of the "political iconomy" ascribed to Central Americanness.[9] This part of the discussion tallies a cultural compendium where Central Americanness morphs into a Guatepeorian iconographic state that enumerates what individuals from the isthmus should look like as well as how and where they should live. I survey how nations and peoples from the region literarily show up to formulate my narrative and outline how Central Americans are introduced and kept at a safe distance so as not to disorient a U.S. Latino and Latina brownness. The space between Latino/a studies and Central Americanness tacitly lays an infrastructure that accentuates a standard Latinoness and Latinaness through a radical otherness inferred as a Guatepeorian Latinidad. Such craftings demand further deliberation about the orientation of Latino and Latina literature. When approaching these Latino/a and Central American specificities, one may want to weigh in on these issues: How correlative is Central Americanness to Latino and Latina literary articulations of a Global South–like discourse and its differentiations (e.g., folkways, distinctive norms and practices, food preferences and traditions, plantation economies, tropical climates, language and speech patterns, and geographic smallness)?[10] Does the content of Latinoness and Latinaness create a "southern literature" that is ultimately wedded to the U.S. literary and national zeitgeist of the "Great American Novel" through the exercising of more untranslatable "southern" walks of life like Central Americanness? Is Central America's regionalism immutably decreed beneath "South of Southern Norths"? Guatepeorianness dots the dissimilar types of southern emergence from this distinct U.S. Central American dark brown space.

The chapter progresses with a review of the discursive American horizon North and South, trying to understand what this map means regionally and hemispherically, and at the level of subjectivation, especially within a Central American–Americanness that attempts to forge an American space in the Americas. Hardly extras playing a minor part in the Latino/a studies triumvirate, modes of U.S. Central Americanness are being staged through a new analytic lexicon. This chapter studies, as a last point for consideration, U.S. Central American subjectivity through the theoretical beginnings proffered by Arturo Arias's Central American–American framework. Scrutinizing how this paradigm might be incorporated in Latino/a studies and how it might submit to Latinidad and an "Other Latino" status, I take to task the promising directions of Central American–Americanness as a hermeneutic opening interrogating the presumed stability of Latinoness and Latinaness. Central American–Americanness points to the need for Central Americans to begin producing other Souths within the nuanced and tense makings of Latino/a, Latin-Americanness, and U.S.-situated Americanness.

Somatic and Geographic Guatepeorianness

This section begins by working through the vast uses of an idiom that texture and lend credibility to my premise of Guatepeorianness as a dismal reflection of Central America. The strange saga of the vernacular phrase "de Guatemala a Guatepeor" drives one to try to make meaning of it, as it cannot be uncoupled from the monological assumptions about Central America's geography and cultural identity. Its origins are indeterminate, but as Arthur Aristides Natella Jr. puts forward in *Latin American Popular Culture*, the "colorful expression" forms part of the region's "traditional wisdom" (2008: 38–39). Curiously, de Guatemala a Guatepeor is one of 986 entries that compose "the wisdom of the folk" catalogued in *A Dictionary of Mexican American Proverbs* (Glazer, 1987: xi).[11] It is summoned in works from the Chicano movement like the Teatro de la Esperanza's play, *Guadalupe* (Huerta, 1989: 224), as well as in life narratives like Gloria López-Stafford's *A Place in El Paso: A Mexican-American Childhood* (1996: 106). The saying also arises in analyses of Chicana and women of color predicaments, as surmised by Paula Moya in *Learning from Experience* (2002: 37). I treat de Guatemala a Guatepeor not as a passing remark, but as a figure of thought and code of knowledge. It is a central theme that gives birth to a system of odd Central American referentials.[12]

The euphemism's equivalences in English range from hitting an excess of rough patches, falling into circumstances that turn from bad to worse, or going from out of the frying pan into the fire. I inject this Guatepeorian examination with the descriptions, sensory encounters, and literary evocations of the isthmus. They are employed as a necessary reiteration of recurring cultural properties not because they are mirror images of Central America but because of the peculiar discourse that stamps the region. Steven Pinker posits that "there are two likely habitats" for "where the meanings of words live." One of them "is the world, where we find the things that a word refers to. The other is in the head where we find the people's understanding of how a word may be used" (2007: 281). A physical world, Guatemala, walks alongside an individual's enunciated conjuration of Guatepeor. It remains to be said that there are individuals who loathe the expression, as evinced by the Guatemalan Facebook group, "yo tambien odio k digan vamos de Guatemala a guatepeor!!!"[13] ("I also hate that they say we're going from Guatemala to guatepeor!!!") Others insist that the name "Guatemala" be changed to

"Guatebella" because of the negative register of meanings in this adage (Valladares Molina, 2008). While drawing on this phraseology, I push for new Latino and Latina ideas and cultural reference points that speak to the realities and practices of Central Americans dwelling in what Oscar Hijuelos presents as the "United Stays" (2011: 3).

So let us briefly approach our first Guatepeorian panorama by leafing through Caryl Phillips's collection of essays, *The Atlantic Sound*, which trails the voyage the author and his parents took from Guadeloupe to England when he was four months old. While traveling on a banana boat, Phillips overhears the captain's navigational frustrations. To get to England, he must coast through one, or more, of the wretched—and in his professional life, inescapable—banal banana republics. The captain proclaims, "it's just another banana republic" in Costa Rica and "fucking banana republic" in Guatemala (2000: 10–12).[14] Under his gaze, there is a collective oneness that appears to be Central America. Yet in this figuration, the banana's "tropicality," paired with its signifier for the corrupt and unpromising Podunk places from which it sprouts, is left behind. But their misery continues to come up through that hackneyed maxim, reducing Guatemala and the rest of Central America to a repetitive reference of abject nothingness.[15]

Isthmian nothingness is hardly discarded literarily. It emerges in Latino and Latina literature as a measuring stick for disaster that also represents people as conditions. Esmeralda Santiago applies this precept for the challenges faced by the Puerto Rican diaspora. Her first memoir casts light on a common conceptual perception of Central America as a grave and anguished space. An epigraph to one of her autobiographical sketches announces, "*De Guatemala a guata-peor* [. . .] From Guatemala to guate-worse" (1993: 133).[16] Despite Santiago's incongruous use of "guata" and "guate," the cloying proverb is far from nebulous. It must draw on Guatemala to be able to function as a criterion for misfortunes. The parallels between Puerto Ricans and Guatemalans notwithstanding, the former have the prospect of leaving both the state of Guatemalan badness and Guatepeorianness. Puerto Ricans, after all, have not been sociohistorically constructed as Central Americans. The island has been a U.S. colony since the advent of the banana republics, and Puerto Ricans are U.S. citizens. Guatepeorianness for Puerto Ricans is discursively temporary, while Central Americans are doomed in Guatepeorianness. One must ask, what can Guatepeorianness ever positively contribute to Latinoness and Latinaness in its pessimistic, negative predicament?

De Guatemala a Guatepeor organizes an understanding of individuals that come from Central America. Extending the breadth of "guate-worse," we come across an official Guatepeor producing a figurative social "territory" and "community." Guatepeor, an index for the isthmus, is idiomatic and seemingly in stasis. Central America, as an amalgam of a repetitive banana republic, is frozen in time. If the U.S. South has been defined "as a national 'other,'" the "central" otherness of Latin America's other South, Central America, is evinced by its departure from U.S. Americanness, Latin Americanness, and the U.S. Latino and Latina triad (Gray, 2002: xvi).

Other scholars have reinscribed this debasing Guatepeorian state to Mexican migrants. It has been written that "for Mexicans to choose the United States, reversed the old Latin American saying, from *de Guatemala a guatepeor* (which, loosely translated, means to go from bad to worse) to *de guatepeor a Guatemala*" (J. Limón, 1998: 101). Things are so bad that Mexicans in the United States cease to be discursively Mexican. They become Guatemalan-like. Things are dreadful—mala Guate*mala* bad—but not as ruinous as they would be under Guatepeorianness, an ambivalent model more in line with the "worse-ness" of Guatemalans and Central Americans. Although Mexico becomes the metaphoric Guatemala, most significant is the afflicted state of Guatepeor. My capitalization of the word "Guatepeor" enhances a formally recognized state that symbolically supersedes Guatemala's meanings as a nation.

Why does this saying make so much sense in Latino and Latina literary creativity and intellectual production? And what might it mean if we drew on U.S. cities from the Global North as a site of insignificance? For instance, the American heartland hosts a small city in central Illinois and a town in central Arizona named "Peoria." People from these locales are known as "Peorians." The *Oxford English Dictionary* (*OED*) elaborates that "Peoria" is "a member of a North American Indian people constituting one of the autonomous groups forming the Illinois people." Peoria is also "the Algonquian language of the Peorias (applied both to the dialect of the Peoria band and to the Illinois language generically)." In terms of its everyday, American uses, Illinois's Peoria "has been proverbially regarded as the typical measure of U.S. cultural and intellectual standards at least since Ambrose Bierce (c. 1890)." Peoria has also functioned as "the butt of baseball player jokes (c. 1920–40, when it was part of the St. Louis Cardinals farm system) and popularized in the catchphrase 'It'll play in Peoria' (often negative), meaning 'the average American will approve,' which was popular in the Nixon White House (1969–74) but seems to suggest a vaudeville origin." On the whole, Peoria is the "embodiment of U.S. small city values and standards [which] include Dubuque, Iowa; Hoboken and Hackensack, N.J.; Oakland (Gertrude Stein: 'When you get there, there isn't any there there'), and Burbank, Calif., and the entire state of North Dakota" (Dictionary.com, n.d.). The "Guate" in Guatemala calls attention to quaint Central America and the "Peoria" of Guatepeorianness takes us to a U.S. rhetoric of geographic smallness and quaintness. Although Peoria is in the hegemonic Global North, it is still the "worst" that the U.S. terrain has to offer vis-à-vis its American ordinariness. The *OED* concisely summarizes Peoria as "any place (in the United States) inhabited by people with plain, down-to-earth, conventional tastes and attitudes." It is unavoidable to speculate, one might add, what a U.S. Central American in Peoria might be called, a Guatepeorian-Peorian?

Guatemala and Guatepeor share an operating system of meaning emphasizing unfavorable states for anyone who may or may not be Guatemalan. These de Guatemala a Guatepeor entailments may be attempts to articulate a common language that aims to capture the tensions of this "American" moment, while also speaking to a referential mode of Latino and Latina hardship, daily indignities, and disadvantage. But the manner in which Central Americanness is being brought up and written dictates a reevaluation. Given the rhetorical value of Guatepeor—one in which many Latinos and Latinas seem to have symbolically passed through—has this site-as-condition changed the subjectivation of a given Latino or Latina? Guatepeorianness inadvertently creates hierarchies that naturalize the presumed inevitable state of Central American calamitousness. Mala (bad) and peor (worse) may change in disagreeable, unsatisfactory, or injurious conditions. But the "Guate" prefix faithfully clings to the mapping of Guatemalan geopolitics. The inactive Central American Guate is, if another colloquial phrase may be permitted, the exclusive gift that keeps on giving to Guatemalans and, by extension, Central Americans: the unquestionable typification of Guatepeorianness.

What does Guatepeorianness look like? And what does the language of Guatepeorian read like? Observe these limners of dark brown Central

American figures and their emergence in the U.S. landscape. Dianne Walta Hart discloses that the physical traits of the Nicaraguan woman in her testimonial, *Undocumented in L.A.*, accentuate the "smallness of her hands and features. She is less than five feet tall with frizzy brown hair that frames her light brown face and a ruddy complexion" (1997: xxii). The nationality and unpleasant appearance of Hart's informant, whom she names Marta, hallmark a mismatched creature. Her light brown face is disproportionate to the reddish complexion. To picture Marta's endemic oddness is to see red: indigenous red skin or ideological red. Her superimposed redness paints a radical leftist in politics, unruly behavior, and the color of blood. Marta is an undesirable citizen from Guatepeor. Yet the undocumented Marta participates in the American everyday.

Marta resembles the "it-ness" of an animal or object introduced by Danzy Senna in *Symptomatic*. This fictional enterprise pens "Menchu" as a doppelgänger for Maya author and human rights activist, Rigoberta Menchú, who received the 1992 Nobel Peace Prize and Príncipe de Asturias de Cooperación Internacional award in 1998. But the region's accomplishments are sullied, diminutivized to their intrinsic feral Guatepeorian nature. Menchu — under this inscription, Menchú's last name lacks a diacritical mark on the "u" — can be extracted as a "poodle-monkey," a living thing "who doesn't like labels" (Senna, 2004: 102). *Symptomatic*'s narrator frugally reveals the reason for the canine-primate denotation: "([I]t was named after the Guatemalan peasant and memoirist Rigoberta Menchu)" (118). Marta's and Menchu's status of belonging is Guatepeorian or, even more incurable, Guatepeorianness: a region-specific, anthropoid diminutive — or demonym — for being almost lovable and fully pitiable. As a social condition, helpless Guatepeorianness embodies any Central American nation. Borrowing from Héctor Tobar, the Cold War Guatepeorian still image depicts "an innocent, provincial, friendly kind of face, the face of someone you feel sorry for because you know they're Guatemalan and thus gullible and luckless by definition, the whole host of things Guatemalans are famous for. *Una cara que da lástima*" (1998: 78).

Guatepeorianness divulges exaggerated webs of difference, as Patricia Engel demonstrates.[17] Her debut novel, *Vida*, describes a cornucopia of Latin American maids employed by a Colombian American family in New Jersey. But it is the recently arrived Guatemalan woman, Deisy — possessing "a mouth full of gold" and whose surprising dietary habits include the unsavory consumption of turtle eggs—that stands outside U.S. suburbia and acceptable Latino and Latina social relations (2010: 90). It goes without saying that my point is not to prove false or erroneous the possibility that a Central American may have gold teeth or unabashedly enjoy the frequent ingestion of turtle eggs. Rather, I seek to problematize the signifying practices and characteristics applied to "parvenus and numerically lesser immigrant Latin American populations" as they textually mingle with other U.S. Latinos and Latinas (R. Rodriguez, 2002: 109). What interests me is how Central American "difference" is managed and represented—how the unequal relations and statuses of U.S. Latinos and Latinas are "acclimated"—so that a cultural precept and politics surface at the expense of Central American outsiderness. It is no accident, for instance, that Deisy makes a deal with Sabina, her employers' daughter, to stop eating the endangered turtle eggs (Engel, 2010: 91). A particular and acceptable kind of Latino and Latina mode comes forth, a type of unifying solidarity where the Guatemalan other hangs on as othered. This otherness hints at the importance of Guatepeorianness: a conflicting ideology that still suggests their Latino and Latina dislocation. But if Guatepeorianness signals a specifically Central American form of Latin underdevelopment, it also codifies Latino and Latina proximity to a simultaneous present and up-and-coming "American" future.

The reader could arrive at a similar conclusion with Cristina García's Salvadoran character, Marta Claros, in *A Handbook to Luck*.[18] Her supposititious lifestyle proves irreconcilable with the customs of Los Angeles's more modern citizenry. Like Deisy, Marta is literarily personified through her obsession with eggs. She has a chicken coop in her backyard, even though such practice is "against city ordinances." She goes as far as sewing clothing for "her" eggs, leaving them on "plump pillows around the house." The third person narrator tells us that at least Marta Claros "didn't sleep with the chickens, the way her mother used to do. What did it matter that she'd bought them a crib and a baby blanket?" (2007: 138–39). Marta Claros's effigy provokes parallels with the informal saying, "to lay an egg," which is tantamount to being unsuccessful before an audience. As a Guatepeorian who lays questionable eggs, Marta Claros is an American failure within the text's performance.

Taken at face value, this "Guatepeorization" stretches to a "Central Americanization" of U.S. urban life with agrarian qualities.[19] Notice the nonfictional comments of Carmen Rivera, a Puerto Rican widowed mother of three sons referenced by De Genova and Ramos-Zayas. Rivera is aware of "the spatialized underpinnings of the racialized distinction between Puerto Ricans and Mexicans in Chicago." But the Windy City's South Side, which includes some of the largest concentrations of Mexicans, is "much poorer [with] lots of vacant buildings." Its indigence seems "like a bit of Central America in the city" (2003: 63). In this grassroots estimation from the bottom up, Puerto Ricans, as U.S. citizens, are entitled to live in an American space that does not contain traces of Central American poverty and underdevelopment. Rivera's assessment of destitution imputes a collective Guatepeorization mindful of Mexicans as they "populate" an impoverished Guatepeorianness whose backwardness essentially belongs in Central America.

This evocation of a certain type of a Latino and Latina collectivity—dependent on a flood of calamities—can be conceived as a Guatepeorian Latinidad for U.S. Central Americans. A Guatepeorian Latinidad punctuates what established U.S. Latinoness and Latinaness are not, for Guatepeorianness is consumed by the plight of undocumented Central American migrations. The compounding of the nation-state borders Central Americans have crossed to get to the United States arouse what De Genova and Ramos-Zayas identify as an "empathetic Latinidad" among other U.S. Latino and Latina groups (2003: 184). Despite this compassion, the Guatepeorian plight is inconsonant with those who classify or issue the empathetic Latinidad. What drives this empathetic Latinidad and what are the objectives of its affect? A Guatepeorian presence is far from therapeutic in the U.S. landscape. Guatepeorianness functions as a contemporary Latino and Latina mode of distanciation. Central Americans appear to enact un-Latinoness and un-Latinaness, one that is relatively analogous to the ideological un-Americanness precipitated by the Cold War.[20] Not unlike Cuban Americans, the 1980s great migration of Central Americans also occurred against the backdrop of the ideological struggle between communism versus capitalism (cf. A. García, 1997). And yet Central Americans have followed a deviating model from Cuban Americans, who received various forms of settlement assistance as well as immigration protection and legal status. The U.S. government and the media portrayed Cuban exiles from the 1960s and 1970s as people who shared American ideals in their unequivocal opposition to communism. By contrast, Central Americans were largely regarded as economic rather than political migrants.

This distinction turned them into undeserving of American protection and assistance within the United States.

Additional Latino and Latina groups like Dominicans could fall under this Cold War lens as well. Junot Díaz has revisited in *The Brief Wondrous Life of Oscar Wao* other forms of corresponding un-Americanness that modify Guatepeorianness by not merely outlining irreversible Guatemalan-like *mala* adversity. He invokes an embryonic process of "becoming" in the Global North: northern New Jersey. A Central American "ethnoracial marginalia" surfaces when the Dominican American protagonist encounters a Salvadoran "who was burned all over his face [. . .] and looked like the Phantom of the Opera" and an undocumented, pregnant Guatemalan hitchhiker (2007: 171, 198). These peripheral figures represent a gathering of inhabitants who have been affected by civil unrest in the Western Hemisphere, catastrophic moments that Díaz references as *fukú*. Described as "the Curse and the Doom of the New World" and "the Great American Doom," fukú applies to the Global South's externally "democratized" nations and the ensuing migrations to the United States from foreign intervention (4–5). These disfigured Cold War Americans — or, Americans of fukú descent — call attention to a different linguistic symbology of Latinoness and Latinaness that needs to be staged. Take note of how fukú distinctively features Cold War ideology and distress without bringing up the grimness of Guatepeor.

The retelling of this American way of life is an important point of U.S. Latino American and Central American–American intertwinement. It allows us to begin theorizing how recent Latino and Latina migrants are created and how they are constructed in literary unravelings of political events orienting readers toward an understanding of American social reality.[21] How to think about Latino and Latina conceptions of "self" as well as literary and theoretical endeavors struggling with hierarchically different southern signifiers and living beings?[22] In 1992 — the year of the quincentenary in the Americas and the year that also marked El Salvador's Peace Accords — the anthology *Iguana Dreams* noted that U.S. Latino and Latina literature "has many points of divergence."[23] The editors found that despite the diversity of Latino and Latina experiences, a central theme in these approaches is "the need for cultural survival," one that adverts to American assimilation and how "Latinos camouflage and adapt to new environments without losing their identity." The continuation of Latino and Latina existence sheds light on what this volume's compilers regarded as a collective preoccupation: "How much of our culture should we be willing to lose or suppress in order to participate in mainstream society" (Poey and Suarez, 1992: xvii–xviii)?

This canvass needs some modification. How are nonnormative ("new") Latino and Latina subjectivities incorporated in mainstream society and in the imperturbable deployment of the Latino and Latina triad? How do Latino and Latina groups—in the broad sense of these terms—survive? As audiences grasp Latino and Latina diversity through a "brown" homogeneity, Latino and Latina novelists become "cultural interpreter[s]" for white audiences (Augenbraum and Stavans, 1993: xvi). Latino and Latina literary approaches to this population's subgroups lead us to contemplate what is at stake when "ethnic insiders" access communities with a makeup similar to their own.[24] Are there any lettered implications to these speculative uses of Central Americans, possibly pointing at an oral, dark brown Indian population whose material basis as Guatepeorians needs to be penned by a Latino and Latina *American* literary culture?[25] I push more questions to the forefront of Latino and Latina literary identities: Can Central Americans be read—and move through Latino and Latina creative thought—without the particular sets of Guatepeorian constraints? How does a "Latino" or "Latina" individual become cognitively visible within Latinoness and Latinaness? We must be heedful to the subjects and themes that forge the directions Latino/a studies assumes now and in the future, supposing that such a category and paradigm continue.

Both Latino/a and Central American are sites under construction. Yet we must invariably question how we are carving up and consolidating a reassuringly comprehensive Latino being, one who constitutes an American personhood by holding up a dark mirror of erupting Central American differences. Central American imperceptibility passes through the circuits and range of vision of Latinoness and Latinaness. These crossings, however, are not yet viable in a Latino/a studies present. Achille Mbembe's observations on African power and subjectivity, as described in *On the Postcolony*, come to mind. "In this book," he writes, "the *subject* emerging, acting effectively, withdrawing, or being removed in the act and context of *displacement* refers to two things: first, to the forms of 'living in the concrete world,' then to the subjective forms that make possible any validation of its contents—that objectify it" (2001: 17). African ways of living, processes of emergence and withdrawal, in line with validation/invalidation and objectification, resonate with this union of Guatepeorian iconographies that draw up a picture of "our" present Latino and Latina moment. But Central American–Americanness stands before us in this contemporary Latino and Latina period too. It is a nascent diagram of incompatible Latino and Latina, U.S., and Latin-American discursive visibilities. And yet Central American–Americanness takes us to other visible facts, perspectives, and the shifting character of Latinoness, Latinaness, and Americanness in the Global South.

Getting an American-American Life

Néstor García Canclini heralded a global task in 2002: to locate Latin Americans in the world as these individuals look for a place in this disparate century. He spoke of Latin America's incompleteness induced by the region's mass migrations and transnational flows. "Latin America," García Canclini reported, "is not complete in Latin America. [. . .] Latin Americanness has come loose, overflowing its territory, drifting toward dispersed routes" (2002: 19–20).[26] His search for a Latin America without Latin America relates to the absence of what has become regionalized bodies lacking specific national problems in the Global North. But Latin America's current unfinished circumstances also signify the dispersal and spurring of Latin America–as–knowledge, or in García Canclini's categorical shorthand, "lo latinoamericano."

Looking for a place in this century, then, entails articulating a sense of self and place at this relatively emptied, de–Latin Americanized juncture. Still, García Canclini's look of inquiry conveys a strict vehicle for finding and expressing a Latin American epistemological space. It presupposes that the continental idea of America comprehensively moves along and segues with the homogenized Latin migrant. Latin Americanness becomes known upon crossing paths with the Global North. García Canclini's reading of Latin Americanness ostensibly relocates to places like the United States. But this hemispherist scope does not suggest a reciprocal way of looking at Latin Americans from U.S. Latino and Latina perspectives. To cite one working illustration, García Canclini does not direct attention to contemporary sociocultural and political processes that predate his dissemination of Latin unity as theoretical knowledge. As we have appraised, this epistemic approach can also be found in U.S. Latinidad, despite its discursive weaknesses and drawbacks. And yet Latino, Latina, and Latin-American mobility serves as a springboard for thinking about such matters as, From where is the next generation of Latinidad or Latin Americanness being engendered? If Latin America is being de-Latinized, are Latino and Latina migrants from the Global North, who return to the region for different reasons and circumstances, "re-Latinizing" it? Or, I should say, could these Latino and Latina bodies in action, new locals and translocals with returning gazes, be enabling a new rehearsal of "Latin-America"?

Far from instituting an inimical opposition of lo latinoamericano versus U.S. Latinidad (lo latino estadounidense), and at great distance from reproducing the common pool of resources bearing Latino- or Latin American–specific frames of reference alone, I examine the elided migratory margins within the constituents of a hemispherist "community" North and South. I am interested in how the Central American diaspora—and its attempts to produce theories and methodologies—fall under what Raewyn Connell (2007) calls "Southern Theory," as presented in this book's first chapter. Guatemalan novelist and critic Arturo Arias has initiated a wide-ranging discussion by pointing to the double deracination of Central Americans across the North/South divide in the Americas. His regional and repetitive unit, "Central American–American," conveys an identity-in-the making that is fomented by displacement and that has yet to arrive in the U.S. Latino and Latina world as well as in Latin-America. This not-so-subtle line of Central American difference—or nontransferable southern likelihood—is disproportionately noticeable: it is south of the U.S. North and South, Mexico, and such normative framings as "Latin America and the Caribbean." Central American–American is the embodiment of a bordered space in a given Global North and a Global South that exempts such geographies.

In view of the bidirectional "Latin" omission in Central America as well as its itinerant designation, Central American–American, I take a conjectural approach by confronting fundamental questions. As I enumerate focal points, my intention is not to pile up question upon question on the subject. I engage with what Edith Grossman describes as "the technique of query-as-response—a traditional, perhaps time-honored method of indicating the almost impenetrable difficulty of the subject" (2010: 5–6). So doing, my open-ended questions as methodology concentrate on how to theorize Latinoness, Latinaness, and Americanness through optics exceeding the ideological foundations of U.S. Americanness, South Americanness/Latin Americanness, and the Hispanic/Latino triad. These concerns reveal the impasse found in the fields that contain and promulgate the meaning of Latin and America: Latin American studies, Latino/a studies, and American studies. The interrogative voice utilized here interpretatively aims to employ interdisciplinarity to get somewhere, that is, to the representation of the "no-places" and the "nobodies" not yet known in discursive sites. It presents us with what artist Kara Walker might call a "continuity of conflict" in a conceptual approach that reinvestigates and reopens what we already think we know, Latinos and Latinas as well as Americanness in the United States (quoted in Halbreich, 2007: 2).

Through the rubric of the Global South and an inspection of how subject formation operates and is produced in multiple Souths, I work through the sources and foundations of knowledge for individuals who have not been fully integrated as Latin American or U.S. Latino and Latina. In the context of a denationalized Central America and subjects from the Global South, we might look into the following questions: How are "origins" and hemispheric belonging redirected when the "Latinness" and "Americanness" of Latinos and Latinas are dislodged and transported into such epistemologies and alterations as Central American–American? What does Global South studies have to offer that border studies, comparative ethnic studies, Latin American studies, and trans-American studies do not? Finally, what comparativist approaches open up due to the hyphenated American-American excess undercurrent in Central American–American, and what does it mean to live with a reiterative Americanness in the Global South?

Unraveling this American twinship and its incapacity to fully dwell in the normative Americas (North America/South America) activates a different future of Americanness that imparts un-Americanness across the Americas. This un-Americanness challenges previous lines of thought on hemispherism and U.S.-centrism. It suspends the elsewhereness of unsettled paradigms that turn "south to the future" (Hobson, 2002). Such intellectual pursuits force one to ask if there is a critical South for Central American–Americanness and if it holds a welcoming promise. "As an open-ended and inclusive category," Matthew Sparke contends, the Global South is not "a fixed territory or geostrategic bloc, but rather a congeries of human geographies that are place-specific and space-making in the face of devastating and far from flattening resources" (2007: 123). Despite the persistence of Americanness, Central American–Americanness is not fixed. Its inward-turned southwardness demands fluctuations in assorted worlds lacking exactitude and rearranging regional and national ways of being, thinking, and living. The Global South affords Central American–Americanness an entryway into this analytic milestone with ever-expanding conversations and political memberships taking on America in a myriad of articulatory forms. In its struggles for getting its own American life, an insistent American-Americanness teases out the Latin American, U.S. Latinidad, and American axis.

I weave a theoretical discussion on the uncertainties conveyed in—and the ambivalent exchange between—Latino/a and Central American-American. These terms exhibit new linguistic fluencies in Latino/a studies and its subgroups. The abridged, identificatory language of "Latino/a studies" indicates that there are subjects standing out of place, alienated from the representative but too precarious ethnoracial signifier Latino and Latina. The track I take brings out what is glossed over in the day-by-day practice of Latino/a studies: from its naming and what is customarily read as its only discursive hegemony (viz. the ethnoracial Latino/a triad) to the function of emergent Latino and Latina lives. The situatedness and modi operandi of Latino/a studies are changing and so is the shifting location (and the naming of an) individual from the Global South. The constitutive elements of Central American–American stage how "multitasking" selfhoods navigate and exceed the current operating connotations of Latino and Latina.

Central American–Americanness becomes an important raison d'être into Latino/a studies, altering the field's directions in the Global South. Central American–American is contiguous to the theories framing the metatext of Latinidad. It is in relation to—and outside the articulatory foundations of—Latinidad, after all, that Central American–Americanness emanates. While Central American–American suggests Latino and Latina as an unattainable state, it also interrogates the presumed stability of Latinoness and Latinaness. Arias's optic allows for "a theoretical space for those dispersed faces of 'otherness' that do not fit within the validated limits of Latin Americanidad or the recognized marginality of the United States" (2003: 170). He acknowledges that Central American–American is "an awkward linguistic oddity, in relation to other U.S. Latino groups" and to other U.S. ethnicities, since Central American–American is a pioneering configuration in the twenty-first century. As of this writing, there are no other ethnoracial models in ethnic studies, American studies, Latin American studies, and Latino/a studies that accentuate reiterative modes of American-American excess to underscore a triumvirate U.S. (American), regional (Central and Latin American), and panethnic (U.S. Latino and Latina) disenfranchisement. Certainly the "double alienness" that Arias configures for transnational Central American gangs applies here (2007: 182).[27] Central American–American is so strange—and estranged—that its insistent claims of American-Americanness seem unbelievable. The credibility adjoined to this American-American incredibility references the sundry kinds of borders Central Americans have crossed to arrive and live in the United States. Central American–Americanness marks the concurrent flows of transnational migration and deportations writing and dividing—in effect, hyphenating and compounding—U.S. American alienation in more than one American setting. Reorienting the boundaries of U.S. Americanness, Latin Americanness, and U.S. Latinoness and Latinaness, Central American–Americanness adjusts to interactive American-Americanness. "As a compression of time and space," this American variant imparts "the *moving* ground between the Americas" and within them (Zilberg, 2007: 493).

Central American–American—with its recurrent but disconnected American twinship—impels subjects to put life into words outside that embodied oddity of what Rubén Darío called, in a *modernista* context, a literary grouping of "los raros" (2005: 400–415).[28] Central Americans as Latino and Latina misfits are not so peculiar when one sorts out the unusual spaces from which the manifold meanings of Central America begin. Some Central American nationalities like Salvadoran fluctuate as less than meticulous references when they turn to such distortions as San Salvadorian or Salvadorian/Salvadorean (with or without the capitalized article "El"). This idiosyncrasy is not unique when evoking a nationality that is unknown or about to be known, like "Porta Ricans" at the turn of the twentieth century and the recent axiomatic summoning of "Columbians" and "Dominican Republicans." Stultifying representations of Central Americans prove as incisive as Central American absence. Between states of becoming and translating into something else, like Guatepeorian, El Salvadorian, or inhabiting an Americanness so undexterous it might as well be called "Central Americanian," Central American–American proposes Latino and Latina as a comparative possibility. Even though there is vagueness to what comprises Latino and Latina subjects, these labels do not have a nebulous reference, academically speaking, in connection to such groups as Chicano and Chicana, Cuban American, and Puerto Rican. Central American–American consequently advances as "an anadiplosis that sounds more like a redundancy, a radically disfigured projection of what 'Latin Americanness' has been assumed to be" (Arias, 2003: 171).

The oddity is the redundancy in the deployment of Central American–American, a perplexing riddle in North America, since it deviates from former president Reagan's interventionist stance that "Central America is America."[29] Central America becomes Central America–America, that which has not been known or geohistorically occupied. Arias's exegesis is worth consulting. The term is a "dissonance" operating as

> a "performative contradidiction" that opens up the possibility for recognition of this as-yet-unnamed segment of the U.S. population. [T]he clumsiness of the sound itself, "Central American–American," underlines the fact that it is an identity which is not one, since it cannot be designated univocally as "Latino" or as "Latin American," but is outside those two signifiers from the very start. It is not quite life on the hyphen as [Gustavo] Pérez Firmat (1994) put it, but more like life off the hyphen, as Juan Flores (2001) asserted in a different sense. Not off the hyphen because these people already inhabit a world that is a montage of cultures, a hybridity so advanced that it has already conformed to a new subjectivity. Rather, they are off the hyphen because they are on the murky margins, not even on the Anglo, North American or South American center: it is life on the margins of those hyphenated others (Cuban-Americans, Mexican-Americans). It is a population that has not earned the hyphen to mark its recognition, its level of assimilation and integration, within the multicultural landscape of the United States. (2003: 171)

Latino or Latina is composed of an unseen, internal hyphenation status. The representational hyphen extends only to groups that have been "seen," historically, "here." Arias's repetition corresponds to marginal versions of America in relation to normative America and the Americas "of color" that are far from murky. Central American–American is an articulation that can transpire "anywhere" due to its U.S. Latino, Latina, and Latin-American ungroundedness. It is regenerated through displacement, and not necessarily from one's compatibility—or incompatibility—with the United States or a Central American nation.

Central American–Americanness is precedently marked, without explicitly being designated as such, by José Luis Falconi and José Antonio Mazzotti's "Other Latino" status.[30] It denotes "new Latin American migrants" outside the scope of the traditionally defined Latino groups: Cuban Americans, Puerto Ricans, and Mexican Americans. The descriptive term includes "three of the most significant sectors within the recent wave of other Latin American migration: Central Americans, Andeans, and Brazilians" (2007: 1–4). Despite the categorical intervention, the necessity behind this conjectural inauguration becomes slippery. Falconi and Mazzotti note that their employment of Latino is informed by an earlier construction of this umbrella label, where "the Latino Population of the United States is a highly heterogenous population that defies easy generalization. . . . We have opted for the broadest, most inclusive, and most generous definition: that segment of the U.S. population that traces its descent to the Spanish speaking, Caribbean, and Latin American worlds." But if Latino ultimately encompasses "all those of Spanish and Latin American origin living within the United States, including peoples of Mexican descent born in the United States and all Spanish and Latin American immigrants and their descendants," why replace the spacious category with an otherizing, alternate group of "marginal" peoples who are presently involved in one aspect or another with Latino and Latina life (6)?

Falconi and Mazzotti's anthology is an invaluable contribution to Latino/a studies. But the Other Latino designation reads rather linearly and in an absolute form. It lacks any kinds of cultural passages and dialogues with "dominant" Latino and Latina groups. Falconi and Mazzotti remark that "there is no guarantee that all the different communities of people of Spanish and Latin American descent that live in this country will some day share a new, singular, hybrid Latino identity, nor that many would desire such an outcome" (2007: 6). But there is no assurance that Other Latinos desire such a qualifier either. Latino and Latina, as exercised by Cuban Americans, Puerto Ricans, and Mexican Americans, have been a foundation for the ever-unfolding Latino and Latina project, since not one of these groups alone has exclusively represented Latinoness and Latinaness. They have concretized, instead, the decisive meanings and local geographies of Cuban Americanness (e.g., Miami and Union City, New Jersey), Puerto Ricanness and Nuyoricanness (e.g., New

York, Chicago, and Philadelphia), and Mexican Americanness/Chicanoness (e.g., the U.S. Southwest).

Although I list Other Latino as a rubric for "secondary" U.S. Central American migrations, it is productive to labor through the meanings of Latino and Latina within the makings and historical demographics of what the editors refer to as "the most established groups in the United States" (Falconi and Mazzotti, 2007: 1). Falconi and Mazzotti acknowledge Latino and Latina heterogeneity. I am cautious, however, about the ways in which Central and South Americans are constellated as a subcategory of otherness to challenge the Latino and Latina discursive space. Central and South American are not symmetrical in their U.S. sociopolitical, cultural, and historical visibility as well as Latin American standing. I by no means apply a "hierarchical invisibility." I interrogate the reasons Latinoness and Latinaness are further otherized and quantified with another umbrella term highlighting distinctiveness from an antecedently "subalternized" category. Latino and Latina constituents need to be reworked not so much by adding more nationalities and regions as aggregate otherizations. Latino, as a category constantly in flux, is a project with no established origins. Before the "established" groups of Mexican-American/Chicano/a, Puerto Rican, and Cuban American enter the dominant U.S. space as "Latino" and "Latina," these groups "exist" through their own ethnoracial particularities and U.S. histories. Latino and Latina come to "be" when the category is articulated in spheres that exceed their nationalist specificity, especially when one's ethnicity or nationality is used as a generic beginning for comparative Latino and Latina possibilities. One specific ethnoracial group alone does not make it "Latino," though its "being" resonates or emulates "Latinness."

Other Latinos overlook the nuances inherent in articulations of Latinidad. Latinidad ought not necessarily be marked through Mexican American, Puerto Rican, and Cuban American. Latinoness and Latinaness are an articulation that necessitates further explanations that capture how one enters this category and why. Is one "naturally" a Latino or Latina, or is it a process of "becoming" through globalized southern and northern locations? Other Latinos, like current U.S. Latinos and Latinas, are imagined as Central and South American aggregates to brown. It is a brownness that is not revamped and that does not cross any ethnoracial borders that attend to divergent forms of the national. How is an Other (U.S.) Latino, vis-à-vis un-Latinoness and un-Americanness, produced? An undisputable dark brown indigenousness could very well be its definitive Central American marker. But more than another form of Latinoness and Latinaness, another type of Central Americanness is emphasized, another neglected un-Latino/Latino simultaneity whose "presencing" has yet to be localized. And, to be sure, that has yet to be fully mobilized in our critical practices and their political implications.

Central American–American anticipates multidirectional processes of Latinities. Such Latinities are joined by multiple semiotics that do not necessarily warrant a hyphen. The three tags of the mutable "Peru Anas," as shown in the photographs — visualized biographical moments in a trio of takes — illuminate this point of becoming a denationalized something else. These Peru Anas splinter and have yet to have categorical language within Latinidad, the United States, and Latin-American spaces. They engulf themselves in the rich parenthetical fringes that are passing by and uncontainable in this articulated U.S. Latino and Latina moment.

The anecdotal Peru Anas, scattered throughout New York City's East Village, are — and are not — from Peru in referential terms. The blank between the first name, Peru, and the last name, Ana (the "same" applies for the "other" Peru Ana that is Ana Peru) is intentional. Its incursion points to versatile but reflecting "Peruvian" configurations that are paradoxically denationalized and renationalized. Peru Ana's and Ana Peru's uncommissioned visual gives rise to our nimble circumstance in the Global South. In their destinationless state, Peru Ana's and Ana Peru's unauthorized public art and unsolicited selfhoods loop and litter the city, challenging notions of vandalism and the public good. Yet they equip us with a determined destination: a public space marking a scrawled being in the populous first world metropole.[31] Ostensibly legible with its capitalized letters, the individualized doubleness of Peru Ana and Ana Peru goes beyond penmanship. Peru Ana–cum–Ana Peru is part of the city's text. The tags are an extension of renamed skyscrapers and street corners with infinite names whose stories are being fleetingly penciled in. The urban patina of Latino and Latina is tarnished with other spontaneous and unmediated compounds. These preliminary sketches turn unsettled "Peruvianness" upside down, setting forth a southern assemblage with motley openings and origins.

Paula Moya has asked a central question that assists and gives important form to this study. "Will there come a point," she inquires, "where we will

DISORIENTING LATINITIES 147

Peru Ana/Ana Peru tags in New York City's East Village. Photos by Frank Augustine. Used by permission of the photographer.

see ourselves primarily as 'Latina,' and secondarily if at all, as 'Chicana,' or 'Puerto Rican,' or 'Cubana'?" (2003: 249). In the general context of one of the most commonly studied ethnoracial groups in Latino/a studies, Moya's solicitude makes sense. I wonder, however, on the congruous inclusion, with a handful of literary exceptions, of Cuban Americans to the study of Latino and Latina lives, identifications, and experiences. Unlike Chicano/a studies and Puerto Rican studies, for example, there is no program or department for Cuban American studies.[32] Another fitting question might be, how does Cuban American exclusion take us to unstable, but recalibrated, directions in the evolving project of Latino/a studies and its challenges? And yet as someone who grew up in the United States, away from my country of birth (El Salvador), and learned to theorize my sense of being and belonging in the U.S. social sphere through Chicananess, my response to Moya's query is, yes.[33] In my U.S. Latina formulation, Salvadoranness, as expressed and theorized in "distant" El Salvador, is an abstraction, as is the "reserved" state of Latinoness and Latinaness. But these unfolding Latinoness and Latinaness have more merit and relevance for me, since this is the space in which I was cast as an ethnoracial other and framed in a different national voice. Latinaness is, conflictingly, where I "unbelong" and where I attempt to find ways of belonging. Central American–Americanness bears importance because it questions these comparable yet incompatible—"irreconcilable," as Du Bois would put it—ways that as, Peru Ana and Ana Peru show, multiply in a Global North. Central American–American pronounces the liminalities that dominant accounts of Latinoness and Latinaness must extricate to theoretically build on Latino and Latina fragmentation.[34]

In the spirit of exercising a dynamic existence, we can cobble through these preoccupations: How to treat and reassemble Latino/a studies in light of the multitudinous subjects and geographies that impart such a project? What generates Latino culture? What *moves* it? Lastly, what might a Latino map look like through the global presencing of voluminous Latino and Latina communities? Although I bring up Central Americanness, I am aware that there are oversights within the isthmus and that much like U.S. Latinoness and Latinaness, its imaginaries and discourse also resonate with "brownness." I propose, however, that Central American–American attends to Central Americanness as a site of neglected multiple subjectivities and geographies that move and alter. In this regard, the standing of problematic blackness and indigenousness in Central America can be adjoined to Central American–American identities-in-the-making. Many Mayas in the 2000 U.S. Census were, in all likelihood, counted as "Hispanics." They were grouped, as Marilyn Moors conjectures, "with other Guatemalan, Mexican, and Central and South American migrants" (2000: 228). Curiously, Moors's nationalities and regions enter a kind of non-Maya Latin American formation in an equalizing manner. One might ask, To what extent does the "Hispanization" of Mayas categorically provide a governmental symbol that embarks on a process of indigenizing the presumed whiteness of the Hispanic category? Does the seeming uncrossability of Maya "Central Americanness" cross over the realm of Central American–Americanness?

A look at the diasporic locations of both Central American indigenousness and blackness would open new sources in—as well as illustrate the limits of—the current Latino and Latina imagination. Sarah England reminds us that Garifunas, also known as "Black Caribs" in the coasts of Belize, Guatemala, Honduras, and Nicaragua, have been more affiliated to the Caribbean than to Central America's interior (2006: 1–2). England finds that Garifuna men began a U.S. process of migration in the 1940s. They worked as merchant marines, whereas Garifuna women, whose migration can be traced to the 1960s, were employed as nannies and home attendants. Yet Garifunas are "present but invisible"; they have a "degree of invisibility" that England dubs "racial camouflaging" in African American and Latino encounters (2009–10: 33).

Given their "propensity to live in African-American neighborhoods," Garifunas "are camouflaged to the general population, including other Latinos" (England, 2009–10: 35). This "art of racial camouflaging," as England sees it, allows Garifunas to "remain under the radar of ethnic/racial stereotyping" (46). England spells out, for instance, Garifuna strategies when dealing with the police. "In this context," she elucidates, "they know that most police will racialize them as African-Americans until they hear them speak and therefore they will be subject to the same racist treatment. Thus in relations with police it is better to be Latino. But on the other hand they also know that to be racialized as Latino has its risks as well, namely being the target of crime and being seen as immigrants, most likely undocumented. In this context the best strategy is to speak Garifuna, which sounds to most people like an African language (even though it is actually Island Carib)" (47). Garifunas are at the interstices of such categories as Central American, Latino and Latina, and African American. Will the presumed African Americanness of these Central American groups be localized within the theoretical directions and dimensions that mark Central American–Americanness: unnameability, invisibility, awkwardness, and off-the-hyphen status? Can the discursive dark brownness of Central Americans in Latino/a studies be analytically joined with the discursive blackening of "other" Central Americans in the isthmus? The semiotic chain of belonging proves abundantly ridden with discrepant elements and formulas: black and indigenous Central Americanness is to Central America what Central American is — as a site with simply too much Guatepeorianness — to U.S. Latinoness, Latinaness, and Latin-Americanness.

Yet as a performed displacement, Central American–American imparts the outcome of invisibility. It calls for Central Americans to begin producing equitable terrains within the nuanced and tense makings of the Latino, Latina, Latin American, and U.S. American triangulation. The critical challenge remains to study how Central American–American "un-hyphenated hyphenation" tags along and molds itself with Mexican-American hyphenation, as it has been mapped, mainly, in Chicana writing (cf. Viramontes, 1985; G. Limón, 1993; D. Martínez, 1994; Benítez, 1998, 2002; Castillo, 2005b).[35] Despite their off-the-hyphen status, Central Americans have been parenthetically integrated into the Chicano/a canon.[36] Through the internal incorporation of Central American–Americans within Latinoness, how are Chicano and Chicana cultural and political specificities complemented and amplified by other Latino and Latina groups? Since Central American cultural workers are not relaxing on the hyphen, as it were, how do other Latinos and Latinas localize and impart the American excess of Central American–American?

From this Central American "silence" and Central American–American emendation, we find omissions speaking to how we can expand margin-to-margin dialogues, as there are many more Guatepeorians, Peru Anas, Americ Anas, and, as Junot Díaz hails them, "*Dominicanis*" to discursively come. Just as the Global South is an undefined but active terrain that is in-the-making, so are the disorienting Central American–American subjects who are transforming an unfolding and associative version of Latinoness and Latinaness. Central American–American veers toward the fissures and gaps inherent in Latino and Latina "southern" living. It also promotes the critical reflection and ongoing mapping of Latino and Latina subjectivities ceasing to be rhetorically submerged in the oddest ways.

EPILOGUE

> We all know what happened next. The @ became a
> supernova of the digital age and part of our daily lives.
> — ALICE RAWSTHORN (2010)

Latining America: Black-Brown Passages and the Coloring of Latino/a Studies has endeavored through the economies of blackness, brownness, and dark brownness. These colorings have marked the necessity for an au courant set of questions and language, as these interrelated Latinities have resonances within and beyond Latino, Latina, and African American domains. Latinoness, Latinaness, and African Americanness are not for "members of the club" only. Their residues and sojourns provide a critical energy for new articulations, signs, color lines, and assemblages of bodies that pass through the apodictic character of U.S. Latino and Latina brownness and dark brownness as well as U.S. African American blackness. Through Latinities, this monograph worked toward a distinct paradigm for Latino/a studies, one that continually seeks to make meaning out of Latino and Latina deletions and oversights. Latinoness, Latinaness, and Latin-Americanness are being positioned and repositioned differently, particularly through the mobility of subjects as well as these categorical designations. And so I conclude not with a complete Latino and Latina picture. My closing observations are put in an open-ended way that is receptive to the incertitude of Latin@ — Latin-*at*, let us call it — futures. But this Latin@ hereafter is not as far down the road as we might think. It is living here and now.

Perhaps no contemporary cultural production encapsulates the vagueness and instability of Latino and Latina futurity better than Nickelodeon's animated television series, *Dora the Explorer*.[1] Much like its Public Broadcasting Service (PBS) predecessor, *Where in the World Is Carmen Sandiego?*, *Dora* familiarizes children with language, geography, history, and global cultures.[2] My course here is not to analytically rehearse how "Nick" gets U.S. Latinidad wrong through this cable show because the character is a corporate construction and worldwide commodity that enacts the market's perceptions about Latinos and Latinas.[3] Instead, I want to rethink Dora Márquez, the protagonist whose surname is an homage to Gabriel García Márquez, as a developing *idea* that harbors Latino and Latina entanglements and out-of-placeness. Latinos and Latinas are a Latin surplus of transitory action and mutability, reflecting new worlds and discoveries outside the Latin milieu of Latin America. Dora is at the cusp of old and new worlds. Like Latinos and Latinas, Dora, the Latin@ explorer who is exploring the globe, is an embryonic reflection of what up-and-coming Latinoness and Latinaness entail. She presents an active world of passages, where her Latin-*at*-ness (Latin@ness) has to be located in different forms and with new peer groups along the way. Dora's national composition is vague, as her deracination ought to be. The issue is not what type of Latina Dora is (as in where she is from) but rather, as Paul Gilroy would say, where she is *at* (1991).[4] As an animated figure, is Dora a "real" Latina or a signifier of indefiniteness and obscurity of what, in effect, Latinness in the United States fundamentally encompasses?

Thus, my question is about not only where the mercurial Dora is but also where do we conclusively find Latinos and Latinas? Semiotically, perhaps the closest yet unintended written Latinity I have seen—one that is, in many cases, facilely inserted within Latino/a studies to signify gender inclusion—is the collective, millennial-friendly moniker "Latin@" and its nascent ilk: Chican@, mestiz@, and Afro-Latin@.[5] Contemporary uses of Latin@ can be assessed through a number of published endeavors evoking these terms. Witness, as examples, Sandra Soto's *Reading Chican@ Like a Queer: The De-Mastery of Desire* (2010); the edited volumes *The Afro-Latin@ Reader: History and Culture in the United States* (Jiménez Román and Flores, 2010); *Latin@s in the World System: Decolonization Struggles in the 21st Century U.S. Empire* (Grosfoguel, Maldonado-Torres, and Saldívar, 2005); and Damián Baca's *Mestiz@ Scripts, Digital Migrations, and the Territories of Writing* (2008). When I first encountered this cryptic term, I found it unbecoming and too digital in its stylistic awkwardness and stuttering unpronounceability. Latin@ also seemed poorly suggestive of a networked social space that duplicated the real world's Latinidad to cyberspace, albeit with the same Latino/a tendencies involving a homogenous brown identification and established group hierarchies.

But the "at," or the approximation sign behind Latin@—Latin-at—pushed me to seriously interrogate where the Latins were really *at* in U.S. Latinoness and Latinaness and in other ambits.⁶ I initially deliberated if there were actual beings behind that symbol and waited, with bated breath, for a Latin@ movement with subjects politically claiming *Latin@ rights*, Latin-*at*-ness, or such Latinities as the ones attended to herewith. The working parameters of *Latining America* have pushed me to revisit and reappraise my initial impressions. Latin@, I would now like to proffer, inadvertently keys into my aims, submitting Latin as the bodily and cultural space of the "at." To rephrase: the Latin behind Latin@ stands for a three-dimensional space where the @—at—is being activated in a myriad of ways in our daily lives. Latin@ can also exercise, to make use of Antonio Viego's insight, a resignification of "temporality, not just race and ethnicity; it should affect how we will tell the time and the history of the Americas in the future" (2007: 121).⁷

Not unlike the perplexing presence of Latinos and Latinas in the United States, "No one knows for sure" when the @ "first appeared," as the *New York Times* reports. The @'s origins are equally nebulous (Rawsthorn, 2010). But my evocation of Latin at-ness is not about flexible, interminable movement or the quest for authentic roots. Neither is it about Nick's little bibliophage, Dora; her best friend, Boots; and her talking backpack, unfailingly luring us into her worldly plans with the travel song, "Come on, vámonos. Everybody let's go." Dora is certainly a starting point for the American conflation of Latin-America and the massive cornucopia of Latin@s (Latin-ats). The looseness of Dora's worldly minded "@-ness" allows us to see imperfections and contradictions beyond Nickelodeon's conjuration. The topic for debate is not so much how the network profits from Dora merchandise. What is at issue is the exploration of the hidden stories of Latinoness and Latinaness and how their forgotten lives must come into play within the playful theming of Dora.

Seen from Izel Vargas's iconological approach, the scattered pieces of this Latin@ness fall under the *Business of Illusion* (2008), as his painting's title emblematizes. The mixed media collage invites purposeful queries: What are the costs of accessing such illusions in the Global North? And who pays for

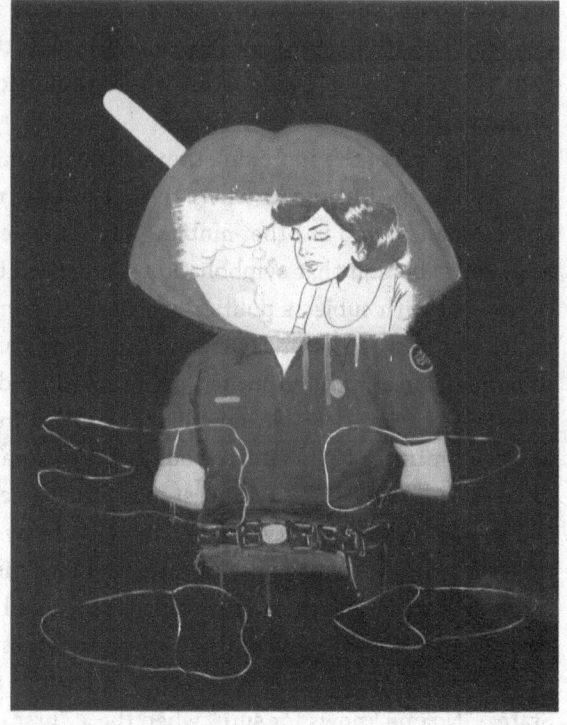

Izel Vargas, *Business of Illusion* (2008). Photo by Benjamin Berry. Used by permission of the artist and photographer.

these costs? The pop iconography advancing Vargas's composition is commanding in its palimpsestic palate. His visual art portrays mundane manifestations of life, physical vulnerability, and cultural consumption: a Dora popsicle, a comic book/graphic novel snapshot, an armless border patrol agent, coyote/teeth/walking tracks, and a black backdrop somberly taking us to what exiled Cuban writer Zoé Valdés so keenly attempted to capture under the literary heading *El dolor del dólar* (The Pain of the Dollar).[8] What might this pain in dolorous dollars be under this gendered representation? The asymmetrical "partnership" between developed nation and underdeveloped migrant is produced by three different experiences of ensnared, or even cornered, "realities": innocence (i.e., Dora), fantasy (i.e., a pop nugget somewhat akin to a *fotonovela* image), and cruelty of civil society (i.e., border patrol agent). They signal selfhoods demarcated by capitalism. Unfulfilled childhoods and adulthoods become the price and pain of personal progress. This dollarized price plays out every industrialized moment of our lives.

Yet it is the seeming omission of violence that grabs one's attention, exposed through torn, bloodied arms. How were the Customs and Border Protection officer's arms cut off? This unexplained affliction also infers social trauma, physical force and laws that limit crossings, and the illusion of almost being. CBP's guardian of American borders meets head-on with embajaDora, a new envoy confronting and negotiating the U.S. American @-ness that eludes so many Latinos and Latinas.[9] This Dora has a covered but mobile face. She accords Latinos and Latinas the multisited @s and Latin dispersals that are already upon us. Vargas's accredited agent, embajaDora, moves imperfectly and dolorously in the existential sense. But the artist's lens allows us to be moved by this Dora that may one day decompose too, since popsicles, after all, dissolve. The public body of the Vargasian Dora follows a different script than Nick's inner workings of her @-ness in the world. The plurality and multidimensionality of embajaDora go where Nickelodeon's "perfect" Latina is not supposed to travel. She is the restless spirit of Latin@ effusion of people making mobile "homes" of belonging through the circulation of ideas, different geographies, and new social contexts.

If we care to look at things differently, we may take up the substratum of Dora and the possibilities of the @ in Latino and Latina daily lives. They direct us on how to think about where Latino/a discourse is *at* as well as how to dwell in the scholarly terrain currently dubbed "Latino/a studies." Latino/a studies in the U.S. Global South augments the struggles of naming and narration. The observant reader may have heard so far a consistent (and inconsistent) phraseology in my referencing throughout this project of the umbrella panethnic terms—or the rugged and ubiquitous panorama of the unequal articulatory balance of—Latino and Latina, Latino/a, Latin@, and Other Latino. Each September, during Hispanic Heritage Month, an array of articles surfaces in the popular press about which U.S. ethnoracial term is the most appropriate to use: Hispanic or Latino. The divergence in these labels is so great that even Wikipedia has a cursory entry about the "Hispanic/Latino naming dispute." I will refrain from contributing my proverbial two cents to the endless flow of processual explanations found in this tireless debate seeking a solidifying truth about—and yet another standardization for—who "those" people are. I briefly allude to it because as these pages come to a close, we must take to task the discursive form that Latinos and

Latinas acquire within academic inquiries framed under what is being called either Latino/a — or Latina/o — studies.

I am interested in how the field calls and accounts for its @-ness through the rubric of the slash found — and the new world conveyed — in Latina/o or Latino/a.[10] As unfolding in the U.S. academy, the term Latino/a breaks with the public and political tradition of the Hispanic/Latino split. The general story of how Latino and Latina is being mapped and theorized within Latino/a studies is forming a new space, a distinct subject, a "Latino/a" that moves differently than the previous Hispanic or Latino characterizations. Throughout *Latining America*, my enunciation of Latino and Latina attempts to point to the labor of attending to the complexities of both gendered categories and experiences. My use of Latinos *and* Latinas strives to show how they are historically inhabited and how they negotiate spaces for a collective cause or singularity. In this manner, I remove the elision of the semiotic slash of Latino/a and shift to the labor signified by the constant practice of the conjunction and — bringing the ardor, agony, and perseverance of theoretical emancipatory work to the fore. I put forth the qualifier Latino and Latina when I refer to individuals and apply Latino/a studies when citing the academic field and its articulation of Latinos/as.

Still, a theoretical undertaking of the topos and praxis of the *meaning* of the slash has been relatively missing in Latino/a studies. I bring it up because I find it compelling as an occupant of the *Latina* space to know not so much *what* to call myself within this political membership but also *how* to call myself. It is imperative to grapple with how to pronounce a cultural and analytic term advancing a scholarly field that also looks unreadable in written form: Latino/a. Let me be clear. I do not turn against the use of Latino/a. I am fully cognizant of the pressing necessity of the ethical inclusion of gender and of the emergence of denominations like Latino/a, Chicano/a, and mestizo/a.[11] But it is important to critically evaluate what is actually included or omitted through the slash — or the process of "o/a-ness." Consult the various essays in Latino/a and Chicano/a readers. There is a body of scholarship that includes these very terms, but that does not give careful and sustained attention to gender analysis. The result is the reification of a Latino subjectivity that often leaves masculinity unquestioned, but what happened to the expressive and relational "a" in Latino/*a*? Latina, as a category and mode of experience, is erased, and the gendering process of the Latino male is not considered either. In all likelihood, a reader who wishes to learn and peruse more about *Latinas* will have to turn to a Latin*a* reader. We paradoxically return to the name "Latino" and the "unknowing" of Latinas — even as Latino/a-ness is evoked.

The ostensibly equitable inclusion of gendered Latino and Latina bodies appears, on the surface, to resolve the other discursive erasures and marginalizations of Latino/a studies. To understand the possibilities, transiency, and routes of Latinoness and Latinaness, one needs to labor through the signification of Latino/a studies and where it is (or is not) going. The realm of language raises some significant propositions with serious implications concerning the idea of Latino and Latina authenticity. If the common historical background of Latinos and Latinas is channeled and contained within the parameters of "Latino/a," we must also reflect on its cognitive function. It is rare to come across, programmatically speaking, gender-inclusive names of institutional departments in the United States akin to the designative purpose of the "Latino/a" in Latino/a studies. To illustrate: official departmental qualifiers, in English, like "African American men and women's studies" or "history and herstory" are uncommon. I turn to these descriptors because they suggest a tension in what is becoming a canonical institutional vocabulary for the status of subjects whose being, although written in equivalizing slashes, provides an enunciatory challenge insofar as such words and subjects do not exist. A Latina would call herself as such, not "Latino/a." Latino/a is disembodied. The term pushes the slashed identities toward ideological terrains that render these Latino/a "bodies" as dislocatable and unmappable to both the U.S. and Latin American landscape. This compressed structuring of Latino and Latina reveals itself as antithetical to the Latino/a project.

We are witnessing the birth of cross-cultural, worldly Latin@ subjects that are constantly and unevenly in flux. Latino/a is at the interstices of national and continental distress. Latin@s allow for new mappings — Latinities — that are not always cohesive and that are oftentimes blurred. There is more than one Latin representation and Latinness at work. Latin@ness repeatedly calls additional Latins in Latined patterns and locations, disrupting the brown borders of Latinidad. The @ engendering Latinness, coupled with a sustained interrogation of the unnamable or linguistically clumsy paths Latinos and Latinas are taking, form part of my vision for molding the new directions of Latino/a studies in the Global South. Equally important, too, is a query about what to do with slashes, *at* signs, and degrees of otherness within a rigid ethnoracial classification, especially as a multitude of Latins pass through it.

Latino/a studies in the Global South is coming into being in fragmented and, at times, unpronounceable forms. The slash, the *at*, and the *this* and *that* of the other demonstrate that this is a field that is in-the-making, much like the Latino and Latina subject that is not fixed or settled. We must acknowledge this, and as the @ in Latin*at* invites, we must not be paralyzed by it. Slashes and *at* signs are far from trivial. These symbols communicate a genealogical trajectory of the field — an intellectual history. They should be treated as spaces of inquiry, possibility, and reconfiguration. The @, above all, is a Latin router, haltingly enunciating yet transporting us to a panoply of fragmented Latined lives.

NOTES

INTRODUCTION. The Copiousness of Latin

1. An explanation is in order for how the categories "U.S. African American" and "Latinos and Latinas" are being referenced in this enterprise. In summoning "U.S. African American," I follow Ifeoma Nwankwo's exercising of the term. She explains her use of this nomenclature: "U.S. African American here refers to people of African descent from the U.S. African American is a general term more appropriate for describing all people of African descent in the Americas. Black here is intended as a general term to index people of African descent more broadly" (2006: 597). Nwankwo also provides Pan-American parameters for analysis. "We need to rethink what we mean when we say 'African American,'" she urges, "so that we include the other Black Americas there (in 'Nuestra América'), as well as here (in the United States)" (2005: 17). My use of this category does not suggest an understanding of U.S. African American as a homogeneous classification and comprehensive experience. Recent scholarship such as Ira Berlin's *The Making of African America: The Four Great Migrations* (2010) documents other groups that are broadening the U.S. meaning of "African America": migrants from the Caribbean and Africa. Berlin notes that after the Immigration and Nationality Act of 1965, which created a yearly limitation of three hundred thousand annual visas on a first-come, first-served basis, "Black America, like white America, was also becoming an immigrant society" (2010: 6). In light of its complex sociohistorical transformations, U.S. African Americanness is also a harbinger of new demographics, representational tensions, and different meanings: "African American migrants," let us say, "have struggled with established residents over the very name 'African American,' as many newcomers — declaring themselves, for instance, Jamaican Americans or Nigerian Americans — shun that title, while other immigrants have denied native black Americans' claim to the title 'African American' since they had never been to Africa" (7). The slavery-to-freedom narrative also diverges. Berlin points out that some of the new arrivals, "rather than being descended solely from those who were sold, [. . .] trace their ancestry to the sellers of slaves" (10). Whereas others,

rather than "condemn[ing] their forced removal from Africa, [. . .] celebrate their arrival in America, in the words of Barack Obama's father, as a 'magical moment'" (11).

Throughout this work, I highlight the separate nature of U.S. Latinos *and* Latinas to concentrate on these two gendered categorizations and experiences. I employ Latino and Latina when referring to individuals and apply Latino/a when citing Latino/a studies as an academic field and its intellectual discourses and practices. This book's epilogue elaborates my concern for the unpronounceable turns Latino and Latina groups are taking through the inclusion of the slash in Latino/a or the "@" sign in Latin@ to detail gender inclusion. As a final note, I use the U.S. Latino and Latina category not as a means to exclusively center and disassociate these U.S. identities from other relational elsewheres. I am also aware that Latinos and Latinas exist in Latin America, Europe, and other locations in the Global South as well as the Global North. I reference U.S. Latino and Latina to provide a context for the population being discussed. This is not to say that U.S. Latino and Latina and Latin American Latino and Latina equivalencies do not exist. Rather, the Latinidad thread I follow and question, as manifested in Latino/a studies, is a U.S. articulation.

2. For additional analyses on Latinidad, consult Beltrán (2010); Caminero-Santangelo (2007); Sugg (2004); J. Rodríguez (2003); Dávila (2001); Aparicio and Chávez-Silverman (1997a); Oboler (1995); Sommers (1991); and Padilla (1985).

3. Further elaborating on her evocation of double consciousness, Portman thoughtfully stated in her apology, "Du Bois writes about how black Americans often view the world simultaneously from other people's point of view (from the outside in), as well as from their own points of view (from the inside out), because they are so aware of how they are scrutinized by other people and prejudices others may have against them. [. . .] I merely related to the overall framework of his idea—what it feels like to always see yourself from within and from without, knowing how other people view you and judge you and knowing how you view and judge yourself, at the same time. [. . .] I tried to explain my experience using a concept written by someone light-years more intelligent than I am, whose writing made me feel like someone else had been through a similar psychological experience to mine in some way. [. . .] I do believe, however, that it is in the small ways we relate to each other, even if we do so inaccurately, that we build our relationships with each other and realize our common humanity" (2004: 32).

4. This is not to say that Du Boisian double consciousness has not been likened to other U.S. contexts as well within U.S. African American studies. Robin D. G. Kelley, for example, tells us to "think of early New World Euro-Americans as possessing what Du Bois called 'double-consciousness': say, English and American, with whiteness as a means of negotiating this double consciousness." These incisive moments of equiva-

lency also have corollaries with other bodies and geohistories, having the potential, as Kelley also sees it, to deepen "our understanding of race, nationality, and culture" (2002: 129).

5. Arlene Dávila has examined how a "commercial Latinidad" (2001: xiv)—as constructed by Hispanic marketing agencies in the United States—promotes the use of Spanish by Latinos and Latinas "to be symbolically moved and touched" through "their language" (71). The value of Spanish "is built as the paramount basis of U.S. Latinidad" (4). As a consequence, the Hispanic marketing industry—or, simply, the Latin market—re-creates "essentialist equations of Latinos" through the continuous reinforcement of Spanish in the advertising world (71). Soetoro-Ng's real-world illustration conveys the different ways that the U.S. category "Latino or Latina" is being inhabited, highlighting other supplemental fashionings of—and constitutions for—the makings and unmakings of a "Spanish people" who are not limited to the Spanish-language world of the Latin market.

6. These migrations to black-brown ways of being can be situated within María Lugones's "'world'-travelling." The working characteristics of this concept "serve to distinguish between a 'world,' a utopia, a possible world in the philosophical sense, and a world-view. By a 'world' I do not mean a utopia at all. A utopia does not count as a world in my sense. The 'worlds' that I am talking about are possible. But a possible world is not what I mean by a 'world' and I do not mean a world-view, though something like a world-view is involved here." Lugones's hermeneutic is outlined in this manner: "For something to be a 'world' in my sense it has to be inhabited at present by some flesh and blood people. That is why it cannot be a utopia. It may also be inhabited by some imaginary people. It may be inhabited by people who are dead or people that the inhabitants of this 'world' met in some other 'world' and now have in this 'world' in imagination. A 'world' in my sense may be an actual society given its dominant culture's description and construction of life, including a construction of the relationships of production, of gender, race, etc. But a 'world' can also be such a society given a non-dominant construction, or it can be such a society or a society given an idiosyncratic construction. As we will see it is problematic to say that these are all constructions of the same society. But they are different 'worlds.' A 'world' need not be a construction of a whole society. It may be a construction of a tiny portion of a particular society. It may be inhabited by just a few people. Some 'worlds' are bigger than others" (1987: 8–9). Soetoro-Ng and Portman's traveling can be regarded as an identifying act that may be *worked on* rather than dismissed for its lack of brown or black "authenticity." Through Lugones's words, we could then "understand *what it is to be them and what it is to be ourselves in their eyes*. Only when we have travelled to each other's 'worlds' are we fully subjects to each other" (17).

7. I do not wish to be misunderstood here: I do not assert that Latinos and Latinas are the only "brown people" in the United States. Rather, I question why brownness has been exclusively designative of U.S. Latino and Latina lives through the dominant framework advancing Latino/a studies—namely, Latinidad. Attempting to find and fully delineate moments of passing among the multitudes of U.S. brown populations would deflect from the groups that I am critically focusing on: Latinos, Latinas, and African Americans. For analyses on the capacious brown canvas, the reader may consult, for example, Vijay Prashad's *The Karma of Brown Folk* (2001).

8. Chapter 3 explores a brown–dark brown symbology and how it is put into use by both U.S. African Americans as well as U.S. Latinos and Latinas.

9. There are changing definitions and transnational dimensions to the nation at hand—in this instance, the United States. In this sense, this monograph concurs with the aims of Nancy Raquel Mirabal and Agustín Laó-Montes's edited volume, *Technofuturos: Critical Interventions in Latina/o Studies*, in which they aim "to provide an intellectual and creative space for destabilizing and reassessing our understanding of Latinidades during a period of accelerated globalization, transnationalism, transmodernity, and reconfigurations of empire," thereby "complicating how we narrate, conceive, and reconstruct the workings of Latinidad and the field of Latina/o studies in the twenty-first century" (Mirabal, 2007: 1). Here, states of U.S. Latinoness and Latinaness are punctuated by "exile, imposed citizenship, 'undocumented' immigrations, colonialism, diaspora, 'legal' residency, cultural citizenship, or historical absorption as a result of the United States–Mexican War of 1846 and the Treaty of Guadalupe Hidalgo of 1848, land and landlessness, whether imagined and/or real, are all fundamental delineators of what constitutes being Latina/o" (8).

10. In employing minoritized or minoritization as particular modes, I echo Michael Dear and Gustavo Leclerc's useful lens for this concept, which refers to "the process by which no racial or ethnic category becomes large enough to command a majority in public dialogue, elections, etc." (2003: xi–xii).

11. Although W. E. B. Du Bois used the term "color line" in the singular, he did not strictly mean *one* arrangement of a line. Lewis Gordon has observed, "The color line is also a metaphor that exceeds its own concrete formulation. It is the race line as well as the gender line, the class line, the sexual orientation line, the religious line—in short, the line between 'normal' and 'abnormal' identities" (2000: 63). I invoke it in the plural, as color lines, to underline the multiple passages that transport us to what Aimee Carrillo Rowe calls the "lines of contact we build with others" (2008: 2).

12. Gavin Jones proposes that "Du Bois's famous aphorism, 'the problem of the Twentieth Century is the problem of the color-line,' can be read as a remotivation of the phrase 'the Negro Problem' itself, a remotivation that identifies the 'problem'

as the paradoxical politics of segregation rather than simply that of racial presence." Jones puts forth that "by locating the true color-line not between black and white society, but at the interface of blackness and a Southern culture that had assimilated that blackness, Du Bois was able to force upon his reader a recognition of a racially hyphenated nation. Du Bois's rhetorical task was to transform the paradoxical America of the color-line." Seen as such, Du Bois's hyphenated structuring of a "color-line" nests, as he wrote in *The Souls of Black Folk*, as a "point of transference where the thoughts and feelings of one race can come into direct contact and sympathy with thoughts and feelings of the other" (Gavin Jones, 1997: 30–31; Du Bois quoted on 31).

13. The *OED* defines a line as signifying "a row of written or printed words" and "the words of an actor's part," thus applying to the world of thespians. Actors perform different characters, adding the features, traits, and peculiarities that they understand to form the individual nature of a person, circumstance, or thing. I make note of actors' lines as these apply to the world of plays, motion pictures, and television broadcasts, among other possibilities, to consider the staging of Latinness, which often surpasses the representation of an "authentic" Latino or Latina subject. As John Leguizamo points out in the context of cinematic passing lines, Latinness moves in various directions. Leguizamo's Colombian and Puerto Rican Latinness were once converted into Italianness. Discussing his role in the 1999 crime drama directed by Spike Lee, *Summer of Sam*, Leguizamo added this autobiographical remark: "I got deep into my character Vinny the hairdresser. Pretty ironic. The story's by an Italian guy [screenwriter Victor Colicchio] who played Puerto Ricans in movies. Now I'm a Puerto Rican playing an Italian in his movie. Holy shit, I crossed over! I figure I was on the Al Pacino exchange program. If he can play Latin twice, I get to be Italian once" (2006: 205).

14. In relation to the exceptionalist tradition of American studies, Brian T. Edwards and Dilip Parameshwar Gaonkar make an assertion that holds relevancy here as well. "We are all studying dying formations," they argue, "with their archives simultaneously ossifying and fragmenting. We are struggling to decipher the new formations as they emerge from the debris of eroding traditions and worlds" (2010: 6).

15. One reason that Latinidad, as a unification strategy, has not adequately focused on "other" forms of Latinness that exceed the consolidation of panethnic subjects may have to do with its "forthcoming" temporality. Antonio Viego submits that "the interpretive contortions necessary to think that Latinos in the United States can constitute a nation in the first place are not only a testament to the ways in which the idea of 'nation' is significantly up for grabs these days. They are also a sign of the more general interpretive contortions that mark the contemporary discourse on *Latinidad*. Theorists of all stripes discuss Latinidad in relation to the future, the tense that ap-

pears to naturally elect itself for these discussions. [. . . T]he broadcasting of the Latino future is intimately dependent upon what will have already been claimed back as evidence of a Hispanic past" (2007: 108). Put another way: the Latinidad "hereafter" also bespeaks of the coming of a "new era" that returns to coherent dispositions of Latinidad.

16. Gayatri Chakravorty Spivak references such grammatical constructions as "to lexicalize." She puts across, "To *lexicalize* is to separate a linguistic item from its appropriate grammatical system into the conventions of another grammar. Thus a new economic and cultural lexicalization [. . .] demands a delexicalization as well" (2004: 118).

17. The colorings of Latinoness and Latinaness illustrate that they are always on the move. As sociologist Clara E. Rodríguez has written, "[A]lthough some Latinos are consistently seen as having the same color or 'race,' many Latinos are assigned a multiplicity of 'racial' classifications, sometimes in one day." She continues, "In addition to being classified by others (without their consent), some Latinos shift their own self-classification during their lifetime. I have known Latinos who became 'black,' then 'white,' then 'human beings,' finally again 'Latino' — all in a relatively short time. [. . .] I have come to understand that this shifting, context-dependent experience is at the core of many Latinos' life in the United States. Even in the nuclear family, parents, children, and siblings often have a wide range of physical types. For many Latinos, race is primarily cultural; multiple identities are a normal state of affairs; and 'racial mixture' is subject to many different, sometimes fluctuating, definitions." In light of these multiple locations, my interest is not so much about finding a subject's definitive ethnoracial identity. It is, instead, about finding relational meaning when a subject taps into another's color line. The idea of Latinoness and Latinaness as provisional states dialogues with Rodríguez's premise: "[F]or many Latinos, 'racial' classification is immediate, *provisional*, contextually dependent, and sometimes contested" (2000: 4–6; emphasis added).

18. An argument can be made that Richard Rodriguez was also searching for, in his third autobiographical project, a verb that would impart expressions of existence by brown actors who defy traditional ways of living and thereby remake, in this process, the United States. Calling himself a Hispanic, "a middle-aged noun" (2002: 105), Rodriguez holds a predilection for this term over "Latino," because it admits "a relationship to Latin America in English" (110). In attempting to find a language for himself, the self-defined "Hispanic memoirist" (111) fluctuates between nouns and adjectives (cf. 103–23). Rodriguez concludes that both Hispanic and Latino honor "linguistic obeisance to Spain" and returns to the Latin location of these categories (109). He asks, "For what, after all, does 'Latin' refer to, if not the imperial root sys-

tem?" Rodriguez narratively progresses by "Latinizing" his categorical preference and discloses, "*Hispanicus sui*." This browned Latin Hispanicity comes out in the United States, for in his estimation, "Only America could create Hispanics, Asians, African Americans" (119). Sociopolitical actors with tangible ethnoracial and national particularities invariably perform Rodriguez's brownness and Hispanization, even though the transgressive future of brown is uncertain in terms of deeds and doers. Latinities anticipate moving actors and geographies beyond Latina, Latino, and Hispanic lives.

19. As Juan Flores claims, "personally and collectively, Puerto Ricans, Mexicans, Cubans, Dominicans, and each of the other groups project their own respective national backgrounds as a first and primary line of identity and on that basis, fully mindful of differences, distances, and particularities, negotiate their relation to some more embracing 'Latino' or 'Hispanic' composite" (1997: 187).

20. Latin body politics have broader implications that go beyond normative American, Latino, and Latina perceptions of the fixed U.S. Latino and Latina subject. Lázaro Lima's deft study provides a lens on "the conditions under which it becomes necessary to create a specific Latino subject of American cultural and literary history." His book, *The Latino Body: Crisis Identities in American Literary and Cultural Memory*, "tells the story of the U.S. Latino body politic and its relation to the state: how the state configures Latino subjects and how Latino subjects have in turn altered the state's appellative assertions of difference (the contemporary emphasis on 'Latino' instead of 'Hispanic,' for example) to their own ends in the public sphere" (2007: 6).

21. U.S. scholarship on "the full range of important historical, political, and cultural connections between Asian Americans and African Americans" is critically unfolding, as evidenced with publications such as Ho and Mullen (2008: 2). Consult also Lee (2011). Asian-Indian connections in Mexico prove equally relevant as well, for "Asians brought to Mexico in slavery on the Manila-to-Acapulco galleons [. . .] were labeled 'African' because the Spanish wanted more slaves, and by law only Africans could be slaves" (Vincent, 2001: 1).

22. Richard Rodriguez's excerpt reads, "My brown is a reminder of conflict. And of reconciliation" (2002: xii).

23. For studies on the African presence in Mexico, consult Gates (2011: 59–90); Vinson and Restall (2009); Bennett (2009); Irwin (2008); Hernández Cuevas (2004); Vinson and Vaughn (2004); and Jiménez Román (n.d.). For analyses on the Africana diaspora in Central America, refer to Feracho, Mosby, and Nwankwo (forthcoming); Gudmundson and Wolfe (2010); Mosby (2003); E. Gordon (1998); and Minority Rights Group (1996).

24. A model for brownness and "brown pride" transpired during the 1960s Chicano movement, when the Brown Berets also materialized. Ian F. Haney López relays that

the political and community organization "adopted the following pledge: 'I wear the Brown Beret because it signifies my dignity and pride in the color of my skin and race'" (2003: 18–19). The Chicano movement—el movimiento, or the Chicano civil rights movement—served as "an insurgent uprising among a new political generation of Mexican-Americans" that "channeled their collective energies into a militant civil rights and ethnic nationalist movement in the late 1960s and 1970s" (A. García, 1997: 1–2). Alma M. García adds that the movement was surrounded by a radical national climate that included "the Black power movement, the anti–Vietnam War movement and the second wave of the women's movement [. . . and] focused on social, political, and economic self-determination and autonomy for Mexican-American communities throughout the United States" (2). Lee Bebout expands on the meanings of el movimiento, noting that it can be described "more accurately [. . .] as a complex, diverse collection of struggles. During the 1960s and 1970s, Chicanos fought for political representation, labor rights, social programs, and access to education. These struggles were undertaken by disparate Chicano communities. Indeed, land grant activists, farm workers, students, and barrio organizers found the movement in their own localized struggles, marking a tension between Chicano diversity and the desire to imagine a national, unified front" (2011: 3–4). In addition, refer to Montejano (2010); C. Jackson (2009); Gonzalez, Fox, and Noriega (2008); Muñoz (2007); Treviño (2001); Saldívar-Hull (2000); and Gaspar de Alba (1998).

25. Cf. R. T. Rodriguez (2010); Flores and Rosaldo (2007); Cabán (2003); Poblete (2003); de la Torre and Pesquera (1993); and Rosaldo (1985).

26. Paul Cuadros suggests another Latinidad that surfaces in connection to the world of high school sports, which we can reference as "Soccer Latinidad." He contrasts this Soccer Latinidad with the "all American" football town of Siler City, North Carolina. Cuadros's delineation of an athletic Latinidad is premised on how the team he coaches, "Los Jets," successfully integrates the three differentiated groups in Siler City's Jordan-Matthews High School (JM): newcomers, immigrant "kids," and "Chicanos." He describes these group's differentiations: "[T]hose feelings of alienation translated into many kids feeling lost, lost in themselves and lost in their communities. You could see that clearly in the halls of JM among the Latino students. There were generally three groups of Latinos at school. There were the 'newcomers,' kids fresh from the border who didn't speak a word of English and were placed in the English As a Second Language classes. Then there were the 'immigrant' kids, like Fish and Indio, who'd come to the United States when they were younger and could speak English. And finally there were the 'Chicanos,' kids like Enrique and Edi who'd been born here and could often speak languages fluently. A newcomer had little in common with a Chicano who perhaps couldn't speak Spanish as well. We had all three groups

on the team—one of the few places at the school where they could come together for something that they all loved" (2006: 155).

This inclusion is significant, as Cuadros expresses his desire for his players to think of themselves as a "Latino" family (2006: 163). His mediated efforts at creating a sense of family, together with a championship team, warrant a Latinidad context, which is organized here around English language proficiency, time of U.S. arrival and/or legal status, and Americanization. This Soccer Latinidad, while not entirely dependent on the Spanish language alone, is framed as a coalitional effort that guides, all the same, the road to American access and success. Cuadros admits as much: "I wanted to make the guys winners—to insulate them from the prejudice, their residency status, and allow them to overcome the barriers erected by the close-minded" (226). Despite Cuadros's best intentions, the highly ethnoracialized features of his players remain untransferable within this coach's Peruvian American gaze and, one must punctuate, within America at large. Cuadros feels inclined to provide not just his players' nationalities but their ethnoracial markers as well. As the soccer players are all referenced through nicknames, the following descriptions follow Cuadros's narrative style. The most light-skinned of the players, "Guero" (spelled without the diaeresis on the "u"), is depicted as having "light brown eyes, beneath the straight, honey-brown hair. [. . .] There was a reason why all the kids called him Guero—he looked white. You'd never know that Guero was a Latino kid until he opened his mouth. He was handsome, strong, a bit dangerous, and naturally all the girls were wild about him" (217). Ironically, in this hierarchical construction of whiteness, the other handsome white figure, distinguished as such, is David Duke, a former Louisiana U.S. Senate candidate and former Grand Wizard of the Knights of the Ku Klux Klan, who attended an anti-immigration rally at Siler City. In one instance, Cuadros writes that Duke possesses "Hollywood good looks" (52). In another, Duke stands out as "the tallest, the best-dressed, and best-looking" in the crowd (55). To return to Cuadros's racialized portrayals of his Latino players: "Oso," from Honduras, is defined as "coffee-bean black" (72). "Lechero" is indigenized: "He had dark-chocolate-colored skin with a triangular-shaped face, large eyes, and a broad nose. You could see the indigenous features in him" (76). Cuadros, on the other hand, appears as the bearer of a Latinidad marked through brownness. He is "short, brown, with dark hair" (113).

27. Expanding the scope of Julia Alvarez's exploration of U.S. Latina *quinceañera* extravaganzas, it can be claimed that an exception to the presumably cogent, Spanish-speaking background that detonates Latinidad is what I am suggesting here as a "Quinceañera Latinidad." This conceptual category refers to the conventional requirements promoted—or to use Alvarez's phraseology, "touted"—by U.S. marketing sectors in the construction of a Latin "traditional" event. To be sure, a Quinceañera

Latinidad depends on the idea of a Latin tradition to explicitly target Latina youth and their parents in what Alvarez identifies as "our Pan-Hispanic United States" (2007: 75). These Latin assemblages are a marker of "an ethnicity with a label that reads MADE IN THE USA (or 'Remade in the USA,' if you will)" since there is sociocultural "pressure to honor a tradition whose content and origins remains vague" (116; 110). The same vagueness is applicable to the subjects and origins subsumed by the U.S. Latino or Latina category. But unlike other kinds of Latinidad, the Spanish language is not a vital part for the manufacturing of a Quinceañera Latinidad. As Will Cain, the president and founder of *Quince Girl* magazine, tells Alvarez, "The Hispanic community is this very fractured community. You have your Mexican Americans and your Puerto Ricans and your Cuban Americans. And the only thing that ties all these separate nationalities together—no, it's not Spanish. [. . .] What ties them together, the one single tie that binds all these cultures . . . is the tradition celebrated across the whole diverse group: the quinceañera. I mean, it is big" (2007: 68–69).

Additional corporate recognition of a Quinceañera Latinidad—mindful of what Alvarez christens as a "flamboyant new kind of American, the Latina American"—includes Kern's Nectar sponsorship of its annual Dulce Quinceañera Sweepstakes and Maggi's Put-Flavor-in-Your-Quinceañera Sweepstakes (2007: 121; 71; 118). The Latinidad that sets the stage for a Quinceañera Latinidad composed of diverse "cultural borrowings" is synthesized as follows: "So that now, Cuban quinceañeras in Miami are hiring Mexican mariachis to sing the traditional 'Las Mañanitas.' The full court of fourteen damas and chambelanes, 'each couple representing a year of the quinceañera's life,' a mostly Mexican practice, is now a traditional must. As is the changing of the shoes to heels, which seems to originally have been a Puerto Rican embellishment. From the Puerto Ricans as well, though some say from the Mexicans, came the tradition of la última muñeca, a 'last doll' dressed exactly like the quinceañera" (78, 75). As is the case with other Latinidades, there are separations and exclusions within the dominant trends mapping U.S. quinceañera festivities and practices. According to Alvarez, the price tag for this festive occasion can range "anywhere from a hundred bucks for a cookout in the backyard and a stereo booming music for the young lady and her friends to fifty grand and up in a hall with a party planner, a limo, dinner for a hundred or more" (64–65). Central Americans—with their frugal cookout quinceañeras—are a group that stands at the lowest socioeconomic echelons of a Quinceañera Latinidad. As Alvarez explains it, "I have to conclude that the cookout quinceañeras are becoming the exception. In the past, perhaps they were the rule. In the old countries, of course. In small homogeneous pockets—a border town in Texas, a barrio composed solely of Central Americans; in other words, a group still largely out of the mainstream loop, perhaps" (65).

A Quinceañera Latinidad, then, emerges among the most visible Latinos and Latinas in terms of buying power, although Alvarez's example of a Latin cultural hodgepodge for quinceañeras largely depends on the "traditional" groups that encompass the U.S. Latino and Latina triad. Those on the margins of a Quinceañera Latinidad — that is, those hosting cookout quinceañeras — fall under the demographic radar because, as Alvarez reports, they are "taking place in segregated, often undocumented populations" (2007: 78). The most conspicuous "Quinceañera Latinos" participating in what Alvarez designates as an American "celluloid dream" are decidedly more marketable, desirable, and memorable in the formation of this Quinceañera Latinidad as well as in Latino and Latina cultural identity–making processes (121).

28. Tronto's ethic of care implicates these four phases: (1) caring about, (2) caring for, (3) caregiving, and (4) care receiving. Caring about implies an awareness of the need to genuinely care in the first place. This "requires listening to the articulated needs, recognizing unspoken needs, distinguishing among and deciding which needs to care about." Caring for entails a "responsibility to meet a need that has been identified." Here "someone has to assume responsibility for organizing [. . . .] The moral dimension of caring for is to assume, and to take seriously, responsibility." Caregiving is a phase in which "individuals and organizations perform the necessary caring tasks. It involves a knowledge about how to care." Care receiving "involves the response of the thing, person, or group that received the caregiving. [It] requires the complex moral element of responsiveness" (1998: 16–17). Tronto's ubiquitous ethic of care is linked to Latinities, because it insists on the significance of analyzing human activities and interactions that, in a way, dismantle "the myth of our own invulnerable autonomy" (19). Tronto's ethic also brings with it gendered and class components that can be attached to ethnoracial factors: "caring is greatly undervalued in our culture — in the assumption that caring is 'women's work,' in perceptions of caring occupations, in the wages and salaries paid to workers in provision of care, in the assumption that care is menial" (16). Consult also Tronto (1993).

29. Regina M. Marchi suggests that the U.S. observance of the Day of the Dead — "a fusion of Indigenous and Roman Catholic rituals for honoring the deceased" in places like Mexico, Guatemala, El Salvador, Bolivia, Peru, and Ecuador (2009: 10–11) — is not limited to U.S. Latinos and Latinas. She remarks that this annual holiday, held on 1 or 2 November, merits greater examination. Marchi insists, "[S]tudies of Latinidad should not be confined to analyses of how Latinos create and fortify cultural ties in response to the dominant U.S. society. They should also examine how phenomena considered Latino enter different cultural spaces and change the dominant culture" (97). One can argue that the U.S. Day of the Dead, as a general manifestation of an ethic of care, has led to the "'Latinization' of U.S. culture" where forms of public mourning

can take place, since "the basic object of the celebration — collectively remembering the dead — is universal enough" (101). Marchi also adds that the Day of the Dead in the United States has been popularized because of a new openness to non-Western spiritualities.

30. With this in mind, I am following a set of paramount questions raised by José Esteban Muñoz: "'Latino' does not subscribe to a common racial, class, gender, religious, or national category, and if a Latino can be from any country in Latin America, a member of any race, religion, class, or gender/sex orientation, who then is she? What, if any, nodes of commonality do Latinas/os share? How is it possible to know *latinidad*?" (2000: 67).

31. A clarification is required for the ways that these Latinidades are manifested in De Genova and Ramos-Zayas's research on the racialized distinctions between Mexicans and Puerto Ricans in Chicago, "one of very few sites where [these two groups] have both settled over several decades" (2003: 1). Latinidad as the "American" abjection of the U.S.-born constitutes the ways that Mexicans and Puerto Ricans perceive this "Latinidad as an identity that fundamentally pertained to many 'second-generation' youth as the effect of a kind of racially subordinate 'Americanization.' This type of 'American' abjection was generally considered to be a degeneration of the 'good' or 'proper' values that migrants prized, and was readily conflated with 'laziness' and welfare system dependency" (179). This Latinidad also demonstrates how migrants view second-generation Latinos and Latinas as "mere 'minorities' who did not speak any language 'properly' [and] embodied values or behaviors more stereotypically associated with African Americans" (180).

The second of these — a Latinidad framed through migrant illegality as well as a Latinidad without Puerto Ricans — emerges through Mexican recognition of other groups, such as Guatemalans, who cross multiple borders to get to the United States. De Genova and Ramos-Zayas further tweak this Latinidad by calling it an "empathetic Latinidad," which is a uniting force with Central American migrants' plight due to the "compounding of nation-state borders" (2003: 184). A Latinidad in opposition to African Americans distrusts and fears African Americans. This Latinidad can also be deemed as "a strategy for the avoidance of blackness" (189). Here, blacks are perceived as too slow, lazy, and with "unfair advantages" at the U.S. workplace. De Genova and Ramos-Zayas elaborate, "It was abundantly evident in these comments that the equation of African Americans with laziness [...] became conjoined with the denigration of racial Blackness, and that this conjuncture became one kind of condition of possibility for the sense of the shared (racialized) identity — as 'Latinos' — to be mutually invoked by Mexican migrants and Puerto Ricans" (188). A Latinidad as an articulation of working-class solidarity is produced "in racialized opposition to whiteness and Blackness [. . .] an unequivocal sameness or equivalence between Mexicans and Puerto Ricans (and also Central Americans) [. . .] in a class-inflected opposition, above else to specifically Latino bosses [. . .] demonstrating their greater loyalty and devotion to whites and Blacks" (195).

A Latinidad as a strategy of middle-class formation relates to "the process of becoming 'middle-class' [as] consonant with 'becoming Latino.'" This way of being both "middle-class" and "Latino" is "rooted in an affirmative sense of 'giving back' or 'serving the community,' and 'remembering where you came from' without 'selling out'" (De Genova and Ramos-Zayas, 2003: 198). Finally, a fractured Latinidad through institutional contexts, whiteness, and power was deployed "in overt relation to whiteness" at institutional settings "traditionally associated with ideas of 'mobility,' 'assimilation,' and 'mainstreaming' (i.e., college)." This Latinidad "became a form of racial identification that held the promises of coalition and solidarity for the sake of contesting the dominant racializations of 'Mexicans' and 'Puerto Ricans' that both groups had to confront" (205).

32. Robin D. G. Kelley sets forth a useful definition of Africana diasporas, explaining that "its contemporary usage emerges clearly in the 1950s and 1960s. It served in scholarly debates as both a political term emphasizing the unifying experiences of African peoples dispersed by the slave trade and an analytical term that enabled scholars to talk about black communities across national boundaries. Much of this scholarship examines the dispersal of people of African descent, their role in the transformation and creation of new cultures, institutions, and ideas outside of Africa, and the problems of building Pan-African movements across the globe. A critical component of this work, as well as all diaspora studies, is the construction and reproduction of a diaspora consciousness. The main elements of such a consciousness (to varying degrees, of course) include a collective memory of dispersal from a homeland, a vision of that homeland, feelings of alienation, desire for return, and a continuing relationship and identity with the homeland" (2002: 126). Frank Andre Guridy cogitates on this diaspora "as both the dispersal of Africans through the slave trade and their ongoing social, political, cultural interactions across various boundaries after emancipation. As a concept that illuminates the creation of cross-border communities, diaspora is a useful way to interpret cross-national, Afro-descended interaction that is not reducible to politicized forms of 'black internationalism' or 'racial solidarity'" (2010: 4–5).

33. Oscar is "a hardcore sci-fi and fantasy man" who cannot surpass his nerd status (Díaz, 2007: 6). Initially, however, "in those blessed days of his youth," Oscar was one "of those preschool loverboys who was always trying to kiss the girls, always coming up behind them during a merengue and giving them the pelvic pump, the first nigger to learn the perrito and the one who danced it any chance he got." Díaz adds, "Because

in those days he was (still) a 'normal' Dominican boy raised in a 'typical' Dominican family, his nascent pimp-liness was encouraged by blood and friends alike" (11). Even though Oscar grows out of his "innate" Dominican dancing skills, the expected and "natural" rhythm of the Latin subject constantly follows him, one can say, through the name association with Oscar D'León. Oscar Emilio León Somoza, otherwise known as Oscar D'León, was born in Caracas in 1943. Reaching musical success in the 1980s, D'León is nicknamed "El Sonero del Mundo" (The Son Singer of the World). He has collaborated with such stars as Celia Cruz, Tito Puente, Arturo Sandoval, and Luís Enrique.

34. Gabriel García Márquez's fictional village of Macondo informs Díaz's moving literary world, which is also in line with its updated, hyperurban space, conceived in the mid-1990s, "McOndo" (Díaz, 2007: 7). The latter refers to a Latin American literary movement taking its root from Macintoshes, McDonald's, and condos (cf. Fuguet and Gómez, 1996). Not to be overlooked is Díaz's gesture to the Anglo- and Francophone Caribbean. Derek Walcott's poem from 1979, "The Schooner 'Flight,'" which speaks to the rich cultural mixtures of the Caribbean and takes the reader to the narrator's brief history of his life, serves as the epigraph to Díaz's book. He also references Martinican intellectual Édouard Glissant, whose theorization of cultural interrelationships in the Caribbean through processes of creolization and conceptual terms like "relation" have served as important landmarks for diasporic studies and the relational links between the Caribbean and the Atlantic world (Díaz, 2007: 92).

35. The complex bridging of high and low popular culture mediums is best raised by Díaz himself, who clues readers on the novel's narration. He told the *New Yorker* that to understand the "narration enigma," readers "have to know a little bit about the comic book series *The Fantastic Four*. Each of the family members is explicitly linked to one of the Four — Oscar is the Thing, Abelard is Mr. Fantastic, Belicia is the Invisible Woman, and Lola is the Human Torch — something I stole from Rick Moody's incomparable novel *The Ice Storm*" (2010).

36. Paula M. L. Moya and Ramón Saldívar, among other literary theorists, have evaluated the shifting articulations of American national identities and literatures through the optic of the "trans-American imaginary" and have called for the need "to see American literature as heterogeneous and multiple." Such a mode requires an alteration of the American corpus, since its influences exceed "nations other than England and idioms that do not originate in the English language have been unevenly and inadequately incorporated into the larger narrative of American literary historiography." Moya and Saldívar provide the hemispheric vantage point — "the interpretive framework that yokes together North and South America instead of New England and England" — of the "transnational imaginary" (2). This literary form of geopolitical

kinship "make[s] visible the centrality of Latinidad to the fictional discourses that continue to shape the American national imaginary" (5). Its theoretical contribution is a "chronotope, a contact zone that is both historical and geographical and that is populated by transnational persons whose lives from an experiential region within which singularly delineated notions of political, social, and cultural identity do not suffice" (2).

This renewed vision of American literature is both opportune and valuable, as Moya and Saldívar seek to extricate the recurring "Americanness" in normative domains that restrict a "national" American corpus. I use a "Latined literature" as a literary resource, rather than the aforementioned terms. Although my perspectives dialogue with Moya and Saldívar, the idea of a Latined literature — or a Latined literary space — diverges insofar as I am interested in the function of U.S. Latino and Latina literature outside the confines of the American geographic, national, cultural, and ethnoracial context that also locates these groups and "their" productions as "Latino" and "Latina." Despite its "trans-Americanness," Latino and Latina writing appears to become standardized within and channeled through the United States, dwelling in literary Americanness. Latino and Latina narrative productions become "naturalized" to the U.S. literary map, as critics seek to find and insist on the centrality of their space in U.S. American literature. But what of such texts as they speak to and restore Caribbean, Central American, and Latin American regional struggles and thinking? I am advancing, then, a rereading — while going beyond the boundaries — of Latinoness, Latinaness, and Latinidad and their insular relation to ideological Americanness. An "American" novel (in the U.S. sense) may herald a Latined perspective, and it may or may not necessarily be written by "Latinos" and "Latinas." Such a text, for instance, could just as well reconstitute a "new" American self — in the continental sense — in the Americas. But it also fashions a new form of writing and engages with hermeneutic turns that integrate and disrupt literary conventions in Latin America *and* the United States. Latin American cultural practices are now gesturing toward Latinos and Latinas, placing their oeuvres in a new regional and historical context, with a literary temporality that is also navigating mass migrations, transnational communities, cultural alterations, and millennial transitions.

Take note of how Junot Díaz and Daniel Alarcón, a Peruvian American writer, are being imported southward. They recently had the distinction of being the only two U.S. Latinos who were named as two of the most renowned thirty-nine authors under thirty-nine (or as pitched in Spanish, *treinta y nueve escritores menores de treinta y nueve*) by the 2007 Bogota World Book Capital. The literary measure of U.S. Latinos and Latinas changes perspective and becomes regional "Latin American." The rest of the "thirty-nine under thirty-nine" authors, selected by a jury composed of Colombian novelists Piedad Bonnett, Hector Abad Faciolince, and Oscar Callazos, write primarily in Spanish and come from Latin America. Díaz's and Alarcón's works are two concrete cases in point of U.S. Latino/a publications that are translated into Spanish. One might ask, where does their "trans-ness" reside, in "trans-America" or "trans-Latin America"? In what ways do their literary forms unsettle both U.S.-based Americanness *and* Latin Americanness? We must bear in mind the different continental understandings of their endeavors, as the American nation and the American hemisphere mark them. In effect, they bear the geo- and biographical distanciation from these spaces, lending themselves to my premise: that the symbolic acts and geographies with which we are grappling constitute Latinings. Such works are not purely (North or Latin) American but an elective representation of a subject with multiple thresholds and continuous denationalizations. What might this mean for hemispherist Latino and Latina creative workers with many detours? What of their translated writings, circulating in more and more globalized settings and linked to other "foreign" aesthetics and literary practices?

37. By separating "re" and "cognition," I am building from the standard meaning of "recognition." The *OED* defines this noun as "the action or process of recognizing or being recognized, in particular" and the "identification of a thing or person from previous encounters or knowledge." But I am also expressing the process of redoing something, like the act of cognition, whose *OED* meaning entails "the mental action or process of acquiring knowledge and understanding through thought, experience, and the senses" and "a perception, sensation, idea, or intuition resulting from this."

38. But this Latining certainly operates in "Latin" America. Just as I explore the itinerant meanings of U.S. Latinoness and Latinaness within an expansive vista of the color line and U.S. borders, Néstor García Canclini's work *Latinoamericanos buscando lugar en este siglo* (2002) seeks to decipher the locations of Latin Americans and Latin Americanness in this century. García Canclini's point of departure includes the following concerns: "What does it mean to be Latin American?" (12); "Where are Latin American accounts located now?" (17); and "Who wants to be Latin American?" (23). The context for the first query reads as follows: "What does it mean to be Latin America? I sought to elaborate an essay about the way in which the question is changing and the new answers that are being constructed. There are still historical voices in this debate, but different ones are being added, and sometimes with new arguments. The scale also has expanded: the present condition of Latin America exceeds its territory. Those who left their countries and are now extending their cultures beyond the region demonstrate the painful dislocation of Latin Americans and the opportunities offered by global exchanges" (12; my translation).

39. Latining also motions toward the critical inclusion of U.S. Latino and Latina cultural and intellectual production in Latin American studies. It is frequently obvious to me how U.S. Latinos and Latinas discursively integrate Latin American history, culture, and politics in their works (e.g., Julia Alvarez, Ana Castillo, Sandra Cisneros, Junot Díaz, Martín Espada, Cristina García, Francisco Goldman, and Héctor Tobar, among many others). This linking, however, is not so apparent when it comes to Latin American literary production and intellectual thought and their examination of — or even interrelation with — U.S. Latinos and Latinas.

40. As geo- and biographical migratory passages, these movements create, as Ira Berlin has elucidated in the context of the transformations underpinning U.S. African American life, "a glimpse of the future, for the new history has not one story line but many and has not one direction but several" (2010: 9). He adds that exploring the complex struggles of the ever-widening African American experience "does not create a single culture, produce an established political goal, or culminate in a pre-established outcome. Rather it raises questions about the character of the master narrative of African American history" (10).

41. At the same time, of course, such subjects may not accept the construction as an accounting of themselves. It is productive to once again turn to Lugones's sagacious observations on "'world'-travelling." She indicates, "In a 'world' some of the inhabitants may not understand or hold the particular construction of them that constructs them in that 'world.' So, there may be 'worlds' that construct me in ways that I do not even understand. Or it may be that I understand the construction, but do not hold it of myself. I may not accept it as an account of myself, a construction of myself. And yet, I may be animating such a construction." The recurring, but differing exercise of "Latin" throughout should be apprehended as a conjectural approach that simultaneously seizes and excoriates stereotypes of the temperamental "Latin." Lugones brilliantly speaks to the meanings behind this construction: "One can be at the same time in a 'world' that constructs one as stereotypically latin, for example, and in a 'world' that constructs one as latin. Being stereotypically latin and being simply latin are different simultaneous constructions of persons that are part of different 'worlds.' One animates one or the other or both at the same time without necessarily confusing them, though simultaneous enactment can be confusing if one is not on one's guard" (Lugones, 1987: 10). Lugones adds, "Given that latins are constructed in Anglo 'worlds' as stereotypically intense — intensity being a central characteristic of at least one of the anglo stereotypes of latins — and given that many latins, myself included, are genuinely intense, I can say to myself 'I am intense' and take a hold of the double meaning. And furthermore, I can be stereotypically intense or be the real thing and, if you are Anglo, you do not know when I am which because I am Latin-

American. As Latin-American I am an ambiguous being, a two-imaged self: I can see that gringos see me as stereotypically intense because I am, as a Latin-American, constructed that way but I may or may not intentionally animate the stereotype or the real thing knowing that you may not see it in anything other than in the stereotypical construction. This ambiguity is funny and is not just funny, it is survival-rich" (13).

42. I interrogate the relevance of double consciousness in light of José Luis Falconi and José Antonio Mazzotti's identification of it as an "old notion" in their edited volume *The Other Latinos: Central and South Americans in the United States*. They ask, "Is the old notion of a 'double consciousness' still useful in depicting these new collective subjectivities?" (2007: 3).

43. I discuss, in chapter 4, José Luis Falconi and José Antonio Mazzotti's "Other Latino" designation in greater length.

44. Cary D. Wintz notes that "taken together," the Harlem Renaissance, the New Negro Movement, and the Negro Renaissance "provide a succinct and remarkably accurate glimpse of the diverse and diffuse currents that surfaced in the mid-1920s and gave rise to a surge of black creativity." But this literary and intellectual movement also poses some definitive chronological limitations. "Generally," Wintz states, "the consensus among scholars has been that the Harlem Renaissance was an event of the 1920s, bounded on one side by the war and the race riots of 1919 and on the other side by the 1929 stock market crash" (1988: 1). Jeffrey B. Perry adds that the Harlem Renaissance "is a much-debated concept — its very existence and name are challenged by some. In general, 'the Harlem Renaissance' refers to the literary outpourings, mostly by Black writers working on Black subject matter with a new sense of confidence and achievement, that reached much wider audiences in the period of the 1920s, particularly the second half of the decade. (Some would date the 'Renaissance' from 1917 through about 1935.) The location of the 'Renaissance' is also contested — some emphasize its national or international character, while most locate it in New York City, particularly Harlem. Much-discussed aspects of the 'Renaissance' concern the authors, their audiences, their themes and subject matter, the quality of their work, and the disproportionate role played by white publishers and white patrons in shaping their artistic works" (2001: 351).

45. Influential literary and cultural vehicles were established during the 1910s and 1920s for these aims, which included the *Crisis*, founded by W. E. B. Du Bois as the official publication of the National Association for the Advancement of Colored People (NAACP), and the Urban League's *Opportunity*, edited by sociologist Charles S. Johnson (1893–1956).

46. And yet ironically *Down These Mean Streets*, a text hailed for its palpable blackness, exposes an anxiety of brownness-cum-blackness. Conversations between

mother and son reveal a concurrent brownness and blackness. In one instance, she reassures him, almost soothingly, "You are not black, you're brown, a nice color, a pretty color" (P. Thomas, 1997: 135). A few pages later, it is the term "*Negrito*" that turns into the problematic loving diminutive, as the mother asks Thomas, "Why does it hurt you to be *un Negrito*?" (148).

47. Thomas misspells *trigueño* and *trigueña* as *tregeño* and *tregeña* in his glossary. The *Diccionario de la Real Academia Española* identifies trigueño and trigueña as "wheat-colored; between dark-skinned and blonde" (my translation). The Spanish definition reads, "de color del trigo; entre moreno y rubio."

48. Although I am borrowing Juan Gonzalez's (2000) apt description and book title in connection to U.S. Latinos and Latinas, I would slightly rearrange it to "harvest of empires," attempting to underscore that interest in Latin America has historically varied and has not been limited just to the United States. For instance, despite the 1823 Monroe Doctrine, which stipulated U.S. protection over the Western Hemisphere, Britain "largely filled the vacuum left by Spain in Central America" (Stiles, 2009: 183). T. J. Stiles recounts, "Leapfrogging from the colonies of Jamaica and British Honduras (later Belize), English merchants had come to dominate the region's trade. In 1841, the British had extended their sway by proclaiming a protectorate over the 'kingdom' of the Miskito (corrupted to 'Mosquito' by the British) Indians on Nicaragua's sparsely populated Atlantic Coast. The Nicaraguans regarded it as an insult to their sovereignty—an insult the British had compounded in 1848, when they had occupied San Juan del Norte and renamed it Greytown to block any canal or transit route" (2009: 183). Another lingering intercontinental example of European and American entrepreneurial and imperial coupling is the initial excavation of the Panama Canal by the French and its subsequent successful construction by the United States in 1914. It illustrates U.S. and European attention for "the fever of the Great Idea" that became the Central American waterway, thereby stressing "the poetry of capitalism" for France and a "strategic and economic crossroads of the Americas" for U.S. military power (Parker, 2009: 86, 238). Matthew Parker writes that Frenchmen were "prepared to die for the Great Idea of the canal," especially because the Central American tropics represented a space in which French planners "were going to engage in the great scientific battle" (90–91). For Americans in the United States, Panama served as an important route that facilitated a link between the East and West Coasts during the Gold Rush, becoming "an American protectorate"—an appendage to U.S. Western expansion and nation formation (36). Parker contends that "between 1861 and 1865, the U.S. was, of course, fighting its own civil war, and the Panama route was used several times for moving troops, materials, and bullion from coast to coast" (37).

49. This absence also lends itself to other levels of nonpresence indicating outsiderness — or even "alienized signification" — within normative mappings of U.S. Latinoness and Latinaness. As Héctor Tobar points out in *The Tattooed Soldier*, this state of unmappable (Central American) "otherworldliness," a Latinity that is not accounted for in Latino/a studies because of its Guatemalan ties, operates as a perpetual U.S. oddity. Central American subjects, under Tobar's literary representation, look "like walking question marks" (1998: 41). Discrepant and irreconcilable, perhaps, but thrusting one to speculate if these question marks, as paradoxically marked invisible beings, require an answer or clarification, since they are beyond the grasp of the American and Latino and Latina social pattern.

50. Nwankwo directs our attention to the proclivity by U.S. "Americanist scholars to think of work by or about U.S. African Americans as falling neatly into one of the two categories — as part of the 'new' hemispherist American studies or as holding firm to academic versions of the national political commitments that undergirded the creation of African-American studies in the first place" (2006: 582).

51. John Hope Franklin also advanced a resonant observation. He had this to say about U.S. African American internationalism and their reactions to Italy's 1935 invasion of Ethiopia: "Almost overnight even the most provincial among the Negroes became international-minded" (quoted in Taketani, 2010: 146).

CHAPTER ONE. Southern Latinities

1. Different scholars attempting to discuss the phenomenon of the Nuevo or New South have employed similar terminology. The designation "Nuevo New South" is traced to Raymond A. Mohl (2005). "New South" was used after the Reconstruction Era (1865–77). Its coinage is generally attributed to Henry Woodfin Grady (1850–89), editor of the *Atlanta Constitution*, who delivered a classic speech before the New England Society in 1886, titled "The New South." Grady's dynamic New South promoted southern industrial growth and northern investment.

2. This tracing of the South's other routes resounds with V. S. Naipaul's preoccupation more than two decades ago in *A Turn in the South*. Naipaul conveyed a nexus with contemporary frameworks that impel further inquiry into what is now framed as the Global South. While acknowledging that his familiarity with the United States was limited to New York and New England, his interest derived from a southern link that binds Naipaul to his homeland, Trinidad (1989: 23). "And for the first time," he writes, "it occurred to me that Trinidad, a former British colony (from 1797), and an agricultural slave colony (until 1833, when slavery was abolished in the British Empire), would have had more in common with the old slave states of the Southeast

than with New England or the newer European-immigrant states of the North." Yet Naipaul's connection was postponed for decades. This personal oversight is induced by the psychological impact that the South's racialized dynamics have had not just in domestic U.S. settings but at an international scale too. This South-South link is so manifest that it "should have occurred to me a long time before, but it hadn't," he concedes (24). "What I had heard as a child about the racial demeanor of the South had been too shocking. It had tainted the United States, and had made me close my mind to the South." But Naipaul's mind, also tainted by U.S. segregationist practices, does not entirely bar the South as a correlational terrain of inquiry. His southern discussion is preoccupied with historical continuity and discontinuity in a landscape — or a "country place" — "where little changed and little happened" (3).

While the landscape may be static in this view, the people of the South are not. Naipaul's prologue bears witness to the region's variegated colorings and developing socioeconomic relations, although the stifling weight of the black-white racial paradigm is skillfully illustrated through the guided tour he received from a North Carolina woman. Calling her remarks "a chant," he describes the comments she furnished him with through two particular repetitions. One of them is: "Black people there, black people there, white people there. Black people, black people, white people, black people. All this side black people, all this side white people. White people, white people, black people, white people" (1989: 10). The other reiteration, more economical with words, is still an echo of the former: "All this side white people, all that side black people. Black people, black people, white people, black people. Black people, white people" (17). Despite this black-white reiterative synonymity, we meet "Indians from India" who are "buying the motels from the South from white people" (6). An older Nuevo South is surfacing also, and it did not escape Naipaul's eye. "The Mexicans did the fruit-picking," he reports, making them an ethnoracial site that provoked a "pro-American attitude [in the South that] extended to foreign affairs" among certain black community members (16–17). Naipaul's undertaking surfaces from his interest in U.S. black responses to "immigrants of a new sort": Latin Americans and Asians (29).

3. While interrogating such boundaries, I attempt to cross and recross these scholarly undertakings, as John Muthyala (2001) has prompted.

4. As a cursory outline on the differences between Hispanics and Latinos, William Luis puts forth a useful, though certainly not definitive, distinction between these categories. I draw on Luis's working definition, because it explains these categories through "writerly" perspectives and traditions: "Hispanics are those who are born or raised and educated in their native country, which they leave for political or economic reasons to reside in the U.S.A. Latinos are those who are born or raised and educated in the U.S.A., and have been subjected to the demands of U.S. society and

culture. Hispanics have closer ties to the language and culture of their country of origin; Latinos recognize their parents' ancestry, but they feel closer to U.S. culture. Hispanic writers tend to write in Spanish; Latino writers tend to write in English, and they contribute to a Latino literature. While I propose a definition for Hispanic and Latino, I also recognize that a Hispanic can identify himself as a Latino and vice versa" (2003: 122).

5. Bernadette Marie Calafell, a Mexican American from Arizona, proposes some interesting insights on what she calls "the new Latina/o South." Calafell begins by telling readers that she followed her Chicana path until she enrolled at the University of North Carolina at Chapel Hill for a doctorate in communication studies. Her self-identification was "forced, for the first time, really to identify myself as a Latina — a Latina in a space that negated Chicana identities." She elucidates, "Latina was a term I had not previously used to describe myself because of its generality. [. . .] Thus, in coming to North Carolina, a land whose population was unknown to me, I chose Latina because of the possibility of identification across ethnic groups" (2007: 14). It is the U.S. Southeast — the new Latina/o South — that opens up Calafell's Chicana consciousness to the emergent possibilities of Latina being. She proffers some considerations for Chicanos and Chicanas in the twenty-first century: "Questions regarding the possibility of Chicana/o as a political and cultural identification for the future suddenly became more and more apparent to me as I forced myself in a world in which very few people knew what Chicana/o meant or identified in that way. What I found instead was a vibrant and growing community of Mexican, Central American, Latina/o, and Arab immigrants who were remaking the face of North Carolina and with it my assumptions about the face of the South. What would Chicana/o come to mean to those children born Mexican American in the South — the next generation? What would Aztlán, our physical and symbolic nation, mean to those who had never visited it or had no concept of it? Would Chicana/o as a term of identification survive once Mexican Americans had moved beyond the Southwest? Or, because of the multiple connections being made in contact zones such as North Carolina would Chicana/o become something else, allowing a new political identification to emerge?" (16).

These conjectural concerns can surface in the Southwest, given that the demographics Calafell references also exist there, with the exception that this area has been historically defined as Aztlán, a Chicano- and Chicana-specific space. Calafell's questions become more tangible for her in light of the black history of the Southeast. She concedes as much, stating that the Southeast imparted a "sense of homelessness that seemed to guide many of our experiences as the weight of the history of the South bore down on our daily lives" (2007: 48). While Calafell's impressions have great promise, they neatly—"authentically"—form a Chicano and Chicana Southwest/ African American Southeast impenetrable dyad. Under this structuring, a "Latina/o" emergence cannot transpire in the "new Latina/o South" because the "I" at hand is invariably—and must be told as—"Chicana/o." What analytically attracts me, nevertheless, are mobile subjects and their impulses toward Latined beginnings and articulations in the U.S. Southeast as well as the Southwest.

6. For Houston A. Baker Jr. "'tight places' are constituted by the necessity to articulate a position that combines the specters of abjection (slavery), multiple subjects and signifiers ([Jim] Trueblood's narrative [in Ralph Ellison's *Invisible Man*] is produced for a rich, northern, white philanthropist), representational obligations of race in America (to speak 'Negro'), and patent sex and gender implications (the role of the Law as the Phallus)" (2001: 15).

7. Lawrence A. Herzog's qualifier of a new borderland urbanism is a locus of a new border city as a tangible living space that crosses national political boundaries, confronting "the conditions under which the global economy collides with social space in a bicultural, first-world–third-world, high density, rapidly urbanizing international boundary region" (2003: 120). In mentioning the black-white plantation South, I am aware that this space is by no means static and monolithic, as Lacy K. Ford and George Brown Tindall, among others, have demonstrated. Ford's examination of the slavery question, which is not one query but a set of interrelated troubling concerns for the upper and lower South during the founding era, "contends that there was not one antebellum South but many, not one southern white mind-set but several" (2009: 4). The following questions reflect Ford's preoccupations, methodologically explored between 1787 and 1840: "Could slavery coexist with the nation's republican ideals? Did the economic benefits of slavery outweigh the costs? Did slavery expand or limit economic and social opportunities for whites? Was there any other way to generate as much wealth in the South as slavery created? Would the wealth held in slaves survive an effort to change systems? Would the spread of evangelical Christianity challenge the dominant slaveholding ethos?" (3). Tindall's *Natives and Newcomers* likens U.S. southerners to migrants: "It had suddenly dawned on me that southeners, white and black, were outsiders in much the same way as were recent immigrants. Southeners differed from immigrants, however, in being home-grown outsiders in the nation" (1995: 23).

8. There are, to be sure, black Latinos and Latinas who migrate to and settle in the U.S. Southeast. As my primary focus is the semiotics of blackness through brownness and dark brownness—and how blackened bodies are constructed and positioned—I defer to future studies on this topic of the politics of space and place for "Afro-Latin@s" in the "New South."

9. This black prominence certainly stands out. Intellectual history discussions verify the importance of a dynamic Durham for U.S. African Americans. Du Bois lauded this urban center in 1912 as an important community that "characterizes the progress of the Negro American" (quoted in Brown, 2008: 12). E. Franklin Frazier denominated it in 1925 as the "Capital of the Black Middle Class" (14). But during the city's "upbuilding," as historian Leslie Brown has shown, "almost everyone who lived in Durham came from someplace else" (16). Brown applies the Du Boisian term of upbuilding in her study to depict the socioeconomic development "of black communities after slavery, upbuilding was the literal and figurative construction of structures African Americans used to climb out of slavery" (10).

10. Texas, as Neil Foley argues, oversteps the U.S. boundaries that mark the South and West. It "fits comfortably within the cultural and historiographical boundaries of the South, with its history of slavery, cotton, and postemancipation society." But Texas also has "cultural elements of the South, the West, and Mexico [that] form a unique borderlands culture" (1997: 2). Mexicans forged new identities in the region by "rupturing the black-white polarity of southern race relations." The cotton culture of central Texas, brought together "by blacks and whites in the South, and Mexicans and Anglos in the Southwest," created a "hybrid southwestern culture" (4–5). That being so, this geography is not "racially static or bipartite but a site of multiple and heterogeneous borders where different languages, experiences, histories, and voices intermingled amid diverse relations of power and privilege. Partly for these reasons, the categories of Anglo, black, and Mexican are wholly inadequate—and even misleading—in describing the highly miscegenated culture of central Texas" (7).

11. The city's shifting entrepreneurial governance in the late 1990s, Thaddeus Countway Guldbrandsen specifies, has been reorganized around a way where "Durham's trajectory resembles most closely that of those cities in the American South whose economic competitive advantage was built partly on the lasting legacy of some aspects of their Southernness, including low property values and low labor costs, as well as on massive public investment in universities, roads, telecommunications, and other infrastructure" (2005: 83). The region's transfigurations can also be accounted for in terms of the bourgeoning Spanish-language press, as newspapers like *La Voz de Carolina* (formerly *La Voz del Pueblo*, 1993, Chapel Hill), *La Conexión* (1995, Raleigh), and *La Noticia* (1997, Charlotte) attest. For an analysis of interethnic relations among African Americans, Latinos, Latinas, and Afro-Latinos, as represented in the Spanish-language media, see Jackson et al. (2008).

12. The *Herald-Sun*, a local newspaper, recently summarized that "the black community decreased" from 2000 to 2006 and estimated a 68 percent growth in Durham among Latinos and Latinas. The Hispanic "population swell," as this venue dubbed

it, is "changing the face" of the medium-sized city and the "contiguous counties" of Durham, Chatham, Orange, Granville, and Person. The boom is attributed to Latino and Latina wage work in agricultural plants and construction jobs, giving way to the *Herald-Sun*'s description of a "flooding of the region" that is "readily apparent by the number of Hispanic *tiendas*, restaurants, laborers, and families" (West and Hoyle, 2007: B1). Adding to this journalistic representation from the celebratory culinary perspective, the now-defunct *Gourmet*, "The Magazine of Good Living," devoted its September 2007 issue to "Carolina Cocina." *Gourmet* illustrated how Durham — and by extension, much of the U.S. South — is becoming "Latin" in its culinary preference. But the food discussion soon turned sociological, noting that approximately "570,000 [Hispanic] people are scattered around the state, many of them living in the so-called Triangle defined by the cities of Raleigh, Durham, and Chapel Hill" (C. Andrews, 2007: 34). There was also a tone of caution as much as a sense of gastronomic discovery in the feature article. Revealing the shared, sustaining sameness between nation and narrator, *Gourmet* observed that in these eateries "you might not hear a word of English spoken for hours at a time" (36).

This uncovering of Durham's surprisingly profitable enterprises — brown and dark brown follies, one might say, in twenty-first-century capitalism — calls for an abridged deliberation of what makes the spice world of a Latino menu so novel in the South? Far from trivial, this concentration on Latino cooking and food choices alludes to how "the South gets defined, by whom, at what time, and why it matters." In a southern meal, Elizabeth S. D. Engelhardt communicates, "you see visible expressions of our background regional identity" (2011: 4). Engelhardt puts forward that "scholars, media, advertisers, and artists not only excavate food practices, we actively shape them as well. Our definitions of 'true' southern foods change and evolve constantly, as some foods are lifted and celebrated while other equally common ones stay in the background waiting for their day" (6–7).

Gourmet's exposure of Latino fare accentuates its estranged, non-black-white southernness at the regional level, while nationwide colloquial truisms take note of how many people in the United States prefer salsa to ketchup. Such propensity for salsa indicates that there is familiarity with Latin ingredients around the American table. Dating further back than the consumption of salsa as an edible phenomenon — and aptly complementary to our lens of the Global South — however, is another demonstrable preference for Latinness and tropicality through the more substantial plant, herb, and grass known as the banana. The fruit, as is widely known, is harvested in Central America, Caribbean posts including Jamaica and Cuba, as well as Colombia and Ecuador. This crop has become the most popular item on supermarket shelves, and "the only other products beating the banana on to our shopping lists" are gasoline and lottery tickets (Chapman, 2007: 17). And yet as a recent pop culture study about the "remarkable culinary evolution" that has "exploded" in the United States points out, "it is a great time to be an eater" in this nation. The researcher adds that "food is an area of American life where things just continue to improve," insofar as "Americans are increasingly sophisticated about what they eat and expansive in their tastes" (Kamp, 2006: xi–xiv). Even though *Gourmet* informed, at the time, middle- or upper-class American subjects about Latino cookery—this type of panethnic food, unlike the more upscale haute cuisine genre of "Nuevo Latino"—is more affordable and crosses into a pan-Latino domain despite its Mexican *taquería* specificity.

13. Latino and Latina national incipiency seems to germinate and become more visible through southern passages and myriad exchanges from the Southwest to the Southeast. According to the *Los Angeles Times* journalist and novelist Héctor Tobar, California is now "sending off its more ambitious and restless" Latino and Latina "sons and daughters to settle in newer places." Tobar records how local gossip about North Carolina stresses that there is "so much work carving up chickens you could save up enough to buy up your own little *rancho*" (2005: 28). Sonia Nazario, also a *Los Angeles Times* reporter, expands on these Southwestern-Southeastern migrations and networks facilitating such geographic exchanges. Her coverage of Lourdes, a Honduran migrant, notes that she moved from the Golden State to the Tar Heel State because "California is too hard." Lourdes's trajectory is retold in this fashion: "She has followed a female friend to North Carolina and started over again. She sold everything in California—her old Ford, a chest of drawers, a television, the bed she shares with her daughter. It netted $800 for the move" (2007: 27). Although Lourdes and her daughter end up moving farther South to Florida, Nazario writes that Lourdes came to love North Carolina. Her daughter, who was born in California, learned to quickly speak English there, "something she hadn't done surrounded by Spanish speakers in California" (186).

Perhaps what is so striking is that North Carolina is providing a more feasible (if not expedient) version of the "American Dream"—or quicker cultural assimilatory evidence—than California. Even so, these questions remain: Why is it so astonishing that Latinos and Latinas are moving out of the Southwest? Is it because they are exceeding the bounds of where they "belong"? How is their incessant movement, as history has shown, continually shifting the geography of "ethnoracial reason" in the U.S. map? I am, of course, echoing the objectives of the Caribbean Philosophical Association (CPA) when I raise this concern. Since its first international conference in 2004, the CPA has organized around the theme of "Shifting the Geography of Reason" in such countries as Barbados (2004), Puerto Rico (2005), Canada (2006), Jamaica (2007), Guadeloupe (2008), Colombia (2010), and Trinidad (2012). The intent behind this analytic geography of reason is to focus "on the broad impact of the rise of Africana and other 'third world' philosophies from geographical notions, metaphors, and assumptions that have long been associated with modern concepts of philosophical reason." The CPA thus "look[s] closely at the variety of intellectual movements that have shaped the development of ideas, especially in the Caribbean, that have contributed to, and continue to have an impact (positive or negative) on, the geography of reason" (Caribbean Philosophical Association, n.d.).

14. Du Bois cautioned on the economic challenges in the South more than a century ago, when he spoke not only of the struggles of the black body but also of the integration of "that" black being into U.S. socioeconomic and nationalist projects. "To be a poor man is hard," Du Bois observed, "but to be a poor race in the land of dollars is the very bottom of hardships" (2003: 12). C. Vann Woodward wrote about the "great changes that are altering the cultural landscape of the South almost beyond recognition." Among those changes, particularly those of the 1940s, is urbanization. To this end, Woodward drew on the symbol of the bulldozer as "the advance agent of the metropolis" to point to the growth of what he terms the "Bulldozer Revolution" (1960: 5–6). The Bulldozer Revolution plowed "under cherished old values of individualism, localism, family, clan, and rural folk culture" in the South, bringing about "industrialism, urbanism, unionism, and big government [that] confirmed or promised too many coveted benefits" (10). By the 1950s a "considerable portion of these Southerners moved from country to suburb," forming a "rurbanization" that "skipped the phase of urbanization entirely" (6–7). The 1950s also signified that "the voice of the South [during this period] had become the voice of the chamber of commerce, and Southerners appeared to be about as much absorbed in the acquirement of creature comforts and adult playthings as any other Americans" (9).

Regarding the Nuevo ("alien") South, Stack's research interposes these public perceptions and interjections, noting that "even after a generation or more of prattle about a new new new South, there still were no jobs to speak of" for the young African Americans of North and South Carolina (1996: 5). And yet does U.S. African American relocation signify erasure from an entire regional and national landscape? Stack's work on U.S. African American migrations to the rural, eastern parts of North and South Carolina presses for the exploration and reflection of the structures that bind individuals to a sense of place and social identities. She notes that figures released by the U.S. Census Bureau as far back as 1975 document the first numbers of a black American exodus from the industrious North to the rural South. Since then, a "small counterstream of perhaps 15,000 people a year [moved] against the overwhelming northward tide that had been flowing throughout the twentieth century" (xiii). So much so that by 1990, "the South had gained more than half a million black Americans who were leaving the North—or more precisely the South had *regained* from the cities of the North the half million black citizens it had lost to northward migration during the 1960s" (xiv). Stack's multilayered ethnographies concerning what she calls an evolving Great Return Migration to southern "homeplaces" stress a reversal of push-and-pull factors anticipating other social dynamics, as internal transformations are bound to take place, and not entirely because of Latinos and Latinas (7). Those returning to the South, Stack insists, "are changed in all the usual mortal ways [. . .] and they are also changed in particular and profound and historical ways, their consciousness shaped by their experience of America at a certain time, in certain American places" (xv). Returning migrants are, in this regard, "more like strangers than homefolk; [. . .] they are very much like migrants moving someplace new," as they seek to develop "a place in which their lives and strivings will make a difference—a place in which to *create* a home" (199).

15. Fink's central focus is Morganton's labor force transformation through Guatemalan and Mexican migrant poultry workers. He inserts scary quotes around the "Hispanic" category under which these groups fall in Morganton, an industrial center whose previous settlers were whites, blacks, and Hmong refugees. Further inquiry into these communities and their demographic shifts demonstrates that the Guatemalans are, in fact, "nearly all" Highland Maya (2003: 2). They are a Q'anjob'al-speaking population "from the mountain villages of the northwestern province of Huehuetenango" that also includes "Awakatekos and Chalchitekos from the commercial agricultural valley of Aguacatán" (4). Fink examines the "cultural adjustment among the new migrant workers," asking, "with what capacity and vision but also at what cost did the Guatemalan Maya transplant themselves to a new North American setting" (2–3)? For the purposes of this study, I am also interested in how these indigenous groups are mutually "Hispanized" or "Latinized" in the United States, particularly through public discourses on "new" migrations and processes of "alienization." As Fink states, "the arriving Guatemala Maya presented a puzzle and a challenge to the established citizenry of Morganton even as this North Carolina town equally presented its own mysteries to the new arrivals. [. . .] [T]he problem was, and remains, more severe—a horde of aliens would ravage the landscape, threatening the very foundation of the community, and deprive others of their chance for the good life" (32). Mayas also pose a form of "Latin" abstraction in the U.S. imaginary. "In this small southern town," Fink writes, "the questions of who is an American, who will do the work, and under what conditions echoed with renewed insistence" (33).

16. I recognize of course the presence of Native Americans in the U.S. South. Although southeastern and southwestern Native populations are not analyzed in a similarly in-depth manner as Africana and Latino and Latina populations in this

book, I am aware that they have navigated geographic and national tensions concerning the U.S. South and Jim Crow laws, notions of U.S. and hemispheric Americanness, and their construction as a "race." Malinda Maynor Lowery's study, *Lumbee Indians in the Jim Crow South: Race, Identity, and the Making of a Nation*, frames the subject formation of North Carolina's Lumbee Indians—also known as Tuscarora, Croatan, Cherokee, and Siouan—through a trifold subject formation that brings in Lumbee identity as well as their southernness and Americanness. Lowery explains that the Lumbee Tribe of Robeson County, North Carolina, has "crafted an identity as a People, a race, a tribe and a nation. They have done so not only as Indians but also as Southerners and Americans. And they have done so against the backdrop of some of the central issues in American history: race, class, politics, and citizenship." Lumbees formed "their own sense of nationhood, [. . .] adopting (and adapting to) racial segregation and creating political and social institutions that protected their distinct identity" (2010: xii).

17. Cuadros characterizes this Latino and Latina silent migration in the rural South to poultry-processing work available in Siler City, North Carolina. This industry is unlike other agricultural enterprises: the meatpacking and poultry-processing plants have a "year-round, six days a week, three shifts" schedule (2006: 12). Cuadros chronicles the ethnoracial and linguistic tensions between white and African American Siler City residents and Latinos and Latinas. He accounts for the latter group's facing of prejudice and fear in that town's public schools. Siler City citizens "needed the Latino workers to man the chicken plants and keep their economy going, but they didn't necessarily want the people or their children to live with them or share their resources" (41). Cuadros perceives that Siler City's townspeople cope with the Latino and Latina presence through "stages similar to the five stages of grief." The steps for such a process brings about "denial, where communities ignore the presence of Latino workers in their town. The next stage is anger. The third stage is bargaining, and sometimes people would say that as soon as the economy took a downturn the Latinos would leave. The fourth is depression. [. . .] The last stage, of course, is acceptance, and in 1999, Siler City was nowhere near accepting the Latino population. Siler City was angry" (42). Most striking is Cuadros's recount of a 2000 KKK rally in Siler City featuring David Duke, "the former grand dragon of the KKK in Louisiana and U.S. Senate candidate" (47). The mass gathering objected to the "unburdenable strain on the indigenous residents here, our traditions, our institutions, and our infrastructure." Whiteness is indigenized in this instance, preceding any "other" group. Siler City's African Americans, however, denounced the protest: "They reasoned that if it were still possible for Klan supporters to hold an open rally after all the previous suffering, there was no guarantee they were any safer than before" (46–47).

18. For Edwards, décalage—"one of the many French words that resists translation into English" but that can nonetheless be thought of as "'gap,' 'discrepancy,' 'time-lag,' or 'interval'"—furnishes a model for Africana groups through "the very weave of culture" that paradoxically brings up "a haunting gap or discrepancy that allows the African diaspora to 'step' and 'move' in various articulations" (2003: 13–15).

19. Conventionally, passing has typified, as historian Martha A. Sandweiss denotes it, a practice that "generally involves adopting a particular identity to move *toward* greater legal and social privilege. It might mean taking on a different gender, or ethnic or national identity, but it most often involves the assumption of a different racial identity. And since, in the United States, social privilege has been associated with lighter-colored skin, passing usually entails concealing one's African American heritage to assume a white identity. The entire practice hinges on a peculiar idea" (2009: 7). Mary Bucholtz also elaborates on the academic fields that dissect this "peculiar idea," making it known that "whereas gender theorists celebrate passing as an achievement, a transcendence of sexual difference, in ethnic studies the phenomenon is generally considered an evasion of racism, an escape that is available only to individuals who can successfully represent themselves as white" (1995: 352). But whiteness is not a linear end for all subjects. There is an overlapping instability within blackness, brownness, dark brownness, and whiteness. These colorings pass and tinge one another in the creation of new biographical moments that attempt to forge a language of selfhood, nation, and ethnicity. Bucholtz is mindful of these possibilities, writing, "passing is not a one-time event but a never-completed process of achieving a position in a recognized category" (354).

20. Charles W. Chesnutt seemed to have this point in mind with his depiction of U.S. African Americans and the alternative routes some took to access the benefits conferred on whiteness within the color line. One of his protagonists in *The House behind the Cedars* (1900) implores that he and his sister must be taken for themselves alone, maintaining "we are a new people" (1993: 57). This newness concentrates on access and self-invention rather than on the exceptionalist idea of being a "rare"—or even a "unique"—American of mixed race.

21. Sonia Saldívar-Hull also applies notions of a "larger political family" (2007: 3)—as evinced in Anzaldúa's *Borderlands/La Frontera*—and a "Familia de Mujeres" in *Feminism on the Border* (2000: 56–57).

22. These equivalencies between what Cohn identifies as the South and Spanish America engender "a fundamental paradigm structuring social organization and relations, as well as leaving a legacy of strict social hierarchization and a deeply rooted aversion to miscegenation" (1999: 6).

23. Though I express and attempt to open a new interpretive window into new

subjectivities, migrants, and migrations, I wish to stress Alfred J. López's productive prompt: "Of course the places and peoples that make up today's Global South are not exactly new; it is rather their commingling and alignment under the banner of globalization and its aftermath, among other things, that distinguishes today's Global South from yesterday's Third World and other such terms" (2007b: v).

24. On this point about African–New World studies, consult Davies et al. (2003).

25. Adams and Phillips Casteel admit that they "are not the first to argue for a connection between Canada and the Americas" (2005: 7). This admission does not diminish their contribution to Canadian, American, and Latin American studies. They offer an intersecting schema between Canadian and broader continental frameworks. Their corollaries for "critical conversations about a hemispheric American Studies" include the following four points: "(1) Canada's place in the history of slavery and the black diaspora; (2) Canada's official policies of bilingualism and multiculturalism and its struggles with linguistic and cultural diversity; (3) The U.S.-Canadian border provides an opportunity to expand the borderlands paradigm from encounters between Mexican and Anglo cultures to a comparative view of contact zones across the Americas; and (4) Canadian discourses of racial hybridity may be seen as counterparts to the more well-known theories of Latin American proponents of mestizaje such as Simón Bolívar, José Martí, José Vasconcelos, and Roberto Fernandez Retámar" (8–11).

26. Juan Flores defines cultural remittances as "the ensemble of ideas, values, and expressive forms introduced into societies of origin by remigrants [returning emigrant nationals] and their families as they return 'home,' sometimes for the first time, for temporary visits or permanent re-settlement, and is transmitted through the increasingly pervasive means of telecommunications" (2009: 4). Cultural remittances are nonmonetary and "may bear even greater consequences than the 'cash transfers.'" We need to "understand the potential deeper significance of all 'transfers' emanating from diasporas," he adds, as "our notion of culture needs to embrace collective, ideological, as well as artistic meanings of the term" (9).

27. One could also take into account Harlem, the urban center of Alain Locke's "New Negro." This neighborhood is represented as a space whose diasporic blackness is not only wedded to the U.S. South. As a "race capital," Harlem "has attracted the African, the West Indian, and the Negro American" (1997: 963). But the characteristics of what can be read as a Global South apply to the "New Negro," as evidenced in the production of linguistically mixed Harlem publications. Locke notes that "Negro" newspapers "carry news material in English, French, and Spanish, gathered from all quarters of America, the West Indies, and Africa has maintained itself in Harlem for over five years" (968).

28. As Sandweiss references in *Passing Strange*, the biography of Clarence King, "an explorer of the American West, a geologist, an accomplished writer and storyteller" (2009: 3), the Southwest—namely, the territory between the Rocky Mountains and the Sierra Nevada—began to be formally surveyed and mapped in 1867 by civilian scientists under the influence of the Northeast's intellectual and political establishments. These men were employed by King, who was appointed and funded by the federal government as U.S. geologist in charge of the U.S. Geological Exploration of the Fortieth Parallel, a Southwest military operation that included graduates from Yale and Harvard Universities (48). Sandweiss writes that King's expedition "represented American ambitions for the West writ at large. And King's efficient field organization, emphasis on the practical uses of basic science, and new, more rigorous methods of topographic mapping provided a model and standard for the rest. The data he and his fellow survey leaders gathered aided economic development in the post–Civil War West, and the scientific reports, maps, popular literature, and stunning photographic views that flowed forth year after year built broad public support for western exploration as a valuable national enterprise" (50). Despite U.S. expansion, King was skeptic about whether "a vibrant American culture could thrive in the West." Unlike Americans in the East, King found that "California people are not living in a tranquil, healthy, social *régime*" (60).

Ana Castillo's query consequently bears pertinence, considering that the U.S. Southwest and West—as they come to be historically recorded—exist from the governmental and institutional circuits of the North. Equally salient is Castillo's point of geographic interest, as it moves out of a U.S. North/U.S. South historical deadlock in terms of nation formation. Herewith, one cannot fail to mention, as well, Saldívar-Hull's fierce remembrance of southern marginality on the U.S.-Mexico borderlands: "Living in Brownsville, Texas, meant living at the southernmost tip of the United States. When I was a child, the knowledge that we were at the bottom of the U.S. map made sense to me" (2000: 12).

29. Hill Collins proceeds to reference the exclusion of educator and activist Septima Clark, who remarked, "I found all over the South that whatever the man said had to be right. They had the whole say. A woman couldn't say a thing" (1990: 8).

30. Palumbo-Liu argues that the "Asia Pacific paradigm is a crucial task for Asian American studies, one that might be facilitated by alternative modernities in South Asia, especially as the momentum toward the Pacific has been modified by the recent instabilities of Asian economies and new waves of South Asian populations have refigured America in critical ways." The modernizing of America excluded certain groups but accommodated others. It framed "the appearance and function of Asian America [. . .] [as] deeply rooted in the histories of both willed and forced migrations, of both

national and global economic change, of wars of colonization, decolonization, and global strife" (1999: 6). U.S. practices of exclusion and accommodation led to a "crisis management," where "American development as a global power sets in motion a complex history of strategizing the precise nature of that [Asian and Asian American] incorporation, and of reading the effects of increased contact upon the national body" (8). Palumbo-Liu asks, "how to understand Asians if not to plumb the psychic content of the body, to see the possible affinities and points of alienation" (7)?

31. It has been assessed that the South's Jim Crow segregation has now become "Juan Crow" due to strict anti-immigration laws and attitudes. The name has been linked to Alabama's anti-immigration measure, HB 56, which directs law enforcement officers to "act as de facto immigration agents during routine traffic stops and requiring school systems to document the citizenship status of new students." Juan Crow is "a play on Jim Crow, the moniker for segregation in the pre–civil rights South—because of the likelihood that Hispanics will be subjected to racial profiling and dubious detentions" (Person, 2011). Roberto Lovato has likened Juan Crow to anti-immigration politics in Georgia. Juan Crow, as a regime, is "the matrix of laws, social customs, economic institutions and symbolic systems enabling the physical and psychic isolation needed to control and exploit undocumented immigrants" (2008).

32. Du Bois described Atlanta's geography as "South of the North, yet North of the South" (1996b: 63). Rubén Martínez synthesized the power dynamics informing the hierarchical normativity of the North/South he encountered—in Los Angeles, Mexico City, and San Salvador—in this manner: "[W]herever I am now, I must be more than two. I must be North and South in the North and in the South" (1993: 5). Martínez's social locations, positionings, and meanings call for linkages that disharmonize the fixity of each location, or in Jon Smith's estimation, "postplantation economies in the New World, and, with appropriate qualification, throughout much of the Third World or Global South" (2004: 144).

33. Robert McKee Irwin, Claudia Sadowski-Smith, and Sophia A. McClennen articulate three notable breaks in the study of the U.S.-Mexico border (Irwin), the Canada–U.S. frontier (Sadowski-Smith), and inter-American studies (McClennen). Irwin upholds that U.S.-Mexico border studies needs to integrate Mexican perspectives into U.S.-based discussions of this southern boundary to challenge "implicit hierarchies that go beyond economics, technology, and military might" and enter "the realms of academics and publishing, the production of knowledges." More scholarly reciprocity is found from South to North, a case advanced by Irwin: "It is certainly more common, for example, for Mexican scholars of Mexican culture to be informed and conscious of what has been published on Mexican culture in English by scholars at U.S. universities than for U.S.-based scholars of American culture to know or care about what Mexicans

working at Mexican universities and publishing in Spanish may contribute to the field" (2001: 510). He adds, "While it is true that Mexican Americans are marginalized in racist U.S. society, in the borderlands themselves, hierarchies are more complex. Chicano culture is not synonymous with U.S.-Mexico border culture. Chicano culture very specifically reflects the lives of Mexican immigrants (first generation or otherwise) in the geopolitical terrain of the United States. The borderlands of Sonora or Nuevo León are not equivalent to those of New Mexico or Southern California" (517). Irwin sparks meaningful and convincing observations. While I understand that he explicitly focuses here on U.S.-Mexico border studies, U.S. border studies and its emergent knowledges should not be limited to the U.S.-Mexico or Mexico-U.S. dyad. Mexico also shares a 750-mile southern border with Belize and Guatemala, and an understanding of U.S.-Canadian border politics necessitates epistemic terms as well.

Sadowski-Smith, for instance, has drawn on Canadian border narratives to consider how this cultural production symbolizes "Canadian internal diversity and its difference from ethnic frameworks in the USA." She marks Canada's "declining economic, political, and cultural autonomy, while also signifying the country's growing relationship to other parts of the hemisphere." In general, Canada's five-thousand-mile border with the United States has indexed a division demonstrating that country's "political and cultural autonomy from the USA, as a marginal space that signifies Canada's marginal position in the world, and as a sanctuary for U.S. Americans, including indigenous peoples and slaves during the nineteenth century and Vietnam War resisters, draft evaders and other political dissenters during the twentieth century" (2005: 65–66).

McClennen calls for the displacement of U.S. culture in inter-American studies to move to other comparative models, as U.S. reference points have served as the predominant "central signifier" to investigate the region. She writes, "If Inter-American Studies are to effectively dislocate the United States from the center of the hemisphere's academic purview, then comparisons of works from within Latin America should also form part of the work of Inter-American Studies." McClennen's illustration of corresponding research includes "a comparison of the feminist theories of Clarice Lispector, Luisa Valenzuela, Diamela Eltit, and Cristina Peri Rossi, or the political aesthetic of the Bolivian Grupo Ukumau and the Peruvian Grupo Chaski" (2005: 393–94). These examples and possible approaches are indisputably important. Yet we should also recall that this proposal suggests a distinctive Inter-South American dialogue that for the most part overlooks Mexico, Central America, and the Caribbean.

34. Jovita González and Eve Raleigh's *Caballero: A Historical Novel* takes us to the slavery that existed in the U.S. South's plantation system. They link it to the lowest

class of workers in Texas as well as in the unfolding U.S. Southwest in 1846. González and Raleigh's fragment on life in the Virginia plantation and its parallel with occupied Texas reads: "Black slaves! [. . .] 'A man should be a slave only if he wishes it. Slavery as such does not exist here [in Texas], but we have peonage which is almost as bad. If your [American] nation is so progressive, why does it not free its slaves? Only freedom of the individual is progress'" (2008: 45).

35. The Great Migration, for example, elicited dreams about America and freedom through the North/South divide and African American odysseys to the North. Hazel Rowley sums it up in *Richard Wright: The Life and Times*: "In the North, wages for blacks could be as much as four times higher than wages in the South. [. . .] You would not be lynched for running a successful business. You could vote. You could live in a brick house and send your children to school for the whole of the school year and you could sit anywhere you liked on public transport and not be bothered. You did not have to step off the sidewalk if a white came along, or raise your hat, or say 'yes-sir,' or wait until all whites were served first before you could buy your newspaper" (2001: 52). Rowley's portrayal of the Ohio River during these migrations evokes a North/South borderland. It functioned as "the border between slavery and freedom. Southern blacks still see it as a gateway to freedom" (50).

36. But we also find a disjunction: while some scholars insist on the academic "openness" of Latino/a studies, such multiple entrances are not extended to the Latino or Latina subject, who is always presumably bound by a discernible way of being "Latino." Angie Chabram-Dernersesian's words hold relevance in terms of the other fields with which Latino/a studies dialogues. At the same time, I am pushing for the study of Latino and Latina theories and bodies through comparative approaches that also focus on the commonplaces and acts through which Latinities speak. Chabram-Dernersesian comments, "With regard to the ways Latina/o studies get articulated in the academy, I would agree with those who propose that what is required is 'numerous entrances, exits,' and 'escape routes' as well as 'collaboration versus subsumption.' Already the trend of Latina/o studies is toward the dispersal of the lines of affiliation, not the promised self-contained overarching umbrella. (The study of Latinas/os can be found in a number of diverse departments including women's studies, law schools, feminist studies, ethnic studies, Native American studies, Black studies, cultural studies, gay and lesbian studies, border studies, and community studies)" (2003: 116).

37. To the notion of "Transamerica," a "Transafrica" can also be appended, as the TransAfrica Forum attests. The TransAfrica Forum is "the oldest and largest African American human rights and social justice advocacy organization promoting diversity and equity in the foreign policy arena and justice for the African World" (2011). Consult also Early (2003).

38. These epistemic terms also have resonances with Mignolo's theory of "border gnosis," where he aspires to "open up the notion of 'knowledge' beyond cultures of scholarships" (2000: 9).

39. For recent contributions to the widening field of inter-American studies, consult Fox (2005).

40. Though not grounding her theoretical contributions through the optic of the Global South, Jody Berland also articulates a double consciousness when it comes to her interrogation of Canadian studies in relation—and contrast—to U.S.-centered Americanisms that slight Canadian discourses. Berland contends in *North of Empire* that Canadians experience "a form of a double consciousness similar to yet profoundly different from the 'doubling' of black consciousness described by race theorists such as W. E. B. Du Bois, Frantz Fanon, and Paul Gilroy. In this writing, the black person sees himself from the vantage point of both the other and himself, and experiences an irresolvable schism between the two perceptions. Rather than remaining invisible behind the veil of the raced body, the Canadian hides behind verisimilitude, 'passing' as the other while recognizing the other not as oneself. This vantage point is double-reflected through a one-way mirror in which 'America' does not see Canada at all. The nonknowing of the other is part of what the Canadian knows, and it shapes her scholarship and art" (2009: 3). Canada's northern subalternity conflicts with the hegemonic neighbor that geographically stands south of its borders.

Taking us to the geopolitics of Panama and the West Indies, Sonja Stephenson Watson implements and problematizes a Du Boisian double consciousness in conjunction with the "'duality' of being both Panamanian and Caribbean" (2009: 231). As she gauges it, specific contemporary Panamanian writers—Carlos Wilson, Gerardo Maloney, and Carlos Russell—negotiate their "Anglophone Caribbean heritage with their Hispanic heritage that is often viewed in conflict with the [nonblack] nation-state" (232). Anglophone West Indians, who are also "bilingual speakers of Spanish and English and navigate culturally and linguistically between Panama, Africa, the Caribbean, and the United States" (231), do not correspond "with the national imaginary, which promoted homogeneity over racial differences" (235). Their oeuvre disputes "national anti-West Indian sentiment and make[s] an effort to integrate the Anglophone Caribbean into the national discourse of *panameñidad*," thus contributing to "debates on race, language, and identity in their 20th-century and 21st-century texts" (237–38).

41. Connell calls attention to the fact that Du Bois "connected race issues in the metropole with movements in the colonial world and, increasingly, with the structure of global capitalism" (2007: 20). Du Bois's double consciousness was undeniably fashioned from an Africana framework that incorporated his genealogical story of

New England, the U.S. South, and the Afro-Caribbean. David Levering Lewis has recounted that class and social interactions were at work also. He writes that Du Bois's "sense of identity or belonging was spun out between the poles of two distinct racial groups — black and white — and two dissimilar social classes — lower and upper — to form that double consciousness of being he would famously describe at age thirty-five" (1993: 12).

42. And yet as Caroline F. Levander has pointed out, Du Bois's Pan-Africanism is hardly linked to other spheres in the Americas like Cuba. "Less familiar" is Du Bois's "interest in Cuba's struggle for independence from Spain. [. . .] Most scholars have tended to overlook the significance of Cuba for Du Bois's thinking, focusing instead on his attention to Haiti and its influence on his commitment to Pan-African nationalism. Yet Du Bois remained interested in Cuba throughout his career, making many trips to Cuba, [and] engaging in extensive correspondence with Cuban political leaders such as Fernando Ortiz" (2006: 158–59). Du Bois's Pan-Africanism can be examined and supplemented through more heterogeneous geographies and knowledges.

43. Carby has noted, Du Bois's "theory of double-consciousness has been so widely adopted to explain the nature of the African American soul." *The Souls of Black Folk*, she adds, "is so frequently taken to be representative of black intellectual, psychological, and existential reality" (1998: 2).

44. Connell further clarifies on this general theory and its possible effects: "Overwhelmingly, general theory is produced in the metropole. Does this matter? The sociology of knowledge would suggest that it does. On the other hand, the very generality of general theory, the aspiration to general relevance, implies that this genre could escape from local determinations" (2007: 28). When I mention general theory and the Global South, I am also inferring its possibility as a shifting intellectual undertaking that labors through ideas and frameworks from "the periphery that have to be considered as part of the dialogue of theory" (46).

45. Provocatively, African American writer Gayl Jones provides a margin-to-margin discussion of the asymmetrical location of Africana and Chicano books. In her novel *Mosquito*, Jones records a Chicana character, Delgadina, as saying, "I figure when they figure out how to commercialize Chicano literature and put us into the category of Entertainment, we'll get some popularity. Well, there are some publishers who are publishing some Chicano-oriented books and books in Spanish, but that's mostly because of the numbers of Chicano readers. We aren't as popular as African-American writers with white readers, though. And mostly we're published by little publishers, like E. D. Santos" (1999: 95).

46. As of this writing, three autobiographical narratives by and about notable men who were born in the United States during the 1910s have been restored and pub-

lished in the first decade of the twenty-first century. These works include Grillo's *Black Cuban, Black American*; John Hope Franklin's *Mirror to America: The Autobiography of John Hope Franklin* (2005); and Ben Vinson III's account, *Flight: The True Story of Virgil Richardson, a Tuskegee Airman in Mexico* (2004). Both Franklin and Grillo wrote their respective stories later on in life as accomplished individuals, whereas Richardson's autobiography, while told in the first person, is registered through Vinson's meticulous historian filter and the questions he solicited from his subject. Richardson's oral reflections were narrated to Vinson. It is striking that Richardson's text is not conceived in ways that parallel testimonial literature and the latter's incorporation of socioeconomic, ethnic, and political marginalities and struggles. I do not seek transparent literary categories for Vinson's characterization of Richardson's life. But as these life narratives are being literarily and historically recuperated, it is important to reflect on these works' solidity. It is not only the autobiographical subject who "is radically in question," as Robert Folkenflik has written, but also the "different vantage points" that publicly shape these modes of self-conception (1993: 12).

In the context of Grillo's memoir, it is worth coupling his life story with a contemporary, such as African American historian John Hope Franklin (1915–2009). Read together, Grillo and Franklin highlight the public representation of a biographical continuity—even literary beginnings—touching not only on the self's reconstruction but also on the importance of restoring particular Jim Crow histories. These projects are attentive to a "collective" (racial) narrative—vis-à-vis individual success—of American achievement. Franklin's autobiography, *Mirror to America*, admits that "Unfortunately, I kept no records of my life until I was a tenured professor and chair of the department at Brooklyn College" (2005: ix). We find a conscientious chronicler who regulates the course of his autobiography through what can be verifiably recorded and granted archival permanence. Grillo's and Franklin's life stories are written after they gained social and political realization, a notable feat since they overcame what Nell Irvin Painter calls the invisible/hypervisible color line at a time prior to the institutionalization of affirmative action (2008: 36).

Ben Vinson's *Flight* has resonances with Grillo insofar as we find correlative Latinities. *Flight* is a historical portrayal of Virgil Richardson (1916–2004), an Arkansas-born African American who was "part of a sub-current of the black diaspora, a member of a small clique of black military servicemen who retired in Mexico" (2004: 2). Arriving in 1950, Richardson lived in Mexico for forty-seven years, returning to Texas in 1997. Virgil's story is notable because he was a former Tuskegee airman, a cluster of elite fliers who inhabit "a special place in the mythology of America." As Richardson recalled his accomplishment, "Learning to fly at Tuskegee was a marvelous and unique opportunity. Most whites in America didn't believe that blacks had the reflexes or intelligence to fly planes" (39). Tuskegee airmen "were among the 'talented tenth' of their generation, whose pedigree among blacks was unquestioned, and whose patriotic service to their country would eventually earn wide respect and praise" (3). Richardson's Mexican migration was part of larger pursuits, as Vinson records it, by African American GIs who "began branching out internationally after World War II, with many taking advantage of the GI bill to improve their education." Mexico provided a "cheap alternative to crowded U.S. schools. In the 1960s and 1970s, black vets from the Korean and Vietnam wars added to the mix. Even wounded soldiers found a new lease on life south of the border, settling, marrying, and thriving in the wonderful Mexican climate" (3).

47. "A common racial identity did not bridge the gulf that existed between the two groups," Grillo mentions. "Black Americans spoke English and followed Protestant religions. Black Cubans spoke Spanish and practiced Catholicism" (2000: 11). These black distinctions differ through Cuban and American nationalities.

48. Gary R. Mormino and George E. Pozzetta record that Ybor City became "a new industrial enterprise" in 1886, the year that "workers put the finishing touches on the magnificent Statue of Liberty" (1987: 63). This industrial boom expanded from 1886 to 1900, a formative period that marked "the rapid and uninterrupted growth of an industry" (68). Curiously, this Latin boom—largely indebted to the recruitment of skilled labor from Spain and Cuba—is characterized through food. Mormino and Pozzetta note that "along with their tote bags, Cubans and Spaniards brought a cultural vitality that helped create an ethnic *paella* unique for the South" (70). Ybor City's Latinness was growing through Sicilian migrants to Florida and New Orleans (81). Italians in Florida "labored in the phosphate mines of Tampa and on construction crews at the magnificent Tampa Bay Hotel" and even went on to establish a "Little Italy" in the mid-1890s (82). For Mormino and Pozzetta, this signifies "the building of a community" in Ybor City that "centered around Seventh Avenue and Eighteenth Street, which remained the settlement's core for the next seventy-five years" (86).

49. Román de la Campa finds that Arte Público Press's RUSHLH's texts are a "major effort" that launch a U.S. Latino and Latina literary boom with beginnings "from each of [the] historically established groups in the United States." This literary heritage is "analogous on a minor scale to the Latin American literary ferment of the past thirty years [that] has provided an interesting retrospective framework, through which the long history of the U.S. Hispanic heritage is now being discovered and rediscovered. Its meaning, as with any other complex historical object-subject, will be open to debate, but it promises to challenge any simple desire to affirm or deny a pan-ethnic Latino identity. It also promises to complicate how these groups and their cultural production are viewed by scholars and critics, though both the Anglo and

Latin American literary establishments—but especially the latter—have resisted acknowledging this considerable corpus" (1994: 63). What interests me about *Black Cuban, Black American* is precisely its embodiment of another literary tension. Grillo's new mode of self-articulation is an immersion into a (Latined) American blackness that is also part of the African American canon.

50. This literary struggle also has implications for how we read Grillo's function as an autobiographer. What are his inquiries into the self, as he develops an epistemology of his existence's coetaneous dimensions? Put another way, what is the larger self-transformation at the level of black and Latin epistemologies? Profoundly embedded to "his" selfhood are the "evidentiary" components of his categorical blackness and Cubanness as well as their textual negation of each other. Grillo's lines of thought as a being-in-the-world are narratively skewed. An autobiographer, William Gass bids, is also "a shaping self: it is the consciousness of oneself as a consciousness among all these other minds, an awareness born out much later than the self it studies, and a self whose existence was fitful, intermittent, for a long time, before it was able to throw a full beam upon the life already lived and see there a pattern, as a plowed field seen from a plane reveals the geometry of the tractor's path" (1994: 51). An autobiographer's new consciousness requires an inner self that also distantiates itself from the representativeness of the narratively constructed self. Such distance—or "othering" of Grillo's Cubanness and blackness—demands that we ask, how does he "rewrite" each black and Cuban situation and their turning points?

51. Wald's take on official stories reads, "I use the term 'official' because of the authority they command, articulated, as they are, in relation to the rights and privileges of individuals. They determine the status of an individual in the community. Neither static nor monolithic, they change in response to competing narratives of the nation that must be engaged, absorbed, and retold: the fashioning and endless refashioning of 'a people'" (1995: 2).

52. Grillo's entry into the "American way of life" is not white Americanness but a black Latined Americanness that also registers—to make use of Anna Julia Cooper's efforts in *A Voice from the South*—dissatisfaction with the American present. This discontentment builds on what Cooper, a North Carolinian, called a "satisfaction in American institutions [that] rests not on the fruition we now enjoy, but [that] springs rather from the possibilities and promise that are inherent in the system, though as yet, perhaps, far in the future" (1998: 54). If the promise of a satisfactory American future is unknowable and unimaginable, so is the arrival of the Latin subject to America. What do we make of such a typically omitted subject—and in changeable manifestations of Latinness? How do we insert it as a possibility and a promise that inher-

ently spring in the American processes and institutions that un-Americanize it? Like Cooper's insistence that the projected voice of the South fails to consider the standpoints of "the expectant Black woman" as an "important witness" to social thought emanating from the South, Grillo's book brings to the fore what Cooper called "one silent strain in the Silent South" (51). Latinity, in this instance, refers to the Cuban cultural practices that Grillo addresses, customs and meanings that do not necessarily impart Cuban but Latin. Despite being told from a racialized man's perspective overlooking Latina voices from the South, Grillo's other layer of the Latino Silent South makes known that Latino and Latina stories are still in the making and have yet to be fully recorded.

53. Jennifer DeVere Brody cogitates on punctuation marks and their proliferation as "visual (re)marks" (2008: 2). She posits, "Punctuation is not a proper object: it is neither speech nor writing; art nor craft; sound nor silence. It may be neither here nor there and yet somehow it is everywhere" (3). Punctuation is marked by "ambiguous movements." Depending on the editorial setting, they "function as shadow figures that both compose and haunt writing's substance" (5). Grillo appears to underscore a robust comma as a subject of punctuation as well as a deferred selfhood that cannot intrude on the present jagged mapping of the past through Arte Público Press's steps to recover the U.S. Hispanic Literary Heritage.

54. We could recollect James Weldon Johnson's discussion in *Along This Way* of the kinds of families he encounters when teaching in rural Hampton, Georgia. During one stop, Johnson meets a homeowner caught between the crevices of being "white" and "colored." The homeowner is described as "an intelligent, light-complexioned man, who had a job with a railroad; the wife was a comely light-brown woman; and there was a pretty little girl named Alma." Johnson does not discount the rich spectrum of the color line as well as the nuances behind the girl's name. He immediately follows with this contention: "I wondered how her parents came to choose the name, a word that in Spanish means soul" (2000: 106). Alma, it should also be noted, means "soul" in Latin. This seeming itinerant moment in Johnson's autobiography pushes the reader to think about black-brown exchanges — lexical doppelgängers — through this family's southern Latinities. One indeed wonders how they — and their names — came to be and how they passed into the racial, historical, and geographic realm of indigent U.S. African American rural life. And yet there is also something obstinately unmoving in this customary mode of passing. The name Alma eclipses, not so subtly, another deviation of *lo negro*. Though Johnson does not expand on other forms of blackness in this rustic part of Georgia (to retain his phrasing), one could interpret such a rupturing moment of the black-white color divide as substantial enough in that it stands out in Johnson's memory as well as text (113).

Karla F. C. Holloway has written about Johnson's representative mode of remembrance in *Along This Way*, alluding to the "fragility of the recollections," in the context of mother-son readerly and artistic formation. Johnson intentionally filled his narrative "spaces with ellipses as if to indicate that even though these are 'intensely vivid' memories, they are vignettes, and they have for him as much visual memory as they do power of recall. He allows his reader to fill in the spaces" (2006: 107). This "Alma vignette" can be framed through a similar literary and interpretive milieu. Johnson's sentence omissions become critical ellipses whose elliptical blanks are filled differently by different readers. What proves extraordinarily elucidating at auditory, linguistic, and visual levels is the possibility that this Alma moment presents: the continuous remix of blackness and brownness as "a sampling machine where any sound can be you" (P. Miller, 2008: 5). This general "you" lends itself to Africana, Latino, and Latina spectrums. This point does not suggest that I am unencumbered by historical accuracy, as assigned to Johnson's period. Rather, I want to access and incorporate another interpretive reentry for evaluating general constructions of U.S. "ethnics." To not be receptive to or deny other readings of a Latin Alma is to endeavor in a literalist analytic take and "translation" of what amounts to, for me, a turning point in perceptions about U.S. African American authenticity in the South. This noteworthy moment can also serve as commentary for readers to extrapolate whether they can hear and tell the difference between an Alma that is U.S. African American or Latina. Since Alma is being narratively represented in a Latined fashion, the question that arises is, what do we care to hear (or not hear) when "something" works against what may be too easily definable?

55. Irving Lewis Allen delineates in *The Language of Ethnic Conflict* that the term *wop* appeared in American slang by the mid-1890s, "near the peak of Italian immigration to the United States," as "a derogatory epithet for Italians." He annotates how "the offensive nickname for an Italian probably derives from the Neapolitan dialect's *guappo*, a dandy (literally a handsome man), later used as a Neapolitan greeting and by other Italians to refer to a Neapolitan" (1983: 118). Allen expounds that "a popular but probably wrong story has it that *wop* derives from the acronym for the phrase With Out Papers (or sometimes Passport). [. . .] The With-Out-Papers story for *wop* is seductive because it is consistent with the fact that later nicknames for other groups did emerge from the bureaucratic insensitivities of the host society" (119). He adds that wop has also signified Work-On-Pavement, "probably inspired by the occupational stereotype of Italians as concentrated in the masonry, construction, and road-building industries" (120).

56. Mormino and Pozzetta note that the Afro-Cuban presence in Ybor City constituted "13 percent of the Cuban population" in 1900. They observe that "Black Cubans,

like white Cubans, were extremely mobile geographically, shuttling frequently between Tampa and the island" (1987: 79).

57. Earl Lewis and Heidi Ardizzone focus on the media uproar resulting from the 1924 interracial marriage between Alice Jones, a black woman, and Leonard Rhinelander, a white trust-fund heir. Their relationship and the court case to annul their marriage "prompted outraged editorials regarding interracial mixing, racial definitions, white manhood, upper-class morals, working class respectability, and the place of racial and class hierarchies in a democratic society" (2001: xiii). The national sensationalism and impact of "The Rhinelander Case," as it has come to be known, was also referenced in Nella Larsen's novel, *Passing* (1929), a connection that has been widely studied (cf. Larsen, 2007; Madigan, 1990). Rhinelander was hailed as a successor to a "well-heeled family" listed in the *Social Register*. The Rhinelanders "descended from several of New York's founding families." They were "an American version of aristocracy" (Lewis and Ardizzone, 2001: xi), making their fortune "as provision merchants, shipping agricultural goods to the West Indies" (9). By contrast, Jones was the daughter of a colored man, and as newspapers of the time described this family's "disparate class standing," a "cabby" (11).

What interests me from Lewis and Ardizzone's discussion is the Latin linkage that surfaces for both Jones and Grillo. In that coloring of blackness, Jones and Grillo point to the roundabout paths that blackness takes, as opposed to steering only toward the "main road": the one-drop rule of black racial identity. Analyzing Jones's media coverage, Lewis and Ardizzone write, "Again and again papers tried to describe Alice, an endeavor that actually painted a range of images of her appearance: She was 'dark'; 'she was 'of light complexion'; she was 'dusky'; she was a 'pretty girl of the Spanish type'; she was 'of medium height, dark and of a Spanish or Latin type of features. Her straight black hair is worn in a long bob'; she was 'a comely young woman with bobbed black hair and a complexion of Spanish tint.'" These statements seem to work through the rich semiotics of blackness and Latinness, an operating Latinities of sorts. Though the remarks seem to invariably translate into blackness, they also paradoxically undermine "the most straightforward definition of blackness [. . .] that someone is black who looks black" (2001: 24).

58. At this point of our discussion, Julie M. Weise's research on the race and class dimensions of the "Mexican generation" and the "Mexican American generation" in New Orleans and the Mississippi Delta demands special note to broaden our Latino and Latina compass of the U.S. South. The former pertains to "Mexican immigrants of the 1910s and 1920s who created homeward-looking cultures as bulwarks against a society that had begun to exclude and racialize them"; the latter speaks to those whose "service in World War II was an integral component of a new political strategy,

and in some cases identity shift, emphasizing U.S. citizenship" (2009: 247). Weise's work, dating from 1908 to 1939, adds an interesting configuration to the corpus of the U.S. South: her analysis revolves around the sociocultural acquisition of whiteness by Mexicans and Mexican Americans, which came into being from abroad. Mexican government representatives, in confronting "the black-white eugenic binary of U.S. white supremacy" (250), exercised a "banner of Mexican nationalism" that granted migrants a social status affiliated with U.S. whiteness (269). Weise contends that "the leadership of Mexico's New Orleans consulate and of its Mexican Honorary Commission in Gunnison, Mississippi [...] [engaged in] distinctly Mexican strategies which Mexicans of all social classes pursued in their quest to attain and retain white status in the U.S. South" (249–50). These commissions "promoted Mexican culture, organized politically, and offered communal support" (258), under a type of Mexicanness—a cultural whitening—that emphasized North-South "cordial relations" (269). This is not to imply, however, that Mexicans and Mexican Americans were not racialized in the South. This point is not amiss in Weise's calculations. "Certainly," she claims, "Mexicans arriving in the South at the close of the Mexican Revolution faced the possibility of becoming racialized not as white nor black, but 'Mexican'" (255). Particularly striking is that although "by 1920 the federal census listed 1,242 Mexican-born whites in New Orleans," it is possible that "an additional ten percent lived there as well, classified as negro or mulatto" (252). All to say, then, that Grillo's coloring has Mesoamerican counterparts, as *negro* and *mulato* are inhabited by Latinos and Latinas. Negro and mulatto do not just stem from U.S. blackness.

59. Still, Grillo expresses disappointment with an institution that did not trust him "in asserting my individuality outside the campus on my own." His individual and institutional differences are framed through political and religious ideologies that are not in line with Xavier University. Since he was considered a "renegade" on campus with "Communist leanings," Grillo intimates that such political differences may have been what led to the university not granting him the highest honors. "Graduation seemed like a bad dream," he bemoans, "with my classmates inquiring, 'What happened?' Visibly embarrassed and upset, I had not learned to be cool under fire." But Grillo, the author with finessed political experience, returns to this moment of disappointment. He seems to want to reconcile these differences by writing, "In the perspective of the years, however, it is not appropriate or necessary to focus on the negative aspects of my largely pleasant years at Xavier. Xavier took me in, one of many penniless if deserving young people of college age." His racial uplift story is obliged to admit that Xavier "provided me with a superb education, which I have used advantageously for my own growth in life, for my family's benefit and, I hope, for the benefit of the many communities that I have served" (2000: 89–90).

60. The organization's website notes, "The Unity Council (officially known as the Spanish Speaking Unity Council) was founded in 1964, incorporated in 1967, and received 501(c)(3) tax-exempt status in 1968. The Unity Council is a non-profit community development corporation committed to enriching the quality of life of families primarily in the Fruitvale District of Oakland. Its mission is to help families and individuals build wealth and assets through comprehensive programs of sustainable economic, social and neighborhood development."

61. With Amparo's exception, members of her household appear as castrated figures, including Grillo's stepfather, Luis, a "classic passive observer." He was "thoroughly defeated and humorless" but played "an indirect role" in Grillo's quest for sex education. Grillo credits Luis with "a few helpful, exciting lessons." Taking "a peep through the keyhole in the bedroom," Grillo saw his mother and stepfather "carry out amazing gyrations under the blanket." They made "intriguing noises, poorly contained by the thin walls" (2000: 25). The mother's repression seems to be released in the bedroom, but it bears mentioning that two humorless individuals perform this undoing. Grillo's undercover investigation made him "wild with excitement" but "afraid of being caught, and guilty, because I knew I was doing something wrong." While illustrating adolescent inadequacies and anxieties around sexual matters, Grillo's representation also intimates a search for who may be symbolically big enough to dominate Amparo. That figure may as well be Grillo, a beneficiary of his mother's "wisdom and strength" (24). Soon after describing his mother's sexual desires, Grillo assigns political respectability to Amparo. He relates that she legally married the passive and seldom employed Luis, thereby recording how his stepfather established "his right to be in the house and to sleep with her" (26).

62. As Gina M. Pérez, Frank A. Guridy, and Adrian Burgos Jr. put across in their edited volume, *Beyond El Barrio: Everyday Life in Latina/o America* (2010), scholars have examined Latinoness and Latinaness as a problem and threat to America. But what also warrants more analytic attention is how Latinos and Latinas become a *problem* with concomitant black problems. Du Bois's problem, let us recall, is about the meaning of blackness. The question remains how Latino and Latina—as an amalgam of many things—pose a particular brown or dark brown problem akin to the meaning of blackness. To borrow from Lawrence D. Bobo (2010), how might we articulate, as a counterpart to blackness, Latino and Latina (brown/dark brown) "human strivings"? By translating the problem as Latino and Latina, Du Bois's formation of the problem stays in its inert blackness, as though the problem of blackness has not migrated to other U.S. ethnoracial domains. The Latino and Latina problem, by contrast, holds a prominent place through the ethnoracially ambiguous Latino/Latina label, not through a dehumanizing symbology of being blackened. I suggest that Latino and

Latina ambiguity, and its appended, monolithized brownness, are part of the contemporary American problem. U.S. Latinoness and Latinaness must be dissected not just through its perceived inherent brownness but also through the overlooked body politics of a problematic, caricatured blackness, brownness, and dark brownness that inform and move through U.S. African Americanness, Latinoness, and Latinaness.

63. Du Bois's peerless excerpt reads, "After the Egyptian and Indian, the Greek and Roman, the Teuton and Mongolian, the Negro is a sort of seventh son, born with a veil, and gifted with second-sight in this American world, — a world which yields him no true self-consciousness, but only lets him see himself through the revelation of the other world. It is a peculiar sensation this double-consciousness, this sense of always looking at one's self through the eyes of others, of measuring one's soul by the tape of a world that looks on in amused contempt and pity. One ever feels his two-ness, — an American, a Negro; two souls, two thoughts, two unreconciled strivings; two warring ideals in one dark body, whose dogged strength alone keeps it from being torn asunder" (2003: 9). For an analysis of the sources from which Du Bois drew his own articulation of double consciousness — that is, European romanticism and American transcendentalism as well as the field of psychology — see Bruce (1992) and Gates and Oliver (1999).

64. My reference to epistemic lines of thinking draws from Mignolo's appraisal that if the problem of the twentieth century was measured through the color line, dilemmas for the twenty-first will fall along what he has identified as the "epistemic line" (2010).

65. This ingression into double consciousness also invites a reinterpretation of how Du Bois's framework has been articulated. For instance, Toi Derricotte could account for such an open double consciousness through the various self-vehicles that are always "there," open for dialogue, and receptive to meanings unmasking the things that estrange us from the world. In her creative nonfiction project, *The Black Notebooks*, Derricotte writes about the many people, subjectivities, and translocations she embodies. Notice the following declaration: "I was watching the world as if I were looking through the eyes of the most vicious racist, but I was also looking through the eyes of white literary critics, black literary critics, of light-skinned black women and dark-skinned black women, of middle class and poor. I was looking through the eyes of my mother, cousins, and aunts. I had to find a way, not only to go around competing and repressive voices, but to address them, to listen and record, to disarm them and to bring them to another perspective, to resolve conflicting aims. Voice becomes, not a synthesis of opposing voices, but rather a path of energy that is allowed by all sides, one that gains egress past restrictions by bowing to them at the same time they are disobeyed, by bargaining and earning" (1997: 20). Derricotte's excerpt zooms

into "the world": the cacophony of conflicting voices that overcrowds and divides her macrocosm. As a manifestation of an unsettled articulation of double consciousness, Derricotte's feelings and thoughts are being opened to a plenitude of social worlds. Derricotte admits another point for deliberation: "Whiteness has to be examined, addressed, not taken as 'normal.' White people have to develop a double consciousness, too, a part in which they see themselves as 'other.' We are all wounded by racism, but for some of us those wounds are anesthetized. When we begin to feel it, we're awake" (125). She promotes the need, for all those wounded by racism, to open up and feel "it" as a problem but not necessarily to be one. On a fictional level, James Weldon Johnson's anonymous narrator in *The Autobiography of an Ex-Coloured Man* articulates a double consciousness embodied through the protagonist's black-and-white biraciality. But since the character's biracial body can signify various readings (and, indeed, misreadings), he moves, I insist, toward an open double consciousness. His namelessness intensifies this "openness." The fact that he is unnamed leads to shifting forms of self-reflection that continually allow him to name—and rename—himself. As he transitions from one world into another, he "looked out through other eyes, my thoughts were coloured, my words dictated, my actions limited by one-dominating, all pervading idea which constantly increased in force and weight until I finally realized in it a great, tangible fact" (1989: 21).

66. For Luis Eduardo Guarnizo, Alejandro Portes, and William Haller "cross-border political relationships" by contemporary U.S. migrants—which in concise form have the tendency to be framed under "transnationalism"—signify "the rise of a new class of immigrants, economic entrepreneurs or political activists who conduct cross-border activities on a *regular* basis" (2003: 1213). The authors opt for a more accurate qualifier, "political transnationalism," to differentiate those actors from migrants who participate in "the simple act of sending remittances to families or traveling home occasionally" (1212). For additional studies on American citizenship, disparate American interests, dual nationalities, and the crafting of "transnational life," consult Oboler (2006); R. Smith (2006); and Duany (2011).

67. Open double consciousness turns the specific double consciousness that Richard Wright postulated in Paris—through the illimitable examination of his handwritten declaration, "I am an American but . . ."—into other Latined realms informed by the conjunction "but" (Wright, n.d.). Wright's "but" can be part of a speculative Latined décalage. It has the potential to modify the meanings and actors behind Americanness through the rotating inhabitants of that inevitable contrarian state enunciated with "but."

68. Perhaps a Mexican American and Chicano and Chicana equivalent to this Du Boisian "other world" could be González and Raleigh's italicized use of the U.S. nation-

ality *Americanos* in their novel, *Caballero*. More than merely applicable to white, U.S. citizens, the idea of Americanos, in Spanish, refers to the unfolding Americanness that awaits the occupied Texan world of González and Raleigh—otherizing not the Mexicanness of what became the U.S. Southwest but the ideological processes that transplant and enforce U.S. Americanness. One of *Caballero*'s characters tries to grasp the meaning of his sudden Americanness by observing, "[C]an't you laugh? Is it not something to laugh at? We are *Americanos*!" (2008: 9). This newly granted and astonishing Americanness is as foreign as the one being brought by the "other world."

69. Richard Wright's quote reads, "There is not a black problem in the United States, but a white problem. The blacks now know what they want.... The whites don't" (quoted in Rowley, 2001: 332).

70. Writing a book review in 1968, the year in which *The Autobiography of W. E. B. Du Bois: A Soliloquy on Viewing My Life from the Last Decade of Its First Century* was published, historian Hugh Davis Graham concurred with Du Bois's own assessment. Graham referred to Du Bois's third and fullest autobiography as a "thoughtful recollection of a high order" (641). Du Bois's extract on a theory of a life reads, "Eager as I am to put down the truth, there are difficulties; memory fails especially in small details, so that it becomes finally but a theory of my life, with much forgotten and misconceived, with valuable testimony but often less than absolutely true, despite my intention to be frank and fair" (1997: 12).

71. Feeling alone cannot fully account for a sustained investigation of Du Bois's centenarian problem. Frantz Fanon's *Black Skin, White Masks*, another seminal text in Africana thought, stresses that his book "should have been written" three years prior to its initial publication in 1952. Echoing Du Bois, where to pen *The Souls of Black Folk* he had to "reduce the boiling to a simmer," Fanon brings to view the fact that "at the time [1949] the truths made our blood boil. Today the fever gas dropped and truths can be said without having them hurled into people's faces" (2008: xiii). Fanon also writes, "if I utter a great shout, it won't be black" (13). Du Bois urged us to think about how "problematic peoples" conceal, disclose, or play with their responses. Feeling *like* a—and not as *the*—problem allows the problematic subject to alter codes of behavior that differ from double consciousness inasmuch as this awareness must make meaning of the problem. Double consciousness is the impetus for making sense of "the problem of the color-line" (Du Bois, 1996b: 5).

CHAPTER TWO. Passing Latinities

1. In addition, Samira Kawash provides these definitional parameters for passing: "Common sense dictates that passing plays only with appearance and that the true identities underlying the deceptive appearances remain untouched. This has

been the accepted understanding of passing, both on the part of social scientists who attempted to study the phenomenon and literary critics who sought to understand the significance of literary representations of passing" (1997: 126). My approach deals with the moving possibilities—passages—from black and Latin to white and vice versa.

2. Two outstanding works on the African diaspora and Latin America include Nwankwo (2005) and Guridy (2010).

3. This assessment is also evidenced in Rampersad's first volume of Hughes's life, whose time in Mexico is described, rather oxymoronically, as a "dull horror" (2002: 32). There may have been dull instants in Hughes's trip, but as I argue, his journeys to that nation unveil an actively working Latinity.

4. As announced in a supplementary page to this same book, "The best biographical material on James Weldon Johnson is his own autobiography, *Along This Way*" (2000: xix).

5. Suzanne Bost's definition of mestizaje provides a good scope of this concept's working directions: "Mestizaje is the Latin American term for the racial and cultural mixture that was produced by the conquest of the so-called 'New World,' in which European colonizers mixed with the darker-skinned colonized subjects. Originally the term was used to describe the Spanish and native heritage, but mestizaje has incorporated additional racial elements. Chicana/o theorists in the United States have drawn attention to the Anglo-American additions to their racial and cultural mixture, but they often elide the African lineage in mestizaje" (2000: 187).

In the context of Nicaragua's mestizaje, Jeffrey Gould explains that the "myth of *Nicaragua mestiza*" depends on "the common sense notion that Nicaragua had long been an ethnically homogeneous society is one of the elite's most enduring hegemonic achievements. The creation of this nationalistic discourse in Nicaragua depended upon the increasing disarticulation of the *Comunidades Indigenas*. This was realized in the highlands departments of Matagalpa, Jinotega, and Boaco through *ladino* pressures on indigenous labor and land, which contributed to the weakening of the *Comunidades*. The incessant questioning of indigenous authenticity that coincided with the *ladino* advance, contributed both to the consolidation of *ladino* power and to the erosion of indigenous communal identity. Moreover, that delegitimization of indigenous authenticity, in turn, was related to the development of a democratic discourse of equal rights and citizenship that effectively suppressed specific indigenous rights to communal land and political autonomy" (2003: 365).

6. Johnson remarked, "occasionally race prejudice bumped into me." Such was the case when a white South Carolinian male was baffled upon encountering the black consul in Nicaragua. "There were several other cases of individuals," Johnson wrote, who were "caught unawares and psychologically unprepared to meet the situation. I

found it best to let them work out their own recovery from the shock and embarrassment" (2000: 258–59).

7. Julie Greene reminds us that empire was a concept that was jettisoned in the United States during Theodore Roosevelt's presidency. The twenty-sixth commander in chief "eschewed the term 'empire' in describing the United States. Instead, he talked about national greatness and the virtues and responsibilities of the Anglo-Saxon race" (2009: 18). As such, Roosevelt needed to win the nation's "citizenry over to a new identity as an imperial power" (35).

8. As a *New York Times* headline on 1 August 1912 announced, "Another Nicaragua Revolt: Mena May Bombard Managua—We Send a Ship to Corinto." The article, a "special to the *New York Times*," informed, "The feud between President [Adolfo] Diaz of Nicaragua and his former War Minister Gen. [Luis] Mena, has developed into a revolution, and to protect American interests the 500-ton gunboat Annapolis has been ordered to proceed from San Juan del Sur to Corinto. There the gunboat will restore communication with American Minister [George T.] Weitzel, who has not been heard from since the rebels cut off Managua from the outside world."

9. On 28 January 1930 Sandino published an opinion piece in the *New York World*, where he declared, "We have understood that the greatest aim of the United States of North America in Nicaragua is to appropriate Central American territory where possibilities exist for the opening of an interoceanic canal route, in addition to the Gulf of Fonseca as a naval base. And that is why our army, together with all the uncorrupted and uncontaminated Nicaraguan people, has determined that the interoceanic canal as much as the naval base in question must be considered within the sovereignty of Latin American nationality for its progress and self-defense" (1988: 305–6; my translation).

10. Robert E. Fleming informs us that literary reception to *The Autobiography of an Ex-Coloured Man* "attracted relatively little attention when it was published in 1912, [but] it remained in print until 1918 as indicated by advertisements in the *Crisis* 'Book Mart' advertisements. However, the 1927 Knopf edition, coming as it did at the height of the Harlem Renaissance and at a time when Johnson was perhaps the best-known member of the older generation of black writers, was considerably more influential. Handsomely printed and well distributed, this edition of the novel was reviewed widely not only in America but in England also. Critics from the 1930s to the present have always considered it one of the most important novels of the early part of the century, and in 1965 it was reprinted, along with Booker T. Washington's *Up From Slavery* and W. E. B. Du Bois's *The Souls of Black Folk*, as *Three Negro Classics*, edited by John Hope Franklin" (1987: 41).

11. The most palpable act of anonymity commonly attributed to Johnson's novel is the leading character's namelessness and the (black) ethnoracial ambiguity that

facilitates his admission, unidirectionally, into whiteness. Overall, however, it can be said that *The Autobiography of an Ex-Coloured Man* interpretively proposes anonymities, since obscurity is attributed to the world that the "ex-coloured man" encounters. Those inhabiting such a world are never formally named, and so the reader, too, goes by the quiddity attributed to the inhabitants of that literary microcosm. This essence has been largely interpreted in black-white terms. Roxanna Pisiak contends, for example, that in the text "[m]uch ambiguity resides in the very personality of the narrator. While he is always careful to describe the exact color of the black people he meets, the reader is never told of the narrator's exact racial status, or of his mother's. This lack of specific racial identity reflects the inanity of the arbitrary racial assumption in American society that any amount of black blood designates an individual as 'black.' Furthermore, because we don't know how 'white' or 'black' the narrator is (biologically), we can only judge him according to his actions and reactions, and not as a 'black man' or a 'white man'" (1993: 86). The simultaneity of both ambiguity and anonymity can be contextualized through Lewis Gordon's theorizing on anonymity and antiblackness. Gordon's premise is that "[o]rdinary existence is an immersion in the bosom of anonymity. Anonymity literally means to be nameless. The context of anonymity with which I am here concerned is an antiblack society. The result in such a society is a violent namelessness committed against blacks whose familiarity is so familiar that it transforms the protective dynamics of anonymity itself. Yet anonymity itself is not the cause of this violence. Anonymity by itself doesn't *cause* anything. In a humane world, anonymity is a blessing that offers human possibility and understanding" (1997: 13–14). Johnson's narrator seems to transcend race through his passing. But his *Latined* blackness (and deviations thereof) are localized within the dynamics of—and Johnson's focus on—an antiblack society.

12. Although Johnson's protagonist travels to Europe, this visit becomes a test for how his ethereal blackness moves through different spectrums outside the United States. Given that a millionaire patron sponsors his trip, it is as though the character becomes a graduate of a European "crash-course" on the Western subject. The narrator mentions that, through this tour of the old world, the white benefactor had made him "a polished man of the world" (1989: 143). The patron concurs, telling him, "my boy, you are by blood, by appearance, by education, and by tastes a white man" (144). Notice that the whiteness proffered is immediately taken back—tinted by the blackness of the light-skinned storyteller through the use of "my boy" as a purported term of endearment.

13. In the case of Hughes's political proclivities, Lawrence P. Jackson has written that "the boy wonder" of the Harlem Renaissance "was vulnerable in the mainstream and on the Left. [. . .] In payment for his commitment to social justice, Hughes spent much of the 1940s and 1950s having to extricate himself from his most radical works

and looking for succor from welcoming black audiences. Despite this sometimes-exhausting trek, Hughes possessed a genuine courage and intellectual flexibility. These qualities enabled him to cultivate the next cadre of artists whose work would project them successfully beyond the confines of racial segregation in the arts. A viable network of writers in Harlem remained, and Hughes, whose regular address shifted only once, from 634 St. Nicholas Avenue to a house at 20 West 127th Street in 1948, often stood at the center" (2011: 19).

14. Latin-America, as "cross-border, transnational zone," symbolizes what Guridy conceives as the "U.S.-Caribbean world." This region "first emerged out of the trade networks of the eighteenth century and came to full fruition after the War of 1898. In the four decades before the outbreak of the Second World War, Caribbean and Central American economies and societies became more integrated into U.S.-controlled cross-border linkages. The boundaries of this supranational configuration stretched from the eastern seaboard of the United States southward along the Atlantic coast to the islands of the Caribbean basin, the shores of the Gulf of Mexico, the nations of Central America, and even the northern reaches of South America" (2010: 7).

15. V. S. Naipaul's insights, as attributed in Patrick French's *The World Is What It Is*, bear significance here. Naipaul speaks of an author's life as a rightful subject of study. His comment reads, "The lives of writers are a legitimate subject of inquiry; and the truth should not be skimped. It may well be, in fact, that a full account of a writer's life might in the end be more a work of literature and more illuminating—of a cultural or historical moment—than the writer's books" (2008: xi). Glimpses of Johnson's and Hughes's lived anecdotal interludes take us to other cultural and historical oversights: the erasure of their fluctuating Latinities.

16. Writing on American Consular Service letterhead, Johnson told his wife, "Everywhere I go, the people, market women, children, everybody ask[s] me about la niña Graciela, and when she is coming" (1912a: 4 Apr.). A little more than a month later, Johnson repeated a similar sentiment, attributing her absence to the heat: "Everybody keeps asking about you. They all seem to miss you very much—but it is as you say, very hot down here" (18 May). It is common, in some Central American nations, to use the term niña, which literally means girl, to respectfully refer to an adult woman, regardless of her age and social class. Salvadoran novelist Jacinta Escudos elaborates on these conventional titles for different stages of "woman-hood." She has written in her blog that the vagueness of niña or even the employment, in Guatemala, of the term *seño* (as an abbreviation for *señora* [woman/Mrs.] or *señorita* [young lady/Miss]) is more welcoming than *doña* (lady, Madame, Mrs., or Ms.). The latter, Escudos has observed, "makes me feel like a decrepit being, and, above all, like a deteriorated 115-year-old [. . .]. Far from being an expression of re-

spect, as it is usually justified, it seems like it has a disparaging connotation. It has always appeared like a guarded way to call me *vieja* [an old woman] to my face" (2008; my translation).

17. Johnson immortalized Manhattan's allure in *The Autobiography of an Ex-Coloured Man*, wherein the protagonist asserts, "New York City is the most fatally fascinating thing in America. [. . .] [A]s I walked about that evening, I began to feel the dread power of the city; the crowds, the lights, the excitement, the gaiety, and all its subtler stimulating influences began to take effect upon me" (1989: 89–90). Stecopoulos has discussed a distinctive "metropolitan superiority" etched in the minds of the period's race men. They had a "sense of 'northerness' and a concomitant feeling of civilized belonging" (2007: 37). Johnson impregnates *Along This Way* with a resonating metropolitanism, as he narratively takes the reader to the summer when he taught "in the backwoods of Georgia." "This was going to be a new experience for me," Johnson confessed. "True, I was born in a very small city, but it was one, nevertheless, that had quite a metropolitan air; and I knew nothing at all of rural life" (2000: 105). Johnson proceeded to equate the inconveniences of his rural life, such as the lack of light, with the kinds of struggles confronted by "the philosophers and poets of Greece in her age of highest culture" (109).

18. Johnson's main character, though, never claims while visiting France that he speaks French better than that nation's citizens. His passage into Latinity is marked through the Spanish language. His French, by contrast, appears a tad rudimentary. He gets by with a vocabulary of "three hundred necessary words"—ergo suggesting that his entrance into Western discourses is unpassable, if not deadlocked (1989: 132–33).

19. The English word that grabs the narrator's attention—it almost shocks him—is the verb "ramify" (Johnson, 1989: 71).

20. Although an argument can be made that Speedy Gonzalez is bound to a Mexican and Mexican American iconography, his symbolic representation codifies a larger Latin population. Carlos Eire's *Waiting for Snow in Havana: Confessions of a Cuban Boy* affords a viewpoint of the representational lineage under which U.S. Latinos and Latinas have fallen vis-à-vis this caricature. Suggesting an afterlife doom for Mel Blanc (1908–89)—the voice of Speedy Gonzalez among a myriad of canonical Warner Brothers and Hanna-Barbera television productions cartoons like Bugs Bunny, Daffy Duck, Porky Pig, and Barney Rubble—Eire utters, "may you burn in hell forever. As one of your God-damned Hispanic Warner Brothers cartoon characters might have said: '*Sí, señor*, firrst I go to zee *fiesta* and zen I tayk-a *siesta*, beeforrre I go to anozzer *fiesta* again. *Ole! Andale, ándale! Arriba, arriba!*' I take it back, Mel. Sorry, I got carried away. Hell might be too harsh a punishment for your sins. You must have been clueless, truly. Maybe a better place for you would be heaven, where you might

be surrounded by lazy, napping, partying spics who talk funny" (2003: 69). Eire also calls Blanc a "spicmeister" and "colonolialist doofus" (81).

21. Train rides prove critically invaluable when canvassing the unsteady linguistic and semiotic divisions that Latined subjects pass through in the U.S. landscape, as we see here with Johnson. Hughes's story "Puerto Ricans" in *The Best of Simple* (1961) also sheds light on how a foreign-sounding Spanish language, as uttered in the United States, deracializes other colored folk. In this piece, Jesse B. Simple boards a New York City subway at 125th and Lenox, hoping to read a recently purchased comic book. During the ride, however, Simple discovers that the book is written in *"Español!"* (1990: 216). Unable to understand — to which Simple merely remarks *"no entiendo"* — he offers the comic to a Puerto Rican passenger, caustically noting, *"Español!* Now that is a language which, if you speak it, will take *some* of the black off of you if you are colored. Just say, *Sí*, and folks will think you are a foreigner, instead of only a plain old ordinary American Negro" (217). Of gleaming significance is Simple's emphasis that español discards *"some* of the black off of you." The Spanish language is not a direct passage into whiteness, but a dissembling utterance of incomprehension on both sides. On the one hand, the white side does not speak Spanish. One could say that since it would take too long for this side to intelligibly and reasonably explain the logic and order of Jim Crow, a temporary passing access is granted to Spanish speakers in this U.S. racial order. On the other hand, we find Latins who claim not to understand the black and white of it and thus provide, like Hughes's character, a simple *"no entiendo."* In this Hughesian sense, this presumed lack of understanding transcends a black-and-white impasse, taking us to the useful purpose of the comic book's narrative value. Toward the story's end, Simple decides he would like to start a series of comics titled *Jess Simple's Jim Crow Jive*. These books would be published in "English and Spanish so Puerto Ricans could laugh, too." *Jess Simple's Jim Crow Jive* would provoke Puerto Rican laughter "because it must tickle them to see what *a little foreignness* will do" (218; emphasis added). Blackness and whiteness cease to be so inchoate and straightforward. The transparency of the color line requires what Hughes called, in this same volume, *"genial* souls" — and I italicize *genial* here since it is a word both in Spanish and English and thus shares passing Latinities — that tap into other colorings of the U.S. panorama (viii).

22. In relation to U.S. West Indian migrations in the early twentieth century, Martha A. Sandweiss interprets this same incident in Johnson's text, concurring with Stecopoulos's analysis. To quote Sandweiss, this was a period where blacks born outside the United States "hung on to their foreign citizenship to assert their social superiority over American-born blacks and shield themselves from some of the most virulent forms of racial discrimination" (2009: 218–19). In connection to Johnson,

we must also consider that Rodriguez Ponce is not so much a bridge to whiteness, but a witness to how varieties of blackness walk in and out of both U.S. blackness *and* whiteness. It is not that Latinos and Latinas, as we now come to know them, are excluded from the black-white binary. Indeed, their racialization processes have been different. This Johnson–Rodriguez Ponce literary episode suggests that U.S. blackness is inclusive of that type of foreign-born blackness. Consider Sandweiss's observation: "the directions to the census takers suggest, the hardening edge of American racial thought at the end of the century had effectively erased the possibility of a category of mixed-race 'mulattoes' with an intermediate status between black and white. If such people had once held a special status that set them apart from 'blacks,' new state laws obliterated the distinction between peoples with different degrees of African heritage" (217). Clearly the black mulatto and the Latino mulato/mestizo, "with different degrees of African heritage," have not been completely removed from the national racial order. Rodriguez Ponce is gaining an instruction on how his Cubanness and Latinoness stand, move, or deadlock in U.S. renditions of unalloyed blackness and whiteness.

23. My uses of Latin@ness/Latin-*at*-ness are explained in this book's epilogue.

24. A Latinity, of course, can also be unpassable, as it has been evidenced for Latinos, Latinas, and Latin Americans. Gabriel García Márquez's biographer, Gerald Martin, chronicles an incident in this writer's journey to the U.S. South—"Faulkner country"—where Latins cannot even pass as culturally white Mexicans. One evening in 1961, García Márquez and his wife "missed a night [in Montgomery, Alabama] because no one would rent 'dirty Mexicans' a room" (2009: 260).

25. Johnson also noted, "Before leaving New York, I had made myself known to Richard Watson Gilder, the editor of the *Century Magazine*, and to William Hayes Ward, the editor of the *Independent*. I began mailing manuscripts to them, and my poems began appearing in the two publications" (2000: 237).

26. The letter was sent to Victor M. Shapiro of the Fox Film Corporation. Shapiro responded on the following day with a tactful and noncommittal note: "My dear Mr. Johnson: I deeply appreciate the autographed copy of your book. I will read it with a great deal of interest as I have heard so much about it. If anything develops when I get to Hollywood, I will communicate directly with you. Best wishes and sincerest regards to yourself and Mrs. Johnson. Sincerely, Victor M. Shapiro" (quoted in Johnson, 1931b).

27. Bok mentions that his Dutch family was able "to make an experiment of Americanization" (1927: x). He interpolated American ideology, noting in his third-person written account, "the American spirit of initiative had entered deep into the soul of Edward Bok" (15).

28. Johnson wrote this poem to honor the fiftieth anniversary of the Emancipation Proclamation, which officially outlawed slavery in 1865.

29. It is worth citing here the 1915 summary of *Fifty Years and Other Poems* provided by the Cornhill Company. The publicity noted, "This volume includes the poem 'Fifty Years' so widely quoted and admired when it was published in *The New York Times* four years ago. Mr. Johnson sings of a variety of themes with the same unerring touch as in the titular poem. There is a group devoted to Latin-American life called 'Down by the Carib Sea,' and a group of 'Folk Runes,' pieces in dialect of the pathetic and humorous aspect of Negro life." Other luminaries who blurbed this book include Elihu Root and Elbridge L. Adams (Johnson, 1915). Root (1845–1937), a lawyer and a recipient of the 1912 Nobel Peace Prize, served as President William McKinley's secretary of war from 1899 to 1904 and as President Theodore Roosevelt's secretary of state in 1905. Adams (1866–1934) was an attorney with literary ties to Joseph Conrad. He served as chair of the Correspondence Committee of the Civil Service Reform Association in 1919 and cofounded the New York–based Fountain Press in 1929.

30. Curtis Márez calls attention to the characteristic employment of "Pancho" for Chicanos. Building on Américo Paredes, Márez asserts, "'Pancho suggests the bandit stereotype, the Mexican with the long mustaches and the cartridge belts crossed over his chest.' In other words, the name calls to mind a stereotyped image of the brown border combatant" (1996: 112).

31. Johnson's monolingual association with American English is worthy of further consideration, as the Spanish language cannot pass. Given Johnson's aptness with various languages, his distinctive bonding at this precise moment with American monolingualism could be fashioned through what Ingrid M. Reneau has called, in the context of "'broad' Belizean Creole (bBC)," a process of "lightening-up one's tongue" (2006: 95). This concept refers to a monolithic tongue that does not migrate or intone "a variety of new U.S. landscapes." In Johnson's Nicaraguan instance, it can be grounded to an un-Americanized race of color that speaks only Spanish (Reneau, 2006: 95). As Reneau writes, "Internal barriers of personal and historical memories and our perceptions of our selves, linguistically and otherwise, can enable as well as disable our abilities to see our commonalities, our wholeness, not only as Belizeans, but as Caribbean and Central American people and people of the world" (2006: 97). Johnson's separation from Spanish, as spoken and embodied in Nicaragua, prompts a disabling of any Latin linkages—punctuating, in this process, a foreignness tinged by his own rendition of a U.S.-based Americanness abroad.

32. Johnson's wife was also learning French, perhaps thinking, like her husband, that they would be going to France in the next consular appointment. Johnson wrote, "Don't get discouraged with your French. You can only master it by *constant* repeti-

tion. You know it was the same with your Spanish, how after hours of repetition, then suddenly you found out that you could speak Spanish and that you knew more than you had any idea that you knew" (1912a: 18 May).

33. The consul's preoccupation with Nicaragua's heat and its tropical nature has resonances with twentieth-century notions on how "the white man 'can never be acclimated in the tropics'" (Greene, 2009: 27). Greene puts forward that "the 'tropics' loomed as a great source of anxiety to many in the early twentieth century. Tropical climates were particularly associated with the absence of civilization" (28).

34. Johnson outlined in one letter the types of transactions for which he was responsible as consul. He confided, "I'm still a bit worried over the responsibility of the Sheridan Estate. In León I collected over $2,000.00 in gold that was due, and $26,000.00 in bills. Mr. L. and I were a whole day counting the bills over. There is still about $6,000.00 in gold to be collected. Besides, his property will amount to about $60,000.00 gold. This is the first big case of the kind I have handled, and, of course, I want every penny to turn just right. My little safe is over loaded with money" (1912a: 5 June).

35. Historian Gerald Horne makes known that Mexico "as a beacon of hope for Negroes was not new. During the antebellum era thousands of enslaved Africans fled to freedom across the border, as Mexico had abolished slavery long before the United States" (2005: 6). Drawing on Hughes's father, Horne explains African American migration to Mexico as follows: "After the death of Reconstruction some African Americans organized to migrate en masse to Mexico. There were also countless individual migrations, as evidenced by the father of Langston Hughes, the writer. Shortly after he was born, his parents separated because his father wanted to escape the United States and go 'where a colored man could get ahead and make money quicker, and my mother did not want to go. My father went to Cuba, and then to Mexico, where there wasn't any color line, or any Jim Crow.' That Langston Hughes's father was not alone in wanting to go to Mexico is indicated by the experience of the Alabama Negro colony in Mexico in the 1890s. Fleeing pell mell from Jim Crow, lynchings, and the rest, Negroes were leaving for Liberia, Central America, and elsewhere. There were 'ten large colonies' in Mexico. A Mexican official had assured the migrants that his nation 'will be their Canaan, the land of hope and promise, where they could find relief from the persecution of southern whites'" (21). Other literary forays into Mexico include Richard Wright's 1940 visit to Cuernavaca. Hazel Rowley, his biographer, reports, "For a black man, Mexico was a welcome heaven" (2001: 197). Wright's observations of that nation are referenced as follows: "'People of all races and colors live in harmony and without racial prejudices or theories of racial superiority.' He added that he only ever experienced racism when he came into contact with

American tourists or businessmen." Wright admitted, "Mexico was beautiful but backward. 'I wanted to go to Europe,' Wright pointed out. [. . .] 'I'm not yet one of those people who can get excited over primitive people. Maybe the reason is that I'm too primitive myself, I don't know'" (2001: 197). By 1954 Mexico was still "populated with expatriates from abroad" (De Veaux, 2004: 50). Audre Lorde, who traveled to Mexico that year, "described it as 'a haven for political and spiritual refugees'" (quoted in De Veaux, 2004: 50).

36. Yet Hughes's mother, who remained in the United States, never quite crossed the Mexican color line. Although she had lived with her former husband, James N. Hughes, in Mexico, she returned to the United States with the "five- or six-year-old" Langston. Hughes recounted their move in this manner: "But no sooner had my mother, my grandmother, and I got to Mexico City than there was a big earthquake, and people ran out from their houses into the Alameda, and the big National Opera House they were building sank down into the ground, and tarantulas came out of the walls—and my mother said she wanted to go back home at once to Kansas, where people spoke English or something she could understand and there were no earthquakes. So we went" (1993: 15–16). Hughes's mother worked as a stenographer for a "colored" lawyer in Topeka, a cook in Chicago, and a waitress in Cleveland. It is hard to miss the classed and gendered dynamics of these racial and geographic passings (or lack thereof). They seem to facilitate, at a larger and perhaps more generous level, processes of reinvention for some of the race men of the period. Charles W. Chesnutt imbued his novel *The House behind the Cedars* (1900) with the limits of racial passing. But it is his heroine, Rena Walden (who uses the moniker Rowena Warwick while passing through the other world) who does not pass, unlike John, her brother. Her concluding comments in the novel underscore this gendered constraint when she tells her intended, a white aristocratic male, "You are white, and you have given me to understand that I am black. I accept the classification, however unfair, and the consequences, however unjust, one of which is that we cannot meet in the same parlor, in the same church, at the same table, or anywhere, in social intercourse; upon a steamboat we would not sit at the same table; we could not walk together on the street, or meet publicly anywhere and converse, without unkind remark. As a white man, this might not mean a great deal to you; as a woman, shut out already by my color from much that is desirable, my good name remains my most valuable possession" (1993: 172–73).

37. By the 1930s Hughes's "revolutionary quality had been recognized before in occasional translations published in Mexico, but the new articles had a more immediate effect. From the mainly apolitical *Contemporáneos* group to the League of Revolutionary Artists and Writers, he was welcomed by the most accomplished

Mexican writers and painters. Among the latter, he met the melancholy Orozco, the mountainous, dark-skinned Diego Rivera (a Negro grandmother, Rivera claimed proudly), Siquieros, Izquierdo, Tamayo, and Montenegro, and was taken up by the flamboyant Lupe Marin, Rivera's estranged wife and his favorite model" (Rampersad, 2002: 303).

38. This key incident is discussed in Rampersad's first volume of *The Life of Langston Hughes*, but it is not assembled within the context of black-brown passing lines that undo the black-white binary or as a border crossing—in effect, a passing—in diasporic blackness (2002: 40). The only time in which Hughes's passing as a Mexican is mentioned in this biography is when Hughes returns, as the biographer puts it, "home" to the United States. Traveling from San Antonio to Cleveland, a clerk in a Saint Louis soda fountain turned the color line into the national line, asking Hughes "bluntly whether he was Mexican or American" (35).

39. Hughes's story is, of course, from the perspective of an everyday black man transitioning into generic white Americanness. Sandweiss's biography of Clarence King, a renowned geologist who passed part-time from distinguished whiteness to anonymous blackness vis-à-vis his common-law marriage to a black woman (née Ada Copeland/Ada Todd) reveals that his written communication with his wife, who had no idea of King's distinguished record of chronicling U.S. Western expansion, was to be destroyed (2009: 144). Sandweiss quotes King's final instructions to his spouse, conveyed in this exclamatory, one-sentence supplement: "P.S. Carefully burn my letters!!" (222). Although some letters survived—and even if they all had been completely destroyed—the story of King's part-time passing lingered. As Sandweiss claims, "'James Todd' was his [King's] greatest fictional work of all" (234).

40. In this way, undocumented migrants can be deported within Mexico or one of its contiguous nations. This passing for a particular nationality facilitates the journey for migrants attempting to cross the Mexico-U.S. border. But in these "brown" Mexico–Central American passages, one seldom hears of Belize and Belizeans, especially when considering Mexico's southern frontier with Guatemala and Belize.

41. Let us briefly recall restrictive 1920s immigration laws such as the Emergency Quota Act (aka the Emergency Immigration Act of 1921) and the Immigration Act of 1924 (also called the Johnson-Reed Act and the National Origins Act). The former was "designed to ensure access for immigrants from northwestern Europe while restricting those from south/central/eastern Europe." The latter remained in effect until 1952, yielding "an annual limit of 150,000 Europeans, a total ban on Japanese" and, among other stipulations, "the creation of quotas based on the contribution of each nationality to the overall U.S. population, rather than on the foreign-born population" (LeMay, 2006: 23).

42. The reader also sees passing Latinities that become "paperless" through the sidestepping of the official documentation required at the crossing of geopolitical borders. This maneuver, as Hughes shows, alludes to a general "education in passing" on national (Mexican or "American") and ethnoracial grounds ("colored," "Latin," or "Mexican"). As these subjects acquire a "mastery of moving back and forth," they authenticate the fact that they can pass, and "no one will ask [them] for [their] papers" (Brady, 2002: 92, 86).

43. These Mexican manifestations of everyday speech reflect Hughes's coruscating attraction with life stories and cultural expressions and their representation in his oeuvre. Certainly his literary construction of the Virginia-born protagonist, Jesse B. Simple, is the typification of someone, who according to the writer, speculates and laughs off "the numerous problems of white folks, colored folks, and just folks—including himself" (1990: viii).

44. The critical literature on this Fanonian moment is copious. Some of the important works include Gooding-Williams (2005b); N. Gibson (2003); Wynter (2001); Alessandrini (1999); Gordon, Sharpley-Whiting, and White (1996); L. Gordon (1995b); and Bhabha (1994).

45. Switching now from sweets to savory food, Eire spills the beans on his white Cuban constitution. He reveals his avoidance of eating the rice and beans that Nilda, his black nanny, would offer him when growing up in Havana. Nilda's invitation to the meal was conveyed through the linguistic nudge, "Here, have some more [rice and beans], you'll grow up to be just like me." Eire fears his "skin would turn black," just like his caregiver's. He states, "I knew even then that there was something awful about being black in Cuba. African Cubans weren't too lucky, from what I could see. They seemed to do all the hard work, and to have inferior bathrooms" (2003: 152). This fear of blackness, which moves synonymously from *Negro* and African to brown and dark, continued "for a very, very long time." Eire adds, "I wouldn't eat any food that was black or brown. Nothing dark. Not even chocolate" (153). He sums his fear along these lines: "Whatever work needed to be done in the house was done by African women. And whatever hard work needed to be done in the world, that is, my world, always fell to African Cubans, men and women alike. [. . .] So when Nilda asked me to join her in being discriminated against, my immediate reaction was to panic. [. . .] I thought it was some kind of curse placed directly on me, and me alone. I was the only white person who would be turned black by dark foods" (159).

46. By 1935 Hughes had published the play *Mulatto* with a double "t," locating the mixed-race matter in the Big House of a Georgia plantation.

47. Guridy's scholarly exploration on the audience reception to Hughes's work in Havana proves stimulating. Cuban disposition during this period toward Hughes and

U.S. black musicians, Guridy finds, "produced new hierarchal and relational understandings of Afro-diasporic cultures in both countries. Cubans celebrated Hughes as a representative of the most advanced sector of the global 'colored race'" (2009: 116).

48. Gustavo Urrutia was a prominent black Cuban journalist and a columnist for the daily Havana newspaper, *Diario de la Marina*.

49. Ortiz is widely recognized as an anthropologist and public intellectual who focused on the study of Afro-Cuban popular traditions. Fernando Coronil's introduction to *Cuban Counterpoint* posits that Ortiz's work practiced the "the self-fashioning of these [Afro-Cuban] peripheries, the counterpoint through which people turn margins into centers and make fluidly coherent identities out of fragmented histories." Coronil adds that this work "helps show the play of illusion and power in the making and unmaking of cultural formations" (1995: xiv). Herewith, Ortiz brought into circulation the notion of "transculturation" in *Cuban Counterpoint* as a means to better express "the different phases of the process of transition from one culture to another." This concept "carries the idea of the consequent of new cultural phenomena" (1995: 102–3). Transculturation conveys "the highly varied phenomena that have come about in Cuba as a result of the extremely complex transmutations of culture that have taken place here, and without a knowledge of which it is impossible to understand the evolution of Cuban folk, either in the economic or in the institutional, legal, ethical, religious, artistic, linguistic, psychological, sexual, or other aspects of life" (98). Ortiz also founded and edited the magazines *Archivos del Folklore Cubano*, *Estudios Afrocubanos*, and *Surco*. He presided over various cultural institutions, including the Society of Cuban Folklore, the Society of Afro-Cuban Studies, and the National Association against Racial Discrimination (cf. M. González, 1946).

50. Ifeoma Nwankwo has put forth that Hughes's "intraracial translation" transformed Nicolás Guillén's poetry into African American English. So doing, Hughes exercised a methodology of translation that undertook "intraracial linguistic difference while also affirming racial connectedness" (1999–2001: 55). Nwankwo contends that Hughes's efforts made Guillén's translated poetry "feel familiar, like one of our own, in order to emphasize the fact that we are all part of one community, the Black community." Nwankwo also submits a key conceptual framework, "transnational Black collectivism," which denotes "a sense of community that prioritizes racial connection over national location. Terms such as 'pan-Africanism' have been used to connote similar notions of a lengthy history or histories that trace them through a fixed genealogy" (56). Transnational black collectivism, more specifically, touches on "the general issue of Black-to-Black translation, of the relationship between translation methodology and the desire for an international Blackness" (60).

51. Rampersad has noted that when Hughes lived in Mexico in 1935, he had become a member "of a tiny international advance guard that would eventually include Pablo Neruda of Chile, Jorge Luis Borges of Argentina, Léopold Sédar Senghor of Senegal, Jacques Romain of Haiti, Aimé Césaire of Martinique, and Nicolás Guillén of Cuba" (2002: 47).

52. As Jean Franco (2002) and Neil Larsen (1995), among others, have brought up, the 1959 Cuban Revolution and the Cold War provoked U.S. academic interest in Latin American literature.

CHAPTER THREE. Indigent Latinities

1. The *Diccionario de la Real Academia Española* enumerates prieto as (1) "said of a color: very dark and almost indistinguishable from black" ("Dicho de un color: Muy oscuro y que casi no se distingue del negro"); (2) as a Cuban term "Said of a person: of the black race" ("Cuba. Dicho de una persona: De raza negra"); and (3) as a Mexican label "Said of a person: of brown skin" ("Méx. Dicho de una persona: De piel morena"). Negro is "Said of a person: Whose skin is of a black color" ("Dicho de una persona: Cuya piel es de color negro"). (All English translations are mine.) I adopt brownish blackness and blackish brownness from W. D. Wright, who takes them up as descriptors in *Black History and Black Identity*. Wright informs us, "Skeptics of a Black ethnic group might point out that all people of that group are not black in color, and thus are not all black people. There is truth in this observation, but some falsity in it as well. What is false about it is the projection of the idea of a pure black race, which has never existed in the world, not even in Africa. In Africa there have always been shades of blackness, including brownish blackness or blackish brownness, or even shades of brownness. [. . .] The amalgamation of white and black people in the United States has not destroyed the black race as such, as that race is still overwhelmingly black, blackish brown, or brownish black, as it was before coming to the United States" (2002: 90).

2. This brownness speaks through a bodily taxonomy. For example, Oscar Hijuelos codifies and naturalizes this Latino brownness in relation to his brother, José-Pascual, whose hair (not skin) "of a brownish-red coloration bespoke somewhat more Latino origins" (2011: 8).

3. See, for example, Christina Sharpe's superb study, *Monstrous Intimacies: Making Post-Slavery Subjects*, where she brings to light formulations of "the (New World) *black* subject" (2010: 3). These subjections—with their routine repetition of sexual violence on these particular bodies—organize the *blackening* of black subjects and how we come to "know" them as both black and blackened. Sharpe calls the routinization of this violence, as her monograph's title elucidates, "monstrous intimacies."

These "awful intimate and monstrous configurations" both in slavery and freedom, from her perspective, rely on "the uses of blackness over time" (14, 4). They link black and blackened diasporic "others" through "everyday mundane horrors that aren't acknowledged to be horrors." Sharpe defines her ongoing processes of subjectification as a "set of known and unknown performances and inhabited horrors, desires and positions produced, reproduced, circulated, and transmitted, that are breathed in like air and often unacknowledged to be monstrous." These productions and reproductions of "fundamental familiar violence" are "the most readable and locatable still through the horrors enacted on the black body after slavery and the official periods of emancipation and through further colonialism, imperialism, and the relative freedoms of segregation, desegregation, and independence, whether the body is in the Caribbean, the Americas, England, or post-independence Africa" (2–3). A provocative question raised in Sharpe's work holds great influence here too: "Do those black and blackened people who can't or don't claim that proximity to whiteness [. . .] as positive inheritance become the sole visible bearers of the trauma of the survival of slavery and racism, sole signifiers of an as yet unerased proximity to the blood-stained gate?" (22).

Please allow me, at this point, to better explain *Latining America*'s analytic quest. I do not make or envision Latino and Latina vocalizations of brownness akin to whiteness. I direct attention to the ways that brownness walks alongside dark brownness *and* blackness in Latino, Latina, and African American contexts—giving weight to how the blackened signifier moves not only through the demonstrably black and blackened body but also through a dark browned subject that has also been blackened. This is not to say that the black body remains locked in its "own" blackened signifiers. This chapter proposes that the blackened signifier is also "popping" up in this Latino and Latina economy of brown and dark brown indigent Latinities. The blackened signifier also migrates and is transmitted through other bodies and narratives. It turns to another doubling of how processes of blackening fracture at the level of meaning for strictly brown (Latino and Latina) and black (African American) signification. To adapt Lewis Gordon's words, "The black, subject to interpretation, becomes a designation that could be held by different groups at different times and as such is both concrete and metaphorical" (2000: 63).

4. As Jennifer P. Mathews reminds us, the *sapodilla* or *chicozapote* tree from which chewing gum, *chicle*, is extracted has Mesoamerican origins. Aztec and Maya pre-Columbian cultures had multiple uses for the sapodilla that ranged from chewing the natural gum and eating the tree's fruit (*sapote*) to using it to treat hemorrhoids and dysentery to exploiting the wood for firewood and building materials (2009: 1–18). The development of chicle as a commercial industry can be traced to the 1870s, when

key entrepreneurial enterprises by Thomas Adams Sr. and William Wrigley Jr. paved the way for "the great American invention" (38). On the other side of this American invention are the gum collectors or rubber tappers, known as *chicleros*, who face natural difficulties in the Mesoamerican jungles where chicle camps are located. The gum collectors largely comprise indigenous workers, who have been viewed rather negatively: "Local peoples generally feared the chicleros and considered them to be one of the dangers of the jungle, as many were rumored to be ex-convicts, Maya rebels, and criminals on the lam" (85). Mathews mentions, "in addition to their violent reputations, chicleros were criticized for being promiscuous vectors of venereal disease" (86). And yet chicleros are a "complex and misunderstood group [that] has played a significant role in a truly American industry" (92). I include this note to indicate the inseparable signifying space of the economically docile Indian: from commercial production and the selling of chicle to the embodiment of a "different" human subject.

5. Apolinar "hardly counted as a male because he did not count as a human being" (Martin, 2009: 37).

6. Castellanos Moya's narrator "passed the time, enjoying the brilliant morning among these hundreds of Indians decked out in their Sunday dress of so many festive colors, among the most salient being that joyous cheerful red, as if red had nothing to do with blood and sorrow but was rather the emblem of happiness for these hundreds of domestic servants enjoying their day off in the large square. [. . .] I realized that not one of those women with slanted eyes and toasted brown skin awoke my sexual appetite or my prurient interests" (2008: 67–68).

7. Mayas are not off the radar in Cancún; they form a visible and significant presence and contribute to the area's way of living. M. Bianet Castellanos's *A Return to Servitude* calls attention to Cancún's tourist industry and how it has fostered, at least since the 1970s, internal indigenous migrations from the Yucatán peninsula to Mexico's most popular traveling destination. Maya workers make up more than one-third of Cancún's population. They are also "the second largest indigenous group in Mexico" (2010: 83; xxxv). They were recruited for wage work "from the surrounding countryside to fill the vast labor supply needed to construct this tourist center" (xviii). The Maya worker "represents the ideal body," since "within the tourist industry, the submissive, exotic, racialized body—which is feminized by the virtue of the work being performed, regardless of the fact that both men and women are employed within this industry—serves as the universal trope by which production is organized and worker subjectivities are constituted" (80).

Castellanos contends that Maya relocation from the countryside to Cancún transforms them "into modern citizens and urban workers," engaged with "the ideological struggles generated by experiencing work and life within export-processing zones dominated by the production of services" (2010: 78). Maya migrant workers employed in service work are transformed into "'modern' citizens." Those previously hired as farm labor underwent corporate "disciplinary tactics" where they "learned to adhere to a time clock, acquired new skills, and adopted new behavior and attitudes (e.g., submissiveness and attentiveness). [. . .] They learned the intricacies of service: setting a table, greeting a client, adopting a hotel's standards of cleanliness, and so forth" (92–93). All the same, Cancún's tourist industry, like maquiladora manufacturing, is typified by "low wages, repetitive motion, attempts to control a worker's sexuality, limited job promotion, a lack of economic security, and a reliance on racialized bodies" (xxx). Castellanos casts light on Mexican modernization projects that required indigenous assimilation into the nation-state. They were forced "by the state to adopt Western dress and stop speaking their language" and "exited the historical stage of national memory in the 1930s, only to be included once again when national discourse embraced multiculturalism in the 1970s" (xxii). Cancún's narrative for the traveling class counts on Maya origins. Yet it is "marked by a growing disconnection with the region [. . .] and a pronounced articulation with a global economy" (81).

8. It remains to be said that not all degrees of black and brown invisibility within these discourses are tantamount to a homogeneously hypothesized black and brown collectivity. Brown critical engagement among U.S. Latinos and Latinas with Afro-Latino populations is, at best, embryonic. Even more, as Ernesto Sagás identifies in the *Latino Studies Journal*, "most Latino studies scholarship" has the tendency to principally concern "itself with the examination of the Chicano, Puerto Rican, and Cuban experiences in the United States" (1998: 5). Sagás conveys, in the context of U.S. Dominican populations, that hierarchical perceptibilities direct which Latino and Latina subgroup has more visibility and legitimate claims to being institutionalized within the field of Latino/a studies. This absence of black Latinos and Latinas and groups outside the aforementioned Latino/a trinity also echoes the types of sedentary African Americanness recognized in U.S. discourses on blackness. Mary Waters discusses, with regard to West Indian migrations to North America, that "the invisibility of the Caribbean immigrants as immigrants [alludes to] their visibility as blacks" (1997: 3). The lives of certain individuals from the Afro-Caribbean imply struggles with processes of negotiating migratory identities from the Americas, of altering such identifications to U.S.-centered notions of Americanness, and of specifically becoming *black* Americans.

9. Vicki L. Ruiz offers this note on Mexican, Mexican American, Chicano, and Chicana categories: "People of Mexican birth or descent refer to themselves by many names—Mexicana/o, Mexican American, and Chicana/o (to name just three). Self-identification speaks volumes about regional, generational, and even political orien-

tations. Mexicana/o typically refers to immigrants, while Mexican American signifies U.S. birth. Chicana/o reflects a political consciousness born of the Chicana/o Student Movement, often a generational marker for those of us coming of age during the 1960s and 1970s. Chicana/o also has been embraced by our elders and our children who share in the political ideals of the movement" (2004: 344).

10. The idea of a linear U.S. Latino and Latina brownness that omits other dark brown tints is particularly evocative post-9/11. Some U.S. Latino and Latina cultural workers are disentangling the meanings of Latino and Latina brownness—engulfed by issues of migration, incarceration, education, employment, political activism, and justice—through the U.S. quest for and a formation of a twenty-first-century brown genealogy. Consider the group the Chicano Messengers of Spoken Word, composed of artists Paul Flores, Amalia Ortiz, and Marc David Pinate. They titled their first play *Fear of a Brown Planet*, dialoguing with Public Enemy's 1990 canonical hip-hop album, *Fear of a Black Planet*. The Chicano Messengers of Spoken Word's piece, which premiered in 2005, was envisioned as a "new spoken word/hip hop theater play." *Fear of a Brown Planet* describes how two Chicanos and a Chicana find themselves in "a psycho-spiritual journey into the dark prison of the mind in a quest for meaning to our collective Brown existence" (Mojica Arts, 2005). But this brownness reads like a referent locked in Latino and Latina specificities. Asked about what sparked the group's enterprise by the *Houston Chronicle* in 2007, Flores touched on the political effects of brownness from a Chicano/Latino composition. He qualified the group's production in this manner: "We invented a scenario commenting on the issue of 'brownness.' If, as projected, by 2050 the majority population will be either Latino or mixed heritage, what is the potential effect of that? We started with three archetypal characters we find in the community. I play a stubborn construction worker who barely graduated high school and was always told he wouldn't amount to anything. Marc's character is a radical labor-party lawyer who's now defending drug dealers. Amalia plays a Hispanic socialite/trophy wife, who's married to a judge. Having them find themselves in an internment camp lets us comment on post-9/11 America" (quoted in Evans, 2007).

11. Caramelo, as a descriptor brought up in the book, implies a "corn teeth smile" (Cisneros, 2002: 36), a brown skin color reminiscent of a peanut (11), a hue "bright as a copper *veinte centavos* color after you've sucked it" (34), a tone "more bright than chicharrón" (74), a shade that is "creamy" (103), and a texture "as dark as cajeta" (116). Even though the streaks of caramelo, "like all mestizos, [come] from everywhere" (96), a caramel state encompasses Indianness in light, intermediate, dark, and extra dark tones.

12. Piri Thomas's phrase from chapter 11 of *Down These Mean Streets* comes to mind: "How to Be a *Negro* without Really Trying" (1997: 95–104). Thomas does not

italicize the word "Negro" in his book, since he uses it in an English-language context. I emphasize the word in this instance to mark its existence in Spanish as well as to bring out its "Latin" brownness.

13. But if blacks-browns have an intimate knowledge of their *negro* location in the U.S. labor force, such approximation also administers blackness as a distant site. This black distance from brownness, as it could play out in the service industry, underscores brown submissiveness and desexualization. Consider, for instance, "wisecracks" about black coffee, or *café negro*. As Renán Almendárez Coello (aka "El Cucuy de la Mañana") recounts it, "¿Usted sabe qué le dice la taza al café? [. . .] ¡Hay, qué negro tan caliente!" (2002: 11). Or, loosely translated, the idiom is, "Do you know what the cup tells its coffee? [. . .] Oh, what a hot *negro*!"

14. Cisneros spells out racial hierarchies through combinations of Indian, black (*negro*), and Spanish ancestry; see the chapter "Echando Palabras" (2002: 79–86). Cisneros's inclusion of this social dictum resonates with another Latin-American aphorism: "trabajo como negro para vivir como blanco" (I work like a *negro*, to live like a white person).

15. In connection to Mexican migrations and Mexican American ethnoracial identity formation, Tomás R. Jiménez proffers the notion of "immigrant replenishment." This concept refers to the ways in which ongoing Mexican migration "sustains both the cultural content of ethnic identity and the ethnic boundaries that distinguish both groups." It is "the means by which Mexican Americans come to feel more positively attached to their ethnic roots." But renewal and attachment also have their implications in U.S. society, as Mexican and Mexican American experiences invariably become "new" to the United States, barring "Mexican Americans from being fully regarded as part of the quilt of ethnic groups that make up the 'nation of immigrants'" (2010: 5). Jiménez elaborates, "The consequences of replenishment depend in large part on the status that the replenishing immigrants occupy in U.S. society. If the immigrant group occupies a low status in the host context—as is the case with the largely poor, laboring, and unauthorized Mexican-immigrant population—then those who are members of the ethnic group being replenished may experience status degradation" (21–22).

16. In Richard T. Rodríguez's words, "If there is a single issue almost always at stake in Chicano/a cultural politics since the Chicano movement of the 1960s and 1970s, it is the family in some shape, form, or fashion. Indeed, the family is a crucial symbol and organizing principle that by and large frames the history of Mexican Americans in the United States" (2009: 2). Rodríguez's work, however, departs from "exclusionary kinship relations" that have provided "the foundation on which la familia become adopted as an organizing strategy for communitarian politics" wedded to masculinity, nationalism, and heteropatriarchy (7, 15). He takes on "the family trope as a double-

edged sword, a signifier with many meanings that both troubles *and* assists in the struggle for communitarian politics" (12).

17. See "Brown, Brownness, Brown Pride, Brownout" and "Brown Berets" (Allatson, 2007: 49–51).

18. I provided some working parameters for the Chicano movement in the notes to the introduction, but we can also profit from this straightforward delineation by sociologist Marta Lopez-Garza. She clarifies, "In the mid-1960s, militant Mexican-American nationalists introduced the word 'Chicano' to the North American vocabulary, and, through the Chicano movement, brought class and race consciousness to Mexican-American politics. The movement was an informal ideological umbrella for a number of Mexican-American (or primarily Mexican-American) organizations. Among the most influential of these were the United Farm Workers, the Federal Alliance of Land Grants in New Mexico, the Brown Berets, Crusade for Justice in Colorado, and Chicano student organizations, such as the Movimiento Estudiantil Chicano de Aztlán (MECHA) and the United Mexican American Students (UMAS). Identifying oneself as Chicano (someone born of Mexican ancestry, but living in the United States) or with 'Chicanismo' became a politically significant factor reflecting political mobilization and active participation in social change. (The leading explanation of the origin of the term 'Chicano' is that the Nahuatl or Aztec pronunciation of the word describing people living in Mexico is *Mechicano*. The term had evolved through various stages of meaning by the time the nationalists appropriated it as a political statement.) A Chicano was one who did not wish to be known as 'American' in the U.S. sense, but whose history and experience were somewhat different from those living in Mexico" (1992: 35).

19. La raza also translates as "the race." I employ "the people" to speak to what Rivera identifies as the "stories of Mexican peoplehood," which are "fundamental to understanding not only the contradictory logic of American democratic culture but also Mexican American cultural production and the ambivalent location of Mexicans as citizen-subjects in the United States." Rivera communicates that "the people" operates as "the cultural framework for democracy, 'the people' have historically become a discursive site that fostered both igalitarianism and egalitarianism, exclusion and inclusion. To this end, defining who counts as 'the people' reveals the contradictory logic of democratic nation-states and the ways in which rhetoric about the people facilitates democratic legitimacy and power for the majority population in the United States" (2006: 3–4). At the same time, I recognize the historical specificity and function of la raza as "the race." Haney López submits that the "repeated use of la raza" in East Los Angeles during the arrests and indictments of the East LA Thirteen "began to translate more readily into 'the race' rather than 'the people.'" For Haney López,

"Mexicans using that phrase [la raza] in East Los Angeles in the late 1960s were not deaf to its resonance when translated into English as 'race.' Increasingly, the U.S. sense of race informed the activist community's invocation of la raza as they moved toward a non-white conception of themselves" (2003: 170). For a critique of la raza as a political movement and its patriarchal cultural nationalism, see Chabram-Dernersesian (1992).

20. I use Chicano in this instance, rather than "Chicano/a," or "Chicano and Chicana," concurring with Ramón A. Gutiérrez's stance in relation to Chicano mobilization from the mid-1960s to the 1970s. He writes, "It is currently common to use the term Chicano/a instead of simply Chicano to indicate that the word includes females too. [. . .] I retain Chicano here for historically specific reasons, namely that Chicano as a political identity was initially claimed largely by men" (2004: 294).

21. Sheila Marie Contreras identifies the movement's indigenous turn as "Chicana/o indigenism." She remarks that "Chicanas and Chicanos are indigenous to the Americas" and "bear the weight of this history of social relations of power as they attempt to conceptualize relationships both to Mexico and to the United States" (2008: 1, 2). The movement's appropriation of iconic signifiers was "[a]rticulated within a matrix of recovered Mesoamerican mythology." Chicana/o indigenism therefore "mobilize[d] the story of the Aztec migration from the ancestral homeland of Aztlán, the cosmogonic narrative of *el Quinto Sol*/the Fifth Sun, and the cross-culturally significant figure of the plumed serpent, also known as the god-king Quetzalcoatl. Indigenism found outlets in fiction and poetry, in public mural art of the period, and in the drama productions of El Teatro Campesino" (71–72).

22. There were some political exceptions in terms of Chicano collaborations with U.S. African Americans, of course, and Haney does bring them to mind in his East Los Angeles discussion of the Chicano movement years. Tatcho Mindiola Jr., Yolanda Flores Niemann, and Nestor Rodriguez also make note that activists from the black and Chicano movements in the Houston area "supported each other ideologically and sometimes cooperated in political work." Still, they underscore that "[l]ong after the Black and Chicano movements subsided, the perception of the need for intergroup political solidarity remained a value for many African Americans and Chicanos. However, stereotypes and competition for resources, among other factors, have mediated this solidarity" (2003: 11). These authors contend that "[s]everal of the terms describing Hispanics [by African American respondents in their research] deal with competition, for example, taking over jobs, [being] underpaid, [becoming a] growing population, [and acting as] opportunistic" (33). They also note that their "results indicate that in general African Americans have more positive views of Hispanics than vice versa" (35).

23. Santa Ana methodologically relies on the *Los Angeles Times*, because "it is the newspaper of greatest distribution in California. It is the local newspaper of California's most populous city and home to the nation's largest Latino population" (2002: 54).

24. "What did Nixon know?" Richard Rodriguez asks. "Did he really devise to rid himself of a bunch of spic agitators by officially designating them a minority, entitled to all rights?" (2002: 117). Nixon is also responsible for a Latino and Latina look southward: "As a result of Nixon's noun, our relationship to Latin America became less remote" (121).

25. Considering Márez's imaginative assembling of the "lowbrow(n)" qualifier, one also wonders if a "highbrow(n)" brown style can emerge. What would be the "highbrow(n)" influences? What would they look and sound like?

26. Cf. Kemo the Blaxican's website (D. Thomas, n.d.).

27. Hazel Rowley explains in her Richard Wright biography that his maternal grandmother, Margaret Bolden, who is also depicted in *Black Boy*, "was so small and slight, with deep set brown eyes and long straight hair. She was so light-skinned that until she opened her mouth and spoke pure Southern Negro dialect, strangers thought she was white. Her grandson Richard Wright believed she was a mixture of Irish, Scottish, and French stock, 'in which somewhere Negro blood had somewhere and somehow been infused'" (2001: 1–2). And "Wright's paternal grandmother, Laura Calvin, was thought to be partly Choctaw Indian" (4).

Audre Lorde's mother, Linda, passed for Spanish in New York (De Veaux, 2004: 11). Alexis De Veaux, Lorde's biographer, writes that Lorde recognized "herself as the darkest child" and illustrates moments that speak to Anzaldúa's struggles with coming to terms for being "la prieta," her family's dark one. De Veaux writes, "Not pretty, not light-skinned, she was the outsider in a family of outsiders" (18). Lorde's 1954 trip to Mexico exhibited fluid states of brownness, blackness, and overlapping Latin-American nationalities. "At times," De Veaux brings up, "she was mistaken for Cuban by Mexicans and for Mexican by Americans" (49). Lorde "was in awe of seeing brown-skinned people, of every hue, wherever she went" in Mexico. She wrote in a missive that "she felt 'like an onion,' peeled of layers of its own smothering skins" (50).

One Zora Neale Hurston comment worth citing here is her reflection, "I feel like a brown bag of miscellany propped against a wall. Against a wall in company with other bags, white, red and yellow" (1997: 1010). This statement on the assortment of inhabitants of this mixed brown bag reflects Latino and Latina states too. Hurston is referring, in this regard, to U.S. African American complexion tests that ranked and organized dark and light blackness around the brown paper bag. These tests connote, as Audrey Elisa Kerr has keenly interpreted it, "degrees of acceptance and inclusion (that is, if one is fairer than the brown bag)." The brown paper bag forms a part of a "complexion lore" that "has been used liberally and with great frequency by African Americans throughout the twentieth and into the twenty-first century, with references to paper bag parties, paper bag churches, brown bag clubs, or brown bag social circles that have resulted in a proscribed language of exclusion and exclusiveness" (2005: 272).

28. Harriet Jacobs expounded on this matter: "Southern women often marry a man knowing that he is the father of many little slaves. [. . .] They regard such children as property [. . .] and it is seldom that they do not make them aware of this by passing them into the slave-trader's hands. [. . .] and *thus getting them out of their sight*" (2000: 37). Once the visible markers that produce black mixture — and the violence attached to the emergence of "black mestizos" — are out of sight, to borrow from the colloquial expression, they are also out of the normative mind. Mestizaje was dropped from black mixture in the United States. There was no room for this type of mestizaje, as U.S. laws of the time mandated. An appendix in the *Narrative of the Life of Henry Box Brown* (1851) notes that the state of South Carolina did not really differentiate between "negroes, mulattoes, or mertizoes" (H. Brown, 2002: 71). The word "mestizos" in this Anglophone context is listed as "mertizoes." Both terms are interchangeable. The misspelling of mestizos signals unfamiliarity with — and a "newness" around — an unrecognizable term as well as population. The incomprehensibility of a classification like mestizo and an ideology like mestizaje still create relative confusion in the twenty-first-century United States. The *PMLA*'s tribute to Anzaldúa in January 2006 included a typographical error that demonstrated the foreignness of mestizaje. A recurring misprint identified mestizaje as *mestizahe* (Martín Alcoff, 2006; emphasis added). Although this typo could be regarded as a genuine oversight, the misprint evokes incomprehensibility about racial mixture in America; perhaps, even a negation of the "unreadable" yet contradictory positions that subaltern subjects can occupy. It is easier to see and differentiate "them" as "nonwhite" than to address the ways mixed whiteness permeates in these supposedly unchanging black (and brown) states.

29. My intent here is to show brownness in all its manifestations and in contexts that cannot be reduced to "brown" Spanish-speaking Latino and Latina bodies. I recognize that the brownness of Senna's dad, Carl Senna, could be attributed to the fact that the family believed he was the son of a Mexican boxer "who had abandoned his wife with three kids and was never seen again" (2009: 16). As far back as 1998 — the year that Senna's first novel, *Caucasia*, was published — the author identified herself as "a black girl with a Wasp mother and a black-Mexican father [with] a face that harkens to Andalusia, not Africa" (1998: 15). But Senna reveals a more complicated

story in *Where Did You Sleep Last Night? A Personal History*, where she uncovers that her paternal grandfather could actually be an Irish priest.

30. The list of racial terms Piri Thomas defines in alphabetical order are "*los blancos*: the whites," "*mi negrito*: my little black one," "*morenito*: little dark brown one," "*moreno*: dark brown, almost black," "*moyeto*: Negro, black man," and "*tregeño, tregeña*: dark-skinned" (1967: 332–33). Although the last two words are not amended in the thirtieth-anniversary edition of *Down These Mean Streets* (1997), Thomas may conceivably mean trigueño and trigueña. Thomas also provides brief definitions for another problematic way of being through sexual orientation. The two debasing labels—the other double haunting a Latino masculinity—are "*maricón*: homosexual, faggot" and "*pato*: faggot, homosexual" (1967: 333). These two derogatory terms in Spanish— maricón and pato—become formalized in translation through the courteous insertion, in English, of homosexual, which needs no translation in either language: they are both written in the same way and have congruous definitions.

31. Santiago's glossary defines negrita or negrito as an "[e]ndearment, little black one" (1993: 273). This theme of abandoning a seemingly authentic national way of life is articulated in Oscar Hijuelos's first book of nonfiction, *Thoughts without Cigarettes* (2011). Hijuelos titles his memoir's first chapter more forcefully than Santiago, calling it "When I Was Still Cuban," leading us to speculate on how his Cubanness was abandoned (or altered) and what he has now become (2011: 3–52).

32. Ginetta E. B. Candelario puts forward that "Dominican whiteness" has been "an explicitly achieved (and achievable) status with connotations of social, political, and economic privilege, and blackness signaled foreignness, socioeconomic subordination, and inferiority." Dominican "blackness"—or, in Candelario's language, "discourses of negritude"—are not utilized as a mode of Dominican national representation and self-identification. Instead, "Dominicans use language that affirms their 'Indian' heritage—*Indio, Indio oscuro, Indio claro, trigüeno* [sic]—and signals their resistance to foreign authority, whether Spanish or Haitian, and their autochthonous claims to sovereignty while accounting for the preponderance of medium to dark skin and complexions in the population" (2007: 5). Candelario's study hinges on "Dominican identity discourses that negotiate blackness and Hispanicity" (6). She adds, "Although Dominicans often share the experience of being Caribbean immigrants who are perceived to be black, unlike British West Indians Dominicans are also Hispanic. Hispanicity in both the United States and the Dominican Republic offers an alternative to blackness. Although 'Hispanic' is a racialized non-white category in the United States, it is also a non-black one" (12).

33. Moraga classifies this approach to and use of "truth" in autobiography as the "fiction of our lives." Give attention to this fragment: "Through the act of writing

that so-called autobiography, I learned that a story well told is a story embellished and re-visioned just like the stories that poured from my mother's mouth in our family kitchen some forty years earlier. The fiction of our lives—how we conceive our histories by heart—can sometimes provide a truth far greater than any telling of a tale frozen to the facts" (2011: 3–4). These autobiographical moments are reinterpretations of past events, with creative and critical emendations, as the memoirist sees fit.

34. Anzaldúa is mindful of the implications of this color consciousness in her essay, "La Prieta." In penning this composition, Anzaldúa records that she "was terrified," because it necessitated that she "be hard on people of color who are the oppressed victims. I am still afraid because I will have to call us on a lot of shit like our own racism, our fear of women and sexuality" (1983: 198).

35. Menchaca notes that in this hierarchical racial structure "[m]estizos enjoyed a higher social prestige than Indians, but were considered inferior to the Spaniards" (2001: 63). As for blacks in Mexico, Menchaca explicates, "Free afromestizos were accorded the same legal privileges as the mestizos. Because they were of partially Africana descent, however, they were stigmatized and considered socially inferior to the Indians and mestizos" (64). Under U.S. expansion in the nineteenth century, "state governments prevented 'American-born' racial minorities from exercising their citizenship rights under the Fourteenth Amendment. Anglo Americans argued that the spirit of the Fourteenth Amendment applied only to Blacks and Whites and that therefore Asians, American Indians, Mexicans, and 'half-breeds' were not entitled to its protection." De jure racial segregation applied to nonwhite Mexicans who "were legally excluded from public facilities reserved for whites" (287). For other studies on the role of pigmentation in the U.S. Southwest and its interconnections with race and gender, vide Haas (1996) and Gutiérrez (1991).

36. The larger impression claimed is that strands of the Caribbean resonate throughout the Americas. Certainly the connection to Mexico and Greater Mexico is fitting, given their prominent associations with indigenousness. As Martin writes, however, the Caribbeanness of Mexico is evident to such cognoscenti as Gabriel García Márquez, whose process of "Latin Americanization" occurred while living in that nation. It was there where García Márquez "absorbed the fact that Mexico, a desert country and a high plains country, was also, in effect, a Caribbean country" (Martin, 2009: 264).

37. It bears mentioning that the articulation—or more accurately phrased, the enunciation—of a *Latina* project appears in an aporetic, if not unconvincing, manner in *Borderlands/La Frontera*. Consider, as a brief illustration, how Anzaldúa presupposes that Latinas are fluent Spanish speakers whose purported linguistic hegemony is at par with the Real Academia Española, or the Royal Spanish Academy. She states,

"Chicanas feel uncomfortable talking in Spanish to Latinas, afraid of their censure. Their language was not outlawed in their countries." Anzaldúa further contends, "We don't say *claro* (to mean yes), *imagínate*, or *me emociona*, unless we picked up Spanish from Latinas, out of a book, or in a classroom" (1999: 79–80). Latinas, in this instance, mean Latin American women in both Latin America and the United States; additionally, they seemingly stand out as more educated. "The first time I heard two women, a Puerto Rican and a Cuban, say the word '*nosotras*,'" she writes, "I was shocked. I had not known the word existed. Chicanas use *nosotros* whether we're male or female. [. . .] Even our own people, other Spanish speakers *nos quieren poner candados en la boca*. They would hold us back with their bag of *reglas de academia*" (76).

These perceptions—which occlude the regionalisms and spoken differences in the Spanish language within the Americas—renders U.S. Latinos and Latinas, many of whom speak, like Anzaldúa, a "border tongue" and are thus neither "fully" fluent in Spanish and English, as more linguistically tied to Latin America than the United States. Such understandings could have precarious effects within "the borderlands," being that Latino and Latina could be read as normative. Their "otherness" is neutralized and, curiously enough, is not "heard" within "brown" border discourses that chronicle "outsiderness" from both English and Spanish. I mention this point not to quibble with Anzaldúa, but as an assigned task—if not an open question—for Latino/a studies scholars to acknowledge: Can Latinoness and Latinaness be disburdened from a suspect state within "established" U.S. groups?

38. Still, there are contradictions in how Chicano, Chicana, Latino, and Latina subjects are often positioned in relatively equivalizing terms—even within these two distinct trajectories that somehow institutionally become one. For instance, Chicanos and Latinos *are* discursively collapsed in many U.S. institutions, as evinced in "Chicano/Latino studies programs" at such institutions as California State University, Long Beach; Eastern Washington University; Sonoma State University; the University of California, Berkeley; the University of California, Irvine; Michigan State University; Portland State University; Scripps College; and University of Wisconsin, Madison, among many others.

39. Du Bois's observations on the term "Negro," and which groups are subsumed as such, prove fruitful: "As long as the majority of men mean black or brown folk when they say 'Negro,' so long will Negro be the name of folks brown and black" (1996a: 70).

40. Moraga's quotation on her mother and how color creates a different class of people reads, "She often called other lower-income Mexicans 'braceros,' or 'wet-backs,' referring to herself and her family as 'a different class of people'" (1983b: 28). Helena María Viramontes's depiction of Mexican American farmworkers in *Under the Feet of Jesus*, a novel dedicated to César Chávez (1927–93), echoes Moraga's take on the racial

connotations of fieldwork. The appearance of Estrella, a central figure in the text, is described as "[d]irty face, fingernails lined with mud [. . .] tennis shoes soiled, brown smears like coffee stains on her dress where she had cleaned her hands" (1995b: 137).

41. Hughes also brings this to view in *The Big Sea*: "On many sides, the color-line barred your way to making a living in America" (1993: 86).

42. In using "cosmic" and "uncosmic," I am referencing José Vasconcelos's theory, from 1925, of la raza cósmica, the cosmic race. For Vasconcelos (1882–1959), Latin America demonstrated greater promise in the development of a new age because of the region's mestizaje. This new age foments aesthetic ideologies, creative endeavors, and racial mixtures that will bring into fruition a new (Latin-American) humanity. Although Vasconcelos embraces the heterogeneity of racial compositions, he does not account for Indianness and blackness. Most provocative about his delineation is its approach to race mixing through an "artistic impulse" dictated by appearance. Vasconcelos's idea of a "new" racial project moves toward the elimination of blackness, or what Frantz Fanon called a process of "lactification" that "whiten[s] the race" and "ensure[s] its whiteness" (2008: 29–30). Vasconcelos forewarns, "in a few decades of aesthetic eugenics, the Black may disappear, together with the types that a free instinct of beauty may go on signaling as fundamentally recessive and undeserving" (1997: 32). Through what he calls "the faculty of personal taste," the quest to eliminate "ugliness" emerges. "The very ugly will not procreate," Vasconcelos instructs. "They will have no desire to procreate. What does it matter, then, that all the races mix with each other if ugliness will find no cradle? Poverty, defective education, the scarcity of beautiful types, the misery that makes people ugly, all those calamities will disappear from the future social change. The fact, common today, of a mediocre couple feeling proud of having multiplied misery will seem repugnant then, it will seem a crime" (30).

This aesthetic breeding process involves what Felix Clay identified, under the framework of "The Origin of Aesthetic Emotion," as "the pleasures of recognition." In it, "we find that rhythmical movement, or a harmonious combination of colour or sound, can by themselves give rise to a simple feeling of pleasure that is instinctive and quite independent of any mental or intellectual appreciation of the cause" (1908: 282). One could conjecture that Vasconcelos seeks an emotional response to the ("cosmic") results based on his theory of race as an art form. Latin American artistic bodies are pushed into the realm of "modern," "first world" visual *pleasure*. This pleasure of the racial text is "naturalized" to the extent that this regional beauty — or even the race of artists — transacts a message for the rest of the world. As works of "art," these Vasconcelian concoctions illuminate this question: how will his cosmic beauties — or, to put it with less veneration, cookie-cutter multiplication of cosmic things — be valued and judged by the white American and European worlds he is trying to mimic? Marilyn Grace Miller substantiates that the rise of Vasconcelos's idea "of a beneficial mixed race was riddled with the numerous obstacles and contradictions imbedded in a colonial history in which questions of racial difference and distinction were paramount. The complexity of the racial discourse produced in the colonies is most graphically portrayed, perhaps, in several sets of paintings which catalogues racial types, or *castas*. Proceeding from a strange racial alchemy, earlier broad divisions of Spaniard, Indian, *negro*, and mestizo or mulatto were splintered into retrograde hybrids such as the *lobo* (wolf) and the *salta atrás*" (2004: 2). Seen in this light, this Vasconcelian structuring of dark Latinness as ugly requires a new visual order of aestheticized pleasure.

43. An incident in Thomas's *Down These Mean Streets* mirrors this conflation of "negrito" and "ugly." Thomas describes how after returning from playing one day, his mother urges him to take a bath. As the fourteen-year-old son bemoans this quotidian activity, the mother responds, "I have to love you because only your mother could love you, *un negrito* and ugly" (1997: 19). The use of the "affectionate" negrito differs from Rodriguez's portrait in that there is not a possessive operating here, just the article *un*. This incident also proves provocative for another set of reasons: the qualifiers employed for the teenage Thomas move through a particular racial hierarchy that builds on his actions. Walking into his apartment and slamming the door shut makes him a simple "*muchacho*." His silliness/"monkeying around" is soon assessed as "a funny *morenito*" (18). His compliments to his mother later earn him the expression, "Ai, qué negrito" (19).

44. Citing the court transcript of the 1946 landmark case *Mendez v. Westminster*, where educational boundaries in Mexican neighborhoods led to school segregation, Ruiz makes note of "a laundry list of hygienic deficiencies peculiar to Mexican children that warranted, in part, their segregation." The Mexican dirtiness to which Rodriguez alludes can infer, as Ruiz lists the deficiencies of the time: "lice, impetigo, tuberculosis, generally dirty hands, face, neck, and ears" (Ruiz, 2004: 356).

45. Just like a passing black figure portrayed in U.S. African American fiction, people nonfictionally wondered if Rodriguez's mother "is Italian or Portuguese" (1982: 114). But the definitive response is "'We are Mexicans,' my mother and father would say, and taught their four children to say whenever we (often) were asked about our ancestry" (115).

46. Moraga speaks to her "white" U.S. American and "brown" Mexican mixture in her latest enterprise also. Consider the following excerpts: "My racial identity has always been more ambiguous," she observes in *A Xicana Codex of Changing Consciousness* (2011: 12). "Me, a light-skinned mixed-blood Chicana with lousy Spanish" (15).

47. Given Moraga's "social advantage" of looking white, as she calls it (2011: 7), Soto emphasizes her capacity to write "herself *into* a narrative of racialized difference,

emerging as they do from a profound desire to be recognized and engaged as a racialized subject. To that end, Moraga rearranges and reconfigures the epistemological and ontological tropes that one expects to find in accounts of difference" (2005: 238).

48. Soto states, "Moraga's self-racialization depends on the idea that even if one's formative socialization did not include the daily experiences and negotiations of being seen and treated by dominant society as racially different and, importantly, racially inferior (the long-term cumulative effects of which presumably could never be alienable), one can grasp the singular concept of race well enough at the theoretical and historical levels to incorporate it decisively into one's personhood as an adult" (2005: 250).

49. Notions of the "American" tragic mulatto come to mind, of the incessantly conflicted, mixed-race subject that has functioned under Donald Bogle's lens as "the third figure of the black pantheon" (2001: 9). Hortense J. Spillers expands that "this peculiar new-world invention" is "stranded in cultural ambiguity" (1989: 165). The mulatto was "created to provide a middle ground of latitude between 'black' and 'white,' the customary and permissible binary agencies of the national adventure, mulatto being, as a neither/nor proposition, inscribed no historic locus, or materiality, that was other than evasive and shadowy on the national landscape." Yet they embody "an alibi, an excuse for 'other/otherness' that the dominant culture could not (cannot now either) appropriate or wish away." Mulattos are "an accretion of signs that embody the 'unspeakable,' of the Everything that the dominant culture would forget, the *mulatto/a*, as term, designates a disguise, covers up, in the century of Emancipation and beyond, the social and political reality of the dreaded African presence." The "mulatto/a," Spillers observes, "exists for others," but he or she is also a "site of contamination" (1989: 165–67; emphasis added).

Spillers's judicious insertion, in the English language, of a slash and an "a" in the masculine word, "mulatto," catches the eye. This use is more common now in a romance language like Spanish where categories such as "Latino/a" are written as such to denote gender inclusion. Spillers's use of mulatto/a as far back as 1989 predates Latino/a studies's employment of "Latino/a" as an analytic classification. Mulatto/a invites other views of the masculine-centered trajectory of the mulatto man and, one might add, moves toward forging new corollaries with the mulato or mulata in Latin-American contexts. Although Anzaldúa refers to "mulatto blood" rather than calling herself "mulata," the same general understanding of the "dreaded African presence" prevails within the indigenous bloodlines her family wishes to advance. On the distinction between mestizos and mulatos in Spanish America, Ilona Katzew submits, "these appellations developed progressively over time and varied from region to region. The terms mestizo and mulato gained widespread popularity from the sixteenth century and remained current until the end of the colonial period. Mestizo referred to culturally mixed peoples in general and to the combination of Spaniards and Indians in particular, while mulatto—a zoologically inspired term that referred to the hybrid nature of mules—designated the offspring of Spaniards and Africans. [...] The term mulatto was appropriate for this kind of mixture instead of the generic mestizo, because this racial combination 'was deemed uglier and stranger, and to make the point of comparing it to the nature of the mule'" (2004: 43–44).

For an analysis of racial mixture in American literature that dissects the ways in which mulatto and mestiza representations are intertwined, refer to Suzanne Bost's *Mulattas and Mestizas: Representing Mixed Identities in the Americas, 1850–2000*. "Just as biracialism leads African-American writers to think about the nature of racial identity," Bost states, "contemporary work by Chicana/o writers often centers on the issue of racial mixture" (2003: 19). There are, of course, moments of divergence. Bost asks, "If mixed-race identity arouses pride for the Latina/o *raza*, why have relatively few African-Americans celebrated the biracialism of the mulatto? Is the mulatto not a border figure and a cultural translator as much as the Mexican-American mestiza? [...] While Mexican and Chicana/o histories feature *Mestizaje* as a central component in defining national identity, African-American identity has been built on greater polarization" (20–21). As the reader can discern, I am interested in the structuring of a "brown"—or, in Bost's phraseology, a "Latina/o *raza*"—mixture that shuns blackness, even one that is mixed, as "mulatto" attests in this Anzaldúan moment of grave concern for her exposing, tumultuous dark marker. African American mixture or fluidity does not become "mixed" only through white contact. Another insightful nexus might be that of the Hispanophone mulata and the function of the mestiza.

50. Soto attends to this reference also, appraising it as a statement that "frame[s] and *enact[s]* 'going brown' as an ongoing discursive process performed at a number of levels, not the least of which is the writing or illocution itself, as the utterances perform the very action they describe. That is, Moraga not only describes a certain kind of speaking to and for her mother (here rendered symbolic of Chicana and Mexicana women) that enables her to 'go brown,' but uses this kind of speech—indeed, repeats it again and again—to speak/write to us, her readers" (2005: 252).

51. It is also a new image of brownness and brown sexuality vis-à-vis *india* love. Observe, for instance, this stanza: "When her India makes love / it is with the greatest reverence / to color, texture, smell" (Moraga, 1993: 91).

52. Brownness and Indianness conflate and participate in a shared danger. "Since my earliest childhood," Moraga attests, "I knew Mexican meant Indian. [...] I knew 'Indian' was dangerous, like lesbianism" (2011: 13).

53. Moraga strives, as well, for these illegitimacies that replenish queerness, unbelonging, and nonnormativity, proclaiming, "May we strive always for illegitimacy

and unlawfulness in this criminal culture. May our thoughts and actions remain illicit. May we continue to make art that incites censorship and threatens to bring the army beating down our desert door" (2011: 17).

54. This is not to say that Anzaldúa's dark brownness has been entirely evaded and discounted at the academic level. Nor do I suggest that Anzaldúa has conveniently, evenly, and facilely fled from dark brownness. And I certainly do not claim that Anzaldúa's theories have not been instrumental for Chicanos, Chicanas, Latinos, and Latinas. I am, however, interested in the further excavation of her *dark* matter, insomuch as she is mostly made out as "a brown-skinned" or brown subject (Keating, 2000: 2; 2009). There are glimpses of Anzaldúa's darkness at the level of criticism. Sonia Saldívar-Hull provides a good example of how Anzaldúa's "New Mestiza revolutionary theory" operates as a way for "dark women to [reclaim] the right to theorize and create new world visions" (2000: 62–63). Anzaldúa thus accomplishes, in Saldívar-Hull's estimation, a "conscious rupture with all oppressive traditions of all cultures and traditions" (Anzaldúa, quoted in Saldívar-Hull, 2000: 63).

Indeed, one is inclined to think that Anzaldúa's personal history of abject dark brownness and her prieta status is hinged on an intrinsically oppressive tradition. As a result, her procurement of brownness is fundamental because she resists and attenuates the "traditional" abject location of dark brownness. This mestiza spin on Anzaldúa's burgeoning brownness becomes a new strategy and symbol for the self as well as for the larger constitution of a Chicano and Chicana—and by extension a Latino and Latina—browned "we," or in Saldívar-Hull's terms, "collective historia" (2000: 71). Yet the thought I do want to advance is that dark brownness has been jettisoned at the discursive level. The social and familial unacceptability of la prieta that the reader witnesses in Anzaldúa's work remains unacceptable and inadmissible. Might there be any limits in a collective self's recreation, as it fixes itself by shedding dark brownness? Are we relegating dark brownness to an autobiographical memory—a scenario from the transcended past? Brownness hovers over dark brownness as a site and framework of subject recognition. And brownness, in turn, becomes a recognizable counterstory to dark brownness. I encourage further critical labor on dark brownness. The asymmetrical and still untold story of the kinship between brown and dark brown needs to be problematized and analogously brought into the conversation. Studying the "other" part of brownness—dark brownness—would give rise to the reshaping and rewriting of "brown" existence. Far from a signifier of brown estrangement, dark brownness would surface as a key component of Latino and Latina subject formations.

55. By interracial literature Sollors means "works in all genres that represent love and family relations involving black-white couples, biracial individuals, their descen-

dants, and their larger kin—to all of whom the phrasing may be applied, be it as couples, as individuals, or as larger family units" (1997: 3).

56. It is not that U.S. Latinos and Latinas, as a plenitude of mixtures, are monoracial, of course. Rather, I am alluding to how a collective articulation of brownness brings about a mestizaje whose new fabric is tinged by a homogeneous, yet stimulative, brownness.

57. A brown space as constitutive of U.S. Latinas and Latinos comes to mind. Shane T. Moreman and Dawn Marie McIntosh build on "brown scriptings and re-scriptings" of Latina drag queens through a "brown space" (2010: 118). Brown, in their view, "more captures the fluidity of cultural identity that is characterized by the fluctuating representations of those who can claim to this identity." Brownness can be captured and enacted only by brown practitioners with their rightful claim to being "Latina/o, Hispanic and even Chicana/o." Informed by Angharad N. Valdivia, they deem Latino and Latina as "the 'Brown race,' falling somewhere between White Eurocentric and Black Afrocentric racial categories. [. . .] Not *purely* a particular race, brown is a 'hybrid of hybrids.' [. . .] Latina/o is not simply brown, but a hybrid negotiation of browns that moves across borders" (119). I concur with brownness as a hybrid negotiation of browns. But I also differ in the sense that this hybrid brownness assumes that its mobility and negotiation can be attained only through Latinoness and Latinaness. Non-"Latino/a" hybrids that have hybridized brownness are shut off from Latinoness and Latinaness.

CHAPTER FOUR. Disorienting Latinities

1. I am following the 1900 introduction of the Du Boisian color line, as Brent Hayes Edwards has underscored, not through the wide currency it later gained with the publication of *The Souls of Black Folk*, but through its international antecedent, the Pan-African conference in London. The color line can be situated beyond the "U.S. debates and civil rights struggles that are commonly taken to be its arena, [and] in the much broader sphere of 'modern civilization' as a whole" (2003: 1–2). Indeed, events in Central America from the beginning of the twentieth century strengthen the weighty significance of places like Panama, particularly through the 1914 U.S. construction of that nation's canal, which underpins additional terrains and dates from the Global South. The year 1903, for example, charts Panamanian independence from Colombia; nine years after the U.S. Congress passed the Panama Canal Act. This date provides a foundation for a Panamanian/Central American scholarly link to American studies, Chicano/a studies, ethnic studies, and Latino/a studies discussions that historically mark deracinated subjects in the Americas, namely through key imperial occurrences

like the 1846–48 Mexican-American War and the 1898 Spanish-American War. The construction of the República de Panamá, largely supported by the United States as a means to control the canal uniting both the Pacific and Atlantic Oceans, provides a correlative model of annexation, nation formation, and expansion. A new Panamanian nationality came into being from the previously recognized Colombian citizenship. There was, as well, the advancement of a new "racial 'ladder'" during this period, celebrating U.S. engineering innovation. As Matthew Parker writes, "the Americans and the hundred or so British [were] at the top; next came the Panamanians and the Spanish 'almost-whites'; at the bottom were the blacks, with the West Indians beneath the locals in status" (2009: 413–14). Salaries were organized in a way where gold coins were largely reserved for white U.S. citizens and local currency, Panamanian silver, for the West Indian darker shades. U.S. segregation in the Canal Zone stressed an acute observation by a patroller in the area that runs thus: "Panama is below the Mason and Dixon Line" (381).

2. As Peter Chapman points out, a banana republic does not "have to produce bananas to qualify for the title. Nicaragua, for example, did not grow bananas in any great commercial quantity. The country's banana republicanism resided in the happy coincidence of views enjoyed by the ruling Somoza family, United Fruit, and the U.S." (2007: 6).

3. Consult, for example, the introductory volume of the journal the *Global South*. Alfred J. López, the editor, wrote that the Global South "can and does serve as a signifier of oppositional subaltern cultures ranging from Africa, Central and Latin America, much of Asia, and even those 'Souths' within a larger perceived North, such as the U.S. South and Mediterranean and Eastern Europe" (2007b: 8). Note López's qualification of "Central *and* Latin America." It seems cognizant of how Central America is excluded from the Latin American map. Central and Latin America need to be named through this conjunction. And yet Central and Latin America simultaneously mark their separateness. Curiously, the Caribbean is omitted from this Latin American equation.

4. U.S. Salvadoran migrants textually appear in Latino/a fiction as fetishized, unassimilated, monstrous bodies, albeit torture and civil strife. Consult, for example, Demetria Martínez's *Mother Tongue*, which occupies a notable literary space in Chicano/Latino literature. Martínez's narrative was first published by the Arizona-based Bilingual Press/Editorial Bilingüe in 1994, and reissued in 1996 through a corporate publisher, One World/Ballantine Books, a division of Random House. Awarded the 1994 Western States Book Award for Fiction, *Mother Tongue* illustrates how Salvadoran refugees inhabit the U.S. terrain. But despite its aims at sociopolitical solidarity, Martínez's work writes Salvadorans outside of U.S. life. The novel is

double voiced: it is told through the two competing narratives of a Chicana, María, and a Salvadoran, José Luis. My observations focus on María's impressions of the Salvadoran figure. Engagement with the novel's first part calls for a pressing attentiveness to how invisible secondary Latino and Latina groups become visible Latinos and Latinas. Martínez provides stimulus for exploring how Salvadoran "silence" speaks through Chicana literature. As I argue, to "be" Central American is to be that which is about to emerge, about to be seen, and possibly, about to be heard. María falls in love with José Luis, a tortured refugee who flees to Albuquerque. José Luis's arrival may be a reference to 1986, when New Mexico governor Toney Anaya declared this state (the first in the nation) as a sanctuary for Central American refugees. Because José Luis is in danger, his name is a pseudonym. (His nom de plum later turns out to be his birth name.) María looks after José Luis in the absence of her godmother and is determined to fall in love with him. Her desire is included in the novel's first sentence: "I knew I would one day make love with him." María adds familiarity to her subject's dark brownness by describing José Luis's features: "His face was a face I'd seen in a dream. A face with no borders: Tibetan eyelids, Spanish hazel irises, Mayan cheekbones. I don't know why I had expected Olmec: African features and a warrior's helmet" (1996: 3–4). María romanticizes a war hero who is anything but Salvadoran, extending her Mexican Olmec past. But how would El Salvador's Pipil Indians fit within José Luis's multiple racial and ethnic compositions? José Luis's facial traits have no borders and add a different twist to José Vasconcelos's cosmic race, as civil war becomes a racializing ingredient. *Mother Tongue* presents the remaking of a new political, Cold War Latino mestizo. As María procreates with José Luis, their child represents the forging of an unnamable Latino union. This Latinized Cold War mestizaje presents a U.S. citizen whose identity is informed by his mother's Chicananess. Through this Cold War mestizo, the reader sees the discursive fracturing of what turns out to be a U.S. Latino disunion. U.S. Salvadoranness is nonexistent, even though its North American rebirth stems from a mixed Indianness in relation to an English-speaking empire. Since José Luis speaks only Spanish, the Americanization of his U.S. Salvadoranness cannot be literally heard. U.S. Salvadoran "speech" is outside of "Latino" (and American) normativity. The new Cold War mestizo is a U.S. inflection of U.S. Salvadoran/"Latino" bastardry.

5. McGrath's narrator, a psychiatrist, explains, "Their buried materials was throwing up nightmares and other symptoms, and would continue to do so until the trauma could be translated into a narrative and assimilated into the self" (2008: 31). It can be said that a discursive Latino or Latina self perceives and chronicles the "buried trauma" of Central American nightmares and their deficient conditions. But what still needs to be translated and assimilated, narratively speak-

ing, is the language of multiple Central American selves, as they resurface in the United States.

6. The armed conflict displaced so many Central Americans that even Gabriel García Márquez's 1982 Nobel Laureate address speaks to the outpouring of Salvadoran migrations: "Since 1979, the civil war in El Salvador has produced almost one refugee every twenty minutes." García Márquez also puts into words the larger diasporic "nation" formed by Latin populations of displacement, adding, "The country that could be formed of all the exiles and forced emigrants of Latin America would have a population larger than that of Norway" (1982).

7. By U.S.-centered American ideologies, I mean to denote nationalist characterizations of citizenship, opportunity, equality and justice, and democracy and order. U.S.-centered forms of Americanisms are localized within U.S. renditions of being American. Nations in the Americas have their own foundations for understanding, using, and claiming their particular American identity in relation to themselves or in a hemispheric context that counters U.S.-centrism.

8. John Rechy, for instance, provides such a glimpse of a disorienting Latino or Latina in *The Miraculous Day of Amalia Gómez*. Facing a day of socioeconomic and individual complications in "East Ellay" that can be resolved only through a miracle, the leading character in this novel thinks about an underlying but unspeakable question. Amalia, the protagonist, contemplates why her son, Juan, allows a motherless Salvadoran teenager to sleep in their garage. The teenager's motherless state is more credible than his nationality, and Amalia asks herself, "*Was* he Salvadoran? Had Juan told her that only to disorient her?" (1991: 94). Representations of refugee and motherlessness notwithstanding, what makes this passing interest of marginal U.S. Salvadoranness so disorienting? Is it because of the contemporaneity of both U.S. Salvadorans and Salvadoranness in a geography that can be bound only to Aztlán? Do these disorienting citizens orient us to graver (U.S. Salvadoran) problems than one's (non-Salvadoran) own?

9. Political iconomy centers on "the operations of the image economy, the now ubiquitous and vastly important system of symbolic exchange between people, interest groups, cultures, an exchange conducted largely but never exclusively through visual images, both actualised and imagined" (T. Smith, 2003: 33).

10. El Salvador, for instance, was dubbed by Nobel Laureate Gabriela Mistral as the Little Tom Thumb of America, el pulgarcito de América. The smallness of the Little Tom Thumb perpetuates the supposition that there is cultural dearth in the region. This "affectionate" diminutive reduces El Salvador to a charming, quaint region whose size is equivalent to that of Massachusetts. Contemporary equations of El Salvador to Tom Thumb echo early European writers who, in the sixteenth and seventeenth

centuries, would contrast a monster, Gargantua, to Tom Thumb, a nameless pigmy. This discourse of smallness indicates that there are many Tom Thumbs within the U.S. and European neocolonial imaginaries. Anne Lake Prescott remarks that "Europeans had in fact long associated giants and pygmies, for both inhabit distant or doubtful terrain and both raise question about size's relation to status (especially as traditional pygmies would be tiny—half a cubit, said one authority)" (1996: 75). While El Salvador is not collapsible to the giant monsterhood that is Gargantua, its anomaly is nonetheless emphasized in size, development, and culture. These aberrations also serve as a threat. The political activities of Tom Thumb could turn the pigmy into the monstrous Gargantua; the 1980s civil war in the region is a case in point.

11. The idiom is indexed in a threefold manner: (1) "De guatemala se fue a guatepeor," (2) "Salió de guatemala y cayó en guatepeor," and (3) "Salí a guatemala y entré a guatepeor" (Glazer, 1987: 148–49).

12. Central America, historian Greg Grandin contends, keeps "showing up" in the United States "in the oddest ways" (2006: 223). It was there that the Republican Party "first combined the three elements that give today's imperialism its moral force: punitive idealism, free-market absolutism, and right-wing Christian mobilization" (3). In the exercising of a "new revolutionary imperialism" after "America's latest episode of imperial overreach in the wake of 9/11 [. . .] a recycling of personnel" was ushered into the George W. Bush administration. They were "veterans of Ronald Reagan's Central American policy in the 1980s," involving advisers and hangers-on like "Elliott Abrams, Bush's deputy national security adviser in charge of promoting democracy throughout the world; John Negroponte, former U.N. ambassador, envoy to Iraq and intelligence czar; Otto Reich, secretary of the state for the Western Hemisphere during Bush's first term, and Robert Kagan, an ardent advocate of U.S. global hegemony." John Poindexter, President Reagan's former national security adviser convicted of lying to Congress during the Iran-Contra scandal, was subsequently appointed by Donald Rumsfeld to direct the Pentagon's Total Information Awareness Program. And John Bolton, who "served as Reagan's point man in the Justice Department," had a role as the twenty-fifth U.S. ambassador to the United Nations (4–5). This cast of political personae is not superfluous. The cabinet members became the political "founding fathers" (or stepfathers, if you will) of Central American–American beginnings.

13. There are various Facebook pages mocking this expression. One of these platforms, which joined Facebook on 2 March 2010, calls itself "Irte de guatemala a guatepeor." As of 8 June 2012, this page had 4,838 "likes." The page's "about" tab lists another Spanish expression, "La suerte de la fea, la guapa la desea," as its main and only source of information. The phrase roughly translates to "The ugly girl's luck is what the good-looking girl wants."

14. As the title of Myra Mendible's anthology *From Bananas to Buttocks: The Latina Body in Popular Film and Culture* (2007) suggests, the banana emerges as a representational icon and marker of U.S. Latino and Latina existence in popular culture typifications of Latinidad. Mendible's volume specifically centers on Latina subjects, although it bears mentioning that the banana has also evoked a "tropical" optic emphasizing, more generally, the differences between countries with varying levels of industrialization. For the most part, U.S. Latino/a cultural studies have turned to the banana from a Hispanophone Caribbean standpoint to stress misrepresentations from the "other" Americas as well. But this banana trope spreads to Central and South America and can be positioned and referenced through its own particularities. The inability to ground the banana in other discursive, Latinized forms overlooks the expansive terrain of Latinidad and the conditions that insert — or "write in" — one's arrival to this realm. Such cultural domain has not been an equitable one, as Kirsten Silva Gruesz has written. She points out "the idea that Central American nations are even later arrivals than the rest of Latin America to the table of modernity" (2008: 141).

One example of a "Caribbeanized" banana, as it has been charted in Latino/a studies, is Frances Aparicio's and Susana Chávez-Silverman's edited volume on cultural representations of U.S. Latinos and Latinas, *Tropicalizations: Transcultural Representations of Latinidad* (1997b), where they draw from Victor Hernández Cruz's work by adding a plurality to their anthology's title, an homage to that poet's first book, *Tropicalization* (1976). The editors elicit Hernández Cruz's alienation from the U.S. metropolis, one in which the poet substitutes snow for green bananas in the cold urban landscape, forecasting a "Weather report: Green bananas have been reported falling from heaven in some parts of the city." Through this verse, U.S. Latino and Latina voices "transform the U.S. landscape into realities informed and subverted by visual icons, cultural practices, texts, and language from the Hispanic Caribbean" (Aparicio, 1997: 194). Aparicio's sharp points Caribbeanize the island of Manhattan from the Global North. But Hernández Cruz's tropical conversation with the frigid "first world" moves toward richer banana connotations that get eliminated from Latinidad. His jocular approach — a retropicalized Caribbean-specific response — is rooted at the level of the witty and has not been placed in interlocutory discussion with the sobering effects of the banana for those in Central and South America whose national identities are shaped by U.S. economic and political interests.

The ways that intellectuals from "banana republics" studiously navigate the transformation of local landscapes need to be conjoined to a Latinidad that would be significantly sharpened by relating to — and often diverging with — how such figures from the Global South may (or may not) be in dialogue with U.S. Latino and Latina cultural producers. The United Fruit Company (UFC), founded in 1899, created a group of "Banana Zone gypsies," to paraphrase from Gerald Martin, that included, in places like Santa Marta, Colombia, "artisans, merchants, boatmen, prostitutes, washerwomen, musicians, [and] bartenders." These migrant, "tropicalized" communities, not unlike U.S. Latinos and Latinas, "became plugged into the international market of goods," a consumptive Americanization, one could claim, with a range of such U.S. products as "Montgomery Ward catalogues, Quaker Oats, Vicks Vaporub, Eno Fruit Salts, [and] Colgate Dental Creme" (2009: 39). I would argue that one pressing preoccupation that can be teased out and rendered more complex in Latino/a studies involves how literary figures from the "tropics" *untropicalize* the banana by transporting us to this fruit as (1) a symbol of labor exploitation (Ernesto Cardenal, Nicaragua), (2) a "civilizing" tool for the developing nation (Carlos Luis Fallas, Costa Rica), (3) an allegory for a "new" quadcultural mestizo and mestiza (Francisco Goldman, Guatemala and the United States); and (4) a haunting national memory (Gabriel García Márquez, Colombia).

Take Cardenal's foundational poem, "Zero Hour," which draws on the ways in which this Nicaraguan poet chronicles the U.S. banana industry in that nation while tracing the life of revolutionary leader Augusto César Sandino. Cardenal's tropicalization stresses a southern Latinity where the crudity of U.S.-sponsored economic and political violence in Nicaragua is implied in location. Cardenal depicts Central America as a place of chaos and dictatorship, tropicalized no less than by the U.S. intervention that propels Nicaraguan struggles for democracy. The poem's opening sentence attests to this point: "Tropical nights in Central America, / with moonlit lagoons and volcanoes / and lights from presidential palaces, / barracks and sad curfew warnings" (1980: 1). Here, bananas—their color, green or yellow, is beside the point—are not merely used to represent an inversion of U.S. climate. They are applied to direct attention to the demands of U.S. capital: "The banana is left to rot on the plantations, / or to rot in the cars along the railroad tracks / or it's cut overripe so it can be rejected / when it reaches the wharf or be thrown into the sea; / the bunches of bananas declared buried, or too skinny, / or withered, or green, or overripe, or diseased: / so there'll be no cheap bananas, / or so as to buy bananas cheap. / Until there's hunger along the Atlantic Coast of Nicaragua" (1980: 3).

Other forms of banana tropicalizations from the Global South include Fallas's novel, *Mamita Yunai* (1966), which focuses on the life and working conditions of *bananeros* in "La Yunai," the popular pronunciation of the UFC. Goldman's *The Long Night of White Chickens* posits that North American market-driven tropicalizations have created a "quadcultural synthesis" in Central America (1992: 242). This quadcultural character accounts for a Guatemalan mixture that reflects "banana-boat loaders and North American fruit company clerks, Indian, African blood, Spanish-Moorish and who knows what else?" (160). Goldman's and Cardenal's analytic acts of southern

Latinities are critiques of a tropicalizing Latinidad that are reported back to North Americans. Indeed, Goldman narrates Guatemala's formation as a banana republic in his third novel, *The Divine Husband*, a provocative representation of the political and economic emergence of Central America in the nineteenth century. He writes about the exotic appropriation of a "nearly naked, vixenish, and seed-eyed Indian woman, wearing a flamboyant serpent-feather headdress, standing in a canoe piled with fruits and paddled by monkey, parrot, and lizard" for the U.S. branding of Chiquita bananas (2004: 142). U.S. capitalist demands vis-à-vis banana investments also extend to South America.

García Márquez reports in *Living to Tell the Tale* about the socioeconomic impact of the investments by the UFC in Colombia. More than countering a northern tropicalization, the economic exploitation of the banana workers marks for Colombians, as García Márquez's mother tells it, a place where the world ends. The Nobel Laureate makes known, "I followed the direction of her [his mother's] index finger and saw the station: a building of peeling wood, sloping tin roofs, and running balconies, and in front of it an arid little square that could not hold more than two hundred people. It was there, my mother told me that day, where in 1928 the army had killed an undetermined number of banana workers. I knew that event as if I had lived it, having heard it recounted and repeated a thousand times by my grandfather from the time I had a memory: the soldier reading the decree by which the striking laborers were declared a gang of lawbreakers; the three thousand men, women, and children motionless under the savage sun after the officer gave them five minutes to evacuate the square; the order to fire, the clattering machine guns spitting in white-hot bursts, the crowd trapped by panic as it was cut down, little by little, by the methodical, insatiable scissors of the shrapnel" (2003: 14–15). The repetition of labor—coupled with the redundancy in telling his story, a political tale that marks the time the author "had a memory"—makes this account part of Colombian national history.

15. "Guatepeorianness" and nothingness, as a conjunction, summarize Goldman's assertion that "Guatemala doesn't exist" in the epistemological sense (1992: 21). Goldman hence qualified this statement about Guatemalan and Central American modernity as "poor little countr[ies], no luck at all, nothing ever goes right" (243).

16. Santiago may mean "guate-peor" instead of "guata-peor," although the latter use coincides with the common misspelling, in English, of Guatemala to Guatamala. Given that Peoria exists as a geographic location in the United States and as a reference point for dull and uninspiring American attitudes, de Guatemala a Guatepeor could be translated as "from Guatemala to Guatepeoria," or simply "from Guatemala to Peoria."

17. Some well-known U.S. Central American authors also reproduce this trope of Guatepeorianness. Mario Bencastro's novel, *Odyssey to the North*, is one example that

molds the untamable lifestyles of Salvadorans in the United States. Primarily the story of Calixto, a dishwasher in a Washington, D.C., hotel, *Odyssey to the North* takes place in the 1980s and early 1990s. Calixto works alongside three other men: the distinctively named Caremacho ("Machoface"), Juancho, and Cali. Other character names include Pateyuca ("Yucafeet"), Lencho, and Chele Chile. The last two designations are too regional and folkloric to attempt to make an English translation. All the same, Bencastro's figures enter the U.S. domestic realm through economic disillusionment. The novel's introduction to U.S. Salvadoranness occurs through the representation of the hardworking Salvadoran — with "enough" victimhood in his narrative to represent these migrants as "likeable" and tolerable but ultimately unacceptable. From the strong Salvadoran matriarch/tamale vendor who hides in the bushes to give birth only to immediately return after this incident to continue selling her cornmeal dish to unruly immigrants in D.C., Bencastro's portrayal of unbefitting Salvadoran attributes dehumanizes them. Calixto, for example, shares a foul-smelling one-bedroom apartment with nineteen other people. Those living in this unit lack documentation and fear having their housing conditions and legal statuses detected by authorities. As a result, they take shifts: ten people live in the apartment during the day, and the other ten at night. The ways that the twenty individuals dispose of their feces is alarming. According to Calixto, the residents "use plastic bags or newspaper and throw everything into the incinerator. The one who was actually renting the apartment used to say that the building superintendent complained of the terrible stench that filled the building when he burned the garbage" (1998: 15). To gain a kind of Latino literary entrance, Bencastro has to adopt a recognizable Guatepeorianness within the broader U.S. Latino and Latina world.

18. Cristina García also created a fictional Central American — Guatepeorian — nation in *The Lady Matador's Hotel*. This tropical Guatepeor is a "wedge of forgotten land between continents, [a] place of hurricanes and violence and calculated erasures" (2010: 4). There are insurmountable deaths in this nation; it has "coffins, pine-wood coffins stacked up to the sky" (8). The violence of the 1980s civil war lingers, even though the region's twenty-first-century forms of violence and fear are due to transnational gangs, or *maras*. The economy of García's nation is predictably tied to bananas, as the "President of the Universal Fruit Company, Federico Ladrón-Benes" makes his home there. The novel also alludes to representations of buried trauma and collective amnesia. One of García's characters, Aura, "is convinced that the entire country has succumbed to a collective amnesia. This is what happens in a society where no one is permitted to grow old slowly. Nobody talks of the past, for fear their wounds might reopen. Privately, though, their wounds never heal" (9).

19. The Salvadoran agricultural landscape is described as full of birds. It also includes tamarind and orange trees. Marta Claros is introduced as a child vendor who walks the "roughly paved streets of her San Salvador" to sell used clothing (C. García, 2007: 18). Her brother Evaristo first lives *in* a coral tree in San Salvador, followed by a banyan tree (22, 87). Both of these branched and leafy homes are later substituted for a eucalyptus tree in Los Angeles. Marta hails from a land where peasant Salvadoran machos fight by avocado trees during *quinceañera* parties. Banana trees are in abundance too. Just as Marta's stepfather dies after a "commotion" during a quinceañera celebration, someone naturally rips off one of the bountiful leaves from a banana tree and begins fanning the dead body (56). Along fairly similar lines, Z. Z. Packer's *Drinking Coffee Elsewhere* offers an analogous comparison. Packer pens the fictional Lupita, a Guatemalan migrant who takes care of the birds owned by the main character's black father in the short story, "The Ant of the Self" (2003: 73–104). The narrator informs us more concretely that "Lupita knew about birds [. . .] because she'd once owned a rooster when she was five back in Guatemala." Lupita, a charming caricature in diminutive, becomes a literary element that emphasizes the black character's pitiful life in the Midwest. To put it boldly, Lupita dresses like a cheaply adorned dissolute woman, wearing "satiny pajamas that show her nipples. Pink curlers droop from her hair like blossoms." Packer's representation reaches laughable proportions when Lupita, echoing Speedy Gonzalez, yells remarks like, "What do *joo* want?" "Enough eez enough!" and "Joo are never thinking about maybe what Lupita feels!" Even the birds echo Lupita's speech, reciting, "*Arriba, 'riba, 'riba*" (82–83).

20. Julia Alvarez presents a revealing autobiographical moment in *Once upon a Quinceañera*, where two distinct episodes of mistreatment in the public sphere build on the racialization of her use of the Spanish language and the presumed communism of both her family's political migration to the United States and their struggles for U.S. socioeconomic advancement in the 1960s. Though told from a Dominican perspective, Alvarez's fragments nonetheless connote strained versions of U.S. belonging and the idea of American success. In effect, Alvarez's Dominicanness can be seen as an embryonic form of a political migration that stands as too ideologically loaded and that somewhat parallels the present Central American–American situation: unpronounceable, estranged, and un-American. Alvarez's passage remaps the Dominican Republic as being next to Cuba—erasing Haiti in this process but still attempting to find Latin corollaries in the United States: "Pale as we were, hadn't my sisters and I been told by passersby on the street who heard us talking loudly in Spanish: *Spics! Go back to where you came from!* There had been several incidents at my school, older boys spitting at me, throwing pebbles at me, chasing me down the block, accusing me of being a Commie because they had overheard me say that our island was next to Cuba,

where the dreaded Castro was getting ready to launch a bomb against the United States" (2007: 26).

21. We could conceive this "pan-third world" literary moment with what Marc Zimmerman has identified as a "literature of settlement," which looks back "on the homebase and immigration, but from a more settled-in framework, with an existing Latino tradition behind it, now reaching out to other minority and mainstream (U.S. mainly but also Latin American, African, etc.) to expand horizons and move either to pan-Latin American, 'pan-third world' or U.S. mainstream identifications" (1992: 21). I insist, however, that the way in which such solidarity among nations is constructed warrants closer scrutiny, especially when "Latino" or "Latina," as we have seen in this book, is not a given but an identificatory process gathered from different perspectives and subject positions that do not always involve the national. Zimmerman is certainly aware of this point, remarking in his book that "of course [. . .] there are no Latinos, that the word is a construct bringing together diverse people who while they clearly share certain bases, are often quite distinct and only identify with each other in opposition to the non-latinos and that usually for very specific, contingent and often political, epiphenomenal and ephemeral concerns" (40). Latinos and Latinas "exist" through Latinidad. This book, however, has strived to show that Latino and Latina textures can and do exist through the variants of Latinities. These referents convey meaning beyond the brown reach of Latinidad.

22. In a Chicano and Chicana context, Francisco A. Lomelí and Donaldo W. Urioste (1976) posit this "sympathetic fiction" as literatura chicanesca, or "Chicanesque literature." Hector Torres writes that "early in the history of Chicano/a critical discourse" literatura chicanesca designated "a body of literature written about the Chicano/a experience by a non-Chicano/a writer" that provided "a valuable external point of view on the Chicano/a experience" (2000: 159).

23. In addition, 1992 heralded, as Arias has pointed out, the Los Angeles uprising. Although this year marked the Peace Accords in El Salvador, the "peace dividend never took place" in that nation. As Arias elaborates, "the arrival of peace did end actual military combat, as guerrillas turned their weapons in and formed legal political parties that now play the role of a loyal opposition in Congress and have, in El Salvador's case, succeeded in winning many municipal elections, including the city of San Salvador. But the much-promised international aid never did arrive in sufficient quantity. What was expected to be a massive Marshall-like plan to fully modernize these nations to uproot a model of underdevelopment marked by massive amounts of landless peasants, racism against Maya indigenous peoples, and an inability to train the bulk of their populations in the basic rudiments of modern life, including reading and writing, all of these major issues that fed into the civil wars' conflicts, became only a trickle that dwindled to almost nothing after 2000" (2007: 175).

24. I have reworked this concern to advance Patricia Zavella's question raised in *Feminist Dilemmas in Fieldwork*: "What happens when ethnic insiders gain access to a community similar to their own?" (1996: 139).

25. Michael Parenti finds that civil conflict in Central America enabled the United States to perform the role of a "'helpless giant' pushed around by third-rate powers" (1989: 1). The position of many Central American nations as third-rate powers also intones matters of cultural dearth and irrelevance on U.S. and Latin-American realms. Arias has pointed out the absence of Central American literature from Latin American and U.S. literary discourses. He notes that work from this region is "almost like an invisible literature to the degree that it is not addressed critically, it doesn't exist. [Literature from Central America is] not in the bibliographies, it's not on the Modern Language Association panels, it's not named, and so it has to be named" (quoted in Roberts, 1997: 32). Arias's comments identify the invisibility of Central American letters within the Americas.

Evidence of this literary absence can also be found within Central America. The editor of a Salvadoran anthology, spanning from 1880 to 1955, wrote, "It has often been said that El Salvador is an intellectual desert, in no way fertile ground for manifestations of the spirit." The text reads, "Se ha dicho repetidas veces que El Salvador es un desierto intelectual, en nada propicio para manifestaciones del espíritu" (Barba Salinas, 1959, 10; my translation). Nearly four decades later, Salvadoran novelist Horacio Castellanos Moya tackles this motif in his existentialist novel, *El asco*. He reappropriates Latin American and U.S. perceptions about El Salvador. Castellanos Moya, possibly distraught by the emptiness that surfaces in relation to most "things" Salvadoran, forces his public to think about the implications of cultural and geographic obscurity. The novel progresses through the often-disgusted monologue of Thomas Bernhard, a Salvadoran émigré, now a naturalized Canadian citizen, who is obliged to visit his birthplace because of a death in the family. The protagonist's countless denunciations are incitations prompting Salvadoran "pathologies," as living subjects, to begin uncriminalizing the misrepresentations of Salvadoranness. The narrator declares, "This race quarrels with knowledge and with intellectual curiosity, this country is out of time and the rest of the world, it only existed when there was carnage, it only existed thanks to the thousands that were assassinated, thanks to the criminal capacity of the military and the communists, outside this criminal capacity [El Salvador] has no possibility of existence" (1997: 57–58; my translation). Central America, far from being an "intellectual desert," has long housed intellectuals and critics of what C. L. R. James calls the role of the United States as "the representative banker, armorer and political mentor of one political system in opposition to another" (1993: 201).

26. The translation of García Canclini's passages is my own. The quoted excerpts, in the original Spanish, read, "América latina no está completa en América latina" and

"Podemos decir que 'lo latinoamericano' anda suelto, desborda su territorio, va a la deriva en rutas disperas" (2002: 19–20).

27. Arias asks, "when we look at the phenomenon of Central American–Americans captured in the United States and deported to their alleged country of origin, where they are perceived as tattooed aliens—that is, doubly alien, alien in the sense of being foreigners to the nation-state that does not recognize their blood tie to it, their belongingness to their particular sovereign space, and aliens in the sci-fi sense of appearing to be a different species altogether with their innumerable tattoos, postmodern space travelers of a sort—who is global, and who is, indeed, local?" (2007: 182).

28. Ilan Stavans, the editor of the Penguin Classics edition of *Rubén Darío: Selected Writings*, explains, "*Modernismo* was, more than anything else, a metaphysical pursuit by a cadre of [Latin American] intellectuals disenchanted with institutionalized religion and with the ideological currents available" (2005: xxx). The modernista movement—or revolution, as Stavans calls it—"occurred roughly between 1885 and 1915 (or with Darío's death, a year later), and although it spilled into other artistic arenas, its central tenets apply to literature almost exclusively, and to poetry most vividly" (xxxi).

29. President Reagan's reminder of this particular territory's value noted, "Central America is a region of great importance to the United States. And it is so close—San Salvador is closer to Houston, Texas, than Houston is to Washington, D.C. Central America is America; it's at our doorstep" (Reeves, 2005: 218).

30. The idea of an "additional otherness" and its connection to other U.S. ethnoracial groups commonly perceived as "homogeneous" is being unraveled in other spheres. Consult, for example, Shaw-Taylor and Tuch (2007), which unsettles the construction of an "insular" blackness in the U.S. racial taxonomy.

31. Peru Ana and Ana Peru manifest a type of "geographic Latinities" that does not extend to just individuals with mercurial sociocultural qualities. Typifying a landscape whose migratory movements and cultural crossings underscore the malleable attributes of the city and its citizens, Peru Ana's and Ana Peru's geographic Latinities delocalize and denationalize—consuming whatever may fall under urbanity. V. S. Naipaul seemingly speaks to this state of urban and national statelessness when he notes, in connection to London life in the 1950s, that "[c]ities like London were to change. They were to cease being more or less national cities; they were to become cities of the world, modern-day Romes, establishing the pattern of what great cities should be, in the eyes of islanders like myself and people even more remote in language and culture" (quoted in French, 2008: 68).

32. I am not making a motion for each Latino and Latina group to have a corresponding field of inquiry apart from Latino/a studies based on their "inherent,"

"all-informing" national identity. Rather, my proposition is that Latino/a studies lacks a feasible comparativist project that, like Latinidad, is "produced in tension," as Mérida Rúa has put it. Rúa has offered some glimpses into Latino and Latina futures categorized by a conjunction of Latin American nationalities that do not only challenge Latino/a studies but also widen its meanings. She deliberates on "interLatino relationships and how prospective identities [. . .] unfold from them" vis-à-vis her research with Puerto Rican–Mexican Chicago residents in their twenties and thirties (2001: 118). Her characterization of "PortoMex" and "MexiRican" subjectivities cues us into the rupturing of the relatively "neat" subject delineations found in Puerto Rican studies, Chicano/a studies, and Latino/a studies. To these modalities, we can also recall Angie Chabram-Dernersesian's (1994) transnational connection and interrogation of her "Chicana-Riqueña" plurality.

Rúa seeks an inter-Latino/a studies model that has not been geographically divided by a U.S. East and West dyad predicated on "when the Chicano encounters the Nuyorican" (2001: 120). Her ethnographic investigation illustrates how a dual Latinoness has been induced by a subject's convergence of coeval Puerto Ricanness and Mexicanness. This nationally mixed Latino and Latina subject "seldom receives scholarly attention" from their "respective" disciplines: Chicano/a studies and Puerto Rican studies (119). I would note, however, that the analytic and conceptual role of Latino/a studies for Latino and Latina multitudes that do not solely and particularly depend on national identities and signifiers has yet to be explored. Rúa's study is certainly instructive, as is her view of Latinidad. The latter is "a cultural expression that embraces blood and fictive kin, lovers, friends, neighbors, co-workers, and even strangers in an everyday form of community building. Individuals engaging in these community-building efforts come to know themselves by way of their interactions with members of diverse Latino ethnoracial groups." I concur with this stance to an extent, but I must also question whether one needs a binationally transmuted Latino or Latina to make sense of one's self. More specifically, does one need a "diverse" Latino and Latina to make sense of one's own diversity? Is a Latino or Latina with one nationality invariably uniform and uninformed about "the malleable boundaries" of Latino and Latina life (120)?

One must be cautious, for to privilege a Latino or Latina based on a double national Latin American background renders this positioning in biological terms. If one is not born into these binational circumstances, one lacks that "lived experience of everyday Latinidad" (Rúa, 2001: 118). Aparicio seems to advance this claim of "hybrid Latino subjects who are the offspring of Latinas/os of two different national groups" and their distinct negotiation of Latino and Latina identity. It varies, Aparicio writes, "from the Anglo-Latino power dyad that has structured most of our understanding about Latinas/os in the United States. [. . .] [They] make strategic decisions about national differentiation based on a variety of contextual, family, and social factors. Thus, their identity constructions tend to be more concentric, multiple, and diffused than what we are accustomed to" (2007: 45). These mixtures propel a panethnicity for certain Latinos and Latinas that moves away from the specificity of being a Chicano, Chicana, or Nuyorican into different processes of binational identification. But we should also question the idea of Latinoness and Latinaness as definitive, determined, and empirical. Latinoness and Latinaness seem to consistently share one agreeable definition because *one* nationality coherently guides a particular Latino or Latina. Aparicio also enumerates other national Latino and Latina varieties, among them, "Cubolivians [and] Mexistanis (Mexican and Pakistani)," which are "but a few of the possible hybrid identities that populate our urban centers" (47).

33. I would venture to add that Juan Gonzalez presents an interesting prototype not just for a U.S. *Latino* Puerto Ricanness but also through his drafting of U.S. Latino and Latina history in *Harvest of Empire: A History of Latinos in America*. Herewith, Gonzalez enacts a fascinating hopscotch of Latin American and U.S. history: his account executes a hemispheric narrative of "states" of Latinaness and Latinoness vis-à-vis a *simultaneous* examination of nation formation in the United States and Latin America. Gonzalez, a Puerto Rican who grew up in New York City, claims a Latino identification not merely as a form of Latinidad but plausibly within the context of my focus here, as a Latinity aware of the many cross-identificatory tenets gestating U.S. Latino and Latina states. Bridging Latino, Latina, and Latin American outlooks from various geohistorical locations, *Harvest of Empire* reminds the U.S. "common reader" that although there may be "a growing number of Latino professionals, students, and intellectuals who may know a great deal about their particular ethnic group—Chicano, Puerto Ricans, Cubans," they understand "little else about other Hispanics" (2000: xvi). Gonzalez situates his writing as one advanced by "the perspective of a Latino," calling it "a frank attempt to make sense of both the Latin American and North American experience" (xvii–xviii). His work underscores that "Latino/a" becoming is tied to U.S. growth and territorial expansion of Latin America.

34. To this end, we can profit from Michaeline Crichlow and Patricia Northover's *Globalization and the Post-Creole Imagination*, where they wrestle with the politics of forging place in the Caribbean, a specificity that resonates with other groups. The Caribbean can be extended to Central America, alongside the traveling meanings of Central American–American, which signals the location of "other" Central Americans within the isthmus and the ongoing mappings of Central American–Americanness. Such a project applies to notions of being as they relate not only to existence but also to articulations of place and space and a subject's capacity to be present. The sup-

posed fixity of a nation and standard identifications of a region must deal with the traveling body. These moving bodies are "journeys toward the refashioning of the self, times, and places and the intertwinement of global and local processes," since they invariably shift and redirect our understanding of creolization (2009: ix). Such maneuvering—or "mobile strategies"—invite theoretical groundings and dynamics (xiv). They provide en entry into a continual "mapping of the present"; new geographic and cultural milieus restart through creolization processes (22). The "original" Caribbean setting of creolization is therefore broadened and becomes an exchange of boundless presencing, or the "ontologies of lived space." These anthologies are driven by multi-directional "hi/stories" delineating human identity stories (18–20).

35. Themes of indigence and underdevelopment, confusion, violence, and monstrosity abound in Graciela Limón's *In Search of Bernabé*, a novel that received the American Book Award from the Before Columbus Foundation in 1994 as well as literary honors, in 1991, from the Chicano Literature Contest at the University of California, Irvine. One of the main characters in Limón's work, Luz Delcano, takes refuge in the Los Angeles–based Casa Andrade, which functions as a "temporary home, town hall, and information center" (1993: 80). The services provided by Casa Andrade become a form of dependency for Luz, who, as Limón writes, "had never lived under the same roof with so many people, some of them crowded into rooms according to families, age or sex. [. . .] Luz had always worked for her keep, and she found her stay at Casa Andrade difficult to accept. She tried to compensate by helping out in the kitchen or by watching children who had no one to take care of them or by cleaning the house. But nothing helped to dispel her feeling of dependency" (1993: 80). Despite Helena María Viramontes's allegiance with U.S. Central Americans, the complexities of revolutionary processes are simplified and commodified for U.S. readers. In "The Cariboo Café," a short story published in *The Moths and Other Stories* (1995a), Viramontes attempts to localize Nicaraguan revolutionary politics in the U.S. realm. But one of the concurrent narratives in this story implies that the loss of a mother's son is linked to the "contras," the Sandinistas. Viramontes has not properly addressed this type of literary obfuscation. To this end, Ellen McCracken attempts to explain this confusion in a chapter footnote of her book, *New Latina Narrative: The Feminine Space of Postmodern Ethnicity*. McCracken notes that Viramontes "intended the term to refer generically to a political group against any government. Given the American media's prevalent usage of the term 'Contra' to refer to anti-Sandinista at the time the story was published (1985), Viramontes' use of the word is overcoded to imply strongly that the Sandinistas are responsible for this woman's misfortune. Perhaps in a subsequent edition of the story, Viramontes will devise a mode to distance the term clearly from its common usage in the United States" (1999: 208–9).

Carole Fernández's *Sleep of the Innocents* takes place in a fictional town of Soledad (solitude, in English), which tropes, to a certain extent, on Gabriel García Márquez's construction of Macondo in *One Hundred Years of Solitude*. Soledad residents live in adobe huts, but the poor village still manages to glow in the afternoon sun (1991: 27).

36. While U.S. Central American bodies can be read as passing into U.S. states of Mexicanness, Chicanoness, or Chicananess, such admissions are not always altogether "complete." As Tobar intimates in *The Tattooed Soldier*, Central Americans incorporate, but do not fully assimilate, Mexican cultural practices in their lives. The Spanish sounds of Los Angeles are a fusion of Central American *and* Mexican Spanish, coupled with English. Tobar's linguistic example reads, "*Fijate vos, que ese vato* from La Mara got in a fight with that dude from *la* Eighteenth Street who lives down the block. Yeah, right there in the class. Real *chingazos. El de La Salvatrucha estaba* bleeding *y todo*" (1998: 59). In the memoir of Los Angeles radio host "El Cucuy de la Mañana" — a story tantamount to a U.S.-Central American testimonial, since Almendárez Coello's autobiographical account is told through interview form — Renán Almendárez Coello also illustrates this point of U.S. Central American–Mexican linguistic fusion. Almendárez Coello expresses himself through Honduran/Central American regionalisms and Mexican expressions. His "Mexicanization," or even Mesoamerican Latinity, can also be due to the fact that as a child he lived for some time in Guarizama, a small town in the department of Olancho, Honduras. Guarizama, in his words, was a "small piece of Mexico hidden in the navel of Honduras." He elaborates that "even the people spoke with a Mexican accent." Almendárez Coello's quote, in Spanish, reads, "era un pedacito de México escondido en el ombligo de Honduras. Hasta las gentes hablaban con el acento mexicano" (2002: 52; my translation).

EPILOGUE. @

1. *Dora the Explorer* made its television debut during the summer of 2000. Dora was first intended as a computer-integrated program for two- to five-year-old children. The *New York Times* makes known that the Latina character "solves every challenge — in English and Spanish" and "builds confidence in children because she shows them how to deal with different situations" (Olson, 2010). National Public Radio (NPR) reported that *Dora* cocreator Chris Gifford and his team "set out to engineer a character who could motivate kids to participate [and initially] tried several animated characters — a squirrel, a martin. One promising idea: a bunny." But the idea of "something altogether different was brewing," in light of the fact that Brown Johnson, the president of Nickelodeon's animated programming, had "learned that Latinos aren't terribly well represented in children's television. And she was out to change that."

NPR's Rolando Arrieta recounted that "schoolteachers, sociologists, historians and cultural and language experts were all brought in to help" in Nick's manufacturing of *Dora*. There were mistakes along the way, like the naming of Dora's friend, Tico, who was always asleep under a tree. Johnson explained, "Our cultural consultant said, 'Not such a good idea.' A Latino character, who only speaks Spanish, the littlest character, always asleep. Just *not* a good idea" (2008).

Most notable is Arrieta's parenthetical clarification, "(If nothing else, such a character might have angered Costa Ricans, who affectionately call themselves 'Ticos')." Carlos Cortes, a history professor at the University of California at Riverside, told Arrieta that Dora was consciously framed as a "pan-Latino character, so she can be a source of pride and identity for anyone of Latino background. [. . .] For example, make sure the words we're using were universal. Not Spanish terms that meant one thing in Cuba and something else in Mexico and something else in Peru" (2008). Rather than seeing this as synthetic, I would add that many Latinos and Latinas speak this kind of generic Spanish—"Telemundo Spanish," as Patricia Engel's protagonist would call it (2010: 120). This version of the Spanish language is perhaps a standardized U.S. form of the language, where many Latinos and Latinas strive to be generally or commonly understood by groups outside their specific national and cultural milieus. The Spanish enacted in the United States may also appropriate many regionalisms from Latin America and infuse such terms with their own ("national") Spanish. Although Dora's age is marked as a seven-year-old, the year 2010 heralded her tenth birthday. Since her first appearance, her cultural influence involves, as Hank Stuever recapitulated it for the *Washington Post*, the selling of "a few billion dollars' worth of toys, books, DVDs and clothing every year." Stuever added, "she's on TV all over the world. The back-to-school industry alone owes her big-time. Macy's made her into its first Thanksgiving parade balloon of a minority cartoon imp" (2010).

2. Airing from 1991 to 1995, the PBS Daytime Emmy Award–winning series *Where in the World Is Carmen Sandiego?* was targeted toward eight- to thirteen-year-olds. It was described as a U.S. phenomenon, with some schools hosting what *USA Today* called "Carmen events" (Woessner, 1992). *Where in the World Is Carmen Sandiego?* was partly a response to that decade's studies, which disclosed "a tremendous ignorance of geography among Americans: according to a National Geographic survey, one in four cannot locate the Soviet Union or the Pacific Ocean. It also comes in the wake of successful game shows for children on commercial television, most notably 'Double Dare,' that offer zany, fast-paced antics but little educational substance" (Rabinovitz, 1991). But as Robert Woessner also cautioned, "don't call [the show] educational to the creators of *Carmen Sandiego* at Broderbund Software Inc., Novato, Calif. To them, educational equals boring. They prefer 'explorational'" (1992). *Carmen Sandiego*'s

explorational qualities, in addition to her geographic approach, are important antecedents to *Dora the Explorer*.

3. Nicole M. Guidotti-Hernández, for example, engages with *Dora the Explorer* through the normative mainstream media venues that create Latinidad, but mostly through Dora as a product and commodity: "The reconfiguration and popularization of Latino/a identity is most effectively analyzed through discourses of Latinidad, which are processes where Latino/a identities and cultural practices are contested and created in media, discourse, and public space. Latinidad influences the construction of Dora, which means that she is not merely created by ideas about Latinas, but she also creates ideas about Latinas." Guidotti-Hernández also comments, "Dora represents no particular Latino/a national identity, but her otherness is not far removed from the U.S. context, so most viewers assume she is Mexican or Puerto Rican" (2007: 212). From my end, I have been attracted to Dora precisely because she is not tied to any Latin American nation. Dora's Latin@ "origins" can be explored not through Latino and Latina "wholeness" but through her animated elation and immersion with other Latinos and Latinas enlivening a new @ genealogy.

4. Nationality, Paul Gilroy reminds us, "conditions the continuing aspiration to acquire a supposedly authentic, natural and stable identity. This identity is the premise of a thinking 'racial' self that is both socialised and unified by its connection with other kindred souls encountered usually, though not always, within the fortified frontiers of those discrete ethnic cultures which also happen to coincide with the contours of a sovereign nation state that guarantees their continuity" (1991: 4).

5. One of the subjects that has yet to be charted within Latinidad also lacks an at-ness within the @ economy: indigenous groups. The emergent categories for indigenous populations could read thus: "indi@," "indigen@," "May@," "Aymar@," and so on. "Afro-Latin@s" are mentioned in this register of at-ness, but the qualifier also poses some questions. As identified in *The Afro-Latin@ Reader* (Jiménez Román and Flores, 2010), for instance, Afro-Latin@s already have an @ within Latin@. But we must also probe into the inclusivity of the category "Afro." As it currently suggests in English, the Latin@ part of "Afro-Latin@" is inclusive of both genders. The Afro component, however, could be read as neutral, since it maintains a gender bias. It can also be ostensibly interpreted as avoiding a responsibility to semiotically include women, in view of the fact that "Afro" is a term in the English language that lacks grammatical gender in words. Under the logic of gender inclusion for U.S. ethnoracial categories with Latin backgrounds, Afro-Latin@ ought to read, "Afr@-Latin@." My purpose is not to pettifog or nitpick over language and seemingly paltry details. My focus is to bring attention to the types of terms summoned in Latino/a studies to *do* the representational work for gender inclusion. *Latino* seems to be the sole word carrying the weight for this type of indexing in the field.

6. On 22 March 2010 the Department of Architecture and Design at the Museum of Modern Art (MoMA) publicly announced that it had acquired the @ symbol. Its value and function, MoMA argued, "has become an important part of our identity in relationship and communication with others." MoMA's *Inside/Out* blog offers a historical commentary on this emblem, which bears Latin and Spanish linguistic similarities in connotation. As clarified, "Some linguists believe that @ dates back to the sixth or seventh century, a ligature meant to fuse the Latin preposition *ad*—meaning 'at', 'to,' or 'toward'—into a unique pen stroke. The symbol persisted in sixteenth-century Venetian trade, where it was used to mean *amphora*, a standard-size terracotta vessel employed by merchants, which had become a unit of measure. Interestingly, the current Spanish word for @, *arroba*, also indicates a unit of measure" (Antonelli, 2010).

7. Viego prompts us to "more productively read the term *Latino* as a term outside and beyond ontologies of race and ethnicity, not because it appears to point to the postraciological but rather because in fact it is a term that is first and foremost remarking on questions of temporality" (2007: 121). Seen in this manner, the Latino category resignifies a temporality that is not just marked by ethnoracial constructs and circumstances. I veer this "Latino temporality" to a *Latin@* direction so that the @ in Latin keeps us "on the run"—that is, it permits us to take the detours of Latinness and to recognize its impermanence.

8. The Valdés title I cite here, *El dolor del dólar*, was actually published in 1999 as *Te di la vida entera* (*I Gave You All I Had*) in Spanish. This descriptive heading has been on my radar since finding Valdés's book at a Parisian bookshop as *La Douleur du dollar* in 1998. Valdés brings to light matters of translation as well as the titular changes of this novel in her blog, zoevaldes.net. She writes in a 16 March 2008 post, "*El dolor del dólar* (The Pain of the Dollar) sounded bad in Spanish, and I had to change it for *Te di la vida entera*. Soon [the significance of] this title in Spanish was lost enormously in translation. [. . .] It sounded better in French than the original one, *La Douleur du dólar* [sic]." In Spanish, Valdés's excerpt reads, "*El dolor del dólar* sonó mal en español y tuve que cambiarlo por *Te di la vida entera*, y luego este título en español perdía enormemente en la traducción, resultada un título cheísimo, y en francés sonó mejor el que fue realmente el original, *La douleur du dólar* [sic]" ("París era una rumba," zoevaldes.net, 16 March 2008; my translation).

9. *Embajadora*, in Spanish, denotes a woman ambassador. I am exercising a playful use of the Spanish noun to form a nexus with Dora. This evocation would translate as "ambassaDora" in English.

10. One of the most persuasive uses of the slash, as applicable to U.S. ethnoracial identity, has come from Asian American studies and its excogitation of what David Palumbo-Liu identifies as "Asian/American." Inserting a slash between Asian and American, Palumbo-Liu states that this Asian/American split "signals those in-

stances in which a liaison between 'Asian' and 'American,' a *sliding* over between two seemingly separate terms, is constituted." He details, "As in the construction 'and/or,' where the solidus at once instantiates a choice between two terms, their simultaneous and equal status and an element of indecidability, that is, as it at once implies both exclusion and inclusion, 'Asian/American' marks *both* the distinction installed between 'Asian' and 'American' *and* a dynamic, unsettled, and inclusive movement" (1999: 1).

11. As an instance of the urgency for referents like Chica*na* and Lati*na*, take note of Sonia Saldívar-Hull's trajectory of renaming herself as a *Chicana* feminist, one who, in her phrasing, "refused the Chica*no*" (2000: 29). She submits, "To my ear, the *o* in *Chicano* struck a dissonant chord. The *o* began to signify that position bajo cero under the o of tradition, costumbres, what *Ms.* [magazine] instructed me to identify as patriarchal constraints" (26). Use of the Chica*na* signifier by "feminists scholars, activists, and writers— who have lived under the *o* in *Chicano*" gives, for this reason, meaningful shape and content to "the historical record written by men and male-identified women" (27).

WORKS CITED

Aching, Gerard. 1997. *The Politics of Spanish American Modernismo: By Exquisite Design.* New York: Cambridge University Press.
Adams, Rachel, and Sarah Phillips Casteel. 2005. "Introduction: Canada and the Americas." *Comparative American Studies* 3, no. 1 (March): 5–13.
Alessandrini, Anthony C., ed. 1999. *Frantz Fanon: Critical Perspectives.* New York: Routledge.
Allatson, Paul. 2004. Foreword to *Killer Crónicas: Bilingual Memories,* by Susana Chávez-Silverman. Madison: University of Wisconsin Press. ix–xiii.
———. 2007. *Key Terms in Latino/a Cultural and Literary Studies.* Malden: Blackwell.
Allen, Irving Lewis. 1983. *The Language of Ethnic Conflict: Social Organization and Lexical Culture.* New York: Columbia University Press.
Almendárez Coello, Renán. 2002. *El Cucuy de la Mañana: En la cumbre de la pobreza.* New York: Rayo/HarperCollins.
Alvarez, Julia. 2007. *Once upon a Quinceañera: Coming of Age in the U.S.A.* New York: Plume.
Andrews, Colman. 2007. "Carolina Cocina: A Wave of Mexican Immigration Is Changing the Definition of Southern Cooking." *Gourmet,* September. 31–36.
Andrews, William L. 1992. Introduction to *Classic American Autobiographies,* edited by William L. Andrews. New York: New American Library. 7–18.
Antonelli, Paola. 2010. "@ at MoMA." *Inside/Out: A MoMA/P.S. 1 Blog.* MoMA, 22 March. http://www.moma.org/explore/inside_out/2010/03/22/at-moma/, accessed on 22 March 2010.
Anzaldúa, Gloria. 1983. "La Prieta." In Moraga and Anzaldúa, 1983: 198–209.
———. 1999. *Borderlands/La Frontera: The New Mestiza.* 2nd ed. San Francisco: Aunt Lute Books. (Orig. pub. 1987.)
Aparicio, Frances R. 1997. "On Sub-Versive Signifiers: Tropicalizing Language in the United States." In Aparicio and Chávez-Silverman, 1997: 194–212.
———. 2007. "(Re)constructing Latinidad: The Challenge of Latina/o Studies." In Flores and Rosaldo, 2007: 39–48.

Aparicio, Frances R., and Susana Chávez-Silverman. 1997a. Introduction to Aparicio and Chávez-Silverman, 1997: 1–17.

———, eds. 1997b. *Tropicalizations: Transcultural Representations of Latinidad.* Hanover: University Press of New England.

Arellano, Gustavo. 2007. *¡Ask a Mexican!* New York: Scribner.

Arias, Arturo. 2003. "Central American-Americans: Invisibility, Power, and Representation in the U.S. Latino World." *Latino Studies* 1, no. 1: 168–87.

———. 2007. "Central American Diasporas: Transnational Gangs and the Transformation of Latino Identity in the United States." In Laó-Montes and Mirabal, 2001: 173–89.

Arrieta, Rolando. 2008. "Me Llamo Dora: An Explorer in Modern America." NPR, 14 April. http://www.npr.org/templates/story/story.php?storyId=89531478, accessed on 31 July 2011.

Arrizón, Alicia. 2006. *Queering Mestizaje: Transculturation and Performance.* Ann Arbor: University of Michigan Press.

Arte Público Press. N.d. "Recovering the U.S. Hispanic Literary Heritage." *Latinoteca. com.* http://www.latinoteca.com/recovery, accessed on 10 June 2012.

Augenbraum, Harold, and Ilan Stavans. 1993. "Introduction: Soldier of the Culture Wars." *Growing Up Latino: Memoirs and Stories*, edited by Harold Augenbraum and Ilan Stavans. Boston: Houghton Mifflin. xv–xxix.

Baca, Damián. 2008. *Mestiz@ Scripts, Digital Migrations, and the Territories of Writing.* New York: Palgrave Macmillan.

Baker, Houston A., Jr. 2001. *Turning South Again: Re-Thinking Modernism/Re-Reading Booker T.* Durham: Duke University Press.

Baldwin, James. 1984. *Notes of a Native Son.* Boston: Beacon. (Orig. pub. 1955.)

Barba Salinas, Manuel, ed. 1959. *Antología del cuento salvadoreño: 1880–1955.* San Salvador: Ministerio de Cultura Departamento Editorial.

Barthes, Roland. 1997. *The Eiffel Tower and Other Mythologies.* Translated by Richard Howard. Berkeley: University of California Press.

Bebout, Lee. 2011. *Mythohistorical Interventions: The Chicano Movement and Its Legacies.* Minneapolis: University of Minnesota Press.

Beltrán, Cristina. 2010. *The Trouble with Unity: Latino Politics and the Creation of Identity.* Oxford: Oxford University Press.

Bencastro, Mario. 1998. *Odyssey to the North.* Translated by Susan Giersbach Rascon. Houston: Arte Público.

Bender, Thomas. 2002. "Historians, the Nation, and the Plenitude of Narratives." *Rethinking American History in a Global Age*, edited by Thomas Bender. Berkeley: University of California Press. 1–21.

Benítez, Sandra. 1998. *Bitter Grounds: A Novel.* New York: Picador.

———. 2002. *The Weight of All Things*. New York: Hyperion.

Bennett, Herman Lee. 2009. *Colonial Blackness: A History of Afro-Mexico*. Bloomington: Indiana University Press.

Benz, Stephen. 1997. "Through the Tropical Looking Glass: The Motif of Resistance in U.S. Literature on Central America." In Aparicio and Chávez-Silverman, 1997: 51–66.

Berland, Jody. 2009. *North of Empire: Essays on the Cultural Technologies of Space*. Durham: Duke University Press.

Berlin, Ira. 2010. *The Making of African America: The Four Great Migrations*. New York: Viking.

Bernabé, Mónica. 2006. Prologue to *Idea crónica: Literatura de no ficción iberoamericana*, edited by María Sonia Cristoff. Buenos Aires: Fundación TyPA/Viterbo. 7–25.

Bhabha, Homi K. 1994. *The Location of Culture*. New York: Routledge.

Bobo, Lawrence D. 2010. "Claiming Human Dignity." *Du Bois Review* 7, no. 2: 253–55.

Bogle, Donald. 2001. *Toms, Coons, Mulattoes, Mammies, and Bucks: An Interpretative History of Blacks in American Films*. New York: Continuum.

Bok, Edward. 1927. *The Americanization of Edward Bok: The Autobiography of a Dutch Boy Fifty Years After*. New York: Scribner's Sons.

Boon, Marcus. 2010. *In Praise of Copying*. Cambridge: Harvard University Press.

Bost, Suzanne. 2000. "Transgressing Borders: Puerto Rican and Latina Mestizaje." *MELUS* 25 (Summer): 187–211.

———. 2003. *Mulattas and Mestizas: Representing Mixed Identities in the Americas, 1850–2000*. Athens: University of Georgia Press.

Brady, Mary Pat. 2002. *Extinct Lands, Temporal Geographies: Chicana Literature and the Urgency of Space*. Durham: Duke University Press.

Brickhouse, Anna. 2004. *Transamerican Literary Relations and the Nineteenth-Century Public Sphere*. Cambridge: Cambridge University Press.

Brody, Jennifer DeVere. 2008. *Punctuation: Art, Politics, and Play*. Durham: Duke University Press.

Brown, Henry Box. 2002. *Narrative of the Life of Henry Box Brown, Written by Himself*. New York: Oxford University Press. (Orig. pub. 1851.)

Brown, Leslie. 2008. *Upbuilding Black Durham: Gender, Class, and Black Community Development in the Jim Crow South*. Chapel Hill: University of North Carolina Press.

Bruce, Dickson D., Jr. 1992. "W. E. B. Du Bois and the Idea of Double Consciousness." *American Literature* 64, no. 2: 299–309.

Bruinius, Harry. 2007. *Better for All the World: The Secret History of Forced Sterilization and America's Quest for Racial Purity*. New York: Vintage.

Bucholtz, Mary. 1995. "From Mulatta to Mestiza: Passing and the Linguistic Reshaping of Ethnic Identity." *Gender Articulated: Language and the Socially Constructed Self*, edited by Kira Hall and Mary Bucholtz. New York: Routledge. 351–73.

Butler, Judith. 2005. *Giving an Account of Oneself*. New York: Fordham University Press.

Cabán, Pedro A. 2003. "Moving from the Margins to Where? Three Decades of Latino/a Studies." *Latino Studies* 1, no. 1: 5–35.

Calafell, Bernadette Marie. 2007. *Latina/o Communication Studies: Theorizing Performance*. New York: Lang.

Calderón, Héctor, and José David Saldívar, eds. 1998. *Criticism in the Borderlands: Studies in Chicano Literature, Culture, and Ideology*. Durham: Duke University Press.

Caminero-Santangelo, Marta. 2007. *On Latinidad: U.S. Latino Literature and the Construction of Ethnicity*. Gainesville: University Press of Florida.

Candelario, Ginetta E. B. 2007. *Black behind the Ears: Dominican Racial Identity from Museums to Beauty Shops*. Durham: Duke University Press.

Carby, Hazel V. 1987. *Reconstructing Womanhood: The Emergence of the Afro-American Woman Novelist*. New York: Oxford University Press.

———. 1998. *Race Men*. Cambridge: Harvard University Press.

Cardenal, Ernesto. 1980. *Zero Hour and Other Documentary Poems*. Translated by Paul W. Borgeson Jr., Jonathan Cohen, Robert Pring-Mill, and Donald D. Walsh. New York: New Directions Books.

Caribbean Philosophical Association. N.d. "CPA Home." Institute for the Study of Race and Social Thought. Temple University. http://www.temple.edu/isrst/events/CPA.asp, accessed on 7 June 2008.

Carrillo Rowe, Aimee. 2008. *Power Lines: On the Subject of Feminist Alliances*. Durham: Duke University Press.

Carroll, Rory. 2007. "Hotel Mistakes Nobel Laureate for Bag Lady." *Guardian*, 17 August. http://www.guardian.co.uk/world/2007/aug/17/international.travelnews, accessed on 10 August 2008.

Castellanos, M. Bianet. 2010. *A Return to Servitude: Maya Migration and the Tourist Trade in Cancún*. Minneapolis: University of Minnesota Press.

Castellanos Moya, Horacio. 1997. *El asco: Thomas Bernhard en San Salvador*. Translated by Katherine Silver. San Salvador: Arcoiris.

———. 2008. *Senselessness*. New York: New Directions.

Castillo, Ana. 2005a. "22 November 2005." Blog entry. http://anacastillo.com/ac/blog/index.shtml, accessed on 12 February 2008.

———. 2005b. *Psst!. . .: I Have Something To Tell You, Mi Amor*. San Antonio: Wings.

Chabram-Dernersesian, Angie. 1992. "I Throw Punches for My Race, but I Don't Want to Be a Man: Writing Us—Chica-nos (Girl, Us)/Chicanas—into the Movement Script." *Cultural Studies*, edited by Larry Grossberg, Cary Nelson, and Paula Treichler. New York: Routledge. 81–95.

———. 1994. "'Chicana! Rican? No, Chicana-Riqueña!': Refashioning the Transnational Connection." *Multiculturalism: A Critical Reader*, edited by David Theo Goldberg. Cambridge: Blackwell. 269–95.

———. 2003. "Latina/o: Another Site of Struggle, Another Site of Accountability." *Critical Latin American and Latino Studies*, edited by Juan Poblete. Minneapolis: University of Minnesota Press. 105–20.

Chaney, Michael A. 2007. "International Contexts of the Negro Renaissance." *The Cambridge Companion to the Harlem Renaissance*, edited by George Hutchinson. Cambridge: Cambridge University Press. 41–54.

Chapman, Peter. 2007. *Bananas: How the United Fruit Company Shaped the World*. Edinburgh: Canongate.

Chesnutt, Charles W. 1993. *The House behind the Cedars*. New York: Penguin Books.

Cisneros, Sandra. 2002. *Caramelo: A Novel*. New York: Vintage Contemporaries.

Clackson, James, and Geoffrey Horrocks. 2007. *The Blackwell History of the Latin Language*. Malden: Blackwell.

Clay, Felix. 1908. "The Origin of Aesthetic Emotion." *Sammelbände der Internationalen Musikgesellschaft* 9, no. 2 (January–March): 282–90.

Cobb, James C., and William Stueck. 2005. Introduction to *Globalization and the American South*, edited by James C. Cobb and William Stueck. Athens: University of Georgia Press. xi–xvi.

Cohn, Deborah N. 1999. *History and Memory in the Two Souths: Recent Southern and Spanish American Fiction*. Nashville: Vanderbilt University Press.

Connell, Raewyn. 2007. *Southern Theory: The Global Dynamics of Knowledge and Social Science*. Cambridge: Polity.

Conrad, Joseph. 1993. *Heart of Darkness*. New York: Knopf. (Orig. pub. 1902.)

Contreras, Sheila Marie. 2008. *Blood Lines: Myth, Indigenism, and Chicana/o Literature*. Austin: University of Texas Press.

Cooper, Anna Julia. 1998. *The Voice of Anna Julia Cooper: Including a Voice from the South and Other Important Essays, Papers, and Letters*. Edited by Charles Lemert and Esme Bhan. Lanham: Rowman and Littlefield.

Cooppan, Vilashini. 2005. "The Double Politics of Double Consciousness: Nationalism and Globalism in *The Souls of Black Folk*." *Public Culture* 17, no. 2 (Spring): 299–318.

Coronil, Fernando. 1995. "Introduction to the Duke University Press Edition: Transculturation and the Politics of Theory; Countering the Center, Cuban

Counterpoint." *Cuban Counterpoint: Tobacco and Sugar*, by Fernando Ortiz, translated by Harriet de Onís. Durham: Duke University Press. ix–lvi.

Coutin, Susan Bibler. 2003. "Suspension of Deportation Hearings: Racialization, Immigration, and 'Americanness.'" *Journal of Latin American Anthropology* 8, no. 2 (June): 58–95.

Crichlow, Michaeline A, and Patricia Northover. 2009. *Globalization and the Post-Creole Imagination: Notes on Fleeing the Plantation*. Durham: Duke University Press.

Cruz, Celia. 1997. *100% Azucar! The Best of Celia Cruz con La Sonora Matancera*. With La Sonora Matancera. Compact disc. B000003426. New York: Rhino/Wea.

Cruz, Nilo. 2003. *Anna in the Tropics*. New York: Dramatists Play Service.

Cuadros, Paul. 2006. *A Home on the Field: How One Championship Soccer Team Inspires Hope for the Revival of Small Town America*. New York: Harper.

Cunningham, George P. 1973. "James Weldon Johnson Papers (Correspondence)." Collection of American Literature. Beinecke Rare Book and Manuscript Library. Yale University, New Haven, Conn. July. http://webtext.library.yale.edu/xml2html/beinecke.JWJ.con.html, accessed on 13 July 2008.

Darío, Rubén. 2005. *Rubén Darío: Selected Writings*. Edited by Ilan Stavans. Translated by Andrew Hurley, Greg Simon, and Steven F. White. New York: Penguin Classics.

Davidman, Lynn. 2000. *Motherloss*. Berkeley: University of California Press.

Davidson, Peter. 2005. *The Idea of the North*. London: Reaktion Books.

Davies, Carole Boyce, Meredith Gadsby, Charles F. Peterson, and Henrietta Williams, eds. 2003. *Decolonizing the Academy: African Diaspora Studies*. Trenton: Africa World Press.

Dávila, Arlene. 2001. *Latinos, Inc.: Marketing and the Making of a People*. Berkeley: University of California Press.

———. 2008. *Latino Spin: Public Image and the Whitewashing of Race*. New York: New York University Press.

Davis, Gregson. 1997. *Aimé Césaire*. Cambridge: Cambridge University Press.

De Acosta, Alejandro. 2007. "Latino/a: A Geophilosophy for Wanderers." *An Atlas of Radical Cartography*, edited by Lize Mogel and Alexis Bhagat. Los Angeles: Journal of Aesthetics Protest Press. 69–76.

Dear, Michael, and Gustavo Leclerc, eds. 2003. *Postborder City: Cultural Spaces of Bajalta California*. New York: Routledge.

De Genova, Nicholas, and Ana Y. Ramos-Zayas. 2003. *Latino Crossings: Mexicans, Puerto Ricans, and the Politics of Race and Citizenship*. New York: Routledge.

De la Campa, Román. 1994. "Latin Lessons: Do Latinos Share a World . . . or a Word?" *Transition* 63: 60–76.

———. 2000. *Cuba on My Mind: Journeys to a Severed Nation*. New York: Verso.

———. 2001. "Latin, Latino, American: Split States and Global Imaginaries." *Comparative Literature* 53, no. 1 (Autumn): 373–88.

De la Torre, Adela, and Beatriz M. Pesquera, eds. 1993. *Building with Our Hands: New Directions in Chicana Studies*. Berkeley: University of California Press.

Derricotte, Toi. 1997. *The Black Notebooks: An Interior Journey*. New York: Norton.

De Veaux, Alexis. 2004. *Warrior Poet: A Biography of Audre Lorde*. New York: Norton.

Díaz, Junot. 1996. *Drown*. New York: Riverhead Books.

———. 2007. *The Brief Wondrous Life of Oscar Wao: A Novel*. New York: Riverhead Books.

———. 2010. "The Book Bench: This Week in Fiction; Questions for Junot Díaz." *New Yorker*, 15 March. http://www.newyorker.com/online/blogs/books/2010/03/this-week-in-fiction-talking-with-junot-diaz.html, accessed on 1 July 2010.

Díaz Neiro, Teresa, Michelle Eistrup, Alanna Lockward, Walter Mignolo, and Rolando Vásquez. 2011. "Decoloniality and Decolonial Aesthetics: A Manifesto." +Decolonial Aesthetics Workshop. Conference program. Duke University, Durham, N.C., 4–6 May.

Dictionary.com. N.d. "Peoria." http://dictionary.reference.com/browse/peorian?qsrc=2446, accessed on 8 June 2012.

Didion, Joan. 1994. *Salvador*. New York: Vintage. (Orig. pub. 1983.)

Douglas, Mary. 2002. *Purity and Danger: An Analysis of Concept Pollution and Taboo*. New York: Routledge.

Douglass, Frederick. 1997. *Narrative of the Life of Frederick Douglass, an American Slave, Written by Himself*. Edited by William L. Andrews and William S. McFeely. New York: Norton. (Orig. pub. 1845.)

Duany, Jorge. 2011. *Blurred Borders: Transnational Migration between the Hispanic Caribbean and the United States*. Chapel Hill: University of North Carolina Press.

Du Bois, W. E. B. 1968. *The Autobiography of W. E. B. Du Bois: A Soliloquy on Viewing My Life from the Last Decade of Its First Century*. New York: International Publishers, 1997.

———. 1988. *The Negro*. Millwood, N.Y.: Kraus-Thomson Organization. (Orig. pub. 1915.)

———.1996a. *The Oxford W. E. B. Du Bois Reader*. Edited by Eric J. Sundquist. New York: Oxford University Press.

———. 1996b. *The Souls of Black Folk*. New York: Penguin Books. (Orig. pub. 1903.)

———. 1998. *W. E. B. Du Bois Speaks: Speeches and Addresses, 1920–1963*. Edited by Philip S. Foner. New York: Pathfinder.

———. 2003. *The Souls of Black Folk*. New York: Barnes and Noble Classics.

Duchon, Deborah A., and Arthur D. Murphy. 2001. "Introduction: From *Patrones* and *Caciques* to Good Ole Boys." *Latino Workers in the Contemporary South*, edited by Arthur D. Murphy, Colleen Blanchard, and Jennifer A. Hill. Athens: University of Georgia Press. 1–9.

Dworkin y Méndez, Kenya. 2000. Introduction to *Black Cuban, Black American: A Memoir*, by Evelio Grillo, vii–xiv. Houston: Arte Público.

Eakin, Marshall C. 2003. "When South Is North: The U.S. South from the Perspective of Brazilianist." Keynote Address Symposium on "The U.S. South in Global Contexts," 1–28. Oxford: University of Mississippi.

Early, James. 2003. "TransAfrica: An Interview with Bill Fletcher Jr." *Radical History Review* 87 (Fall): 127–37.

Edwards, Brent Hayes. 2003. *The Practice of Diaspora: Literature, Translation, and the Rise of Black Internationalism*. Cambridge: Harvard University Press.

Edwards, Brian T., and Dilip Parameshwar Gaonkar. 2010. "Introduction: Globalizing American Studies." *Globalizing American Studies*, edited by Brian T. Edwards and Dilip Parameshwar Gaonkar. Chicago: University of Chicago Press. 1–44.

Eire, Carlos. 2003. *Waiting for Snow in Havana: Confessions of a Cuban Boy*. New York: Free Press.

Engel, Patricia. 2010. *Vida*. New York: Black Cat.

Engelhardt, Elizabeth S. D. 2011. *A Mess of Greens: Southern Gender and Southern Food*. Athens: University of Georgia Press.

England, Sarah. 2006. *Afro Central Americans in New York City: Garifuna Tales of Transnational Movements*. Gainesville: University Press of Florida.

———. 2009–10. "Afro-Hondurans in the Chocolate City: Garifuna, Katrina, and the Advantages of Racial Invisibility in the Nuevo New Orleans." *Journal of Latino-Latin American Studies* 3, no. 4 (Fall–Spring): 31–55.

Epps, Brad. 2001. "Passing Lines: Immigration and the Performance of American Identity." *Passing: Identity and Interpretation in Sexuality, Race, and Religion*, edited by María Carla Sánchez and Linda Schlossberg. New York: New York University Press. 92–134.

Escudos, Jacinta. 2005. "Literatura en Centro América: Invisibles a plena vista." Paper presented at the Valiente Mundo Nuevo: Encuentro de Escritores Latinoamericanos. La Caixa Foundation, Lleida-Barcelona, Spain, April 2005.

———. 2008. "Niña, doña, seño: Modismos centroamericanos (I)." *Jacintario*, 29 April. Espacio Filmica. http://www.filmica.com/jacintaescudos/archivos/007601.html, accessed on 11 August 2008.

Espada, Martín. 1999. *Zapata's Disciple: Essays*. Cambridge: South End.

Evans, Everett. 2007. "Brown Planet Speaks to Liberation." *Houston Chronicle*, 28

June. http://www.chron.com/disp/story.mpl//4925389.html, accessed on 30 May 2011.

Falconi, José Luis, and José Antonio Mazzotti, eds. 2007. *The Other Latinos: Central and South Americans in the United States*. Cambridge: Harvard University Press.

Fallas, Carlos Luis. 1966. *Mamita Yunai*. San José, Costa Rica: Principios. (Orig. pub. 1941.)

Fanon, Frantz. 1963. *The Wretched of the Earth*. Translated by Constance Ferrington. Introduction by Jean-Paul Sartre. New York: Grove.

———. 2008. *Black Skin, White Masks*. Translated by Richard Philcox. New York: Grove.

Faulkner, William. 1990. *Light in August*. New York: Vintage International. (Orig. pub. 1932.)

Femalefirst.co.uk. 2004. "Natalie Portman Apologises for 'Feeling Black.'" *Female First*, 30 November. http:www.femalefirst.co.uk/celebrity/17612004.htm, accessed on 15 December 2004.

Feracho, Lesley G., Dorothy E. Mosby, and Ifeoma Kiddoe Nwankwo, eds. Forthcoming. "Black Is Black? Rethinking Diaspora, Blackness, and Gender in Central American Literary and Cultural Production." Special issue, *Afro-Hispanic Review*.

Fernández, Carole. 1991. *Sleep of the Innocents*. Houston: Arte Público.

Fink, Leon. 2003. *The Maya of Morganton: Work and Community in the Nuevo New South*. Chapel Hill: University of North Carolina Press.

Fleming, Robert E. 1987. *James Weldon Johnson*. Boston: Twayne.

Flores, Juan. 1993. *Divided Borders: Essays on Puerto Rican Identity*. Houston: Arte Público.

———. 1997. "The Latino Imaginary: Dimensions of Community and Identity." In Aparicio and Chávez-Silverman, 1997: 183–93.

———. 2009. *The Diaspora Strikes Back: Caribeño Tales of Learning and Turning*. New York: Routledge.

Flores, Juan, and Renato Rosaldo, eds. 2007. *A Companion to Latina/o Studies*. Malden: Wiley-Blackwell.

Flores, Juan, and George Yúdice. 1990. "Living Borders/Buscando America: Languages of Latino Self-Formation." *Social Text* 24: 57–84.

Foley, Neil. 1997. *The White Scourge: Mexicans, Blacks, and Poor Whites in Texas Cotton Culture*. Berkeley: University of California Press.

Folkenflik, Robert. 1993. "Introduction: The Institution of Autobiography." *The Culture of Autobiography: Constructions of Self-Representation*, edited by Robert Folkenflik. Stanford: Stanford University Press. 1–20.

Fontova, Humberto. 2007. *Exposing the Real Che Guevara and the Useful Idiots Who Idolize Him*. New York: Sentinel.

Ford, Lacy K. 2009. *Deliver Us from Evil: The Slavery Question in the Old South*. New York: Oxford University Press.

Fox, Claire F. 2005. Special issue, *Comparative American Studies: An International Journal* 3, no. 4 (November).

Franco, Jean. 2002. *The Decline and Fall of the Lettered City: Latin America in the Cold War*. Cambridge: Harvard University Press.

Franklin, John Hope. 2005. *Mirror to America: The Autobiography of John Hope Franklin*. New York: Farrar, Straus and Giroux.

French, Patrick. 2008. *The World Is What It Is: The Authorized Biography of V. S. Naipaul*. New York: Knopf.

Fuguet, Alberto, and Sergio Gómez, eds. 1996. *McOndo*. Barcelona: Mondadori.

Gallop, Jane. 2002. *Anecdotal Theory*. Durham: Duke University Press.

García, Alma M. 1997. *Chicana Feminist Thought: The Basic Historical Writings*. New York: Routledge.

García, Cristina. 2007. *A Handbook to Luck*. New York: Knopf.

———. 2010. *The Lady Matador's Hotel*. New York: Scribner.

García, María Cristina. 1997. *Havana USA: Cuban Exiles and Cuban Americans in South Florida, 1959–1994*. Berkeley: University of California Press.

———. 2006. *Seeking Refuge: Central American Migration to Mexico, the United States, and Canada*. Berkeley: University of California Press.

García Canclini, Néstor. 2002. *Latinoamericanos buscando lugar en este siglo*. Buenos Aires: Paidós.

García Márquez, Gabriel. 1982. "The Solitude of Latin America." Nobel Lecture, 8 December. http://www.nobel.se/literature/laureates/1982/marquez-lecture.html, accessed on 19 October 2003.

———. 1998. *One Hundred Years of Solitude*. Translated by Gregory Rabasa. New York: Harper Perennial. (Orig. pub. 1970.)

———. 2003. *Living to Tell the Tale*. Translated by Edith Grossman. New York: Knopf.

Gaspar de Alba, Alicia. 1998. *Chicano Art: Inside/Outside the Master's House*. Austin: University of Texas Press.

Gass, William. 1994. "The Art of Self: Autobiography in an Age of Narcissism." *Harper's Magazine*, May, 43–52.

Gates, Henry Louis, Jr. 1994. *Colored People: A Memoir*. New York: Knopf.

———. 2011. *Black in Latin America*. New York. New York University Press.

Gates, Henry Louis, Jr., and Nellie Y. McKay. 1997. "Preface: Talking Books." *The Norton Anthology of African American Literature*, edited by Henry Louis Gates Jr. and Nellie Y. McKay. New York: Norton. xxvii–xli.

Gates, Henry Louis, Jr., and Terri Hume Oliver, eds. 1999. *The Souls of Black Folk*. New York: Norton.
Gibson, Donald B. 1993. Introduction to *The House behind the Cedars*, by Charles W. Chesnutt. New York: Penguin Classics.
Gibson, Nigel C. 2003. *Fanon: The Postcolonial Imagination*. Cambridge: Polity.
Gilroy, Paul. 1991. "It Ain't Where You're From, It's Where You're At: The Dialectics of Diasporic Identification." *Third Text* 13, no. 3: 3–16.
———. 2003. *The Black Atlantic: Modernity and Double-Consciousness*. Cambridge: Harvard University Press.
Glazer, Mark, ed. 1987. *A Dictionary of Mexican American Proverbs*. New York: Greenwood.
Gobat, Michel. 2005. *Confronting the American Dream: Nicaragua under U.S. Imperial Rule*. Durham: Duke University Press.
Goffman, Erving. 1963. *Stigma: Notes on the Management of Spoiled Identity*. New York: Touchstone.
Goldman, Francisco. 1992. *The Long Night of White Chickens*. New York: Atlantic Monthly.
———. 2004. *The Divine Husband*. New York: Atlantic Monthly.
González, Jovita, and Eve Raleigh. 2008. *Caballero: A Historical Novel*. College Station: Texas A&M University Press.
Gonzalez, Juan. 2000. *Harvest of Empire: A History of Latinos in America*. New York: Penguin Books.
González, Manuel Pedro. 1946. "Cuba's Fernando Ortiz." *Books Abroad* 20, no. 1 (Winter): 9–13.
Gonzalez, Rita, Howard N. Fox, and Chon A. Noriega, eds. 2008. *Phantom Sightings: Art after the Chicano Movement*. Berkeley: University of California Press.
Gonzalez, Veronica. 2007. *Twin Time: Or, How Death Befell Me*. Los Angeles: Semiotext(e).
Gooding-Williams, Robert. 2005a. "Du Bois, Politics, Aesthetics: An Introduction." *Public Culture* 17, no. 2 (Spring): 203–15.
———. 2005b. *Look, a Negro! Philosophical Essays on Race, Culture and Politics*. New York: Routledge.
Gordon, Edmund T. 1998. *Disparate Diaspora: Identity and Politics in an African Nicaraguan Community*. Austin: University of Texas Press.
Gordon, Lewis R. 1995a. *Bad Faith and Antiblack Racism*. Atlantic Highlands, N.J.: Humanities International.
———. 1995b. *Fanon and the Crisis of European Man: An Essay on Philosophy and the Human Sciences*. New York: Routledge.

———. 1997. *Her Majesty's Other Children: Sketches of Racism from a Neocolonial Age*. Lanham: Rowman and Littlefield.

———. 2000. *Existentia Africana: Understanding Africana Existential Thought*. New York: Routledge.

Gordon, Lewis R., T. Denean Sharpley-Whiting, and Renée T. White, eds. 1996. *Fanon: A Critical Reader*. Malden: Blackwell.

Gould, Jeffrey. 2003. "Gender, Politics, and the Triumph of *Mestizaje* in Early 20th-Century Nicaragua." *Perspectives of Las Américas: A Reader in Culture, History, and Representation*, edited by Matthew C. Gutman, Félix V. Matos Rodríguez, Lynn Stephen, and Patricia Zavella. Malden: Blackwell. 365–82.

Grady, Henry W. 2012. "The New South." *The Gilded Age and Progressive Era: A Documentary Reader*, edited by William A. Link and Susannah J. Link. Malden: Wiley-Blackwell. 19–22.

Graham, Hugh Davis. 1968. "*The Autobiography of W. E. B. Du Bois: A Soliloquy on Viewing My Life from the Last Decade of Its First Century* by W. E. B. Du Bois." *Journal of Southern History* 34, no. 4 (November): 640–41.

Grandin, Greg. 2006. *Empire's Workshop: Latin America, the United States, and the Rise of the New Imperialism*. New York: Owl Books.

Gray, Richard. 2002. "Inventing Communities, Imagining Places: Some Thoughts on Southern Self-Fashioning." *South to a New Place: Region, Literature, Culture*, edited by Fred Hobson. Baton Rouge: Louisiana State University Press. xiii–xxiii.

Greene, Julie. 2009. *The Canal Builders: Making America's Empire at the Panama Canal*. New York: Penguin Books.

Grillo, Evelio. 2000. *Black Cuban, Black American: A Memoir*. Houston: Arte Público.

Grosfoguel, Ramón, Nelson Maldonado-Torres, and José David Saldívar, eds. 2005. *Latin@s in the World System: Decolonization Struggles in the 21st Century U.S. Empire*. Boulder: Paradigm.

Grossman, Edith. 2010. *Why Translation Matters*. New Haven: Yale University Press.

Gruesz, Kirsten Silva. 2002. *Ambassadors of Culture: The Transamerican Origins of Latino Writing*. Princeton: Princeton University Press.

———. 2008. "The Mercurial Space of 'Central' America." *Hemispheric American Studies*, edited by Caroline F. Levander and Robert S. Levine. New Brunswick: Rutgers University Press. 140–65.

Guarnizo, Luis Eduardo, Alejandro Portes, and William Haller. 2003. "Assimilation and Transnationalism: Determinants of Transnational Political Action among Contemporary Migrants." *American Journal of Sociology* 108, no. 6 (May): 1211–48.

Gudmundson, Lowell, and Justin Wolfe, eds. 2010. *Blacks and Blackness in Central America: Between Race and Place*. Durham: Duke University Press.

Guidotti-Hernández, Nicole M. 2007. "*Dora the Explorer*: Constructing 'Latinidades' and the Politics of Global Citizenship." *Latino Studies* 5, no. 2: 209–32.

Guldbrandsen, Thaddeus Countway. 2005. "Entrepreneurial Government in the Transnational South: The Case of Durham, North Carolina." *The American South in a Global World*, edited by James L. Peacock, Harry L. Watson, and Carrie R. Matthews. Chapel Hill: University of North Carolina Press. 83–98.

Guridy, Frank Andre. 2003. "From Solidarity to Cross-Fertilization: Afro-Cuban/African American Interaction during the 1930s and 1940s." *Radical History Review* 87 (Fall): 19–48.

———. 2009. "Feeling Diaspora in Harlem and Havana." *Social Text* 27, no. 1 98 (Spring): 115–40.

———. 2010. *Forging Diaspora: Afro-Cubans and African Americans in a World of Empire and Jim Crow*. Chapel Hill: University of North Carolina Press.

Guterl, Matthew Pratt. 2007. "South." *Keywords for American Cultural Studies*, edited by Bruce Burgett and Glenn Hendler. New York: New York University Press. 230–33.

Gutiérrez, Ramón A. 1991. *When Jesus Came, the Corn Mothers Went Away: Marriage, Sexuality, and Power in New Mexico, 1500–1846*. Stanford: Stanford University Press.

———. 2004. "Internal Colonialism: An American Theory of Race." *Du Bois Review* 1, no. 2: 281–95.

Haas, Lisbeth. 1996. *Conquests and Historical Identities in California, 1769–1936*. Berkeley: University of California Press.

Halbreich, Kathy. 2007. Foreword to *Kara Walker: My Complement, My Enemy, My Oppressor, My Love*. Minneapolis: Walker Art Center. 1–3.

Hamilton, Nora, and Norma Stoltz Chinchilla. 2001. *Seeking Community in a Global City: Guatemalans and Salvadorans in Los Angeles*. Philadelphia: Temple University Press.

Haney López, Ian F. 2003. *Racism on Trial: The Chicano Fight for Justice*. Cambridge: Belknap Press of Harvard University Press.

Hart, Dianne Walta. 1997. *Undocumented in L.A.: An Immigrant's Story*. Wilmington: SR Books/Scholarly Resources.

Henríquez, Cristina. 2009. *The World in Half*. New York: Riverhead Books.

Henry, O. 1922. *Cabbages and Kings*. Garden City: Doubleday, Page.

Hernández Cuevas, Marco Polo. 2004. *African Mexicans and the Discourse on Modern Nation*. Lanham: University Press of America.

Herzog, Lawrence A. 2003. "Global Tijuana: The Seven Ecologies of the Border."

Postborder City: Cultural Spaces of Bajalta California, edited by Michael Dear and Gustavo Leclerc. New York: Routledge. 119–42.

Hijuelos, Oscar. 2011. *Thoughts without Cigarettes: A Memoir*. New York: Gotham Books.

Hill Collins, Patricia. 1990. *Black Feminist Thought: Knowledge, Consciousness, and the Politics of Empowerment*. New York: Routledge.

Ho, Fred, and Bill V. Mullen, eds. 2008. *Afro Asia: Revolutionary Political and Cultural Connections between African Americans and Asian Americans*. Durham: Duke University Press.

Hobson, Fred, ed. 2002. *South to the Future: An American Region in the Twenty-First Century*. Athens: University of Georgia Press.

Holloway, Karla F. C. 2006. *BookMarks: Reading in Black and White*. New Brunswick: Rutgers University Press.

Horne, Gerald. 2005. *Black and Brown: African Americans and the Mexican Revolution, 1910–1920*. New York: New York University Press.

Huerta, Jorge, ed. 1989. *Necessary Theater: Six Plays about the Chicano Experience*. Houston: Arte Público.

Hughes, Langston. 1920. "A Diary of Mexican Adventures (If There Be Any)." Box 492. Folder 12432. Series 14. Langston Hughes Papers. James Weldon Johnson Collection in the Yale Collection of American Literature. Beinecke Rare Book and Manuscript Library. Yale University, New Haven, Conn.

———. 1929. "Loose Journal Papers and Notes/1929." Box 492. Folder 12,434. Series 14. Langston Hughes Papers. James Weldon Johnson Collection in the Yale Collection of American Literature. Beinecke Rare Book and Manuscript Library. Yale University, New Haven, Conn.

———. 1930. "The Trip to Havana." Box 492. Folder 12436. Series 14. Langston Hughes Papers. James Weldon Johnson Collection in the Yale Collection of American Literature. Beinecke Rare Book and Manuscript Library. Yale University, New Haven, Conn.

———. Circa 1934–37. "Mexico a Spanish Lessons." Box 492. Folder 12441. Series 14. Langston Hughes Papers. James Weldon Johnson Collection in the Yale Collection of American Literature. Beinecke Rare Book and Manuscript Library. Yale University, New Haven, Conn.

———. 1990. *The Ways of White Folks*. New York: Vintage. (Orig. pub. 1934.)
———. 1993. *The Big Sea*. New York: Hill and Wang. (Orig. pub. 1940.)
———. 1997. *The Best of Simple*. New York: Hill and Wang. (Orig. pub. 1961.)

Hurston, Zora Neale. 1997. "How It Feels to Be Colored Me." *The Norton Anthology of African American Literature*, edited by Henry Louis Gates Jr. and Nellie Y. McKay. New York: Norton. 1008–11.

Irwin, Robert McKee. 2001. "Toward a Border Gnosis of the Borderlands: Joaquín Murrieta and Nineteenth-Century U.S.-Mexico Border Culture." *Nepantla: Views from South* 2, no. 3: 509–37.

———. 2008. "Memín Pinguín, Rumba, and Racism: Afro-Mexicans in Classic Comics and Film." *Hemispherist American Studies*, edited by Caroline F. Levander and Robert S. Levine. New Brunswick: Rutgers University Press. 249–65.

Jackson, Carlos Francisco. 2009. *Chicana and Chicano Art: ProtestArte*. Tucson: University of Arizona Press.

Jackson, John, Jr., David Sartorius, Carlos Tovares, Bobby Vaughn, and Ben Vinson III. 2008. "Charting Racial Formations in the New U.S. South: Reflections on North Carolina's Latino, African-American, and Afro-Latino Relations." Center for Africana Studies Working Paper Series. Working Paper 010. Johns Hopkins University. http://www.jhu.edu/africana/news/working_papers/index.html, accessed on 7 October 2008.

Jackson, Lawrence P. 2011. *The Indignant Generation: A Narrative History of African American Writers and Critics, 1934–1960*. Princeton: Princeton University Press.

Jacobs, Harriet. 2000. *Incidents in the Life of a Slave Girl*. New York: Signet Classic. (Orig. pub. 1861.)

James, C. L. R. 1993. *American Civilization*. Cambridge: Blackwell.

Jiménez, Tomás R. 2010. *Replenished Ethnicity: Mexican Americans, Immigration, and Identity*. Berkeley: University of California Press.

Jiménez Román, Miriam. N.d. "Africa's Legacy in Mexico: What Is a Mexican?" Smithsonian Institution. http://www.smithsonianeducation.org/migrations/legacy/almmx.html, accessed on 5 June 2011.

Jiménez Román, Miriam, and Juan Flores, eds. 2010. *The Afro-Latin@ Reader: History and Culture in the United States*. Durham: Duke University Press.

Johnson, James Weldon. 1912a. Letters to Grace E. Johnson. Box 41. Folder 21. Series 3: Family Correspondence. James Weldon Johnson Papers. James Weldon Johnson Collection in the Yale Collection of American Literature. Beinecke Rare Book and Manuscript Library. Yale University, New Haven, Conn.

———. 1912b. Letters to Sherman, French and Company. Box 18. Folder 435. Series 1: James Weldon Johnson Correspondence, 1896–1972. Se-Sh General Correspondence. James Weldon Johnson Papers. James Weldon Johnson Collection in the Yale Collection of American Literature. Beinecke Rare Book and Manuscript Library. Yale University, New Haven, Conn.

———. 1915. Announcement from the Cornhill Company. Letters to Grace Nail Johnson. Box 41. Folder 23. Series 3: Family Correspondence. James Weldon Johnson Papers. James Weldon Johnson Collection in the Yale Collection of American Literature. Beinecke Rare Book and Manuscript Library. Yale University, New Haven, Conn.

———. 1916. Letters to Grace E. Johnson. Box 41. Folder 25. Series 3: Family Correspondence. James Weldon Johnson Papers. James Weldon Johnson Collection in the Yale Collection of American Literature. Beinecke Rare Book and Manuscript Library. Yale University, New Haven, Conn.

———. 1917. *Fifty Years and Other Poems*. Boston: Cornhill.

———. 1931a. Letter to Victor M. Shapiro, 27 April. Box 18. Folder 431. Series 1: James Weldon Johnson Correspondence, 1896–1972. Se-Sh General Correspondence. James Weldon Johnson Papers. James Weldon Johnson Collection in the Yale Collection of American Literature. Beinecke Rare Book and Manuscript Library. Yale University, New Haven, Conn.

———. 1931b. Letter from Victor M. Shapiro, 28 April. Box 18. Folder 431. Series 1: James Weldon Johnson Correspondence, 1896–1972. Se-Sh General Correspondence. James Weldon Johnson Papers. James Weldon Johnson Collection in the Yale Collection of American Literature. Beinecke Rare Book and Manuscript Library. Yale University, New Haven, Conn.

———. 1933a. Letter from Eleanor Roosevelt, 15 November. Box 17. Folder 409. Series 1: James Weldon Johnson Correspondence, 1896–1972. Rh-Rn General Correspondence. James Weldon Johnson Papers. James Weldon Johnson Collection in the Yale Collection of American Literature. Beinecke Rare Book and Manuscript Library. Yale University, New Haven, Conn.

———. 1933b. Letter to Eleanor Roosevelt, 6 November. Box 17. Folder 409. Series 1: James Weldon Johnson Correspondence, 1896–1972. Rh-Rn General Correspondence. James Weldon Johnson Papers. James Weldon Johnson Collection in the Yale Collection of American Literature. Beinecke Rare Book and Manuscript Library. Yale University, New Haven, Conn.

———. 1989. *The Autobiography of an Ex-Coloured Man*. New York: Vintage. (Orig. pub. 1912.)

———. 2000. *Along This Way: The Autobiography of James Weldon Johnson*. New York: Da Capo, 2000. (Orig. pub. 1933.)

Jones, Gavin. 1997. "'Whose Line Is It Anyway?': W. E. B. Du Bois and the Language of the Color-Line." *Race Consciousness: African-American Studies for the New Century*, edited by Judith Jackson Fossett and Jeffrey A. Tucker. New York: New York University Press. 19–34.

Jones, Gayl. 1999. *Mosquito*. Boston: Beacon.

Jonnes, Jill. 2009. *Eiffel's Tower: And the World's Fair Where Buffalo Bill Beguiled Paris, the Artists Quarreled, and Thomas Edison Became a Count*. New York: Viking.

Kamp, David. 2006. *The United States of Arugula: The Sun-Dried, Cold-Pressed, Dark-Roasted, Extra Virgin Story of the American Food Revolution*. New York: Broadway Books.

Kanellos, Nicolás. 2012. "Recovering the U.S. Hispanic Literary Heritage." *PMLA* 17, no. 2 (March): 371–374.

Kaplan, Amy. 2002. *The Anarchy of Empire in the Making of U.S. Culture*. Cambridge: Harvard University Press.

Katzew, Ilona. 2004. *Casta Painting: Images of Race in Eighteenth-Century Mexico*. New Haven: Yale University Press.

Kawash, Samira. 1996. "*The Autobiography of an Ex-Coloured Man*: (Passing for) Black Passing for White." *Passing and the Fictions of Identity*, edited by Elaine K. Ginsberg. Durham: Duke University Press. 59–74.

———. 1997. *Dislocating the Color Line: Identity, Hybridity, and Singularity in African-American Narrative*. Stanford: Stanford University Press.

Keating, AnaLouise. 2000. "Risking the Personal: An Introduction." *Gloria E. Anzaldúa: Interviews/Entrevistas*, edited by AnaLouis Keating. New York: Routledge. 1–15.

———, ed. 2009. *The Gloria E. Anzaldúa Reader*. Durham: Duke University Press.

Kelley, Robin D. G. 2002. "How the West Was One: The African Diaspora and the Re-Mapping of U.S. History." *Rethinking American History in a Global Age*, edited by Thomas Bender. Berkeley: University of California Press. 123–47.

Kennedy, Charles Stuart. 1990. *The American Consul: A History of the United States Consular Service, 1776–1914*. Westport: Greenwood.

Kerr, Audrey Elisa. 2005. "The Paper Bag Principle: Of the Myth and the Motion of Colorism." *Journal of American Folklore* 118, no. 469 (Summer): 271–89.

Kirkpatrick, Jeane. 1987. "Dictatorships and Double Standards." *El Salvador: Central America in the New Cold War*, revised and updated, edited by Marvin E. Gettleman, Patrick Lacefield, Louis Menashe, David Mermelstein, and Ronald Radosh. New York: Grove. 14–39.

Laó-Montes, Agustín. 2001. "Introduction: Mambo Montage; The Latinization of New York City." *Mambo Montage: The Latinization of New York*, edited by Agustín Laó-Montes and Arlene Dávila. New York: Columbia University Press. 1–52.

———. 2007. "Decolonial Moves: Trans-locating African Diaspora Spaces." *Cultural Studies* 21, nos. 2–3 (March–May): 309–38.

Larsen, Neil. 1995. *Reading North by South: On Latin American Literature, Culture, and Politics*. Minneapolis: University of Minnesota Press.

Larsen, Nella. 1929. *Passing. Quicksand and Passing*, edited by Deborah E. McDowell. New Brunswick: Rutgers University Press, 1986.

———. 2007. *Passing*. Edited by Carla Kaplan. New York: Norton.
Lasch, Pedro. 2008. "Epics of Black and Brown: A Public Panel on the Representation, Culture, and Experience of African American and Latino/a Migrations." Panel discussion on Jacob Lawrence's "The Migration of the Negro" series. Golden Belt, Durham, N.C., 2 October.
Latinoteca.com. 2010. "U.S. Hispanic Recovery." http://www.latinoteca.com/app-home/app-inprints/recovery-project, accessed on 10 February 2010.
Lee, Julia H. 2011. *Interracial Encounters: Reciprocal Representations in African and Asian American Literatures, 1896–1937*. New York: New York University Press.
Leguizamo, John. 2006. *Pimps, Hos, Playa Hatas, and All the Rest of My Hollywood Friends: My Life*. New York: Ecco.
LeMay, Michael C. 2006. *Guarding the Gates: Immigration and National Security*. Westport: Praeger.
Levander, Caroline F. 2006. *Cradle of Liberty: Race, the Child, and National Belonging from Thomas Jefferson to W. E. B. Du Bois*. Durham: Duke University Press.
Lewis, David Levering. 1993. *W. E. B. Du Bois: Biography of a Race, 1868–1919*. New York: Henry Holt.
Lewis, Earl, and Heidi Ardizzone. 2001. *Love on Trial: An American Scandal in Black and White*. New York: Norton.
Lima, Lázaro. 2007. *The Latino Body: Crisis Identities in American Literary and Cultural Memory*. New York: New York University Press.
Limón, Graciela. 1993. *In Search of Bernabé*. Houston: Arte Público.
Limón, José E. 1998. *American Encounters: Greater Mexico, the United States, and the Erotics of Culture*. Boston: Beacon.
Locke, Alain. 1997. "The New Negro." *The Norton Anthology of African American Literature*, edited by Henry Louis Gates Jr. and Nellie Y. McKay. New York: Norton. 961–70.
Lomelí, Francisco A., and Donaldo W. Urioste. 1976. *Chicano Perspectives in Literature: A Critical and Annotated Bibliography*. Albuquerque: Pajarito.
López, Alfred J. 2007a. "Introduction: The (Post)global South." *Global South* 1, no. 1 (Winter): 1–9.
———. 2007b. "Preface and Acknowledgments." *Global South* 1, no. 1 (Winter): v–vi.
Lopez-Garza, Marta. 1992. "Los Angeles: Ascendant Chicano Power." *NACLA: Report on the Americas* 26, no. 2 (September): 34–38.
López-Stafford, Gloria. 1996. *A Place in El Paso: A Mexican-American Childhood*. Albuquerque: University of New Mexico Press.
Lovato, Roberto. 2008. "Juan Crow in Georgia." *Nation*, 26 May. http://www.thenation.com/article/juan-crow-georgia, accessed on 12 February 2012.

Lowery, Malinda Maynor. 2010. *Lumbee Indians in the Jim Crow South: Race, Identity, and the Making of a Nation*. Chapel Hill: University of North Carolina Press.

Lugones, María. 1987. "Playfulness, 'World'-Travelling, and Loving Perception." *Hypatia* 2, no. 2 (Summer): 3–19.

———. 2006. "On Complex Communication." *Hypatia* 21, no. 3 (Summer): 75–85.

Luis, William. 2003. "Latino U.S. Literature." *The Companion to Latin American Studies*, edited by Philip Swanson. London: Arnold. 122–53.

Madigan, Mark J. 1990. "Miscegenation and 'The Dicta of Race and Class': The Rhinelander Case and Nella Larsen's *Passing*." *Modern Fiction Studies* 36, no. 4 (Winter): 523–29.

Mahler, Sarah J. 1995. *American Dreaming: Immigrant Life on the Margins*. Princeton: Princeton University Press.

———. 1996. *Salvadorans in Suburbia: Symbiosis and Conflict*. Needham Heights, Mass.: Allyn and Bacon.

Marchi, Regina M. 2009. *Day of the Dead in the U.S.A.: The Migration and Transformation of a Cultural Phenomenon*. New Brunswick: Rutgers University Press.

Márez, Curtis. 1996. "Brown: The Politics of Working-Class Chicano Style." *Social Text* 48, no. 3 (Fall): 109–32.

Marrow, Helen B. 2009. "New Immigrant Destinations and the American Colour Line." *Ethnic and Racial Studies* 32, no. 6 (July): 1037–57.

Martin, Gerald. 2009. *Gabriel García Márquez: A Life*. New York: Knopf.

Martín Alcoff, Linda. 2006. "The Unassimilated Theorist." *PMLA* 121, no. 1 (January): 255–59.

Martínez, Demetria. 1994. *Mother Tongue*. Tempe: Bilingual Press/Editorial Bilingüe.

———. 1996. *Mother Tongue*. New York: One World/Ballantine Books.

Martínez, Rubén. 1993. *The Other Side: Notes from the New L.A., Mexico City, and Beyond*. New York: Vintage Books.

Mathews, Jennifer P. 2009. *Chicle: The Chewing Gum of the Americas, from the Ancient Maya to William Wrigley*. Tucson: University of Arizona Press.

Mbembe, Achille. 2001. *On the Postcolony*. Berkeley: University of California Press.

McClennen, Sophia A. 2005. "Inter-American Studies or Imperial American Studies." *Comparative American Studies* 3, no. 4 (November): 393–413.

McCracken, Ellen. 1999. *New Latina Narrative: The Feminine Space of Postmodern Ethnicity*. Tucson: University of Arizona Press.

McGrath, Patrick. 2008. *Trauma: A Novel*. New York: Vintage Books.

McKee, Kathryn, and Annette Trefzer. 2006. "Preface: Global Contexts, Local Literatures; The New Southern Studies." *American Literature* 78, no. 4 (December): 677–90.

Menchaca, Martha. 2001. *Recovering History, Constructing Race: The Indian, Black, and White Roots of Mexican Americans*. Austin: University of Texas Press.

Menchú, Rigoberta. 1994. *I, Rigoberta Menchú: An Indian Woman in Guatemala*. Edited by Elisabeth Burgos-Debray. Translated by Ann Wright. New York: Verso.

Mendible, Myra. 2007. "Embodying Latinidad: An Overview." *From Bananas to Buttocks: The Latina Body in Popular Film and Culture*, edited by Myra Mendible. Austin: University of Texas Press. 1–28.

Menjívar, Cecilia. 2000. *Fragmented Ties: Salvadoran Immigrant Networks in America*. Berkeley: University of California Press.

Mignolo, Walter. 2000. *Local Histories/Global Designs: Coloniality, Subaltern Knowledges, and Border Thinking*. Princeton: Princeton University Press.

———. 2005. *The Idea of Latin America*. Malden: Blackwell.

———. 2009. "Epistemic Disobedience, Independent Thought, and Decolonial Freedom." *Theory, Culture and Society* 26, nos. 7–8 (December): 1–23.

———. 2010. "Closing Reflections." Education, Development, Freedom: The Annual Workshop of the Center for Global Studies and the Humanities. Duke University, Durham, N.C., 25–27 February.

Milian, Claudia. 2004. "Studying New World Negro Problems: Open Double Consciousness and Mulatinidad in Edwidge Danticat's *The Farming of Bones*." *C.L.R. James Journal: A Review of Caribbean Ideas* 10, no. 1 (Winter): 123–53.

———. 2006. "Playing with the Dark: Africana and Latino Literary Imaginations." *A Companion to African-American Studies*, edited by Lewis R. Gordon and Jane Anna Gordon. Malden: Blackwell. 543–68.

———. 2007. "*Mestizaje: Critical Uses of Race in Chicano Culture*. By Rafael Pérez-Torres." *Aztlán: A Journal of Chicano Studies* 32, no. 1 (Spring): 237–42.

Miller, Marilyn Grace. 2004. *Rise and Fall of the Cosmic Race: The Cult of Mestizaje in Latin America*. Austin: University of Texas Press.

Miller, Nancy K. 2000. "But Enough about Me, What Do You Think of My Memoir?" *Yale Journal of Criticism* 13, no. 2 (Fall): 421–43.

Miller, Paul D. 2008. "In through the Out Door: Sampling and the Creative Act." *Sound Unbound: Sampling Digital Music and Culture*, edited by Paul D. Miller, aka DJ Spooky That Subliminal Kid. Cambridge: MIT Press. 5–19.

Mindiola, Tatcho, Jr., Yolanda Flores Niemann, and Nestor Rodriguez. 2003. *Black-Brown Relations and Stereotypes*. Austin: University of Texas Press.

Minority Rights Group, ed. 1996. *Afro-Central Americans: Rediscovering the African Heritage*. London: Minority Rights Group.

Mirabal, Nancy Raquel. 2007. "Introduction: Historical Futures, Globality, and Writing Self: An Introduction to Technofuturos." In Mirabal and Laó-Montes, 2007: 1–27.

Mirabal, Nancy Raquel, and Agustín Laó-Montes, eds. 2007. *Technofuturos: Critical Interventions in Latina/o Studies*. Lanham: Lexington Books.

Mohl, Raymond A. 2005. "Globalization, Latinization, and the *Nuevo* New South." *Globalization and the American South*, edited by James C. Cobb and William Stueck. Athens: University of Georgia Press. 66–99.

Mojica Arts. 2005. "Youth Speaks and the National Performance Network Present the World Premiere of Fear of a Brown Planet." Press release. http://mojicaarts.com/pr/brownplanet/, accessed on 8 June 2012.

Montejano, David. 2010. *Quixote's Soldiers: A Local History of the Chicano Movement, 1966–1981*. Austin: University of Texas Press.

Moors, Marilyn M. 2000. "Conclusion: The Maya Diaspora Experience." *The Maya Diaspora: Guatemalan Roots, New American Lives*, edited by James Loucky and Marilyn M. Moors. Philadelphia: Temple University Press. 223–30.

Moraga, Cherríe L. 1983a. "For the Color of My Mother." In Moraga and Anzaldúa, 1983: 12–13.

———. 1983b. "La Güera." In Moraga and Anzaldúa, 1983: 27–34.

———. 1993. *The Last Generation: Prose and Poetry*. Boston: South End.

———. 2011. *A Xicana Codex of Changing Consciousness: Writings, 2000–2010*. Durham: Duke University Press.

Moraga, Cherríe L., and Gloria Anzaldúa, eds. 1983. *This Bridge Called My Back: Writings by Radical Women of Color*. New York: Kitchen Table/Women of Color. (Orig. pub. 1981.)

Morales, Ed. 2003. *The Latin Beat: The Rhythms and Roots of Latin Music from Bossa Nova to Salsa and Beyond*. New York: Da Capo.

Moreman, Shane T., and Dawn Marie McIntosh. 2010. "Brown Scripting and Rescriptings: A Critical Performance Ethnography of Latina Drag Queens." *Communication and Critical/Cultural Studies* 7, no. 2 (June): 115–35.

Mormino, Gary R., and George E. Pozzetta. 1987. *The Immigrant World of Ybor City: Italians and Their Latin Neighbors in Tampa, 1885–1985*. Urbana: University of Illinois Press.

Mosby, Dorothy E. 2003. *Place, Language, and Identity in Afro-Costa Rican Literature*. Columbia: University of Missouri Press.

Mountford, Peter. 2011. *A Young Man's Guide to Late Capitalism*. New York: Mariner Books.

Moya, Paula M. L. 2002. *Learning from Experience: Minority Identities, Multicultural Struggles*. Berkeley: University of California Press.

———. 2003. "With Us or Without Us." *Nepantla: Views from South* 4, no. 2: 245–52.

Moya, Paula M. L., and Ramón Saldívar. 2003. "Fictions of the Trans-American Imaginary." *Modern Fiction Studies* 49, no. 1 (Spring): 1–18.

Muñoz, Carlos, Jr. 2007. *Youth, Identity, Power: The Chicano Movement*. New York: Verso.

Muñoz, José Esteban. 2000. "Feeling Brown: Ethnicity and Affect in Ricardo Bracho's *The Sweetest Hangover (and Other STDs)*." *Theatre Journal* 52, no. 1 (March): 67–79.

———. 2006. "Feeling Brown, Feeling Down: Latina Affect, the Performativity of Race, and the Depressive Position." *Signs: Journal of Women in Culture and Society* 31, no. 3 (Spring): 675–88.

———. 2007. "'Chico, What Does It Feel Like to Be a Problem?': The Transmission of Brownness." In Flores and Rosaldo, 2007: 441–51.

Muthyala, John. 2001. "Reworlding America: The Globalization of American Studies." *Cultural Critique* 47 (Winter): 91–119.

Naipaul, V. S. 1989. *A Turn in the South*. New York: Knopf.

Napier, Winston. 2000. Introduction to *African American Literary Theory: A Reader*, edited by Winston Napier. New York: New York University Press. 1–13.

Natella, Arthur Aristides, Jr. 2008. *Latin American Popular Culture*. Jefferson, N.C.: McFarland.

Nazario, Sonia. 2007. *Enrique's Journey: The Story of a Boy's Dangerous Odyssey to Reunite with His Mother*. New York: Random House.

Nericcio, William Anthony. 2007. *Tex[t]-Mex: Seductive Hallucinations of the "Mexican" in America*. Austin: University of Texas Press.

Noriega, Chon A. 2008. "The Orphans of Modernism." *Phantom Sightings: Art after the Chicano Movement*, edited by Rita Gonzalez, Howard N. Fox, and Chon A. Noriega. Berkeley: University of California Press. 16–45.

Nwankwo, Ifeoma Kiddoe. 1999–2001. "Langston Hughes and the Translation of Nicolás Guillén's Afro-Cuban Culture and Language." *Langston Hughes Review* 16, nos. 1–2 (Fall–Spring): 55–72.

———. 2005. *Black Cosmopolitanism: Racial Consciousness and Transnational Identity in the Nineteenth-Century Americas*. Philadelphia: University of Pennsylvania Press.

———. 2006. "The Promises and Perils of U.S. African-American Hemispherism: Latin America in Martin Delany's *Blake* and Gayl Jones's *Mosquito*." *American Literary History* 18, no. 3 (Fall): 579–99.

Oboler, Suzanne. 1995. *Ethnic Labels, Latino Lives: Identity and the Politics of (Re)Presentation in the United States*. Minneapolis: University of Minnesota Press.

———, ed. 2006. *Latinos and Citizenship: The Dilemma of Belonging*. New York: Palgrave Macmillan.

Olson, Elizabeth. 2010. "'Dora' Special Explores Influence on Children." *New York Times*, 8 August. http://www.nytimes.com/2010/08/09/business/media/09dora.html, accessed on 31 July 2011.

Ortiz, Fernando. 1995. *Cuban Counterpoint: Tobacco and Sugar*. Translated by Harriet de Onís. Durham: Duke University Press. (Orig. pub. 1940.)

Ostler, Nicholas. 2007. *Ad Infinitum: A Biography of Latin*. New York: Walker.

Oxford English Dictionary. http://www.oed.com/, accessed on 11 June 2012.

Packer, Z. Z. 2003. *Drinking Coffee Elsewhere: Stories*. New York: Riverhead Books.

Padilla, Felix M. 1985. *Latino Ethnic Consciousness: The Case of Mexican Americans and Puerto Ricans in Chicago*. Notre Dame: University of Notre Dame Press.

Painter, Nell Irvin. 2008. "Un Essai d'Ego-Histoire." *Telling Histories: Black Women Historians in the Ivory Tower*, edited by Deborah Gray White. Chapel Hill: University of North Carolina Press. 28–41.

Palumbo-Liu, David. 1999. *Asian/American: Historical Crossings of a Racial Frontier*. Stanford: Stanford University Press.

Paredez, Deborah. 2009. *Selenidad: Selena, Latinos, and the Performance of Memory*. Durham: Duke University Press.

Parenti, Michael. 1989. *The Sword and the Dollar: Imperialism, Revolution, and the Arms Race*. New York: St. Martin's Press.

Parker, Matthew. 2009. *Panama Fever: The Epic Story of the Building of the Panama Canal*. New York: Anchor Books.

Peacock, James L. 2007. *Grounded Globalism: How the U.S. South Embraces the World*. Athens: University of Georgia Press.

Peacock, James L., Harry L. Watson, and Carrie R. Matthews, eds. 2005. *The American South in a Global World*. Chapel Hill: University of North Carolina Press.

Pérez, Emma. 2003. "Queering the Borderlands: The Challenges of Excavating the Invisible and Unheard." *Frontiers: A Journal of Women's Studies* 24, nos. 2–3: 122–31.

Pérez, Gina M., Frank A. Guridy, and Adrian Burgos Jr., eds. 2010. *Beyond El Barrio: Everyday Life in Latina/o America*. New York: New York University Press.

Perez, Hiram. 2005. "You Can Have My Brown Body and Eat It, Too!" *Social Text* 23, nos. 3–4 84–85 (Fall–Winter): 171–91.

Pérez Firmat, Gustavo. 2010. *The Havana Habit*. New Haven: Yale University Press.

Pérez-Torres, Rafael. 2006. *Mestizaje: Critical Uses of Race in Chicano Culture*. Minneapolis: University of Minnesota Press.

Perry, Jeffrey B., ed. 2001. *A Hubert Harrison Reader*. Middletown: Wesleyan University Press.

Person, David. 2011. "Column: 'Juan Crow' Law Alive and Well in Alabama." *USA Today*, 1 November. http://www.usatoday.com/news/opinion/forum/story/2011

-11-01/alabama-illegal-immigration-law/51031138/1, accessed on 15 February 2012.
Phillips, Caryl. 2000. *The Atlantic Sound*. New York: Knopf.
Piñero, Miguel. 1980. *La Bodega Sold Dreams*. Houston: Arte Público.
Pinker, Steven. 2007. *The Stuff of Thought: Language as a Window into Human Nature*. New York: Penguin Books.
Pisiak, Roxanna. 1993. "Irony and Subversion in James Weldon Johnson's *The Autobiography of an Ex-Coloured Man*." *Studies in American Fiction* 21, no. 1 (Spring): 83–96.
Poblete, Juan, ed. 2003. *Critical Latin American and Latino Studies*. Minneapolis: University of Minnesota Press.
Poey, Delia, and Virgil Suarez. 1992. Introduction to *Iguana Dreams: New Latin Fiction*, edited by Delia Poey and Virgil Suarez. New York: HarperPerennial. xv–xix.
Portman, Natalie. 2004. "Natalie Portman Responds." *Allure*, December. 32.
Prashad, Vijay. 2001. *The Karma of Brown Folk*. Minneapolis: University of Minnesota Press.
Prescott, Anne Lake. 1996. "The Odd Couple: Gargantua and Tom Thumb." *Monster Theory: Reading Culture*, edited by Jeffrey Jerome Cohen. Minneapolis: University of Minnesota Press. 75–91.
Rabinovitz, Jonathan. 1991. "The Case of the Game-Show Ploy." *New York Times*, 6 October. http://www.nytimes.com/1991/10/06/arts/television-the-case-of-the-game-show-ploy.html, accessed on 26 July 2011.
Ramos, Julio. 2001. *Divergent Modernities: Culture and Politics in Nineteenth-Century Latin America*. Translated by John D. Blanco. Durham: Duke University Press.
Rampersad, Arnold. 1993. Introduction to *The Big Sea*, by Langston Hughes. New York: Hill and Wang. xiii–xxvi.
———. 1997. Introduction to *Short Stories: Langston Hughes*, by Langston Hughes. New York: Hill and Wang. xiii–xix.
———. 2002. *The Life of Langston Hughes*. Vol. 1, 1902–1941: *I, Too, Sing America*. Oxford: Oxford University Press.
Rawsthorn, Alice. 2010. "Why @ Is Held in Such High Design Esteem." *New York Times*, 21 March. http://www.nytimes.com/2010/03/22/arts/design/22ihtdesign22.html?adxnnl=1&ref=technology&adxnnlx=1311741691-wrWcT6nGlv0+v3aarPdiaA, accessed on 27 July 2011.
Real Academia Española. *Diccionario de la lengua española*. http://www.rae.es/rae.html., accessed on 11 June 2012.
Rechy, John. 1991. *The Miraculous Day of Amalia Gómez*. New York: Grove.
———. 2008. *About My Life and the Kept Woman: A Memoir*. New York: Grove.

Reeves, Richard. 2005. *President Reagan: The Triumph of Imagination*. New York: Simon and Schuster.
Reneau, Ingrid M. 2006. "Da Inna Who Fa Mout' Mi Tongue/In Whose Mouth Is My Tongue: Writing as a Belizean American." *Small Axe* 10, no. 1 (February): 94–99.
Rigg, Jonathan. 2007. *An Everyday Geography of the Global South*. London: Routledge.
Rivera, John-Michael. 2006. *The Emergence of Mexican America: Recovering Stories of Mexican Peoplehood in U.S. Culture*. New York: New York University Press.
Roberts, Cheryl A. 1997. "An Interview with Arturo Arias." *Speaking of the Short Story: Interviews with Contemporary Writers*, edited by Farhat Iftekharuddin, Mary Rohrberger, and Maurice Lee. Jackson: University Press of Mississippi. 22–34.
Rodríguez, Clara E. 2000. *Changing Race: Latinos, the U.S. Census, and the History of Ethnicity in the United States*. New York: New York University Press.
Rodríguez, Ileana. 2004. *Transatlantic Topographies: Islands, Highlands, Jungles*. Minneapolis: University of Minnesota Press.
Rodríguez, Juana María. 2003. *Queer Latinidad: Identity Practices, Discursive Spaces*. New York: New York University Press.
Rodriguez, Richard. 1982. *Hunger of Memory: The Education of Richard Rodriguez*. Boston: Godine.
———. 1992. *Days of Obligation: An Argument with My Mexican Father*. New York: Viking.
———. 2002. *Brown: The Last Discovery of America*. New York: Viking.
Rodríguez, Richard T. 2009. *Next of Kin: The Family in Chicano/a Cultural Politics*. Durham: Duke University Press.
———. 2010. "The Locations of Chicano/a and Latino/a Studies." *A Concise Companion to American Studies*, edited by John Carlos Rowe. Malden: Wiley-Blackwell. 190–209.
Rosaldo, Renato. 1985. "Chicano Studies, 1970–1984." *Annual Review of Anthropology* 14: 405–27.
Rowley, Hazel. 2001. *Richard Wright: The Life and Times*. New York: Holt.
Rúa, Mérida M. 2001. "*Colao* Subjectivities: PortoMex and MexiRican Perspectives on Language and Identity." *Centro Journal* 8, no. 2 (Fall): 117–33.
Ruiz, Vicki L. 2004. "Morena/o, blanca/o y café con leche: Racial Constructions in Chicana/o Historiography." *Mexican Studies/Estudios Mexicanos* 20, no. 2 (Summer): 343–60.
Sadowski-Smith, Claudia. 2005. "Canada-U.S. Border Narratives and U.S. Hemispheric Studies." *Comparative American Studies* 3, no. 1 (March): 63–77.
Sagás, Ernesto. 1998. "Recently 'Discovered': Dominicans in the United States." *Latino Studies Journal* 3: 4–10.

Saldívar, José David. 1997. *Border Matters: Remapping American Cultural Studies.* Berkeley: University of California Press.

———. 2012. *Trans-Americanity: Subaltern Modernities, Global Coloniality, and the Cultures of Greater Mexico.* Durham: Duke University Press.

Saldívar, Ramón. 2007. "Social Aesthetics and the Transnational Imaginary." In Flores and Rosaldo, 2007: 406–16.

Saldívar-Hull, Sonia. 2000. *Feminism on the Border: Chicana Gender Politics and Literature.* Berkeley: University of California Press.

———. 2007. "Introduction to the Second Edition." *Borderlands/La Frontera: The New Mestiza*, by Gloria Anzaldúa. 3rd ed. San Francisco: Aunt Lute Books. 1–15.

Sánchez, George J. 1993. *Becoming Mexican American: Ethnicity, Culture, and Identity in Chicano Los Angeles, 1900–1945.* New York: Oxford University Press.

Sánchez Korrol, Virginia. 1996. "The Origins and Evolution of Latino History." *OAH Magazine of History* 10, no. 2 (Winter): 5–12.

Sandino, Augusto César. 1988. *Pensamiento político.* Caracas: Biblioteca Ayacucho.

Sandweiss, Martha A. 2009. *Passing Strange: A Gilded Age of Love and Deception across the Color Line.* New York: Penguin.

Santa Ana, Otto. 2002. *Brown Tide Rising: Metaphors of Latinos in Contemporary American Public Discourse.* Austin: University of Texas Press.

Santiago, Esmeralda. 1993. *When I Was Puerto Rican.* New York: Vintage.

Sassen, Saskia. 2009. "Incompleteness and the Possibility of Making: Towards Denationalized Citizenship?" *Cultural Dynamics* 21, no. 3 (November): 227–54.

Schlossberg, Linda. 2001. "Introduction: Rites of Passing." *Passing: Identity and Interpretation in Sexuality, Race, and Religion*, edited by María Carla Sánchez and Linda Schlossberg. New York: New York University Press. 1–12.

Scott, A. O. 2005. "A Complex Metamorphosis of the Most Fundamental Sort." *New York Times*, 2 December. http://movies.nytimes.com/2005/12/02/movies/02trans.html, accessed on 5 June 2012.

Senna, Danzy. 1998. *Caucasia.* New York: Riverhead Books.

———. 2004. *Symptomatic.* New York: Riverhead Books.

———. 2009. *Where Did You Sleep Last Night? A Personal History.* New York: Farrar, Straus and Giroux.

———. 2011. *You Are Free.* New York: Riverhead Books.

Sharpe, Christina. 2010. *Monstrous Intimacies: Making Post-Slavery Subjects.* Durham: Duke University Press.

Shaw-Taylor, Yoku, and Steven A. Tuch, eds. 2007. *The Other African Americans: Contemporary African and Caribbean Immigrants in the United States.* Lanham: Rowman and Littlefield.

Singh, Amritjit, and Peter Schmidt. 2000. "On the Borders between U.S. Studies and

Postcolonial Theory." *Postcolonial Theory and the United States: Race, Ethnicity, and Literature*, edited by Amritjit Singh and Peter Schmidt. Jackson: University of Mississippi. 3–69.

Smith, Jon. 2004. "Postcolonial, Black, and Nobody's Margin: The U.S. South and New World Studies." *American Literary History* 16, no. 1: 144–61.

Smith, Jon, and Deborah N. Cohn, eds. 2004. *Look Away! The U.S. South in New World Studies*. Durham: Duke University Press.

Smith, Robert Courtney. 2006. *Mexican New York: Transnational Lives of New Immigrants*. Berkeley: University of California Press.

Smith, Sidonie, and Julia Watson. 2001. *Reading Autobiography: A Guide for Interpreting Life Narratives*. Minneapolis: University of Minnesota Press.

Smith, Terry. 2003. "The Dialectics of Disappearance: Architectural Iconotypes between Clashing Cultures." *Critical Quarterly* 45, nos. 1–2 (July): 33–51.

Sollors, Werner. 1997. *Neither Black nor White Yet Both: Thematic Explorations of Interracial Literature*. New York: Oxford University Press.

Solomon, Deborah. 2008. "All in the Family." *New York Times Magazine*, 20 January. http://www.nytimes.com/2008/01/20/magazine/20wwln-Q4t.html?_r=1&oref=slogin, accessed on 1 August 2008.

Sommer, Doris. 1999. "Be-Longing and Bi-Lingual States." *Diacritics* 29, no. 4 (Winter): 84–115.

Sommers, Laurie Kay. 1991. "Inventing Latinismo: The Creation of 'Hispanic' Panethnicity in the United States." *Journal of American Folklore* 104, no. 411 (Winter): 32–53.

Soto, Sandra K. 2005. "Cherríe Moraga's Going Brown: 'Reading Like a Queer.'" *GLQ: A Journal of Lesbian and Gay Studies* 11, no. 2: 237–63.

———. 2010. *Reading Chican@ Like a Queer: The De-Mastery of Desire*. Austin: University of Texas Press.

Sparke, Matthew. 2007. "Everywhere but Always Somewhere: Critical Geographies of the Global South." *Global South* 1, no. 1 (Winter): 117–24.

Spillers, Hortense J. 1989. "Notes on an Alternative Model—Neither/Nor." *The Difference Within: Feminism and Critical Theory*, edited by Elizabeth Meese and Alice Parker. Amsterdam: Benjamins. 165–87.

Spivak, Gayatri Chakravorty. 2004. "Harlem." *Social Text* 22, no. 4 (Winter): 113–39.

Stack, Carol. 1996. *Call to Home: African Americans Reclaim the Rural South*. New York: Basic Books.

Stam, Robert. 1999. "Palimpsestic Aesthetics: A Meditation on Hybridity and Garbage." *Performing Hybridity*, edited by May Joseph and Jennifer Natalya Fink. Minneapolis: University of Minnesota Press. 59–78.

Stavans, Ilan. 2005. Introduction to *Rubén Darío: Selected Writings*, edited by Ilan

Stavans. Translated by Andrew Hurley, Greg Simon, and Steven F. White. New York: Penguin Classics. xvii–lix.

Stecopoulos, Harilaos. 2007. "Up from Empire: James Weldon Johnson, Latin America, and the Jim Crow South." *Imagining Our Americas: Toward a Transnational Frame*, edited by Sandhya Shukla and Heidi Tinsman. Durham: Duke University Press. 34–62.

Stiles, T. J. 2009. *The First Tycoon: The Epic Life of Cornelius Vanderbilt*. New York: Knopf.

Stokes, Doug. 2003. "Countering the Soviet Threat? An Analysis of the Justifications for U.S. Military Assistance to El Salvador, 1979–92." *Cold War History* 3, no. 3 (April): 79–102.

Stuever, Hank. 2010. "A Landmark in Familiar Territory: 'Dora the Explorer' Turns 10 on Nickelodeon." *Washington Post*, 14 August. http://www.washingtonpost.com/wp-dyn/content/article/2010/08/13/AR2010081306131.html, accessed on 31 July 2011.

Sugg, Katherine. 2004. "Literatures of the Americas: Latinidad, and the Reformation of Multi-ethnic Literatures." *MELUS* 29, nos. 3–4 (Fall/Winter): 227–42.

Sundstrom, Ronald R. 2008. *The Browning of America and the Evasion of Social Justice*. Albany: State University of New York Press.

Taketani, Etsuko. 2010. "Colored Empires in the 1930s: Black Internationalism, the U.S. Black Press, and George Samuel Schuyler." *American Literature* 82, no. 1 (March): 121–49.

Tarica, Estelle. 2008. *The Inner Life of Mestizo Nationalism*. Minneapolis: University of Minnesota Press.

Thomas, David L. K. N.d. "Kemo the Blaxican." http://www.kemotheblaxican.com, accessed on 8 June 2012.

Thomas, Piri. 1967. *Down These Mean Streets*. New York: Knopf.

———. 1997. *Down These Mean Streets*. New York: Vintage Books. (Orig. pub. 1967.)

Tindall, George Brown. 1995. *Natives and Newcomers: Ethnic Southerners and Southern Ethnics*. Athens: University of Georgia Press.

Tobar, Héctor. 1998. *The Tattooed Soldier: A Novel*. Harrison: Delphinium Books.

———. 2005. *Translation Nation: Defining a New American Identity in the Spanish-Speaking United States*. New York: Riverhead Books.

Torres, Hector A. 2000. "The Ethnographic Component in Chicano/a Literary Discourse." *Aztlán* 25, no. 1 (Spring): 151–66.

TransAfrica Forum. 2011. "Justice for the African World." http://transafrica.org/home/, accessed 10 April 2012.

Treviño, Jesús Salvador. 2001. *Eyewitness: A Filmmaker's Memoir of the Chicano Movement*. Houston: Arte Público.

Tronto, Joan C. 1993. *Moral Boundaries: A Political Engagement for an Ethic of Care*. New York: Routledge.

———. 1998. "An Ethic of Care." *Generations* 22, no. 3 (Fall): 15–20.

Tyler, Carole-Anne. 1994. "Passing: Narcissism, Identity, and Difference." *Differences* 6, nos. 2–3: 212–48.

Unity Council. N.d. Home page. http://www.unitycouncil.org/, accessed on 10 June 2012.

Valdés, Zoé. 2008. "París era una rumba." *zoevaldes.net*, 16 March. http://zoevaldes.skyrock.com/91.html, accessed on 2 August 2011.

Valencia Ramírez, Cristóbal. 2009. "Active Marooning: Confronting *Mi Negra* and the Bolivarian Revolution." *Radical History Review* 103 (Winter): 117–30.

Valladares Molina, Acisclo. 2008. "De Guatemala a Guatepeor. . . Y retacho penguén." *El Periódico*, 31 March. http://www.elperiodico.com.gt/es/20080331/opinion/51337, accessed on 7 July 2011.

Vargas, Izel. 2008. *Business of Illusion*. http://izelvargas.com/home.html, accessed on 10 June 2012.

Vasconcelos, José. 1997. *The Cosmic Race/La raza cósmica*. Translated by Didier T. Jaén. Baltimore: Johns Hopkins University Press.

Viego, Antonio. 2007. *Dead Subjects: Toward a Politics of Loss in Latino Studies*. Durham: Duke University Press.

Vincent, Theodore G. 2001. *The Legacy of Vicente Guerrero, Mexico's First Black Indian President*. Gainesville: University Press of Florida.

Vinson, Ben, III. 2004. *Flight: The True Story of Virgil Richardson, a Tuskegee Airman in Mexico*. New York: Palgrave McMillan.

Vinson, Ben, III, and Matthew Restall, eds. 2009. *Black Mexico: Race and Society from Colonial to Modern Times*. Albuquerque: University of New Mexico Press.

Vinson, Ben, III, and Bobby Vaughn. 2004. *Afroméxico: El pulso de la población negra en México; Una historia recordada, olvidada y vuelta a recordar*. Translated by Clara García Ayluardo. Mexico City: Centro de Investigación y Docencia Económicas/Fondo de Cultura Económica.

Viramontes, Helena María. 1995a. *The Moths and Other Stories*. 2nd ed. Houston: Arte Público. (Orig. pub. 1985.)

———. 1995b. *Under the Feet of Jesus*. New York: Dutton.

Wald, Priscilla. 1995. *Constituting Americans: Cultural Anxiety and Narrative Form*. Durham: Duke University Press.

Waters, Mary C. 1997. *Black Identities: West Indian Immigrant Dreams and American Realities*. New York: Sage.

Watson, Sonja Stephenson. 2009. "Are Panamanians of Caribbean Ancestry an Endangered Species? Critical Literary Debates on Panamanian Blackness in the

Works of Carlos Wilson, Gerardo Maloney, and Carlos Russell." *Latin American and Caribbean Ethnic Studies* 4, no. 3 (November): 231–54.

Weise, Julie M. 2009. "Mexican Nationalisms, Southern Racisms: Mexicans and Mexican Americans in the U.S. South, 1908–1939." *Nation and Migration: Past and Future*, edited by David G. Gutiérrez and Pierrette Hondagneu-Sotelo. Baltimore: Johns Hopkins University Press. 247–75.

West, William F., and Ginny Hoyle. 2007. "Hispanics Big Part of Growth: Minority Group Makes Up Half of Counties' Population Swell." *Herald-Sun*, 11 August.

White, Hayden. 1975. *Metahistory: The Historical Imagination in Nineteenth-Century Europe*. Baltimore: Johns Hopkins University Press.

Wintz, Cary D. 1988. *Black Culture and the Harlem Renaissance*. Houston: Rice University Press.

Woessner, Robert. 1992. "Carmen Sandiego Maps a Learning Course." *USA Today*, 18 February.

Woodard Maderazo, Jennifer. 2006. "Manuel Rosales: The Alternative to Chavez in Venezuela." *Vivirlatino.com*, 13 October. http://vivirlatino.com/2006/10/13/manuel-rosales-the-alternative-to-chavez-in-venezuela.php, accessed on 1 June 2011.

Woodward, C. Vann. 1960. *The Burden of Southern History*. Baton Rouge: Louisiana State University Press.

Wright, Richard. N.d. "I Am an American, but . . ." Box 5. Folder 107. Series 1. Writings. Richard Wright Papers. Yale Collection of American Literature. Beinecke Rare Book and Manuscript Library. Yale University, New Haven, Conn.

Wright, W. D. 2002. *Black History and Black Identity: A Call for a New Historiography*. Westport: Praeger.

Wynter, Sylvia. 2001. "Toward the Sociogenic Principle: Fanon, Identity, the Puzzle of Conscious Experience, and What It Is Like to Be 'Black.'" *National Identities and Sociopolitical Changes in Latin America*, edited by Mercedes F. Durán-Cogan and Antonio Gómez-Moriana. New York: Routledge. 30–66.

Zavella, Patricia. 1996. "Feminist Insider Dilemmas: Constructing Ethnic Identity with Chicana Informants." *Feminist Dilemmas in Fieldwork*, edited by Diane L. Wolf. Boulder: Westview. 138–59.

Zilberg, Elana. 2007. "Inter-American Ethnography: Tracking Salvadoran Transnationality at the Borders of Latina/o and Latin American Studies." In Flores and Rosaldo, 2007: 492–501.

Zimmerman, Marc. 1992. *U.S. Latino Literature: An Essay and Annotated Bibliography*. Chicago: MARCH/Abrazo.

INDEX

Note: Page numbers in italics indicate illustrations.

Abrams, Elliott, 242n12
Aching, Gerard, 23
Adams, Elbridge L., 214n29
Adams, Rachel, 34, 189n25
Adams, Thomas, Sr., 222n4
advertising, Latino, 13, 161n5, 167n27
Africana diasporas, 29, 90, 171n32, 219n47
African Americans, 16, 19–21; categories of, 178n50; Chicano/a movement and, 227n22; definitions of, 159n1; future of, 175n40; Grillo on, 43–54; Northern migrations of, 193n35; Southern relocation of, 185n14; un-Latinized, 48
African American studies, 19, 24, 25, 33, 36, 37, 64, 160n4
Afro-Cubans, 218–19nn47–49; Grillo on, 43–54; mestizaje and, 113. *See also* Africana diasporas
Afro–Latin Americans, 8–9
Afro-Latin@s, 8–9, 13, 19, 152, 181n8, 256n5
afromestizos, 231n35
Afro-Venezuelans, 95
Alabama, 191n31, 196n46, 213n24, 215n35

Alarcón, Daniel, 173n36
alienation, 20, 57, 141–42, 166n26, 171n32, 178n49, 191n30, 243n14, 250n27
Allatson, Paul, 21, 101
Allen, Irving Lewis, 200n55
Almendárez Coello, Renán ("El Cucuy de la Mañana"), 225n13, 254n36
Along This Way (James Weldon Johnson), 62, 68–76, 79, 200n54
Alvarez, Julia, 167n27, 175n39, 247n20
American-Americanness, 140–41
American studies, 19, 24–25, 33–39, 65, 140–42, 163n14, 192n33
Anaya, Toney, 240n4
Andrews, William L., 113
Anzaldúa, Gloria, 21, 30, 57, 92; on brownness, 110, 114–15, 118–21, 228n27, 235n49; "New Mestiza revolutionary theory" of, 237n54; on Spanish speakers, 231n37
Aparicio, Frances, 243n14, 251n32
Ardizzone, Heidi, 201n57
Arellano, Gustavo, 125
Arias, Arturo, 22, 128, 139, 141–43, 248n23, 249n25, 250n27
Arrieta, Rolando, 255n1
Arte Público Press, 19, 43–46; de la Campa on, 197n49; Grillo and, 44, 52

Asian American studies, 190n30, 257n10
Asians, 165n21; immigration quotas for, 217n41; segregation laws and, 231n35
Autobiography of an Ex-Coloured Man (James Weldon Johnson), 64, 67, 70–73, 79–80, 96, 205n65, 208–9nn10–12

Baca, Damián, 152
Baker, Houston A., Jr., 27, 181n6
Baker, Josephine, 89
Baldwin, James, 58
banana republics, 124, 130–31, 239n2, 243n14
Barba Salinas, Manuel, 249n25
Barthes, Roland, 83
Bebout, Lee, 166n24
Belize, 124, 177n48, 217n40; creole language of, 214n31. *See also* Central Americans
Bencastro, Mario, 245–46n17
Bender, Thomas, 30
Benz, Stephen, 78–79
Berland, Jody, 194n40
Berlin, Ira, 159n1, 175n40
Bernabé, Monica, 65
Bierce, Ambrose, 131
Big Sea, The (Langston Hughes), 62, 80–81, 111, 233n41
blackness, 2–9, 21–24; Afro-Latinidad and, 13; brownness of, 109–14, 220n1; Central Americanness and, 124; Indianness as, 93–101, 112, 118–19; Vasconcelos on, 233n42; whiteness and, 106–7, 160n4, 221n3. *See also* brownness
Blanc, Mel, 211n20
Bogle, Donald, 235n49
Bok, Edward, 73, 213n27

Bolton, John, 242n12
Boon, Marcus, 3–4
borderlands, 21, 30, 92; "global," 40; Texan culture of, 182n10; urbanism of, 181n7
Borges, Jorge Luis, 220n51
Bost, Suzanne, 207n5, 236n49
Brady, Mary Pat, 84
Brazilians, 144
Brief Wondrous Life of Oscar Wao, The (Junot Díaz), 13–15, 35, 113, 136
Brody, Jennifer DeVere, 199n53
Brown, Leslie, 182n9
brownness, 2–9, 21–24, 148; Afro-Latinidad and, 13; blackness of, 109–14, 220n1; dark, 2–9, 13–17, 21–24, 93–101, 114–21, 146; of Latinidad, 162n7; and Latino/a studies, 121–22; whiteness and, 106–7, 160n4, 221n3. *See also* blackness
Bucholtz, Mary, 59, 188n19
"Bulldozer Revolution," 185n14
Bush, George H. W., 127
Bush, George W., 242n12
Business of Illusion (Vargas), 153–54, 154
Butler, Judith, 108

Cain, Will, 168n27
Calafell, Marie, 180–81n5
Calderón, Felipe, 94–95
Calderón, Héctor, 39–40
Canada, 34, 189n25, 191n33
Canadian studies, 194n40
Cancún, Mexico, 94–95, 222n7
Candelario, Ginetta E. B., 230n32
caramelo, 86–87, 90, 98–99, 224n11
Carby, Hazel V., 48–49
Cardenal, Ernesto, 244n14

care, ethic of, 11, 169n28
Caribbean: Anglophone, 177n48, 194n40; immigrants from, 10, 159n1, 212n22, 230n32; Mexico and, 231n36
Caribbean Philosophical Association (CPA), 185n13
Carrillo Rowe, Aimee, 162n11
Carroll, Rory, 95
Carruthers, Ben Frederic, 90
Carter, Jimmy, 52
casta system, 114, 234n42
Castellanos, M. Bianet, 222n7
Castellanos Moya, Horacio, 94, 222n6, 249n25
Castillo, Ana, 35, 175n39, 190n28
Central American–Americanness, 22, 126–28, 136–50, 242n12, 247n20, 250n27, 252n34
Central Americans, 9, 10, 22–23, 123–29, 137–38, 144; British heritage of, 177n48; Cold War and, 127, 133, 135–36, 240n4; iconography of, 127–28; indigenousness of, 146; Mexican cultural practices and, 254n36; in New Mexico, 240n4; Parenti on, 249n25; quinceañeras of, 168n27; Reagan on, 250n29; Tobar's representations of, 178n49; transnational gangs of, 142, 246n18. *See also specific countries*
Césaire, Aimé, 220n51
Chabram-Dernersesian, Angie, 16, 193n36, 251n32
Chapman, Peter, 239n2
Chávez, César, 232n40
Chávez, Hugo, 95
Chávez-Silverman, Susana, 243n14
Chesnutt, Charles W., 188n20, 216n36

Chicago, Latinos in, 12, 135, 170n31, 251n32
Chicano/a culture, 115, 192n33; brownness and, 93–122; literature of, 248n22
Chicano/a movement, 101–2, 165n24, 224n9; African American collaboration in, 227n22; development of, 226n18; "Guatepeorianness" and, 129
Chicano/a studies, 36, 40, 64, 115, 147–48, 238n1, 251n32; Central Americanness and, 126; Latino/a studies and, 232nn37–38
Chicano Messengers of Spoken Word, 224n10
Chicanos/Chicanas, 144–45; borderland theories and, 39–40; Brown Berets of, 165n24, 226n18; Brown Pride among, 101; Calafell on, 180–81n5; definition of, 223n9; identity markers of, 21; with indigenous ancestry, 102; as manual laborers, 116, 232n40; new immigrants and, 166n26; origin of term, 226n18; as "Panchos," 214n30; Spanish of, 231n37. *See also* Latinos/Latinas; Mexican Americans
chicle workers, 221–22n4
Cisneros, Sandra, 85, 87, 98–99, 175n39, 225n14
Clark, Septima, 190n29
Claros, Marta (fictional character), 134, 247n19
Clay, Felix, 233n42
Cohn, Deborah N., 33, 34
Cold War: Central America and, 127, 133, 135–36, 240n4; Cuba and, 220n52
Collins, Patricia Hill, 35
Connell, Raewyn, 18, 40, 42, 139

Conrad, Joseph, 124, 214n29
Contreras, Sheila Marie, 227n21
Cooper, Julia, 198n52
Cooppan, Vilashini, 19
Coronil, Fernando, 219n49
Cortes, Carlos, 255n1
Cortés, Hernán, 74
Costa Rica, 75–76, 124, 130, 244n14. *See also* Central Americans
Coutin, Susan Bibler, 54–55
Crichlow, Michaeline, 252n34
crónica genre, 21, 65–66
Crusade for Justice, 226n18
Cruz, Celia, 87, 172n33
Cruz, Nilo, 35
Cuadros, Paul, 29, 166n26, 187n17
Cuba, 30, 195n42, 220n52
Cuban Americans, 10, 124, 135, 144–48; Grillo on, 43–53; James Weldon Johnson on, 69; quinceañeras of, 168n27

Darío, Rubén, 65, 142, 250n28
dark brownness (*lo prieto*), 2–9, 13–17, 21–24, 93–101, 114–21, 146. *See also* brownness
Davidman, Lynn, 53
Davidson, Peter, 58
Dávila, Arlene, 61, 161n5
Davis, Gregson, 66
Day of the Dead, 169n29
de Acosta, Alejandro, 3
Dear, Michael, 45, 162n10
décalage, 29, 47, 188n18, 205n67
De Genova, Nicholas, 12, 127, 135, 170n31
de la Campa, Román, 39, 112–13, 197n49
Derricotte, Toi, 204n65

De Veaux, Alexis, 228n27
Díaz, Adolfo, 76, 208n8
Díaz, Junot, 57, 150, 175n39; on blackness, 113; on brownness, 103; popularity in Latin America of, 173n36
—works of: *The Brief Wondrous Life of Oscar Wao*, 13–15, 35, 113, 136; *Drown*, 35, 113
Díaz Neiro, Teresa, 106
Didion, Joan, 124
D'León, Oscar, 14, 172n33
"Dollar Diplomacy," 63, 78
Dominican Americans, 10, 14–15, 35, 142, 150, 230n32, 247n20
Dora the Explorer (TV show), 152–56, 254–56nn1–3
double consciousness: Canadian, 194n40; of Du Bois, 2, 19–20, 160nn3–4; Falconi and Mazzotti on, 176n42; Kelley on, 160n4; Moraga on, 118; open, 19–20, 54–58, 205n67; Sparke on, 41
Douglas, Mary, 104
Douglass, Frederick, 110
Down These Mean Streets (Piri Thomas), 22, 112, 176n46, 224n12, 230n30, 234n33
Drown (Junot Díaz), 35, 113
Du Bois, W. E. B., 18, 110; autobiography of, 56; on blackness, 97, 232n39; on colorism, 111–12, 119, 123, 162–63nn11–12, 238n1; double consciousness of, 2, 19–20, 160nn3–4; on Durham, N.C., 182n9; as editor of *Crisis*, 176n45; as Pan-Africanist, 41, 195n42; on poverty, 185n14; on race "problem," 55–57, 203n62; on white otherness, 22–23

INDEX 293

Duke, David, 167n26, 187n17
Dworkin y Méndez, Kenya, 44

Eakin, Marshall C., 29, 31–33
Edwards, Brent Hayes, 29, 188n18, 238n1
Edwards, Brian T., 163n14
Eiffel Tower, 83–84
Eire, Carlos, 104–5, 211n20
Ellison, Ralph, 181n6
El Salvador, 124, 136, 142, 148, 239n4; Arias on, 248n23; García Márquez on, 241n6; literature of, 249n25; Mistral on, 241n10. *See also* Central Americans
Emancipation Proclamation, 214n28
Emergency Immigration Act, 217n41
Engel, Patricia, 133–34, 255n1
Engelhardt, Elizabeth S. D., 183n12
England, Sarah, 149
Epps, Brad, 15, 30
Escudos, Jacinta, 124, 210n16
Espada, Martín, 175n39

Falconi, José Luis, 144–45, 176n42
Fallas, Carlos Luis, 244n14
Fanon, Frantz, 87, 206n71, 233n42
Faulkner, William, 59, 60
Fernández, Carole, 254n35
Fink, Leon, 28, 186n15
Fleming, Robert E., 208n10
Flores, Juan, 13, 51, 92, 143, 165n19, 189n26
Flores, Paul, 224n10
Flores Niemann, Yolanda, 227n22
Foley, Neil, 182n10
Folkenflik, Robert, 196n46
Fontova, Humberto, 44
Ford, Lacy K., 181n7

Fourteenth Amendment, to U.S. Constitution, 231n35
Franklin, John Hope, 178n51, 196n46
Frazier, E. Franklin, 182n9
French, Patrick, 210n15

Gallop, Jane, 23, 47
gangs, 142, 246n18
Gaonkar, Dilip Parameshwar, 163n14
García, Alma M., 166n24
García, Cristina, 134, 175n39, 246n18
García Canclini, Néstor, 138, 174n38
García Márquez, Gabriel, 94, 152, 254n35; in Alabama, 213n24; Junot Díaz and, 14, 172n34; on Mexico, 231n36; Nobel Laureate address of, 241n6; on United Fruit Company, 245n14
Garifunas ("Black Caribs"), 149
Gass, William, 198n50
Gates, Henry Louis, Jr., 46, 111
Georgia, 191n31, 199n54, 211n17, 218n46
Gifford, Chris, 254n1
Gilder, Richard Watson, 213n25
Gilroy, Paul, 152, 256n4
Gobat, Michel, 77, 78
Goffman, Erving, 120
Goldman, Francisco, 93, 96, 175n39, 244n14, 245n15
González, Jovita, 192n34, 205n68
González, Juan, 22, 177n48, 252n33
Gonzalez, Veronica, 15
Gooding-Williams, Robert, 19–20
Gordon, Lewis, 53, 162n11, 221n3; on anonymity, 209n11; on relational theory of race, 99–100
Gould, Jeffrey, 207n5
Grady, Henry Woodfin, 178n1
Graham, Hugh Davis, 206n70

Grandin, Greg, 242n12
Greene, Julie, 208n7, 215n33
Grillo, Evelio, 19, 26, 43–54
Grossman, Edith, 139
Gruesz, Kirsten Silva, 243n14
Guantánamo naval base, 30
Guarnizo, Luis Eduardo, 205n66
Guatemala, 124–26, 244n14. *See also* Central Americans
Guatemalan Maya immigrants, 186n15
"Guatepeorian Latinidad," 22, 126–38, 142, 150, 242n11, 245–46nn15–18
"Güera, La" (Moraga), 104
Guidotti-Hernández, Nicole M., 256n3
Guillén, Nicolás, 89, 90, 219n50, 220n51
Guldbrandsen, Thaddeus Countway, 182n11
Guridy, Frank Andre, 66; on Africana diaspora, 90, 171n32, 219n47; on Spanish-American War, 210n14
Guterl, Matthew Pratt, 35–36
Gutiérrez, Ramón A., 227n20

Haiti, 62, 113, 195n42, 220n51, 247n20
Haney López, Ian F., 101–2, 165n24, 226n19
Harlem Renaissance, 20–21, 60, 64, 176n44, 208n10
Hart, Dianna Walta, 133
Henríquez, Cristina, 25, 31
Henry, O., 124
Hernández Cruz, Victor, 243n14
Herzog, Lawrence A., 181n7
Hijuelos, Oscar, 130, 220n2, 230n31
Hill Collins, Patricia, 35, 190n29
hip-hop music, 106, 224n10
Hispanic Heritage Month, 155

Hispanics, 165nn19–20; Latinos versus, 155–56, 164–65nn18–20, 179n4; as racialized category, 230n32
hispanidad, 16
Holloway, Karla F. C., 200n54
Honduras, 124, 149, 254n36. *See also* Central Americans
Horne, Gerald, 215n35
Hughes, James N., 80–81, 215–16nn35–36
Hughes, Langston, 20–21, 60–62; on colorism, 86–88, *88*; in Cuba, 67, 89–91; James Weldon Johnson and, 82; in Mexico, 62, 65–67, 80–89; on passing, 82–83, 217n38; politics of, 209n13; private papers of, 62; on Spanish speakers, 212n21; in Texas, 81–82; translations of, 90–91, 219n50
—works of: *The Big Sea*, 62, 80–81, 86, 111, 233n41; *Mulatto*, 218n46; *The Ways of White Folks*, 82; *The Weary Blues*, 89
Hurston, Zora Neale, 110, 228n27

immigration policies, 108–9, 217n41
Indianness, 21–22; as blackness, 93–101, 112, 118–19; Chicanoness and, 102; Maya, 94–95, 148–49, 186n15, 222n7; mestizaje and, 231n35, 233n42. *See also* Native Americans
inter-American studies, 39, 192n33. *See also* American studies
Iran-Contra scandal, 242n12
Irwin, Robert McKee, 191n33
Italian immigrants, 197n48, 200n55

Jacobs, Harriet, 229n28
Jackson, Lawrence P., 209n13

Jamaican Americans, 159n1
James, C. L. R., 249n25
Jefferson, Thomas, 77
Jim Crow laws, 36, 196n46; Langston Hughes on, 212n21; "Juan Crow" policies and, 191n31; as motive for emigration, 215n35; Naipaul on, 179n2. *See also* segregation
Jiménez, Tomás R., 225n15
Jiménez Román, Miriam, 13
Johnson, Grace Nail, 68, 74–77, 214n32
Johnson, James Weldon, 20–21, 49, 60–62, 199n54; in Costa Rica, 75–76; Langston Hughes and, 82; on New York City, 211n17; in Nicaragua, 63, 66–80, 214n31, 215n34; private papers of, 68
—works of: *Along This Way*, 62, 68–76, 79, 200n54; *Autobiography of an Ex-Coloured Man*, 64, 67, 70–73, 79–80, 96, 205n65, 208–9nn10–12
Johnson-Reed Immigration Act, 217n41
Jones, Alice, 201n57
Jones, Gavin, 162n12
Jones, Gayl, 195n45
Jonnes, Jill, 83–84
"Juan Crow" policies, 191n31

Kagan, Robert, 242n12
Kanellos, Nicolás, 44–45
Kaplan, Amy, 36
Katzew, Ilona, 235n49
Kawash, Samira, 206n1
Kelley, Robin D. G., 160n4, 171n32
"Kemo the Blaxican" (David L. K. Thomas), 106
Kennedy, Charles Stuart, 80

Kerr, Audrey Elisa, 228n27
King, Clarence, 190n28, 217n39
Kirkpatrick, Jeane, 127
Ku Klux Klan, 167n26, 187n17

Laó-Montes, Agustín, 10–11, 13, 55, 162n9
Larsen, Nella, 201n57
Lasch, Pedro, 1
"Latin," 1–2, 7, 9
Latin Americans, 1–2, 17, 123, 138–40; "intensity" of, 175n41; as second-class Europeans, 9–10
Latin American studies, 19, 25, 33, 64–65, 140, 142, 175n39. *See also* Latino/a studies
"Latin-at-ness" (Latin@ness), 70, 151–58
Latinidad, 2–6, 8–10, 145; brownness of, 162n7; "empathetic," 135; "Guatepeorian," 22, 126–38, 142, 150, 245–46nn15–18; Latinities versus, 9–16; Muñoz on, 12, 170n30; Quinceañera, 167n27; Soccer, 166n26
Latinity(ies), 2–7; Latinidad versus, 9–16; "passing" and, 213n24
Latino/a studies, 2, 8–9, 15–16, 115, 156–58, 160n1; brownness and, 121–22; Central Americanness in, 124, 126; Chabram-Dernersesian on, 193n36; Chicano/a studies and, 232nn37–38; comparativist project for, 251n32; inclusive language for, 235n49, 256n5
Latinoness/Latinaness, 2–8, 123, 145, 160n1; as "problem," 53–58, 203n62; re-cognition of, 15, 22, 43, 81, 92, 174n37

Latinos/Latinas, 1–11, 144, 147–48; advertising to, 13, 161n5, 167n27; brownness and, 93–101; definitions of, 160n1; Hispanics versus, 155, 164–65nn18–20, 179n4; "intensity" of, 175n41; marketing to, 13, 161n5; *la raza* and, 101, 120–21, 226n19, 233n42, 236n49; Spanish of, 231n37. *See also* Chicanos/Chicanas

Latinoteca.com, 45

League of Revolutionary Artists and Writers, 216n37

League of United Latin American Citizens, 102

Leclerc, Gustavo, 45, 162n10

Lee, Spike, 163n13

Leguizamo, John, 57, 163n13

Levander, Caroline F., 195n42

Lewis, David Levering, 195n41

Lewis, Earl, 201n57

Liberia, 215n35

Lima, Lázaro, 165n20

Limón, Graciela, 253n35

Limón, José, 39–40

Locke, Alain, 189n27

Lomelí, Francisco A., 248n22

López, Alfred J., 189n23, 239n3

Lopez-Garza, Marta, 226n18

López-Stafford, Gloria, 129

Lorde, Audre, 110, 216n35, 228n27

Lovato, Roberto, 191n31

Lowery, Malinda Maynor, 187n16

Lugones, María, 12, 17, 37; on world-travelling, 161n6, 175n41

Luis, William, 179n4

Lumbee Indians, 186n16

lynchings, 193n35, 215n35

Maceo, Antonio, 50

Malcolm X, 110

Malinche, La, 74

Maloney, Gerardo, 194n40

Manifest Destiny, 78

Marchi, Regina M., 169n29

Márez, Curtis, 103, 105–6, 214n30

marriage, interracial, 110–11, 201n57, 217n39

Marrow, Helen B., 26

Martí, José, 65

Martin, Gerald, 94, 213n24, 243n14

Martínez, Demetria, 239n4

Martínez, Rubén, 191n32

Massaguer, Conrado, 89

Mathews, Jennifer P., 221n4

Mayas, 94–95, 148–49, 186n15, 222n7

Mazzotti, José Antonio, 144–45, 176n42

Mbembe, Achille, 137

McClennen, Sophia A., 191n33

McCracken, Ellen, 253n35

McGrath, Patrick, 123, 126

McIntosh, Dawn Marie, 238n57

McKay, Nellie Y., 46

McKee, Kathryn, 39

Mena, Luis, 208n8

Menchaca, Martha, 114, 231n35

Menchú, Rigoberta, 94–95, 118, 133

Mendez v. Westminster, 234n44

Mendible, Myra, 12–13, 243n14

mestizaje, 101, 104–9; Afro-Cubans and, 113; Bost on, 207n5; de la Campa on, 112–13; Fourteenth Amendment and, 231n35; among Indians, 231n35, 233n42; literature of, 121, 237n55; mulattos and, 118, 213n22, 235n49; Clara Rodríguez on, 164n17; segregation

laws on, 231n35; among slaves, 98–99, 110, 114, 229n28; terms for, 235n49
Mexican Americans, 10, 124, 144–45, 201n58; as "MexiRican," 251n32. See also Chicanos/Chicanas
Mexicans, 125, 131; in Chicago, 12, 135, 170n31, 251n32; U.S. segregation laws and, 231n35, 234n44
Mexico, 165n21; as Caribbean country, 231n36; Revolution of, 84; U.S. African Americans in, 81, 215n35; U.S. war with, 78, 162n9, 239n1
Mignolo, Walter, 9, 17, 39; on "border thinking," 48, 83
Miller, Marilyn Grace, 234n42
Miller, Nancy K., 46
Miller, Paul, 58
Mindiola, Tatcho, Jr., 227n22
minoritization, 5, 26, 109, 162n10
Mirabal, Nancy Raquel, 162n9
Mistral, Gabriela, 241n10
Mohl, Raymond A., 28, 178n1
Moody, Rick, 172n35
Moors, Marilyn, 148–49
Moraga, Cherríe, 21, 102; on autobiography, 230n33; on brownness, 110, 114–16, 118; on double consciousness, 118; "La Güera" by, 104; on Indianness, 119, 236n52
Morales, Ed, 3–4
Moreman, Shane T., 238n57
Mormino, Gary R., 197n48, 200n56
Mountford, Peter, 125
Movimiento Estudiantil Chicano de Aztlán (MECHA), 226n18
Moya, Paula M. L., 129, 146–48, 172n36
Mulatto (Langston Hughes), 218n46

mulattos, 118, 213n22, 235n49. See also mestizaje
multiculturalism, 48, 107, 189n25, 223n7
Muñoz, José Esteban, 12, 55–56, 107–8, 170n30
Museum of Modern Art (MoMA), 257n6
Muthyala, John, 179n3

Naipaul, V. S., 178n2, 210n15, 250n31
Natella, Arthur Aristides, Jr., 129
National Association for the Advancement of Colored People (NAACP), 176n45
Native Americans, 109, 118–19; mestizaje and, 231n35, 233n42; Peorian, 131; segregation of, 231n35; in U.S. Southeast, 186n16; in U.S. Southwest, 102. See also Indianness
Nazario, Sonia, 184n13
negritude, 230n32
Negroponte, John, 242n12
Nericcio, William Anthony, 59
Neruda, Pablo, 220n51
New Mexico, 226n18, 240n4
New Orleans, 201n58
New South, 178n1
Nicaragua, 124, 143, 244n14; Iran-Contra scandal and, 242n12; mestizaje in, 207n5; 1912 revolution in, 63, 76–78, 208n8. See also Central Americans
9/11 attacks, 103, 107, 224n10, 242n12
Nixon, Richard M., 103–4, 132, 228n24
Northover, Patricia, 252n34
Nuevo South, 178n1, 183n12, 185n14
Nuyoricans, 22, 57, 112, 145, 251n32. See also Puerto Ricans

Nwankwo, Ifeoma, 24, 159n1, 178n50, 219n50

Oboler, Suzanne, 10
open double consciousness, 19–20, 54–58, 205n67
Orozco, José Clemente, 217n37
Ortiz, Amalia, 224n10
Ortiz, Fernando, 90, 219n49
Ostler, Nicholas, 7
otherness, 17, 22–23, 53, 107, 128, 131, 145, 158, 250n30

Packer, Z. Z., 247n19
Padilla, Felix, 10
Painter, Nell Irvin, 196n46
Palumbo-Liu, David, 35, 190n30, 257n10
Panama, 124; California gold rush and, 77; independence of, 238n1. *See also* Central Americans
Panama Canal, 177n48, 238n1
Panamanian writers, 194n40
"Pancho," 214n30
Paredes, Américo, 214n30
Paredez, Deborah, 11–12
Parenti, Michael, 249n25
Parker, Matthew, 177n48, 239n1
"passing," 59–67, 91–92, 188n19; definitions of, 59, 188n19, 206n1; Epps on, 15, 30; Langston Hughes on, 82–83, 217n38; Kawash on, 206n1; Latinity and, 213n24
Peacock, James L., 28, 39, 42
Pedroso, Regino, 89
Peoria, 131–32, 245n16
Pérez, Emma, 119–20
Perez, Hiram, 106–7, 109
Pérez Firmat, Gustavo, 3, 143

Pérez-Torres, Rafael, 115
Perry, Jeffrey B., 176n44
"Peru Ana/Ana Peru" tags, 146, 147, 148, 150, 250n31
Phillips, Caryl, 130
Phillips Casteel, Sarah, 34, 189n25
Pinate, Marc David, 224n10
Piñero, Miguel, 57
Pinker, Steven, 129
Pisiak, Roxanna, 209n11
Poey, Delia, 137
Poindexter, John, 242n12
Porter, William Sydney, 124
Portman, Natalie, 2–3, 160n3
Pozzetta, George E., 197n48, 200n56
Prescott, Anne Lake, 242n10
prieto, 220n1
Puerto Ricans, 10, 124, 142, 144–45; in Chicago, 12, 135, 145, 170n31, 251n32; "Guatepeorianness" and, 130; Langston Hughes on, 212n21; in New York City, 22, 57, 112, 145, 251n32; as "PortoMex," 251n32; quinceañeras of, 168n27
Puerto Rican studies, 148, 251n32

queerness, 57, 106, 120, 236n53
quinceañeras, 167n27, 247n20

race, 171n32; mixed marriages and, 110–11, 201n57, 217n39; relational theory of, 99–100; stereotypes of, 149. *See also* blackness; mestizaje
Raleigh, Eve, 192n34, 205n68
Ramos, Julio, 65–66
Ramos-Zayas, Ana Y., 12, 135, 170n31
Rampersad, Arnold, 62, 90, 207n3, 220n51

ranchera music, 105
Rawsthorn, Alice, 151, 153
raza, la, 101, 120–21, 226n19, 233n42, 236n49
Reagan, Ronald, 143, 242n12, 250n29
Real Academia Española, 231n37
Rechy, John, 112, 241n8
re-cognition, 15, 22, 43, 81, 92, 174n37
Reich, Otto, 242n12
Reneau, Ingrid M., 214n31
Rhinelander, Leonard, 201n57
Richardson, Virgil, 196n46
Rigg, Jonathan, 18, 23
Rivera, Diego, 217n37
Rivera, John-Michael, 103, 226n19
Rodríguez, Clara E., 164n17
Rodríguez, Ileana, 78–79
Rodriguez, Nestor, 227n22
Rodriguez, Richard, 8, 21; on brownness, 94, 97, 103–4, 115–18, 121; on "Hispanic," 164n18; on Nixon, 103–4, 228n24
Rodríguez, Richard T., 225n16
Rodriguez Ponce, Ricardo, 69–70, 213n22
Romain, Jacques, 220n51
Roosevelt, Eleanor, 73
Roosevelt, Franklin D., 73
Roosevelt, Theodore, 63, 74, 208n7
Root, Elihu, 214n29
Rosales, Manuel, 95
Rowley, Hazel, 193n35, 215n35, 228n27
Rúa, Mérida, 251n32
Ruiz, Vicki L., 114, 223n9
Rumsfeld, Donald, 242n12
Russell, Carlos, 194n40

Sadowski-Smith, Claudia, 191–92n33
Saldívar, José David, 34–35, 37, 39–40
Saldívar, Ramón, 42, 172n36
Saldívar-Hull, Sonia, 190n28, 237n54, 258n11
Sánchez, George J., 67
Sánchez Korrol, Virginia, 10–11, 22
Sandino, Augusto César, 63, 208n9, 244n14
Sandweiss, Martha A., 188n19; on Caribbean immigrants, 212n22; on King, 190n28, 217n39
Santa Ana, Otto, 102–3
Santiago, Esmeralda, 112, 130, 230n31, 245n16
Sassen, Saskia, 1, 5
Schlossberg, Linda, 30
Scott, A. O., 38
segregation, 163n1, 231n35, 234n44; Naipaul on, 179n2; in Panama Canal zone, 239n1; in U.S. Army, 51. *See also* Jim Crow laws
Senghor, Léopold Sédar, 220n51
Senna, Danzy, 58, 93–94, 110–11, 133, 229n29
September 11. *See* 9/11 attacks
Shapiro, Victor M., 213n26
Sharpe, Christina, 220n3
Shaw-Taylor, Yoku, 250n30
Siler City, N.C., 166n26, 187n17
Singh, Amritjit, 34
Siquieros, David Alfaro, 217n37
slavery, 181n7, 221n3; Africana diasporas of, 29, 90, 171n32, 219n47; Asian Mexicans and, 165n21; mestizaje and, 98–99, 110, 114, 229n28; in Texas, 182n10, 193n34
Smith, Jon, 34, 191n32
Soccer Latinidad, 166n26
Soetoro-Ng, Maya, 2–3, 161n5

Sollors, Werner, 121
Somoza Debayle, Anastasio, 127, 239n2
Sonora Matancera, La (Cuban band), 87
Soto, Sandra K., 118, 152, 235n48, 236n50
Southerland, Adm. William Henry Hudson, 77, 80
Spanish-American War, 210n14, 239n1
Sparke, Matthew, 40–41, 140–41
"Speedy Gonzalez" (caricature), 69–70, 211n20, 247n19
Spillers, Hortense J., 235n49
Spivak, Gayatri, 164n16
Stack, Carol, 40, 185n14
Stavans, Ilan, 250n28
Stecopoulos, Harilaos, 68, 70, 71, 211n17, 212n22
Stein, Gertrude, 132
Stiles, T. J., 177n48
Stokes, Doug, 127
Stuever, Hank, 255n1
Suarez, Virgil, 137
Sundstrom, Ronald R., 108

Taft, William Howard, 79
Tarica, Estelle, 114
Texas, 32, 91, 182n10, 193n34, 196n46
Thomas, David L. K. ("Kemo the Blaxican"), 106
Thomas, Piri, 22, 112, 176n46, 224n12, 230n30
Tindall, George Brown, 181n7
Tobar, Héctor, 133, 175n39, 178n49, 184n13, 254n36
TransAfrica Forum, 193n37
Transamerica (film), 38–39
transnationalism, 20, 33, 38, 66, 205n66; brownness and, 98, 104, 106

Trefzer, Annette, 39
Tronto, Joan C., 11, 169n28
Trujillo, Rafael Leónidas, 13–14
Tuch, Steven A., 250n30
Tuskegee airmen, 196n46
Tyler, Carole-Anne, 79

United Farm Workers (UFW), 226n18
United Fruit Company (UFC), 239n2, 243n14
United Mexican American Students (UMAS), 226n18
Unity Council, 52, 203n60
Urban League, 176n45
Urioste, Donaldo W., 248n22
Urrutia, Gustavo, 90
utopia, 161n6

Valdés, Zoé, 154, 257n8
Valdivia, Angharad N., 238n57
Valencia Ramírez, Cristóbal, 95
Vallejo, César, 65
Vargas, Izel, 153–55, 154
Vasconcelos, José, 189n25, 233n42, 240n4
Viego, Antonio, 153, 163n15, 257n7
Vietnam War, 126, 166n24, 192n33, 197n46
Vinson, Ben, III, 196n46
Viramontes, Helena María, 232n40, 253n35

Walcott, Derek, 172n34
Wald, Priscilla, 2, 45, 198n51
Walker, Kara, 88, 140
Walker, William, 78
Ward, William Hayes, 213n25

Washington, Booker T., 208n10
Ways of White Folks, The (Langston Hughes), 82
Weary Blues, The (Langston Hughes), 89
Weise, Julie M., 84, 201n58
Weitzel, George T., 208n8
Where in the World Is Carmen Sandiego? (TV show), 152, 255n2
White, Hayden, 66
whiteness, 106–7, 160n4, 221n3. *See also* blackness
Wilson, Carlos, 194n40
Wintz, Cary D., 176n44
Woessner, Robert, 255n2

Woodward, C. Vann, 185n14
Wright, Richard, 56, 110, 193n35, 205n67; grandparents of, 228n27; in Mexico, 215n35
Wright, W. D., 220n1
Wrigley, William, Jr., 222n4

Xavier University (La.), 49–51, 202n59
xenophobia, 108–9

Ybor City, Fla., 43, 44, 197n48, 200n56
Yúdice, George, 92

Zavella, Patricia, 249n24
Zimmerman, Marc, 17, 248n21

THE NEW SOUTHERN STUDIES

*The Nation's Region: Southern Modernism,
Segregation, and U.S. Nationalism*
by Leigh Anne Duck

*Black Masculinity and the U.S. South:
From Uncle Tom to Gangsta*
by Riché Richardson

*Grounded Globalism: How the U.S. South
Embraces the World*
by James L. Peacock

*Disturbing Calculations: The Economics of Identity
in Postcolonial Southern Literature, 1912–2002*
by Melanie R. Benson

American Cinema and the Southern Imaginary
edited by Deborah E. Barker and Kathryn McKee

*Southern Civil Religions: Imagining the Good Society
in the Post-Reconstruction Era*
by Arthur J. Remillard

*Reconstructing the Native South: American Indian
Literature and the Lost Cause*
by Melanie Benson Taylor

*Apples and Ashes: Literature, Nationalism,
and the Confederate States of America*
by Coleman Hutchison

*Reading for the Body: The Recalcitrant Materiality
of Southern Fiction, 1893–1985*
by Jay Watson

*Latining America: Black-Brown Passages
and the Coloring of Latino/a Studies*
by Claudia Milian

www.ingramcontent.com/pod-product-compliance
Lightning Source LLC
Chambersburg PA
CBHW011622250426
43672CB00038B/2960